PAGE
26

ON THE ROAD

YOUR COMPLETE DESTINATION GUIDE
In-depth reviews, detailed listings
and insider tips

TOP EXPERIENCES MAP NEXT PAGE

DISCARDED

Newfoundland & Labrador p162

Prince Edward Island p133

New Brunswick p90

Nova Scotia p28

PAGE
247

SURVIVAL GUIDE

YOUR AT-A-GLANCE REFERENCE
How to get around, get a room,
stay safe, say hello

Directory A-Z

THIS EDITION WRITTEN AND RESEARCHED BY

Celeste Brash

Emily Matchar, Karla Zimmerman

48°W
50°W
52°W
54°W
56°W
58°W

58°N
56°N
54°N
52°N

60°N
58°N
56°N

62°W
64°W
66°W
68°W

60°N

ATLANTIC
OCEAN

ELEVATION

	1500m
	1000m
	500m
	200m
	0

100 km
60 miles
0
0

N

Labrador
Sea

QUÉBEC

Ungava
Bay

Torngat Mountains

▲ Mont d'Iberville
(1652m)

Hebron

Kaumajet
Mountains

Nain

Mistastin
Lake

Fraser River

Davis Inlet

Harp
Lake

Hopedale

Postville

Makkovik

Cape
Harrison

LABRADOR

Nipishish
Lake

Rigolet

Hamilton Inlet

Lake
Melville

North West
River

Happy Valley-
Goose Bay

International
Military Base

500

Churchill River

Smallwood
Reservoir

Churchill
Falls

Atikonak
Lake

Lake
Joseph.

Eskec

500

Schefferville

Labrador
City

Wabush

Ashuanipi
Lake

Lac
Caniapiscau

Cartwright

Paradise
River

Port Hope
Simpson

Mary's
Harbour

Belle

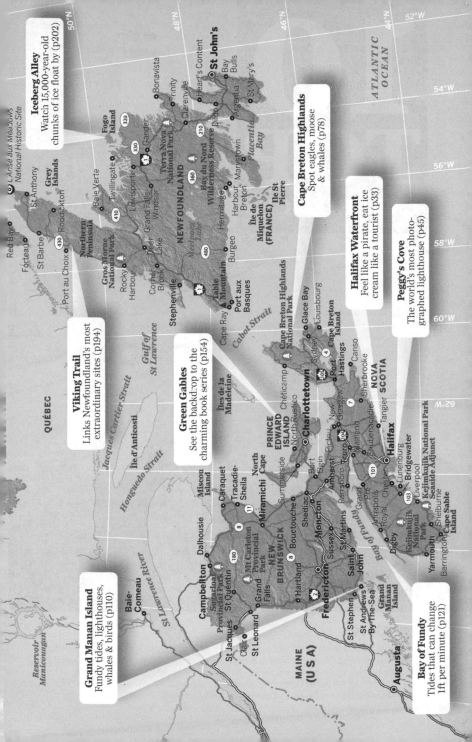

Iceberg Alley
Watch 15,000-year-old chunks of ice float by (p202)

Cape Breton Highlands
Spot eagles, moose & whales (p78)

Halifax Waterfront
Feel like a pirate, eat ice cream like a tourist (p33)

Peggy's Cove
The world's most photo-graphed lighthouse (p45)

Viking Trail
Links Newfoundland's most extraordinary sites (p194)

Green Gables
See the backdrop to the charming book series (p154)

Grand Manan Island
Fundy tides, lighthouses, whales & birds (p110)

Bay of Fundy
Tides that can change 1ft per minute (p121)

ATLANTIC OCEAN

QUÉBEC

NEWFOUNDLAND

PRINCE EDWARD ISLAND

NOVA SCOTIA

NEW BRUNSWICK

MAINE (USA)

St John's
L'Anse aux Meadows National Historic Site
Bay Bulls
St Mary's
Heart's Content
Trinity
Bonavista
Clarenville
Argentia
Placentia Bay
Marystown
Harbour Breton
Île St Pierre
Île de Miquelon (FRANCE)
Hermitage
Burgeo
Bay du Nord Wilderness Reserve
Terra Nova National Park
Gander
Twillingate
Fogo Island
Grey Islands
St Anthony
Red Bay
Forteau
St Barbe
Port au Choix
Roddickton
Baie Verte
Lewisporte
Grand Falls
Windsor
Deer Lake
Corner Brook
Rocky Harbour
Gros Morne National Park
Northern Peninsula
Stephenville
Port aux Basques
Cape Ray
Table Mountain
Meelpaeg Lake

Gulf of St Lawrence
Jacques Cartier Strait
Île d'Anticosti
Honguedo Strait
Cabot Strait

Reservoir Manicouagan
St Lawrence River
Baie-Comeau

Îles de la Madeleine
Chéticamp
Cape Breton Highlands National Park
Cape Breton Island
Glace Bay
Sydney
Louisbourg
Canso
Sherbrooke
Tangier
New Glasgow
Pictou
Antigonish
Truro
Maitland
Shubenacadie
Chester
Lunenburg
Bridgewater
Liverpool
Shelburne
Barrington
Cape Sable Island
Yarmouth
Digby
Annapolis Royal
Kejimkujik National Park
Kejimkujik National Park Seaside Adjunct
Halifax
Grand Pre

Charlottetown
North Rustico
Summerside
Port Elgin

Campbellton
Dalhousie
Sugarloaf Provincial Park
St Quentin
Grand Falls
Mt Carleton Provincial Park
Hartland
Fredericton
St Leonard
St Jacques
Clair
Edmundston
Miscou Island
Caraquet
Tracadie-Sheila
Miramichi
North Cape
Bouctouche
Shediac
Moncton
Sussex
Amherst
Parrsboro
St Martins
Saint John
Grand Manan Island
St Andrews By-The-Sea
St Stephen
Augusta

Bay of Fundy

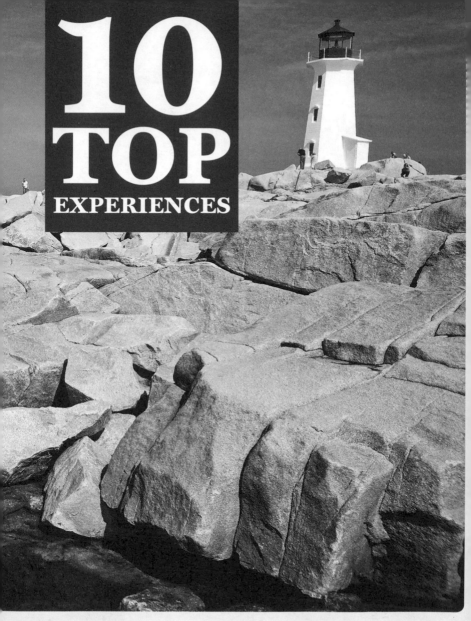

10 TOP EXPERIENCES

Peggy's Cove

1 It's on all the postcards and is clogged with tour buses throughout summer, yet Peggy (p45) enchants all who visit. The lighthouse, the blue-grey sea and the tiny sheltered bay scattered with crab traps and Popeye-esque boat docks are all straight out of a sailor's yarn. To get beyond the snapshot take the time to meander, and experience a glimpse of life in a very, very small Maritime village. It's surprising Disney hasn't made a film here yet.

Bay of Fundy Tides

2 The Bay of Fundy (p121) is home to the highest tides in the world. Boats look hopelessly beached on mud flats and piers look ridiculously lofty at low tide. Then, when one billion tonnes of water flow back into the bay, boats bob up to 15m above where they were six hours earlier – it's surreal. Get right into the tidal action by rafting the tidal bore, or relax with a whale-watching cruise, on which you might see blue whales or the rare fin whale.

Halifax Waterfront

3 When the fog is in, the tall ships, piers and harbor take on the air of an eerie pirate-movie set. A foghorn blows and you can almost imagine the cold, dingy scene of yesteryear. Then the sun comes out and everything turns festive: street buskers, laughter peeling from outdoor pub seating and kids with ice-cream cones fill the waterfront; container ships and sailboats chug across the sparkling bay. Hop on the Dartmouth ferry to get a view back to shore of Halifax's boxy downtown (p33).

ANDREW BAIN

Scottish & Acadian Music

4 Long cold winters have been endured for centuries with the help of lively fiddle playing and dancing. Call it a ceilidh, kitchen party or concert (p228), but don't miss the chance to experience something that brings joy to much of this part of the world. Listen to bagpipes or watch young fiddle virtuosos play while the oldies get up and step dance. Music is practiced indoors all winter to be let loose to party in summer at community halls, pubs, parks and festivals.

ANDREW BAIN

Viking Trail

5 The Viking Trail (p194), aka Rte 430, connects Newfoundland's two World Heritage sites on the northern peninsula. Gros Morne National Park, with its fjordlike lakes and geological oddities, rests at its base, while the sublime, 1000-year-old Viking settlement at L'Anse aux Meadows – Leif Eriksson's pad – stares out from the peninsula's tip. The road is an attraction in its own right, holding close to the sea as it heads resolutely north past Port au Choix' ancient burial grounds and the ferry jump-off to big bad Labrador.

EMILY RIDDELL

Lobster Suppers

6 Slapping on a bib was never so much fun. Join the crowds of hungry revelers attacking their plate-sized, orange-red crustacean with forks, pickers and nutcrackers. Get covered in lobster juice; dunk each mouthful in butter and enjoy. Don't forget to leave room for the feast's common accompaniments: mussels, chowder, fresh biscuits, salad and strawberry shortcake for dessert. You can get the lobster supper experience (p234) at restaurants but the best, cheapest and most fun meals are at local churches and town halls.

Iceberg Alley

7 They shimmer from white to electric blue as they float down the grey-black Atlantic. It's a wonder that these icebergs (p202) have broken away from their Greenland home to create such a show, but even more amazing is that some of the ice is more than 15,000 years old. Having this ancient ice to cool down a summer drink is an odd sensation – are you really enjoying global warming or will this drink give you Paleolithic superpowers?

Cape Breton Highlands National Park

8 Circuitous roads wind along evergreen ridgelines and dramatic coastal cliffs. Eagles soar above, whales spout in the distance and moose can be seen along the roadside. Tackle this national park (p77) as a drive or a peddle but be sure to buckle up your hiking boots at least once to explore the trails, which lead past streams, waterfalls and wildflowers to even more stunning vistas. On the coast, paddle a kayak or take a whale-watching tour to look for minke whales, seabirds and seals.

CHERYL FORBES

RADIUS IMAGES/PHOTOLIBRARY

Grand Manan Island

9 From windy, jagged cliffs and marshland, to spruce forests and sloping points with storybook lighthouses, Grand Manan (p110) has incredible natural diversity along its 30km length. There are dozens of trails to wander and coves to explore but no fast-food restaurants or traffic. The silence is broken only by the rhythmic ocean surf. You feel about a million nautical miles away from anything not windswept, rugged or overwhelmingly natural. To get out of a peaceful stupor, go kayaking, cycling, whale watching or birding.

Green Gables

10 Let the stories of your childhood come alive at the real-life sites (p154) that provided the backdrop to the beloved Anne of Green Gables series. All over Prince Edward Island you'll find kitsch gift shops, little girls dressed up in red polyester 'Anne' braids, and antiques and old-time memorabilia, as well as places that understandably inspired names such as the 'Lake of Shining Waters' and 'White Way of Delight.'

EMILY RIDDELL

Welcome to
Nova Scotia, New Brunswick & Prince Edward Island

Delimited and fashioned by the mighty Atlantic, these down-home Canadian provinces call you 'Deary,' offer you hot seafood chowder then ask you to dance as whales breach in the distance.

Water World

'Water everywhere,' you think, as you scan the horizon from the cliff top to which this path has led. The surf crashes, the tides pull, the wind slaps you with a briny smell. It's forever about the sea here.

Then you see it. No, not the bank of fog rolling in over the hill. You see that too, curse it, but out on the water you spot a fine spray emanating from what appears to be a log. Then it happens! The log morphs into two giant tail flukes arching up, cascading water from their scalloped edges before it slaps down upwelling a fan of water. Seconds later the slick arch of a whale body roll-slides on the inky ocean surface once more, and then it's gone.

It's a freeze-frame moment, one of many to experience in Atlantic Canada. Such flashes might occur as you whiz past a lupine-fringed sienna-colored beach on your bike in Prince Edward Island (PEI), fly-fish the mythical rivers of French-tinged New Brunswick, watch icebergs float by in Newfoundland or hit a 90-degree angle mounting a tidal bore wave in an inflatable dinghy in Nova Scotia. This is Atlantic Canada and it's tops for hiking, biking, kayaking, whale watching or anything having to do with the sea and outdoors.

A Foot-tapping Good Time

What happens to people when the cold keeps them indoors a good part of the year? They learn to play the fiddle, cook up a mighty fine chowder (plus maybe a little homebrew) and wear out their dancing shoes. Yes, this is a culture well-practiced in the art of partying and it likes nothing more than to share the good times with all who visit; if these come-one-come-all get togethers don't make you tap your feet, check your pulse. Outdoor music and food festivals fill up the summer calendar that much more as the good times expand with the sunshine. Everyone is in on the festivities – Acadian and Scottish each have their own distinct music – and you're all invited, so be there by six.

Shellfish Bliss

Gear-up for some serious crustacean battles by wearing a bib and not worrying about getting butter in your hair. Lobster, scallops, crab, mussels and oysters form one of the best bounties the sea has on offer. Confused about how to get the meat out of that crustacean leg? These thoughtful Canadians often supply you with instructions on the placemat of how to master the beast with your supplied utensils. Part surgeon, part warrior, part gourmet, the experience of eating these critters is almost as good as they taste. Eat your way around from the scallops of Nova Scotia to the oysters of PEI to more adventurous cod tongues of Newfoundland; lobster is everywhere.

need to know

Currency
» Canadian dollars ($)

Language
» English and French

When to Go?

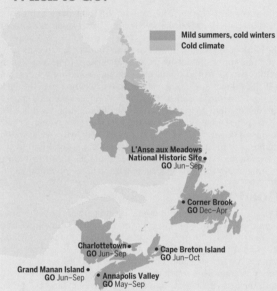

Mild summers, cold winters
Cold climate

L'Anse aux Meadows National Historic Site •
GO Jun–Sep

• **Corner Brook**
GO Dec–Apr

Charlottetown •
GO Jun–Sep

• **Cape Breton Island**
GO Jun–Oct

Grand Manan Island •
GO Jun–Sep

• **Annapolis Valley**
GO May–Sep

High Season
(Jul & Aug)

» Sunshine and warm weather prevail

» The whole region plunges into festival mode, with theater, music and food extravaganzas

» Attractions and visitor information centers keep longer summer hours

Shoulder
(May–Jun & Sep–Oct)

» Wildflowers bloom in the spring and leaves turn gold and red in the fall

» Temperatures are cool but comfortable

» Some lodgings and restaurants shut

Low Season
(Nov–Apr)

» Few lodgings and attractions outside the big cities and ski resorts remain open

» Darkness and cold take over

» Christmas festivals liven up December and January

Set Your Budget

Budget less than
$90

» Dorm bed: $25–38

» Campsite: $20–30

» Plenty of markets and supermarkets for self-catering

Midrange
$90–250

» B&B or room in a midrange hotel: $70–180

» Restaurant meal: from $20 plus drinks

» Rental car: $35–65 per day

» Attraction admissions: $5–15

High end more than
$250

» Four-star hotel room or luxury B&B: from $180

» Three-course meal in a top restaurant: from $40 plus drinks

» Sea kayaking or canoe day-tour: $55–120

Money
» ATMs widely available. Credit cards accepted in most hotels and restaurants.

Visas
» Generally not required for stays of up to 180 days; some nationalities require a temporary resident visa.

Mobile Phones
» Local SIM cards can be used in European and Australian phones. Other phones must be set to roaming.

Driving
» Drive on the right; steering wheel is on the left side of the car.

Websites
» **Nova Scotia Tourism** (www.novascotia.com)

» **Tourism New Brunswick** (www.tourismnewbrunswick.ca)

» **Tourism PEI** (www.tourismpei.com)

» **Newfoundland & Labrador Tourism** (www.newfoundlandlabrador.com)

» **Parks Canada** (www.pc.gc.ca)

» **Lonely Planet** (www.lonelyplanet.com/canada)

Exchange Rates

Australia	A$1	C$0.94
Europe	€1	C$1.34
Japan	¥100	C$1.25
New Zealand	NZ$1	C$0.74
UK	UK£1	C$1.64
US	US$1	C$1.05

For current exchange rates see www.xe.com.

Important Numbers

Nova Scotia and PEI's area code is 902, New Brunswick is 506, and Newfoundland and Labrador is 709. Many accommodations have toll-free numbers that are free to dial from Canada and the USA. For local calls you need to use the area code but not the country code.

Country Code	1
International Access Code	011
Emergency	911
Directory Assistance	411

Arriving
» **Halifax Stanfield International Airport**
Airbuses – Every 45 minutes 5am to 11pm
Taxis – $54; 30 minutes to downtown

» **St John's International Airport**
Taxis – $22.50 plus $3 for each additional passenger; 10 minutes to downtown

» **Land Border Crossings**
Canadian Border Services Agency (www.cbsa-asfc.gc.ca/general/times/menu-e.html) posts updated wait times hourly; usually less than 30 minutes

Keep in Mind
Perhaps the important thing to remember is Canada's immense scale: distances can be deceivingly long and travel times slow due to single-lane highways and even a lack of highways (such as on the east and west coasts, when ferries take over from roads). Don't try to pack too much into your itinerary and do consider limiting your explorations to one or two regions in depth.

Also, blackflies and mosquitoes can be a major annoyance in the summer. Bring insect repellent and clothing to cover up with, especially in northern and woodsy regions. Your flesh will thank you.

Transportation (rental car, ferry) and sleeping reservations are important in July and August.

what's new

For this new edition of Nova Scotia, New Brunswick & Prince Edward Island, our authors have hunted down the fresh, the revamped, the transformed, the hot and the happening. These are some of our favorites. For up-to-the-minute reviews and recommendations, see lonelyplanet.com/canada.

Wineries, Nova Scotia

1 Several new wineries have opened in the Bear Valley and Annapolis Valley regions making the west coast a bona fide destination for wine tasting (p55).

Marble Zip Tours, Newfoundland

2 Marble Mountain strung up the highest zipline in Canada, and it cruises right by a waterfall throughout the seasons (p203).

Joggins Fossil Center, Nova Scotia

3 Soon after the Joggins Fossil Cliffs became a World Heritage site, the town opened a state-of-the-art museum dedicated to the scene, with excellent cliff tours offered (p71).

Distilleries, Prince Edward Island

4 Prince Edward Distillery in Hermanville cooks up potato vodka, putting the province's abundant tuber to good use, while Myriad View Distillery in Rollo Bay produces legal, knee-buckling moonshine (p147).

Hostels, Nova Scotia

5 Excellent new hostels have opened in Digby (Digby Backpackers Hostel; p58), Caledonia (Caledonia Country Hostel; p52), Five Islands (Mo's at Five Islands; p68) and Lawrencetown Beach (Lawrencetown Beach House; p44) making it easier to tour the province on the cheap.

Evandale Resort, New Brunswick

6 By the ferry landing on the Saint John River, this once-abandoned Victorian inn has been restored to its former opulence amid white farmhouses and wildflower fields (p99).

Cupids Legacy Centre, Newfoundland

7 Over 150,000 artifacts have been unearthed on this site of England's first Canadian colony and you can tour the archaeological dig where they're still finding treasures (p180).

Ship to Shore Restaurant, Prince Edward Island

8 John Bil, founder of the now-departed Flex Mussles and three-time oyster-shucking champion, has opened a humble shrine to fresh shellfish (p156).

Montgomery Theatre, Prince Edward Island

9 This theater in a renovated 19th-century church presents plays from the life and times of Lucy Maud Montgomery, author of *Anne of Green Gables* (p153).

Wild Caraway Restaurant & Cafe

10 Find locally sourced foodie goodness at this cafe that's so cute you'll never want to leave – and you won't have to, because there are great rooms upstairs (p70).

if you like...

Seafood

If you're a seafood lover with a weakness for shellfish, then you've come to the right place. Sweet Atlantic lobsters are ubiquitous and other underwater delicacies such as Digby scallops and Malpeque oysters are world-famous for their quality.

Lobster Suppers A Maritime seafood feast found mostly in Nova Scotia and Prince Edward Island (PEI), best taken in churches and town halls (p234)

Ship to Shore The freshest critters of the sea are prepared by PEI's 'shellfish shaman' (p155)

Royal Fundy Seafood Market Tuck into this fishmonger's shop for fresh-from-the-wharf Digby scallops and more (p58)

Norseman Restaurant & Art Gallery Put on rubber boots to handpick your lobster right on the shore (p201)

Roland's Sea Vegetables Buy some nori, sea lettuce or Irish moss that are purported to be the best in the world (p111)

Wine & Spirit Tasting

Hard to believe, but Nova Scotia's Annapolis Valley has the same latitude as Bordeaux, France and was probably the first place that wine grapes were grown in the New World. Other areas produce harder stuff: whisky, vodka and good 'ole fashioned moonshine.

Annapolis Valley & Bear River regions Wineries are popping up everywhere through these two adjacent areas perfect for touring (p55)

Glenora Inn & Distillery Canada's only single malt whisky is produced here; tour the distillery and take a swig of the spirits (p76)

Rossignol Winery Specializes in fruit wines including an award-winning (and delicious) blackberry meade (p144)

PEI Distilleries One makes fine potato vodka and the other makes Canada's first legal moonshine so potent it evaporates on the tongue (p147)

Auk Island Winery Try fruit wines made with iceberg water and local fruit (p191)

Historic Sites

Leif Eriksson was probably the first European to set foot in the Americas in Newfoundland, marking the beginning of this region's rich European history. Folks get into it too, dressing up in period garb and acting the part bringing the sites to life.

Louisbourg The mother of this region's historical sites – the size and authenticity of the recreated sites make you feel like you time-warped to the 18th century (p86)

L'Anse aux Meadows National Historical Site Seriously, this is where the Vikings landed? Yup and it's just as cool as you hoped it would be (p199)

King's Landing Historical Settlement Woo hoo! It's a recreated 19th-century Loyalist village including pub food and children's programs (p98)

Pier 21 Over a million immigrants landed here to start their lives anew in Canada or the USA. Prepare to be moved by true heartwarming stories and maybe find the names of your ancestors (p33)

If you like... **surfing**, head to Lawrencetown Beach,
Nova Scotia to find several surf schools (p44)
If you like... icebergs, head to 'Iceberg Alley,'
Newfoundland. Watch them float by and even find
pieces of them cooling your drink (p202)

Lighthouses

When most people envision the Atlantic and Maritime provinces, there's a lighthouse in the image somewhere. A drive out to any coastal spit will usually turn up a red-and-white beacon just waiting to be photographed.

Peggy's Cove The quintessential Maritime image: a red-and-white storybook lighthouse on rolling granite backed by the cold Atlantic (p45)

Cape Enrage Watch the rise and fall of the Fundy tides from this windswept, 150-year-old beacon (p121)

Long Point Spot icebergs in May and June from the 360-degree view in this 1876 lighthouse (p191)

Swallowtail Lighthouse Whitewashed perfection on a grassy bluff where you can watch seals raiding ancient fish traps (p110)

Point Amour Lighthouse Provincial Historic Site The tallest lighthouse in Atlantic Canada also has a small maritime history museum (p212)

Point Prim PEI's prettiest beacon with views over the island; climb up and try the hand-pump fog horn (p144)

Hiking & Walking

This is a forested region with so many fantastic hiking possibilities that we can hardly list them all in this book. From coastal jaunts to deep woods, mountains, lakes and valleys, you'll be looking out for birdlife and moose, and will surely spot a rabbit or four.

Cape Breton Highlands National Park Winding roads to ocean vistas perfect for spotting whales, moose or eagles (p77)

Fundy National Park See the highest rise and fall of the tides from forested bliss (p119)

Mt Carleton Start out in French cowboy country to discover rugged hiking and quiet lakes (p100)

Southeastern Avalon Peninsula So many parks and reserves you'll be spoiled for choice and are guaranteed to see plenty of birds (p178)

Cape Split There's no better place to hike along the Fundy tidal shore then reward yourself afterwards with a glass of red (p62)

Kayaking & Canoeing

Perhaps the most Canadian of sports and a spectacular way to experience this region from a watery perspective, kayaking and canoeing are activities that you should try at least once on your trip. From mellow lake paddles to high action in the waves past spouting whales, the water is a huge part of what makes these provinces tick.

Eastern Shore Nova Scotia's forgotten coast is studded with islands and calm bays, perfect for paddling, all beautiful even in dense fog (p87)

Mt Carleton Gorgeous wilderness canoeing through a string of wilderness lakes surrounded by tree-clad mountains (p100)

North Rustico Scoot off from the red-sand beach and burn the calories you'll replenish at a lobster supper that night (p153)

Chiputneticook Lakes Take a four-day camping and canoeing trip through this spectacular wilderness lake area (p104)

>> Swallowtail Lighthouse (p110), Grand Manan Island, New Brunswick

GUYLAIN DOYLE

Whale Watching

Thar she blows! Humpbacks and minke are the most common whales you'll spot in this region but lucky souls will see elusive blue whales and the endangered fin whale, two of the largest creatures on Earth. It's worth the chill and seasickness. Really.

Digby Neck Get way out into the Bay of Fundy for your best chances to see blue and fin whales (p57)

Pleasant Bay You'll find plenty of folks leading tours up here and you'll probably see eagles soaring close to shore too (p79)

Fundy Isles The whales are here but you'll surely also get to see plenty of seals and bird life including puffins (p108)

Witless Bay Ecological Reserve Just when you thought your dreams had been realized with whale, seal and puffin sightings, an iceberg floats by. Yeah, this place has it all (p178)

Music

Whether it's Scottish, folk or rock, music rings everywhere in this corner of Canada. Ceilidhs, kitchen parties and some awesome festivals liven up the summer and extend into the fall.

Ceilidh Trail Nonstop kitchen parties and ceilidhs await along this highway; finish up in Chéticamp for a taste of Acadian rhythms (p76)

Halifax It's got one of the highest rates of bars per capita in the world and nearly every one of them swells with live music. You'll find everything here, but this is your best stop for modern and hip sounds (p40)

Stan Rogers Folk Festival It ain't Glastonbury but even the most seasoned festival-goers rave about the intimate vibe and quality of music here that ranges from bluegrass to Celtic (p88)

Cavendish Beach Festival Camp on the beach and enjoy the best modern country music scattered with some rock and folk acts. Big names show up at this one (p153)

Acadian Culture

No, they aren't Québecois, these French speakers have their own unique culture that is directly linked to the Cajuns in southern US. The proud culture has a soulful brand of fiddle music, their own tricolor flag and a delicious cuisine specializing in delicately spiced meat pies.

Northeastern New Brunswick Staunchly Acadian and sporting one of the region's best historical sites, the Acadian Historic Village (p129)

Chéticamp, Nova Scotia Probably the best place to get into the culture via summer music, theater performances and Acadian restaurants (p77)

Pubnico, Nova Scotia Out of the way but so friendly with its own historical recreation, Le Village Historique Acadien (p54)

French Shore, Nova Scotia Less touristed than Chéticamp, find nightly concerts in summer and roadside eateries serving rappie pie (p55)

Région Évangeline, PEI Small but with a punch: this was the first region where the Acadian flag was ever unfurled (p159)

month by month

February

This is not a popular month to visit this part of Canada unless you're looking for deep snow and hard ice. Expect a warm welcome during one of the coldest months of the year.

Skiing

Atlantic Canada's best skiing is at Marble Mountain in Corner Brook, Newfoundland, open from December to April. It's challenging terrain but lift lines are short and the snow is plentiful.

World Pond Hockey Tournament, Plaster Rock, New Brunswick

Hokey purists, don't miss this event. All proceeds go towards building an arena for the folks of Tobique Valley but until then, the ponds are cleared and over 120 teams come to shoot pucks around the ice.

April

The land is usually thawing by April and trees are sprouting new leaves but if you visit, you'll be enjoying it all with very few other people around.

Mi-Carême

Mid-Lent, usually in March or April, is marked in the Acadian town of Chéticamp by getting in disguise and visiting neighborhood homes to see if anyone can guess who you are. Meanwhile music, feasts and entertainment are found around town.

May

If you don't like crowds, May can be a lovely time to visit this region. Apple trees are blossoming and many attractions and accommodations start to open around the middle of the month.

Snow Crab Season

Snow crab season runs from May 1 to August 31 in Labrador and Newfoundland, while it goes from mid-April to late-July in the more southern provinces.

June

Dodge the crowds by showing up in June when the weather can be sunny but brisk and wildflowers are blooming. In some areas many tourist-oriented attractions may still be shut or keep low-season hours.

Whale Watching

Whales begin to be seen in the Bay of Fundy and off the coast of Newfoundland this month then hang around to feed till around October or November. Meanwhile on Nova Scotia's Southshore the season runs from July to October.

Drifting Icebergs

Spring and early summer are the best times to see some of the tens of thousands of icebergs that break off in Greenland to sail down the coast of Newfoundland's 'Iceberg Alley.' The iceberg-tracking site www.icebergfinder.com can help you plan where to go and what times of year are best to visit.

☆ Acadian Concerts

In late June you'll start to find summer Acadian concerts and kitchen parties along the Nova Scotia coast between Yarmouth and Digby. More are scheduled through July and by August you can find a performance most nights of the week.

✱ Nova Scotia Multicultural Festival

For 25 years Dartmouth has celebrated its diversity with a weekend of waterfront concerts. It was moved to Halifax in 2010 but many are hopeful it will be back at Alderney Landing in Dartmouth by 2011.

July

Summer starts to heat up, festivals bring music and food to the streets and all outdoor activities are a go. Yet early in the month things can still be relatively un-crowded.

✕ Lobster Suppers

During the summer lobster season (which changes throughout the region), tasty crustations get boiled up en masse and served to hungry crowds with all-you-can-eat fixings and pie for dessert.

☆ Ceilidhs

Cape Breton is the capital of these foot-tapping Scottish music performances where most people in the small communities participate, show up as audience and get up and dance. While found year-round, you can find them nightly in July and August.

✱ Canada Day

Canada's national holiday is celebrated throughout the region with parades, fireworks, music and picnics. Many businesses shut in observance so make sure you have plans and a picnic packed before the big day, July 1.

✱ Cavendish Beach Festival

Some of the biggest names in country music come up to Cavendish, Prince Edward Island, to play beachside while campers get their party on. This is one of the largest outdoor music festivals in North America and the island swells with people.

✱ Indian River Festival

As an antidote to Cavendish partying, this festival from the end of June into October showcases classical, jazz and world music in an acoustically sublime St Mary's Church. The French Gothic architecture warms up the beautiful music into a wonderful summer experience.

◉ Peak of Lupine Season

Lupine usually begin blooming in June but by July they cover hillsides, colorfully border the highways and decorate home fronts. Purple is the dominant color but you'll also see scatterings of pink lupine, especially in PEI.

✱ Halifax Pride Week

Halifax booms with events for Pride Week, the largest this side of Montréal. Don't miss the annual highly entertaining Dykes vs Divas Softball game, the Queer Acts Theatre Festival, dance party and the extravagant parade.

✱ Tall Ships, Nova Scotia

It's magical watching tall ships sail through Halifax Harbour. Unfortunately, the Tall Ship Festival isn't a yearly event and the next one is scheduled for 2012. However, there are always a few ships docked along the waterfront.

☆ Nova Scotia Tattoo

If you're into military marching bands and WWII reminiscing, this event, the 'largest annual indoor show in the world,' will appeal to you. Some international performers including clowns, comics, acrobats and bagpipers are thrown in for good measure.

✱ Bastille Day

Celebrate the July 14 French national holiday with bona fide French nationals in St-Pierre. The town comes alive with music, food stalls and family-oriented games for nonstop fun. Stop in for a few éclairs while you're there as well.

August

High season is in full-swing by August when the weather is at its sunniest, everything is open on extended hours and festivals are going on everywhere.

Stan Rogers Folk Festival

The tiny remote seaside town of Canso swells with visitors once a year for what many claim is one of the best music festivals in the Maritimes. It's a mellow scene with camping, easy-going people and amazing live performances.

Halifax International Busker Festival

Comics, mimics, daredevils and more from Canada and around the world perform on several outdoor stages over 11 days. This is the oldest festival of its kind in Canada and the audience usually exceeds 500,000 people.

Bakeapple Season

Called 'cloudberries' throughout much of the rest of the world, this rare and delectable berry is in full season by mid-August – then it's tossed liberally into pies and jam and is even given its own August festival in Labrador.

Digby Scallop Days

Celebrating Digby's massive scallop fleet, this five-day festival in early August lets you try out different styles of preparation (all good). Alongside are parades, dances, car shows and even a kids' pie-eating contest.

Miramichi Folksong Festival

Another superlative event, this is North America's oldest folk fest set along the winding namesake river in New Brunswick. Expect a low-key family vibe set to the tune of fiddlers and singers with all the old folks getting up to boogie.

Newfoundland & Labrador Folk Festival

Celebrating traditional Newfie music and storytelling over three days, this festival has been a huge hit for over 34 years. A scattering of performers from outside the province also turn up to spark the summer St John's atmosphere even more.

Royal St John's Regatta

Just after the Folk Festival, Newfoundland keeps up the action with this rowing regatta, claimed to be the oldest sporting event in North America, on Quidi Vidi Lake. St John's becomes a ghost town as thousands head to watch and enjoy the sunshine.

September

Summer gets extended for a slew of music festivals while the harvest of food and wine is enjoyed to the fullest. Temperatures become more brisk but the sun still makes regular appearances.

PEI International Shellfish Festival

Called 'the biggest kitchen party in Canada,' here you get your hands juicy with interactive culinary demos, gorge on the best seafood in the world and enjoy two chowder championships. Meanwhile there's live music, a widely regarded oyster-shucking contest and chef challenges.

Surf's Up

Hurricane season runs from August to November kicking up swells that hit Nova Scotia's Atlantic Coast, creating surprisingly fun waves. The water is the warmest in September so if you hate ice-cream headaches, go now.

Atlantic Film Festival

Atlantic Canada and Canada's best films plus some gems from around the world get screened at this intimate yet internationally recognized festival in Halifax. Of course, this is Nova Scotia so there are plenty of music performances scheduled alongside.

Canadian Deep Roots Festival

Enjoy live folk and rock to Mi'kmaw, Acadian and other unique music, all with Canadian roots, in the fun university town of Wolfville. Workshops are available with some of the artists.

Nova Scotia Fall Wine Festival

There's no better moment to enjoy Nova Scotia's wines than at this event where you can meet wine makers and enjoy their vintages paired with meals prepared by renowned chefs.

October

Ah, the colors of fall. As the world turns from green to red and the temperatures start to really drop, there are

still plenty of music events plus Canadian Thanksgiving to keep you warm.

Fall Foliage

One of nature's most spectacular shows of color begins late September and peaks in October. Panoramas are filled with brick reds, rust, gold and copper that eventually turn brown before dropping to the ground.

Thanksgiving

Unlike the US, Canadian Thanksgiving is celebrated the first Monday in October in thanks of the harvest, not of aboriginal hospitality. Families tend to eat their big meal over the weekend and a few fall festivals surround the big day.

Celtic Colours

Big names in Nova Scotian music make it up to this music festival that runs for nine days. Expect appearances from the rest of the Celtic music world as well, as the fall colors reach their peak.

Halifax Pop Explosion

About 130 bands show up for this event, with a bit of everything from punk and indie to hip-hop and folk. Whatever your tastes, look forward to being introduced to new talent.

December

Christmas

The festivities begin in November with Christmas parades and festivals of light that then move into Father Christmas greetings and Christmas markets. The big day is of course on December 25 when most families get together for holiday supper.

itineraries

Whether you've got six days or 60, these itineraries provide a starting point for the trip of a lifetime. Want more inspiration? Head online to lonelyplanet. com/thorntree to chat with other travelers.

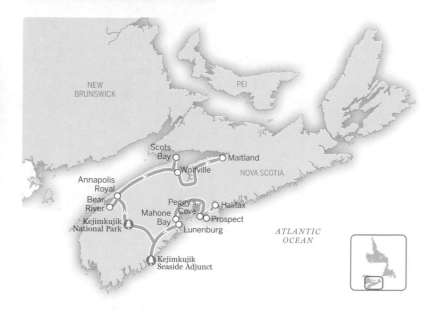

One Week to 10 Days
Essential Nova Scotia

> Soak up some music and culture in **Halifax** then travel to nearby **Peggy's Cove**. Jostle for position to snap the most photographed lighthouse in the world, or have a more subdued experience picnicking in equally pretty **Prospect**. Don't forget your sunscreen in **Mahone Bay**, where the sun shines bright on great craft shopping and sea kayaking. Move on slightly south to **Lunenburg**, a World Heritage site known for its colorful boxy buildings, *Bluenose* schooner and lobstering tours. The **Kejimkujik Seaside Adjunct** provides miles of unspoiled white beaches (and maybe seals), while its big brother **Kejimkujik National Park** lies inland and is a prime place to float a canoe and drift through the woods. Cross the province to **Annapolis Royal** to stay at a heritage bed and breakfast, explore its fort by day and graveyard by night. The next day visit the wineries of **Bear River** and around **Wolfville** before stopping to wolf down a meal at a fine restaurant. Lastly explore the Fundy coast by hiking around **Scots Bay** or go to **Maitland** to get right in and raft the tidal bore.

Two to Three Weeks

Cabot & Viking Trails

Spend a couple days in **Halifax** enjoying lively bars and a nonstop music scene then hit the road up the Atlantic Coast. Stop for a chilly surf at **Lawrencetown Beach** or a hike through pine forest to a spectacular white-sand beach at **Taylor Head Provincial Park**. Visit the historical village at **Sherbrook** then either cut up Hwy 7 for a shortcut to Cape Breton Island or, with an extra day or two, continue on the coast to the isolated, windswept village of **Canso** and the more sheltered picture-perfect hamlet of **Guysborough**. Just after arriving on Cape Breton from the causeway, veer left towards Hwy 30 and stop in at one of the many ceilidh music gatherings along this route. Hook up with the **Cabot Trail**, at **Chéticamp**, a deeply Acadian town. Aah, now you're getting your money's worth. Next you can watch whales or chant with monks at the Tibetan monastery in **Pleasant Bay** and look for moose and nesting bald eagles in **Cape Breton Highlands National Park**. It's always nice to stretch your legs with a hike at **Meat Cove**. And don't forget to get your art fix at the studios along the **St Ann's Loop** before heading over to **Baddeck** to learn everything you ever wanted to know about Alexander Graham Bell at the town's fabulous museum. From here take a jaunt east to **Louisbourg** to visit the massive, windy restored French Fort complete with costumed thespians and activities to bring you back to the 18th century. Stop at the Miner's Museum in **Glace Bay** before arriving in industrial North Sydney for the ferry to Newfoundland.

It's a six-hour sail over the sometimes-rough swell of the Cabot Strait to **Port aux Basques**. Alight and drive north to **Gros Morne National Park**, rich with mountain hikes, sea-kayak tours, fjords and weird rock formations. Take the Viking Trail from here to its awe-inspiring endpoint: **L'Anse aux Meadows National Historic Site**, North America's first settlement. Leif Eriksson and his Viking pals homesteaded the place 1000 years ago, and it probably looked much the same then as it does now. After coming all this way, you too will feel like an Atlantic explorer.

10 Days to Two Weeks
Bay of Fundy Tidal Tour

❯ Experience the dramatic Fundy tides and its wildlife on this loop that could be tackled from Maine, USA. Cross the bridge to **Campobello Island**, the childhood home of 32nd US president Franklin D Roosevelt, from Lubec, Maine then visit the Roosevelt's home that's now a fascinating museum. Take the car ferry to fisherman-funky **Deer Island** to check out **Old Sow**, the world's second-largest natural tidal whirlpool, before boarding another ferry that shuttles you to the mainland. Drive north to gritty yet cosmopolitan **Saint John**, to fill up on fine dining, and warm up your hiking boots at **Irving Nature Park** to see hundreds of birds and possibly seals. Spend the next few days really breaking your boots in throughout **Fundy National Park** and its extensive coastal trails. Continue north to **Cape Enrage** to take a tour of the lighthouse, sea kayak or rappel down the rock cliffs that meet the rise and fall of the powerful tides. Move on to the bizarre **Hopewell Rocks** formations, a must-see, but with the hundreds of visitors you might be a little disappointed after the more pristine experience at Cape Enrage.

Now it's time to change provinces. Drive across the border to Nova Scotia and down the coast of Chignecto Bay to **Joggins** to see the Unesco Heritage fossil cliffs. Continue along driftwood-strewn Chignecto Bay to stop for lunch in **Advocate Harbour** then move onto **Parrsboro** to look for semiprecious stones on the beach. Enjoy the views of the Cobequid Bay tides, which can change up to a foot per minute till you reach **Maitland**, where you can get into inflatable dinghies for an exhilarating rafting adventure on the tidal bore. Get your hiking boots on again around **Scots Bay** where you'll be rewarded with some of the best views of the tides on this entire route. Reward your physical exertion in **Digby** where you can dine on succulent scallops and explore **Digby Neck**, home to the region's most spectacular whale watching and even more hiking trails. From Digby, take the car ferry back to Saint John, New Brunswick to complete the loop.

One Week
Foodie Loop

❭ Eat and drink your way through **Halifax**, then drive to the lively town of **Pictou** to take the car ferry to Wood Islands, Prince Edward Island. Spend your first day in Canada's cutest province exploring the east; stop at **Rossignol Winery**, quirky distilleries and stroll on gorgeous **Basin Head Beach**. Dine in **St Peters** before moving on to **Charlottetown** where you can base yourself for the next few days as you explore the central part of the province. Learn about Anne of Green Gables in **Cavendish**, gorge on lobster in **New Glasgow**, oysters in **Malpeque** and enjoy Charlottetown itself by dining at Lot 30.

Spend a night or two in **Summerside** to explore western PEI with a drive up the scenic west coast through Acadian villages to lighthouse vistas. Gape at the giant windmills of **North Cape** before looping back on the east coast, stopping to learn about Mi'kmaq culture on lovely **Lennox Island**.

Take the **Confederation Bridge** to drive back to Halifax via the bucolic wine region around **Tatamagouche** or, with more time, head down the Fundy Coast to **Parrsboro** as described in the Bay of Fundy Tidal Tour.

Eight Days
Maritime Drive-Through

❭ Short on time but want to see as much as possible? Enjoy **Halifax** for a day before swinging down to snap a few photos at **Peggy's Cove**, then stop for the night in World Heritage–listed **Lunenburg** and spoil yourself with dinner at Fleur de Sel. The next day cross via Bridgewater up Hwy 8 stopping for a day hike or a paddle in **Kejimkujic National Park** then stay in **Annapolis Royal** and take the town's famous nighttime graveyard tour. Take a short drive to **Digby**, perhaps enjoying a scallop lunch, then take the ferry to **Saint John**, New Brunswick. Stay or camp in **Fundy National Park** or in adorable **St Martins**, spending the next day hiking and continuing up the Fundy Coast to view the tides at **Cape Enrage** and **Hopewell Rocks**. The next day drive across the Confederation Bridge into PEI and **Charlottetown**. Explore Anne's Land around **Cavendish**, have a lobster supper then take a tour of PEI's east coast the following day before taking the car ferry back to Nova Scotia. From here it takes an hour and 45 minutes to drive back to Halifax.

regions at a glance

Yaar! This is the Canada for enjoying steel-colored seascapes and salt air with a big bowl of chowder and a pint of ale to wash it down. Everything here revolves around the cold Atlantic Ocean, from today's whale-watching adventures and lobster feasts to the history of Vikings and pirates. While tied together by geography and history, each province has its own personality, from the iceberg-clad desolation of Newfoundland to the forested inland rivers and lakes of New Brunswick, the storybook farmlands of PEI and the never-ending coastal and cultural variations of Nova Scotia. Wherever you choose to go, you'll never be far from the sound of waves crashing on a beach or a simple supper of fresh fish.

Nova Scotia

Culture ✓✓
Activities ✓✓
History ✓✓

Cultural Mishmash

Tartan shops, French-speaking villages and Aboriginal communities are all within kilometers of each other. Throw in some African Nova Scotians and Pier 21, Canada's entry point for over a million immigrants, and you have the definition of a cultural melting pot.

Coves, Cliffs & Tides

Coastal coves between evergreen islets are bird and marine-mammal habitats that beg you to go paddling. On the Fundy Coast see the highest tides in the world that constantly change the landscape. Cape Breton Island's vertiginous coastal cliffs are home to moose and nesting bald eagles.

Time Warp

Nova Scotians don't just preserve their historical vestiges, they get in period costume and do old-time activities from lace making to blacksmithing, recreating the scene as it might have been hundreds of years ago.

p28

New Brunswick

Activities ✓✓
Fishing ✓✓✓
Wildlife ✓✓

You in a Canoe
From the tranquil Chiputneticook Lakes to the quicksilver Tobique River, New Brunswick is tops for canoeing, the most Canadian of activities. You can even meet artisans who still make canoes the old-fashioned way – a dying art.

Tie your Flies
Baseball stars and captains of industry used to come to New Brunswick to cast their fly rods into the province's salmon- and trout-choked rivers. Why not do the same?

Puffin Lovin'
Whether you're a hardcore birdwatcher or just want to be able to tell your friends you saw a moose, New Brunswick's got plenty of animal action to go around. Your best bet: observing rare Atlantic puffins on desolate Machias Seal Island.

p90

Prince Edward Island

Culture ✓✓
Cuisine ✓✓
Beaches ✓✓

It's All About Anne
Personified by Anne Shirley, LM Montgomery's spunky red-headed star of the *Anne of Green Gables* series, Prince Edward Island (PEI) is as sweet and pretty as it's portrayed in the books. Red dirt and sands mimic Anne's hair, while white picket fences and fields of wild flowers paint the real-life backdrop.

Lobster Suppers, Oysters & Potatoes
Vying with Idaho as potato capital of the Americas, you'll pass vine-covered hills to reach town halls serving fisherman-sized suppers of PEI's second most famous food, lobster. Then hit coves of sunlit fishing boats pulling up succulent Malpeque oysters.

White & Pink Beaches
PEI has sienna beach flats topped by red-and-white lighthouses, cream-colored road-eating dunes and stretches of white sands that 'sing' when you walk on them.

p133

Newfoundland & Labrador

Seascapes ✓✓✓
Culture ✓✓
History ✓✓

Great Big Sea
'There's one!' someone shouts, and sure enough, a big, barnacled humpback steams through the water. Or maybe they're referring to the icebergs. Whether you're hiking along shore, out in a boat or sitting by your window, Newfoundland's sea delivers.

Strange Brew
The peculiar brogue is vaguely Irish, the slang indecipherable enough to merit its own dictionary. Plates arrive with cod tongues, bakeapple jam and figgy duff. Towns have names like Dildo and Jerry's Nose. This place is so offbeat it even has its own time zone: a *half* hour ahead of the mainland.

Viking Vestiges
They've taken a low-key approach at L'Anse aux Meadows, Leif Eriksson's 1000-year-old settlement, but the forlorn sweep of land is more powerful that way. You can feel the Vikings' isolation.

p162

Look out for these icons:

 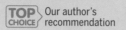 Our author's recommendation   A green or sustainable option   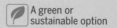 No payment required

On the Road

Nova Scotia

Best Places to Eat

» Fid (p39)

» Jane's on the Common (p39)

» Fleur de Sel (p50)

» Red Shoe Pub (p77)

» Lobster suppers (at town halls and churches around the province)

Best Places to Stay

» Waverley Inn (p38)

» Desbarres Manor (p87)

» Lightkeeper's Kitchen & Guest House (p70)

» Cranberry Cove Inn (p86)

» Digby Backpackers Hostel (p58)

Why Go?

At first glance, Nova Scotia appears sweet as a storybook: lupin-studded fields, gingerbread-like houses, picture-perfect lighthouses and lightly lapping waves on sandy shores make you want to wrap it all up and give it to a cuddly kid as a gift. Then another reality creeps up on you: this is also the raw Canada of fishermen braving icy seas, coal miners, moose, horseflies and hockey. Even so, locals remain the most down-to-earth folk you'll ever meet; Scottish, Acadian or Mi'kmaq, they all enjoy a drink, a song, a dance and a new face to share it with. During daylight hours it's easy to discover empty coastal beach trails and wilderness paths through mixed forest to vistas with briny breezes. For something more cosmopolitan, head to Halifax for some world-class dining and a rocking music scene.

When to Go
Halifax

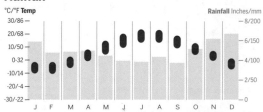

June to August Wildflowers carpet the country while whales come in close to feed

September & October Trees aflame with golds and reds provide the backdrop to fall music festivals

August to November Put on a thick wetsuit, hood and booties to surf icy hurricane swells

History

From time immemorial, the Mi'kmaq lived throughout present-day Nova Scotia. When the French established the first European settlement at Port Royal (today's Annapolis Royal) in 1605, Grand Chief Membertou offered them hospitality and became a frequent guest of Samuel de Champlain.

That close relationship with the French led to considerable suspicions by the British after they gained control of Nova Scotia, and rewards were offered for Mi'kmaq scalps. Starting in 1755, most French-speaking Acadians were deported to Louisiana (where they became 'Cajuns') and elsewhere for refusing to swear allegiance to the British Crown (see the boxed text, p65).

Nova Scotia was repopulated by some 35,000 United Empire Loyalists retreating from the American Revolution, including a small number of African slaves owned by Loyalists and also freed Black Loyalists. New England planters settled other communities and, starting in 1773, waves of Highland Scots arrived in northern Nova Scotia and Cape Breton Island.

Most Nova Scotians trace their ancestry to the British Isles, as a look at the lengthy 'Mac' and 'Mc' sections of the phone book easily confirms. Acadians who managed to return from Louisiana after 1764 found their lands in the Annapolis Valley occupied. They settled instead along the French Shore between Yarmouth and Digby, on Cape Breton Island, around Chéticamp, and on Isle Madame. Today Acadians make up some 18% of the population, though not as many actually speak French. African Nova Scotians make up about 4% of the population. There are approximately 20,000 Mi'kmaq in 18 different communities, which are concentrated around Truro and the Bras d'Or lakes on Cape Breton Island.

Local Culture

With nearly 8000km of coastline, Nova Scotia has a culture that revolves around the sea. Historically, this has been a hard-working region of coal mines and fisheries. The current culture is still very blue collar, but with the decline of the primary industries, many young Nova Scotians are forced to leave their province in search of work.

Perhaps because of the long winters and hard working days, an enormous number of Nova Scotians play music. Family get-togethers, particularly Acadian and Scot-tish, consist of strumming, fiddling, foot-tapping and dancing.

ⓘ Getting There & Away

Air

Most flights go to/from Halifax but there's also an international airport in Sydney on Cape Breton. Airlines include Air Canada, Air Canada Jazz, WestJet, United and Continental. There are multiple flights daily between Halifax and cities such as Toronto, Montréal, Ottawa, Saint John (New Brunswick), Moncton and Boston (Massachusetts). In summer and fall there's a weekly direct flight to London.

Bus

Acadian Lines (☑902-454-9321, 800-567-5151; www.acadianbus.com) provides a bus service through the Maritimes and connects Voyager buses from Quebec and Ontario, and Greyhound from the USA (see p264). From Halifax, destinations include Charlottetown ($70, 5½ hours, two daily), Moncton ($57, four hours, three daily) and Bangor (Maine; $105, 11 hours, daily), where there are connections for Boston and New York. All fares for Acadian Lines are tax-inclusive, and there are discounts for children aged five to 11 years (50%), students (15%) and seniors (25%).

Contactable through Acadian Lines, **Trius Lines** (☑902-454-9321, 800-567-5151) travels along the South Shore from Halifax to Yarmouth ($50, 5½ hours, daily) with connections to the ferries (below). There are discounts for students (15%) and seniors (25%) and for purchasing return tickets.

Boat

NEW BRUNSWICK Bay Ferries (☑888-249-7245; www.bayferries.com; adult/child under 6yr/child 6-13yr/senior $40/5/25/30, car/motorcycle/bicycle $80/50/10) has a three-hour trip from Saint John (New Brunswick) to Digby. Off-season discounts and various packages are available.

NEWFOUNDLAND Marine Atlantic (☑800-341-7981; www.marine-atlantic.ca) operates ferries year-round to Port aux Basques (Newfoundland) from North Sydney (adult/child/car $29/14/81.50). Daytime crossings take between five and six hours, and overnight crossings take about seven hours. Cabins and reclining chairs cost extra. In summer, you can opt for a 14-hour ferry ride (adult/child $80/40.25, car/motorcycle $165/83.50) to Argentia on Newfoundland's east coast. Reservations are required for either trip.

PRINCE EDWARD ISLAND Northumberland Ferries (☑902-566-3838, 888-249-7245; www.peiferry.com; adult/child $16/free, car/motorcycle/bicycle incl passengers $61/40/20)

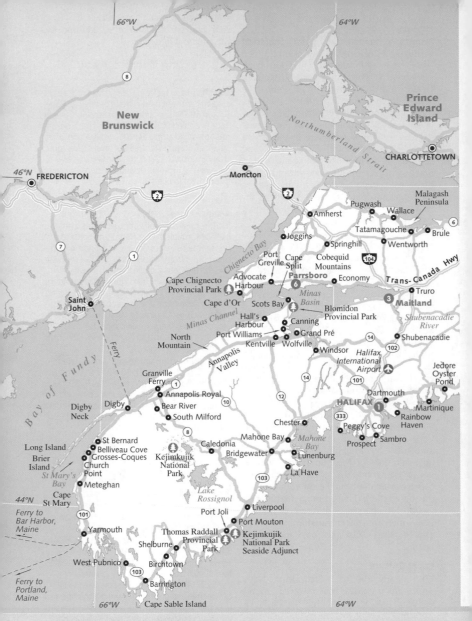

Nova Scotia Highlights

① People-watch along the waterfront and take in an unforgettable meal in **Halifax** (p32)

② Sample French soldiers' rations or a general's feast c 1744 at **Louisbourg National Historic Site** (p86)

③ Get your adrenaline fix by smashing through the waves of the tidal bore at **Maitland** (p66)

④ Experience the misty peace of kayaking through the deserted islands and protected coves around **Tangier** (p89)

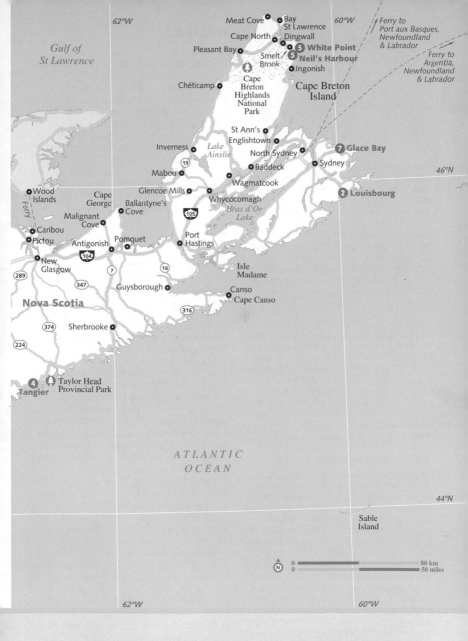

Gulf of St Lawrence

Meat Cove ● ● Bay
● St Lawrence
Cape North ● ● Dingwall
Pleasant Bay ● ⑤ **White Point**
Smelt ● / ⑤ **Neil's Harbour**
Brook
● Ingonish
Chéticamp ●
Cape Breton Highlands National Park
Cape Breton Island

St Ann's ●
Englishtown ●
Inverness ● *Lake Ainslie*
North Sydney ●
⑦ **Glace Bay**
Mabou ● (19)
● Baddeck
● Sydney
46°N
Glencoe Mills ● Wagmatcook ●
Wood Islands ●
Cape George
Ballantyne's Cove ●
Whycocomagh ●
Bras d'Or Lake
② **Louisbourg**
Malignant Cove ●
(105)
Antigonish ●
Pomquet ●
Port Hastings ●
(104)
New Glasgow ●
(7) (16)
Isle Madame
(289)
Caribou ● Pictou ●
(347)
Guysborough ●
Canso ● Cape Canso
Nova Scotia
(316)
(374) Sherbrooke ●
(224)
④ ⑤ Taylor Head Provincial Park
Tangier

ATLANTIC OCEAN

44°N

Sable Island

Ⓝ 0 _____ 80 km
0 _____ 50 miles

62°W   60°W

Ferry to Port aux Basques, Newfoundland & Labrador
Ferry to Argentia, Newfoundland & Labrador

⑤ Eat hot chowder after looking for eagles and whales from **White Point to Neil's Harbour** (p82)

⑥ Search the sand flats exposed by extreme Fundy tides for semiprecious stones around **Parrsboro** (p68)

⑦ Voyage under the ocean floor to the coal mines of **Glace Bay** (p86) while listening to the yarns of a retired miner

NOVA SCOTIA FAST FACTS

» Population: 932,966

» Area: 55,491 sq km

» Capital: Halifax

» Quirky Fact: Home to the only tidal power plant in the Western Hemisphere

cruises between Wood Islands (Prince Edward Island; PEI), and Caribou, near Pictou, up to nine times daily (1¼ hours). You only pay when leaving PEI so it's slightly cheaper to arrive by ferry then exit PEI via the Confederation Bridge (see p137). No reservations are required, but it's wise to show up half an hour before the sailing.

USA Ferry service between Bar Harbor (Maine) and Yarmouth has been running since the 1950s but it was halted in 2010 due to funding issues. It's expected that the service will start up again in 2011 with a new boat so check online for details.

Train

VIA Rail (www.viarail.ca) runs services between Montréal and Halifax (one-week advance purchase adult/child $182/80, 21 hours, daily except Tuesdays) with stops in Amherst (advance purchase adult/child $137/69, 17 hours from Montréal) and Truro (advance purchase adult/child $148/74, 18 hours from Montréal). Students pay the same as adults with no need for advance purchase; adult discount fares may sell out so it's best to book as early as possible.

ℹ Getting Around

Renting a car is by far the easiest way to get around and can be more economical than taking the bus. Shuttle buses (p43) are another alternative. Distances are very manageable; you can easily stay in the Annapolis Valley and do day trips to the South Shore and vice versa. The longest drive most people will do is the four-hour haul to Cape Breton Island from Halifax.

The direct route to most places will be on a 100-series highway (eg 101, 102, 103), which have high speed limits and limited exits. There is usually a corresponding older highway (eg 1, 2, 3) that passes through communities and has varying speed limits, but none higher than 80km/h. The Trans-Canada Hwy (Hwy 104/105) cuts directly across the province from Amherst to Sydney without passing through Halifax. Other back roads snake across rural Nova Scotia, usually numbered 200 to 299 when traveling vaguely east–west and 300 to 399 going north–south. You'll find more potholes than gas stations along these.

HALIFAX

POP 360,000

Halifax is the kind of town that people flock to, not so much for the opportunities, but for the quality of life it has to offer. Sea breezes off the harbor keep the air clean, and parks and trees nestle between heritage buildings, cosmopolitan eateries and arty shops. Several universities ensure that the population is young and the bars and nightclubs full. Stroll the historic waterfront, catch some live music and enjoy the best of what the Maritimes have to offer. In summer, never-ending festivals ignite the party ambience that much more.

History

Pirates, Indians, warring colonialists and exploding ships make the history of Halifax read like an adventure story. From 1749, when Edward Cornwallis founded Halifax along what is today Barrington St, the British settlement expanded and flourished. The destruction of the French fortress at Louisbourg in 1760 increased British dominance and sealed Halifax as Nova Scotia's most important city.

Despite being home to two universities from the early 1800s, Halifax was still a rough and ready sailors' nest that became a center for privateer black-market trade during the War of 1812. As piracy lost its government endorsement, Halifax sailed smoothly into a mercantile era, and the city streets (particularly Market and Brunswick Sts) became home to countless taverns and brothels.

On April 14, 1912, three Halifax ships were sent in response to a distress call: the 'unsinkable' *Titanic* had hit an iceberg. Many of those killed were buried at Fairview Cemetery, next to the Fairview Overpass on the Bedford Hwy.

Soon after, during WWI in 1917 the *Mont Blanc,* a French munitions ship carrying TNT and highly flammable benzol, collided with another ship. The 'Halifax Explosion,' the world's biggest man-made explosion prior to A-bombs being dropped on Japan in 1945, ripped through the city. More than 1900 people were killed and 9000 injured. Almost the entire northern end of Halifax was leveled.

Orientation

The downtown area, three universities and older residential neighborhoods are contained on a compact peninsula cut off from mainland Halifax by an inlet called the North West Arm. Almost all sights of interest to visitors are concentrated in this area, making walking the best way to get around. Point Pleasant Park is at the extreme southern end of the peninsula, and the lively North End neighborhood – home to African Nova Scotians, art-school students and most of Halifax' gay bars – stretches from the midpoint to the northern extreme.

Two bridges span the harbor, connecting Halifax to Dartmouth and leading to highways north (for the airport) and east. The MacDonald Bridge at the eastern end of North St is closest to downtown. The airport is 40km northwest of town on Hwy 102.

⊙ Sights

DOWNTOWN HALIFAX

Historic Properties   NOTABLE BUILDINGS
The Historic Properties is a group of restored buildings on Upper Water St, built between 1800 and 1905. Originally designed as huge warehouses for easy storage of goods and cargo, they now house boutiques, restaurants and bars and are connected by the waterfront boardwalks. Artisans, merchants and buskers do business around the buildings in the summer.

The 1814 **Privateer's Warehouse** is the area's oldest stone building. The privateers were government-sanctioned and -sponsored pirates who stored their booty here. Among the other vintage buildings are the wooden **Old Red Store** – once used for shipping operations and as a sail loft – and **Simon's Warehouse**, built in 1854.

Alexander Keith's Nova Scotia Brewery
BREWERY
(☏902-455-1474; www.keiths.ca; Brewery Market, 1496 Lower Water St; adult/child $16/8; ⊙11am-8pm Mon-Thu, 11am-9pm Fri & Sat, noon-4pm Sun) A tour of this brewery takes you to 19th-century Halifax via costumed thespians, quality brew and dark corridors. Finish your hour-long tour with a party in the basement pub with beer on tap and ale-inspired yarns. Note that you'll need your ID. (Kids are generally kept happy with lemonade.)

Maritime Museum of the Atlantic   MUSEUM
(☏902-424-7490; www.museum.gov.ns.ca/mma; 1675 Lower Water St; adult/child $8.50/4.50; ⊙9:30am-5:30pm Wed-Mon, to 8pm Tue) Part of this fun waterfront museum was a

DON'T MISS

HALIFAX HIGHLIGHTS

» **Halifax Farmers Brewery Market** (p42) – have breakfast here on Saturday mornings

» **Dartmouth Ferry** (p43) – enjoy a breezy budget cruise

» **Maritime Museum of the Atlantic** (below) – learn all about the Halifax Explosion and the *Titanic*

» **Citadel Hill National Historic Site** (below) – for history and a view

» **Live music** (p41) – at a variety of pubs or venues

chandlery, where all the gear needed to outfit a vessel was sold. You can smell the charred ropes, cured to protect them from saltwater. There's a wildly popular display on the *Titanic* and another on the Halifax Explosion. The 3-D film about the *Titanic* costs $5. Outside at the dock you can explore the CSS *Acadia*, a retired hydrographic vessel from England.

The last WWII corvette **HMCS Sackville** (adult/child $3/2; ⊙10am-5pm) is docked nearby and staffed by the Canadian Navy.

Pier 21 Centre   MUSEUM
(☏902-425-7770; www.pier21.ca; 1055 Marginal Rd; adult/child $8.50/5; ⊙9:30am-5:30pm) Named by CBC (Canadian Broadcasting Company) as one of the Seven Wonders of Canada, Pier 21 was to Canada what Ellis Island was to the USA. Between 1928 and 1971 over a million immigrants entered Canada through Pier 21. Their stories and the historical context that led them to abandon their homelands are presented in this museum. Researchers fanned out across Canada to get first-hand testimonials from immigrants who passed through Pier 21. These moving videos are shown in screening rooms off a railcar – bring your hankie.

Citadel Hill National Historic Site
HISTORICAL SITE
(☏902-426-5080; off Sackville St; adult/child $11.70/5.80; ⊙9am-6pm) Canada's most visited national historic site, the huge and arguably spooky Citadel is a star-shaped fort atop Halifax' central hill. Construction began in 1749 with the founding of Halifax; this version of the Citadel is the fourth, built

To Little Dutch
Church (50m)

To Fresh Start B&B (750m);
Maritime Command
Museum (750m)

34

10

43

17

3

Cornwallis St

Brunswick St

Maitland St

Barrington St

Gottingen St

41

Creighton St

To Jane's on
the Common
(500m)

Maynard St

Agricola St

Cogswell St

Halifax
Common

To Heartwood Vegetarian
Cuisine & Bakery (1km)

Scotia
Square

28

Duke St

2

**Art Gallery
of Nova Scotia**

Upper Water St

Hollis St

1

6

39

**Citadel Hill National
Historic Site**

9

Brunswick St

George St

38

21   30

37

32

42

40

4

24

Granville St

Barrington St

Argyle St

Grafton St

Market St

Bell Rd

Summer St

8

Sackville St

Blowers St

11

5

29

25

Spring Garden Rd

20

35   26

Brenton St
Pl

Brenton St

Dresden Row

Clyde St

Birmingham St

Queen St

South Park St

Tower Rd

To Dalhousie University,
Howe Hall (400m)

College St

Morris St

Robie St

To Point Pleasant
Park (1.4km)

from 1818 to 1861. Guided tours explain the fort's shape and history. The grounds inside the fort are open year-round, with free admission when the exhibits are closed.

Art Gallery of Nova Scotia
ART GALLERY
(☎902-424-7542; www.agns.gov.ns.ca; 1723 Hollis St; adult/child $12/3; ⊙10am-5pm Fri-Wed, to 9pm Thu) Don't miss the permanent, tear-jerking Maud Lewis Painted House exhibit that includes the 3m x 4m house that Lewis lived in most of her adult life. The main exhibit in the lower hall changes regularly, featuring anything from ancient art to the avant-garde. Free tours are given at 2pm Sunday year-round (daily during July and August).

Halifax Public Gardens
GARDEN
At the corner of Spring Garden Rd and South Park St, these are considered the finest Victorian city gardens in North America. Oldies bands perform off-key concerts in the gazebo on Sunday afternoons in summer, tai chi practitioners go through their paces, and anyone who brings checkers can play on outside tables.

Titanic Burial Grounds
HISTORICAL SITES
When the *Titanic* sank, the bodies not buried at sea were brought to Halifax. Today there are 19 graves at Mount Olivet Catholic Cemetery (7076 Mumford Rd), 10 in the Baron de Hirsch Jewish Cemetery at the north end of Windsor St, and 121 in the adjacent Fairview Lawn Cemetery; 40 graves are still unidentified. J Dawson, whose name was the basis for Leonardo DiCaprio's character in the film *Titanic,* is at Fairview Cemetery.

FREE Anna Leonowens Gallery
ART GALLERY
(☎902-494-8184; 1891 Granville St; ⊙11am-5pm Tue-Fri, noon-4pm Sat, show openings 5:30-7:30pm Mon) Off the pedestrian area on Granville St, this gallery shows work by students and faculty of the Nova Scotia College of Art & Design. The gallery is named for the founder of the college, who was immortalized in *The King and I* for her relationship with the King of Siam.

St Paul's Church
CHURCH
(☎902-429-2240; 1749 Argyle St; ⊙9am-4pm Mon-Fri) Established in 1749 with the founding of Halifax, Anglican St Paul's Church once served parishioners from Newfoundland to Ontario. Across the square, Halifax' **City Hall** is a true gem of Victorian architecture.

Halifax

St Mary's Cathedral Basilica CHURCH
(☎902-423-4116; 1508 Barrington St; ⊘free tours 10am & 2pm Jul-Sep) You can't miss this cathedral which purportedly has the largest free-standing spire in North America.

Old Town Clock NOTABLE BUILDING
At the top of George St, at Citadel Hill, the Old Town Clock has been keeping time for 200 years. The inner workings arrived in Halifax from London in 1803 after being ordered by Prince Edward, the Duke of Kent.

NORTH END
The North End has been a distinct neighborhood for almost as long as Halifax has existed. In the early 1750s this 'North Suburbs' area became popular and subsequently grew because of its larger building lots.

Churches
St George's Round Church (☎902-423-1059; http://collections.ic.gc.ca/churchandcommunity; 2222 Brunswick St) was built in 1800 and is a rare circular Palladian church with a main rotunda 18m in diameter. Tours are by arrangement. Tours of the 1756 **Little Dutch Church** (2405 Brunswick St), the second-oldest building in Halifax, can also be arranged through St George's. The **Cornwallis St Baptist Church** (5457 Cornwallis St) has been serving African Nova Scotians since the 1830s. Walk by on Sunday

morning and hear the gospel music overflow its walls.

FREE **Maritime Command Museum**

MUSEUM

(☏902-427-0550, ext 6725; 2725 Gottingen St; ☺9:30am-3:30pm Mon-Fri) The admiral of the British navy for all of North America was based in Halifax until 1819 and threw grand parties at Admiralty House, now the Maritime Command Museum. Apart from the beautiful Georgian architecture, the museum is worth a visit for its eclectic collections: cigarette lighters, silverware and ships' bells, to name a few.

OUTSIDE THE CITY CENTER

Point Pleasant Park NATURE RESERVE

Some 39km of nature trails, picnic spots and the **Prince of Wales Martello Tower** – a round 18th-century defensive structure – are all found within this 75-hectare sanctuary, just 1.5km from the city center. Trails around the perimeter of the park offer views of McNabs Island, the open ocean and the North West Arm. Bus 9 along Barrington St goes to Point Pleasant, and there's ample free parking off Point Pleasant Dr.

McNabs Island NATURE RESERVE

Fine sand and cobblestone shorelines, salt marshes, abandoned military fortifications and forests paint the scenery of this 400-hectare island in Halifax harbor. Staff of the **McNabs Island Ferry** (☏902-465-4563; www.mcnabsisland.com; Government Wharf; round-trip adult/child $12/10; ☺24hr) will provide you with a map and an orientation to 30km of roads and trails on the island. For camping reservations contact the **Department of Natural Resources** (☏902-861-2560; www.parks.gov.ns.ca/mcnabs.htm). The ferry runs from Fisherman's Cove in Eastern Passage, a short drive through Dartmouth. When the ferry staff are not too busy, they'll pick you up in Halifax for the same fare.

🏃 **Activities**

Cycling

Cycling is a great way to see sites on the outskirts of Halifax – you can take bikes on the ferries to Dartmouth or cycle over the MacDonald Bridge.
Pedal & Sea Adventures (☏902-857-9319, 877-772- 5699; www.pedalandseaadventures.com; per day/week incl tax from $35/140) will deliver the bike to you, complete with helmet, lock and repair kit. It also leads

good-value tours (one-/two-day trips including taxes and meals cost $105/235) and also offers self-guided tours, starting from $69.

Hiking

There are both short and long hikes surprisingly close to downtown. **Hemlock Ravine** is an 80-hectare, wooded area that has five trails, suitable for all levels. To get there take the Bedford Hwy from central Halifax then turn left at Kent Ave – there is parking and a map of the trail at the end of this road. See www.novatrails.com for more detailed trail descriptions and directions to other trailheads. There's also hiking in **Point Pleasant Park** and on **McNabs Island**.

☞ **Tours**

Bluenose II HARBOR TOURS

(☏902-634-1963, 800-763-1963; www.bluenose2.ns.ca; Lower Water St) This replica of the famous two-masted racing schooner, the *Bluenose*, seen on the back of Canada's 10¢ coin, runs harbor tours when it's in town. It was completely restored in 2010 – check the website for pricing.

Tall Ship Silva HARBOR TOURS

(☏902-429 9463; www.tallshipsilva.com; Queen's Wharf at Prince St; ☺noon, 2pm, 4pm, 6pm & 10:30pm daily May-Oct) You can choose whether to lend a hand or simply sit back and relax while taking a one-hour ($12 per person), 1½-hour (adult/child $20/14) or evening party two-hour ($20 per person) cruise on Halifax' square masted tall ship.

Tattle Tours WALKING TOURS

(☏902-494-0525; www.tattletours.ca; per person $10; ☺7:30pm Wed-Sun) Lively two-hour tours depart from the Old Town Clock and are filled with local gossip, pirate tales and ghost stories. Walking tours are also available on demand – ask at any Visitor Information Centre (VIC).

Salty Bear Adventure Tours BUS TOURS

Salty Bear is the sociable backpacker's choice for touring the province.

Great E.A.R.T.H Expeditions ECO TOURS

(☏902-223-2409; www.greatearthexpeditions.com; half-/full-day tours from $60/90) Eco half- and full-day tours led from Halifax can include hiking, kayaking or historical themes. Longer four-day tours up the Cabot Trail and through Kejimikujic are also on offer.

HALIFAX FOR CHILDREN

Discovery Centre
MUSEUM

(☎902-492-4422; www.discoverycentre.ns.ca; 1593 Barrington St; adult/child $8.50/6; ⊘10am-5pm Mon-Sat, 1-5pm Sun) Hands-on exhibits, live shows and movies make science fun for all ages.

Museum of Natural History
MUSEUM

(☎902-424-7353; http://museum.gov.ns.ca/mnh/index.htm; 1747 Summer St; adult/child $5.75/3.75; ⊘9am-5pm Tue-Sat, to 8pm Wed, noon-5pm Sun year-round, 9am-5pm Mon Jun-Sep) Daily summer programs introduce children to Gus the toad and demonstrate the cooking of bugs. Exhibits on history and the natural world will keep parents engaged, too.

Theodore Too Big Harbour Tours
HARBOR TOURS

(☎902-492-8847; www.theodoretoo.com; 1751 Lower Water St; adult/child $20/15; ⊘11am, 12:30pm, 2pm, 3:30pm & 5pm daily mid-Jun–Sep) One-hour tours on this funny-looking cartoon character boat of book- and television-fame are particularly good for under-sixes.

Murphy's Cable Wharf HARBOR TOURS
(☎902-420-1015; www.murphysonthewater.com; 1751 Lower Water St) This tourism giant runs a range of tours on Halifax Harbour, from deep-sea fishing and two-hour scenic cruises to the popular 55-minute **Harbour Hopper Tours** (adult/child $26/15) on an amphibious bus.

✰ Festivals & Events

Halifax is at its most vibrant during its variety of jovial festivals. Check out volunteering opportunities through festival websites.

Nova Scotia Tattoo CULTURAL
(www.nstattoo.ca; tickets $27-65; ⊘early Jul) The world's 'largest annual indoor show' is a military-style event with lots of marching bands.

Atlantic Jazz Festival MUSIC
(www.jazzeast.com; ⊘mid-Jul) A full week of free outdoor jazz concerts each afternoon, and evening performances ranging from world music to classic jazz trios (tickets $15 to $30).

Halifax International Busker Festival
BUSKING
(www.buskers.ca; ⊘early Aug) Comics, mimics, daredevils and musicians from all over the world perform along the Halifax waterfront.

Atlantic Fringe Festival THEATER
(www.atlanticfringe.com; ⊘mid-Sep) Offbeat and experimental theatre from both emerging and established artists.

Atlantic Film Festival FILM
(www.atlanticfilm.com; tickets $10-15; ⊘mid-Sep) Ten days of great flicks from the Atlantic region and around the world.

Halifax Pop Explosion MUSIC
(www.halifaxpopexplosion.com; wristbands $50; ⊘mid-Oct) Some 130 concerts are spread out over 12 clubs during a five-day period and include hip-hop, punk, indie rock and folk. A wristband gets you into as many shows as you can manage to see.

🛏 Sleeping

TOP CHOICE **Waverley Inn** INN $$
(☎902-423-9346, 800-565-9346; www.waverleyinn.com; 1266 Barrington St; d incl breakfast $130-240; 🅿@) Every room here is furnished uniquely and nearly theatrically with antiques and dramatic linens. Both Oscar Wilde and PT Barnum once stayed here and probably would again today if they were still living. The downtown location can't be beat.

Pebble Bed & Breakfast B&B $$
(☎902-423-3369, 888-303-5056; www.thepebble.ca; 1839 Armview Tce; r $110-225; 🅿) Bathroom aficionados will find heaven at this luxurious B&B. The tub and shower are in a giant room that leads to a terrace overlooking a leafy garden. The bedrooms are equally generous with plush, high beds and a modern-meets-antique decor. Irish owner Elizabeth O'Carroll grew up with a pub-owning family and brings lively, joyous energy from the Emerald Isle to her home in a posh, waterside residential area.

Halliburton INN $$$
(☎902-420-0658; www.thehalliburton.com; 5184 Morris St; r $145-350; P⊜@) Pure, soothing class without all that Victorian hullabaloo can be found at this exceedingly comfortable and well-serviced historic hotel right in downtown.

Lord Nelson Hotel HOTEL $$$
(☎902-423-5130, 800-565-2020; www.lordnel sonhotel.com; 1515 South Park St; d $140-360; P@) When rock stars (such as the Rolling Stones) come to Halifax, they stay here. It's an elegant yet not stuffy 1920s building right across from Halifax Public Gardens. Rates drop dramatically in the off-season.

Prince George Hotel HOTEL $$$
(☎902-425-1986, 800-565-1567; www.prince georgehotel.com; 1725 Market St; d $170-300; P@) A suave and debonair gem, central Prince George has all the details covered. Garden patios are a great place to take a drink or a meal or even work as an alternative to indoor meeting areas. Parking is $15.

Marigold B&B B&B $
(☎902-423-4798; www.marigoldbedandbreak fast.com; 6318 Norwood St; r $70; P) Feel at home in this artist's nest full of bright floral paintings and fluffy cats. It's in a tree-lined residential area in the North End with easy public transport access.

Fresh Start B&B B&B $$
(☎902-453-6616, 888-453-6616; freshstart@ ns.sympatico.ca; 2720 Gottingen St; r $90-130; P@) Run by two retired nurses, this majestic yet lived-in-feeling Victorian is in a quiet part of the North End. Rooms with en-suite bathrooms are the best value. Gay friendly.

Halifax Backpackers Hostel HOSTEL $
(☎902-431-3170, 888-431-3170; www.halifax backpackers.com; 2193 Gottingen St; dm/d/f $20/57.50/80; P) Co-ed dorms at this hip, 36-bed North End hostel hold no more than six beds. It draws a funky young crowd and everyone congregates at the downstairs cafe to swill strong coffee, eat cheap breakfasts and mingle with the eclectic local regulars. City buses stop right in front, but be warned: it's a slightly rough-edged neighborhood.

HI Nova Scotia HOSTEL $
(☎902-422-3863; www.hihostels.ca; 1253 Barrington St; member/nonmember dm $27/32, r $57; ⊙check-in 2pm-midnight) Expect a dark and dormy night and a bright and cheery do-it-yourself breakfast at this exception-ally central 75-bed hostel. Staff is friendly, the shared kitchen lively and the house Victorian. Reserve ahead in summer.

Dalhousie University HOSTEL $
(☎902-494-8840; www.dal.ca/confserv; s/tw $45/70; ⊙mid-May–mid-Aug; P≋) Dorm rooms with shared bathrooms are nearly sterile (read: posterless and beer-bottle-free). Most people stay at **Howe Hall** (6230 Coburg St), which is adjacent to all the included university amenities and is a short walk to the Spring Garden Rd area. Check the website for other halls that may be available and for student and senior rates.

✖ Eating

Bars and pubs (p40) often serve very good food; kitchens close around 10pm.

TOP CHOICE **Fid** FUSION $$
(☎902-422-9162; www.fidcuisine.ca; 1569 Dresden Row; mains lunch $14-16, dinner $22-27; ⊙lunch Wed-Fri, dinner Tue-Sun; ⌖) Slow-food proponent Dennis Johnston buys all his ingredients from the local farmers' market, then concocts dishes such as monkfish with shell peas, asparagus, maple-glazed pork belly with sweet potato and a beautiful pad thai. It's a great place to sample regional foods; the menu changes weekly and carries vegetarian options.

TOP CHOICE **Jane's on the Common** CANADIAN $$
(☎902-431-5683; 2394 Robie St; mains lunch $11-13, dinner $16-19; ⊙lunch Tue-Fri, dinner Tue-Sun, brunch Sat & Sun) The shiny black diner-style tables fill up early at this increasingly popular eatery. Try a delectable starter such as the arugula, apple and ricotta tart or seared scallops in a curried apricot vinaigrette, then move on to the to-die-for mains such as a smoked pork chop stuffed with spinach, sage and cheddar. Divine!

Bish CANADIAN $$$
(☎902-425-7993; 1475 Lower Water St; mains $30-36; ⊙dinner Mon-Sat) If a sizzling platter of shellfish including king crab, scallops and lobster doesn't up the ante of Maritime cuisine, not much will. There's no better place to celebrate or get very, very romantic than waterside Bishop's Harbour.

Da Maurizio ITALIAN $$$
(☎902-423-0859; 1496 Lower Water St; mains $28-34; ⊙dinner Mon-Sat) Many locals cite this as their favorite Halifax restaurant. The ambience is as fine as the cuisine; exposed

brick and clean lines bring out all the flavors of this heritage brewery building. Reservations strongly recommended.

Epicurious Morcels FUSION **$$**
(☎902-455-0955; Hydrostone Market, 5529 Young St; mains around $12; ⊗11:30am-8pm Tue-Thu, 10:30am-8pm Fri & Sat, 10:30am-2:30pm Sun) The specialties here are smoked salmon, *gravlax* (dill-cured salmon) and unusual but extremely tasty homemade soups. The rest of the internationally inspired menu is also fantastic.

Morris East ITALIAN **$$**
(☎902-444-7663; 5212 Morris St; 10in pizzas $14-17; ⊗lunch Tue-Sat, dinner Tue-Sun) You'll find creative wood-fired pizzas (try the peach, rosemary aioli and prosciutto) on your choice of white, whole-wheat or gluten-free dough, and snazzy cocktails (like basil, lime and vodka punch) at this cosmopolitan cafe.

Brooklyn Warehouse CANADIAN **$$**
(☎902-446-8181; 2795 Windsor St; mains lunch $8-14, dinner around $18; ⊗lunch Mon-Fri, dinner Mon-Sat; ✈) This North End hot spot is loaded with vegetarian and vegan options (the eggplant moussaka stack is excellent), has a huge beer and cocktail menu, and has an atmosphere that feels like a modern, hip version of Cheers – but with way better food.

Il Mercato ITALIAN **$$**
(☎902-422-2866; 5650 Spring Garden Rd; mains $10-24; ⊗11am-11pm) This long-standing Italian favorite doesn't take reservations; come early or late on weekends, or wait a short while.

Chives Canadian Bistro CANADIAN **$$$**
(☎902-420-9626; 1537 Barrington St; mains $17-35; ⊗dinner) With a menu that changes with what's seasonably available using mostly local ingredients, the food is fine dining while the low-lit cozy ambience is upscale casual.

Sushi Nami Royal JAPANESE **$$**
(☎902-422-9020; 1535 Dresden Row; lunch bento boxes from $10; ⊗lunch Mon-Sat, dinner Mon-Sun) Bento box lunch specials with a choice of chicken, pork, eel and more served with rice salad, miso soup and a sushi or tempura option are one of Halifax' better bargains. The sushi is excellent as well.

Wooden Monkey CANADIAN **$$**
(☎902-444-3844; 1707 Grafton St; mains $14-23; ⊗11am-10pm; ✈) This dark, cozy nook with outdoor sidewalk seating on sunny days adamantly supports local organics and is a fab place to get superb gluten-free and vegan meals as well as humane meat dishes.

Heartwood Vegetarian Cuisine & Bakery VEGETARIAN **$**
(☎902-425-2808; 6250 Quinpool Rd; light meals from $5; ⊗10am-8pm Mon-Sat; ✈) Try the local organic salad bar or amazing baked goods along with a cup of fair trade coffee.

Scotia Square Mall Food Court FAST FOOD **$**
(cnr Barrington & Duke Sts) If you're not fussed about ambience, get surprisingly authentic Indian, Korean, Italian food and more for around $5 a plate at this food court. Favorites here are **Ray's Falafel** (⊗8am-6pm Mon-Wed, 8am-9pm Thu & Fri, 9am-6pm Sat) and **Cafe Istanbul** (⊗8am-6pm Mon-Wed, 8am-9pm Thu & Fri, 9am-6pm Sat).

🍷 Drinking

Halifax rivals St John's, Newfoundland, for the most drinking holes per capita. The biggest concentration of attractive bars is on Argyle St, where temporary streetside patios expand the sidewalk each summer. Pubs and bars close at 2am (a few hours earlier on Sunday).

Lower Deck PUB
(☎902-422-1501; 1869 Lower Water St) A first stop for a real Nova Scotian knee-slapping good time. Think pints in frothy glasses, and live music all spilling out over the sidewalks on summer nights. When someone yells 'sociable!' it's time to raise your glass.

Economy Shoe Shop PUB
(☎902-423-8845; 1663 Argyle St) This has been the 'it' place to drink and people-watch in Halifax for almost a decade. On weekend nights actors and journalists figure heavily in the crush. It's a pleasant place for afternoon drinks and the kitchen dishes out tapas until last call at 1:45am.

Onyx BAR
(☎902-428-5680; 5680 Spring Garden Rd) A sultry place for a chic cocktail, the Onyx has a backlit white onyx bar that serves a huge selection of fine wines, single malt whiskeys and nine signature mojitos. Imbibe small plates of Asian-French cuisine made with local ingredients.

Cabin Coffee CAFE
(☎902-422-8130; 1554 Hollis St; ⊗6:30am-6pm Mon-Fri, 7:30am-5pm Sat, 9am-5pm Sun) As cozy as a cabin living room, this place

Halifax has a thumping and thriving gay and lesbian scene with most of the nightlife action concentrated around Gottingen St. In the city center, **Reflections Cabaret** (902-422-2957; 5184 Sackville St) is a wild disco that attracts a mixed crowd. It opens at 4pm, but the action really starts after 10pm (it stays open until 3am).

Lesbian travelers can stop by **Venus Envy** (902-422-0004; 1598 Barrington St; 10am-6pm Mon-Wed & Sat, 10am-7pm Thu & Fri, noon-5pm Sun) to network, browse books and check out fun toys. Squeaky clean **Seadog's Sauna & Spa** (902-444-3647; www.seadogs.ca; 2199 Gottingen St; 4pm-1am Mon-Thu, from 4pm Fri through 1am Mon) is the largest private men's club east of Québec City and has all the spa fixings. The same folks have opened **Menz Bar** (2182 Gottingen St; 3pm-2am), which offers its own Menz Pale Ale on tap. A map of the heart of the gay community is available on the Seadog's website.

Halifax Pride Week (www.halifaxpride.com) takes place every year around the second week of July. Don't miss the Dykes versus Divas softball game that usually kicks off the week.

serves excellent coffee as well as light meals and all-day breakfasts from $4.

☆ Entertainment

Check out the *Coast* to see what's on – a free weekly publication available around town, it's the essential guide for music, theater, film and events.

Live Music

Halifax seems to be fueled on music, with folk, hip-hop, alternative country and rock gigs around town every weekend. Cover charge depends on the band.

Paragon   LIVE MUSIC
(902-429-3020; 2037 Gottingen St) Halifax' choice venue for touring bands and big-name local acts.

Carelton   LIVE MUSIC
(902-422-6335; 1685 Argyle St) Catch acoustic sets then enjoy the reasonable meals including a late-night menu.

Bearly's House of Blues & Ribs   LIVE MUSIC
(902-423-2526; 1269 Barrington St; cover $3) The best blues musicians in Atlantic Canada play here at incredibly low cover charges. Wednesday karaoke nights draw a crowd and some fine singers.

Seahorse Tavern   LIVE MUSIC
(902-423-7200; 1665 Argyle St) The place to see punk, indie and metal bands.

Nightclubs
Dome   NIGHTCLUB
(902-422-5453; 1740 Argyle St) Dubbed the 'Liquordome,' with four establishments under one roof. The Attic has live music; the others are nightclubs that stay open until 3am.

Theater
The two professional theaters in and around Halifax – Neptune Theatre and Eastern Front Theatre in Dartmouth – take a break in summer, with their last shows typically playing in May. However, Shakespeare by the Sea provides diversion through the summer.

Neptune Theatre   THEATER
(902-429-7070; www.neptunetheatre.com; 1593 Argyle St) This downtown theater presents musicals and well-known plays on its main stage (tickets starting from $35), as well as edgier stuff in the studio (tickets from $15).

Shakespeare by the Sea   THEATER
(902-422-0295; www.shakespearebythesea. ca; Point Pleasant Park; suggested donation $15; Jun-Sep) Fine performances of the Bard's works at the Cambridge Battery, an old fortification, in the middle of Point Pleasant Park. Check the website for a map and details.

Sports
The Halifax Mooseheads junior hockey team plays at the **Halifax Metro Centre** (902-451-1221; 5284 Duke St; tickets $15).

🔒 Shopping
Halifax has some truly quirky shops to discover in the city center between Spring Garden Rd and Duke St.

Halifax Farmers' Brewery Market

FOOD & DRINK

(902-492-4043; 1496 Lower Water St; ⊘8am-1pm Sat Jan-mid-May, 7am-1pm Sat mid-May-Dec) North America's oldest farmers market, in the 1820s Keith's Brewery Building, is the ultimate shopping experience. Head here to people-watch and buy organic produce, locally crafted jewelry, clothes and more. In fact, the market has become so popular it's going to be expanded in 2011 to the newly built **Seaport Market**, a second location near Pier 21 – it will be a daily event with more vendors and cafes and more parking.

Nova Scotian Crystal

SOUVENIRS

(☑888-977-2797; 5080 George St; ⊘9am-6pm Mon-Fri, 10am-5pm Sat & Sun) As much of a show as a place to shop. Watch glass blowers form beautiful crystal glasses and vases then pick the ones you want in the classy adjacent shop.

❶ Information

Bookstores

Book Room (☑902-423-8271; 1546 Barrington St; ⊘9am-7:30pm Wed-Fri, 9am-5pm Mon, Tue & Sat, noon-5pm Sun) Around for nearly 160 years, it stocks a good selection of maps and travel guides, plus books by local authors.

John W Doull Bookseller (☑902-429-1652; 1684 Barrington St; ⊘10am-6pm Mon & Tue, 9:30am-9pm Wed-Fri, 10am-9pm Sat) This secondhand store has more books than many libraries.

Internet Access

Many cafes, restaurants and public spaces have wi-fi.

Spring Garden Road Memorial Library (☑902-490-5723; 5381 Spring Garden Rd; ⊘10am-9pm Tue-Thu, 10am-5pm Fri & Sat) Computers on a first-come, first-served basis.

Medical Services

Family Focus (☑902-420-2038; 5991 Spring Garden Rd; consultation $65; ⊘8:30am-9pm Mon-Fri, 11am-5pm Sat & Sun) Walk-in or same-day appointments.

Halifax Infirmary (☑902-473-3383/7605; 1796 Summer St; ⊘24hr) For emergencies.

Money

Bank branches cluster around Barrington and Duke Sts.

Post

Lawton's Drugs (☑902-429-0088; 5675 Spring Garden Rd; ⊘8am-9pm Mon-Fri, 8am-6pm Sat, noon-5pm Sun) Post office inside.

Main Post Office (☑902-494-4670; 1680 Bedford Row; ⊘7:30am-5:15pm Mon-Fri) Pick up mail sent to General Delivery, Halifax, NS B3J 2L3 here.

Tourist Information

Check out posters for performances and events on the bulletin boards just inside the door of the Spring Garden Road Memorial Library.

Tourism Nova Scotia (☑902-425-5781, 800-565-0000; www.novascotia.com) Operates Visitor Information Centres (VICs) in Halifax and other locations within Nova Scotia province, plus a free booking service for accommodations, which is useful when rooms are scarce in midsummer. It publishes the *Doers & Dreamers Guide* that lists places to stay, attractions and tour operators.

Visitor Information Centre (VIC) Argyle St (☑902-490-5963; cnr Argyle & Sackville Sts; ⊘8:30am-8pm Jul & Aug, to 7pm May, Jun & Sep, to 4:30pm Mon-Fri rest of year); Halifax International Airport (☑902-873-1223; ⊘9am-9pm); Waterfront (☑902-424-4248; 1655 Lower Water St; ⊘8:30am-8pm Jun-Sep, to 4:30pm Wed-Sun Oct-May).

Websites

Destination Halifax (www.halifaxinfo.com) Halifax' official tourism site has information on everything from events to package bookings.

Halifax Regional Municipality (www.halifax.ca) Info on everything from bus schedules to recreation programs.

Studio Map (www.studiorally.ca) An up-to-date guide to art and craft studios across the province, plus a shortlist of spot-on recommendations for eateries and B&Bs.

❶ Getting There & Away

Air

Most air services in Nova Scotia go to/from Halifax and there are multiple daily flights to Toronto, Calgary and Vancouver. See p29 for more information.

Bus

Acadian Lines (☑902-454-9321, 800-567-5151; www.acadianbus.com; 1161 Hollis St) The Acadian terminal is at the train station next to the Westin Hotel. Its buses travel daily to Truro (1½ hours) and Amherst (2¾ hours) and connect to Montréal and New York. It also goes to Digby (four hours), with stops throughout the Annapolis Valley, and to Sydney (6½ hours), stopping in Antigonish (3½ hours).

Trius Lines (☑902-454-9321, 800-567-5151) Has a daily route from Halifax to Yarmouth (4½ hours) that serves towns along the South Shore. Call Acadian for information on prices and departure points.

Shuttle Bus

Private shuttle buses compete with the major bus companies. They usually pick you up and drop you off; with fewer stops, they travel faster, but the trade-off is a more cramped ride.

Cloud Nine Shuttle (☑902-742-3992, 888-805-3335; www.thecloudnineshuttle.com) Does the Yarmouth–Halifax–Yarmouth (3½ hours each way) route, stopping along the South Shore; airport pickup or drop-off is an extra $5.

Campbell's Shuttle Service (☑800-742-6101; www.campbell-shuttle-service.com) Goes to Yarmouth.

Inverness Shuttle Service (☑902-945-2000, 888-826-2477; www.invernessshuttle.com) Travels between Halifax and Chéticamp on Cape Breton Island every day but Saturday and Monday (six hours).

Kathleen's Shuttle & Tours (☑903-834-2024; www.digbytoursandshuttle.webs.com) Halifax airport to Digby and Annapolis areas.

PEI Express Shuttle (☑902-462-8177, 877-877-1771; www.peishuttle.com) Goes to Charlottetown (PEI), with early morning pickups.

Scotia Shuttle (☑902-435-9686, 800-898-5883; www.scotiashuttle.com) Travels to Sydney on Cape Breton Island (five hours, daily).

Train

One of the few examples of monumental Canadian train station architecture left in the Maritimes is found at 1161 Hollis St. Options with **VIA Rail** (www.viarail.ca) include overnight service to Montréal (20½ hours, daily except Tuesdays).

❶ Getting Around

To/From the Airport

Halifax International Airport is 40km northeast of town on Hwy 102 toward Truro. **Airbus** (☑902-873-2091; one-way/return $19/27) runs between 5am and 11pm and picks up at major hotels. If you arrive in the middle of the night, as many flights do, your only choice is a taxi, which costs $54 to downtown Halifax. There are often not enough taxis so it's prudent to reserve one in advance. Try **Satellite Taxi** (☑902-445-3333), which has 24-hour airport service.

Car & Motorcycle

Pedestrians almost always have the right-of-way in Halifax. Watch out for cars stopping suddenly!

Outside the downtown core you can usually find free on-street parking for up to two hours. Otherwise, try private **Impark** (1245 Hollis St; per hr/12hr $1.50/8) or the municipally owned **Metro-Park** (☑902-830-1711; 1557 Granville St; per hr/12hr $2.25/15). Halifax' parking meters are enforced from 8am to 6pm Monday to Friday.

It costs considerably more to rent a car at the airport than in town. All the major national chains (see p265) are represented there and also have offices in Halifax.

Public Transportation

Metro Transit (☑902-490-6600; one-way fare $2.25) runs the city bus system and the ferries to Dartmouth. Transfers are free when traveling in one direction within a short time frame. Maps and schedules are available at the ferry terminals and at the information booth in Scotia Square mall.

Bus 7 cuts through downtown and North End Halifax via Robie St and Gottingen St, passing both hostels. Bus 1 travels Spring Garden Rd, Barrington St, and the south part of Gottingen St before crossing the bridge to Dartmouth. 'Fred' is a free city bus that loops around downtown every 30 minutes in the summer.

Taking the **Dartmouth ferry** (one-way fare $2.25; every 15 to 30 minutes from 6am to 11:30pm) from the Halifax waterfront is a nice way of getting on the water, even if it's just for 12 minutes. Woodside, where another ferry goes in peak periods, is a good place to start a bike ride to Eastern Passage or Lawrencetown.

AROUND HALIFAX

Dartmouth

Founded in 1750, one year after Halifax, Dartmouth is Halifax' counterpart just across the harbor. It is more residential than Halifax, and the downtown area lacks the capital's charm and bustle, but it can make a pleasant base since getting to Halifax by bus or ferry is so easy.

Even if you don't stay here, don't miss a harbor cruise via the ferry, the oldest saltwater ferry system in North America. Alderney Gate houses Dartmouth's ferry terminal.

The city swells during the **Nova Scotia Multicultural Festival** (www.mans.ns.ca) in late June. This weekend festival on the waterfront celebrates diversity with great performances and even better food.

Dartmouth Heritage Museum (☑902-464-2300; www.dartmouthheritagemuseum.ns.ca; 26 Newcastle St; admission $3; ☉10am-5pm Tue-Sun mid-Jun–Aug, 1:30-5pm Wed-Sat Sep–mid-Jun) displays an eclectic collection in **Evergreen House**, the former home of folklorist Helen Creighton (who traversed the province in the early 20th century recording stories and songs). Tickets include admission on

FISHERMAN'S COVE

If you're heading up the Eastern Shore from Dartmouth or Halifax, detour onto Hwy 322 to Fishermen's Cove in Eastern Passage, a Popeye-esque fishing port with some of the region's best seafood samplings. **Wharf Wraps** (104 Government Wharf Rd; fish & chips $12; ⊙10am-6pm Jun-Sep) has an outdoor seating area and deservedly famous (and huge) portions of fish and chips, or head next door to the **Fish Basket** (100 Government Wharf Rd; ⊙9am-6pm) for fish and lobster by the pound or a delicious fresh lobster sandwich ($8) for the road.

the same day to the 1786 **Quaker House** (59 Ochterloney St; ⊙10am-5pm Tue-Sun Jun-Aug), the oldest house in the Halifax area, which was built by Quaker whalers from Nantucket who fled the American Revolution. Entertainment can be found at **Eastern Front Theatre** (☑902-463-7529; www.easternfrontthe atre.com; Alderney Gate, Dartmouth; tickets $25), which debuts several works by Atlantic playwrights each year.

Close to both bus routes and the ferry, **Caroline's B&B** (☑902-469-4665; 134 Victoria Rd; s/d $50/60; ⊙Apr-Dec) is run by a charming woman. Check out the cool mosaics on the walls.

Shubie Campground (☑902-435-8328, 800-440-8450; www.shubiecampground.com; Jaybee Dr, off Waverley Rd), the only campground accessible from Halifax on public transportation, is privately run and municipality owned. Facilities include showers and a laundromat.

Haligonians head to Dartmouth just for the massive buttery chocolate croissants available at **Two If By Sea** (66 Ochterloney St; chocolate croissants $3; ⊙7am-6pm Mon-Fri, 8am-5pm Sat &Sun) – but be warned they are usually sold out by about 1pm. Even without the pastries, it's a hip place to stop for a coffee and some people-watching on a sunny day, and has a distinctly Dartmouth atmosphere.

Eastern Shore Beaches

When downtown-dwellers venture over the bridge to Dartmouth on a hot summer's day, it's most likely en route to a beach. There are beautiful, long, white-sand beaches all along the Eastern Shore, and although the water never gets very warm, brave souls venture in for a swim or a surf, particularly if the fog stays offshore.

The closest – and therefore busiest – of the Eastern Shore beaches, **Rainbow Haven**, is around 1km long. Available are washrooms, showers, a canteen and a boardwalk with wheelchair access to the beach. Lifeguards supervise a sizable swimming area.

The most popular destination for surfers, cobblestone **Lawrencetown Beach** faces directly south and often gets big waves compliments of hurricanes or tropical storms hundreds of kilometers away. It boasts a supervised swimming area, washrooms and a canteen. To surf, learn to surf, or just enjoy the view, stay at **Lawrencetown Beach House** (☑902-827-2345; www. lawrencetownbeachhouse.com; dm/d $28/75), a comfy hostel with 10 beds and three private rooms beautifully nestled in the beach grass above one of the only stretches of real sand. There are several places in the area to rent surf boards (around $15 per day) and wetsuits (also $15 per day). Surf lessons are around $75 for 1½ hours including equipment; try **Dacane Sports** (☑902-431-7873; www.hurricanesurf.com), **NovaScotia Surf School** (www.quiksilvercamps.com) or the all-women-run **One Life Surf School** (☑902-880-7873; www.onelifesurf.com).

With more than 3km of white sand backed by beach grass, **Martinique** is the longest beach in Nova Scotia and one of the prettiest in the area. Even if you find the water too cold for a swim, this is a beautiful place to walk, watch birds or play Frisbee.

Sambro

Just 18km south of Halifax, **Crystal Crescent Beach** is on the outskirts of the fishing village of Sambro. There are actually three beaches here in distinct coves; the third one out – toward the southwest – is clothing-optional and gay friendly. An 8.5km **hiking trail** begins just inland and heads through barrens, bogs and boulders to Pennant Point. To get here, take Herring Cove Rd from the roundabout in Halifax all the way to Sambro, then follow the signs.

Prospect

As pretty as Peggy's Cove, Prospect doesn't attract a fraction of the tourist traffic. An undeveloped **trail** starts at the end of Indian Point Rd and leads 3km along the coast past plenty of perfect picnic spots. There's not a lot of room to park at the trailhead, so you may need to leave your vehicle on the roadside into the village.

Prospect Village B&B (☑902-850-1758, 877-850-1758; www.prospectvillagebb.ca; 1758 Prospect Bay Rd; r $135-160) is in a restored nunnery that nearly glows on the misty shores. The warm owners use organics for everything from soaps to the ingredients of their tasty breakfasts.

Peggy's Cove

Peggy's Cove is one of the most visited fishing towns in Canada but for a good reason: the rolling granite cove highlighted by a perfect red-and-white lighthouse exudes a dreamy seaside calm even through the parading tour buses. Most visitors hop off their air-con bus, snap a few pictures then get right back on the bus. If you stick around you'll find it surprisingly easy to chat with the friendly locals (there are only 45 of them) and settle into a fishing village pace. At 43km west of Halifax on Hwy 333 it makes a mellow day trip from the city.

It's best to visit before 10am in the summer as tour buses arrive in the middle of the day and create one of the province's worst traffic jams. There's a free parking area with washrooms and a **tourist information office** (☑902-823-2253; 109 Peggy's Cove Rd; ⊙9am-7pm Jul & Aug, to 5pm mid-May–Jun, Sep & Oct) as you enter the village. Free 45-minute walking tours are led from the tourist office daily from mid-June through August.

◉ Sights & Activities

Peggy's Cove Lighthouse NOTABLE BUILDING
(⊙9:30am-5:30pm May-Oct) The highlight of the cove is this picture-perfect lighthouse, which for many years was a working post office where visitors could send post cards to be stamped with a famed lighthouse-shaped post mark. Unfortunately water damage from storms has shut the long-running post office.

DeGarthe Gallery ART GALLERY
(☑902-823-2256; admission $2; ⊙on demand) See paintings here by local artist William deGarthe (1907–83), who sculpted the magnificent 30m-high *Fishermen's Monument* into a rock face in front of the gallery.

☆ Entertainment

Old Red School House THEATER
(☑902-823-2099; www.beales.ns.ca; 126 Peggy's Point Rd; suggested donation $10) This performance venue puts on comedies and music performances through the high season. A few shows per season are serviced by shuttle vans that offer round-trip to Halifax hotels. Check the website for details.

⛏ Sleeping & Eating

Peggy's Cove Bed & Breakfast B&B $$
(☑902-823-2265, 877-725-8732; www.nsinns. com; 19 Church Rd; r $100-145) The only place to stay in the cove itself, this B&B has an enviable position with one of the best views in Nova Scotia, overlooking the fishing docks and the lighthouse; it was once home to artist William deGarthe. You'll definitely need advance reservations.

Oceanstone Inn & Cottages INN $$
(☑902-823-2160, 866-823-2160; www.ocean stone.ns.ca; 8650 Peggy's Cove Rd, Indian Harbour; r $95-145, cottages $185-265; @) Whimsically decorated cottages are a stone's throw from the beach and just a short drive from Peggy's Cove. Guests can use paddleboats to venture to small islands. Rhubarb, the inn's dining room, is considered one of the best seafood restaurants in the region.

Wayside Camping Park CAMPGROUND $
(☑902-823-2271; wayside@hfx.eastlink.ca; 10295 Hwy 333, Glen Margaret; tent/RV sites $20/32) Ten kilometers north of Peggy's Cove and 36km from Halifax, this campground has lots of shady sites on a hill. It gets crowded in midsummer.

SOUTH SHORE

This is Nova Scotia's most visited coastline and it's here you'll find all those quintessential lighthouses, protected forested coves with white beaches and plenty of fishing villages turned tourist towns. The area from Halifax to Lunenburg is cottage country for the city's elite and is quite popular with day-tripping tourists and locals. Hwy 3 – labeled the 'Lighthouse Route' by tourism officials – can be slow as a result. Take this scenic route if you're not pressed for time and want to check out antique shops or artisans' wares en route. Travel times can be halved by taking Hwy 103 directly to the closest exit for your destination.

Chester

Established in 1759, the tiny town of Chester has today become a choice spot for well-to-do Americans and Haligonians to have a summer home. It's had a colorful history as the haunt of pirates and Prohibition-era bathtub-gin smugglers and it keeps its color today via the many artists' studios about town. There's a large **regatta** in the tranquil harbor in mid-August.

◉ Sights & Activities

FREE **Lordly House Museum**   MUSEUM
(☑902-275-3842; 133 Central St; ☺10am-4pm Tue-Sat) A fine example of Georgian architecture from 1806, the Lordly House Museum has three period rooms illustrating 19th-century upper-class life and Chester history. The museum is also an artists' studio.

Tancook Island   NATURE RESERVE
This island (population 190) is a 45-minute ferry ride from Chester's government wharf (round-trip $5, four services daily Monday to Friday, two daily on weekends; schedule at http://freepages.history.rootsweb.com/~tancook/ferry.htm). Walking trails crisscross the island. Settled by Germans and French Huguenots in the early 19th century, the island is famous for its sauerkraut. The last ferry from Chester each day overnights in Tancook Island.

🛏 Sleeping & Eating

Mecklenburgh Inn B&B   B&B $$
(☑902-275-4638; www.mecklenburghinn.ca; 78 Queen St; r $95-155; ☺May-Jan) This casual four-room inn, built in 1890, has a breezy 2nd-floor veranda; some rooms have private adjacent balconies, most have private bathrooms. The owner is a Cordon Bleu chef so expect an excellent breakfast.

Graves Island Provincial Park
          CAMPGROUND $
(☑902-275-4425; www.parks.gov.ns.ca; campsites $24) An island in Mahone Bay connected by a causeway to the mainland has 64 wooded and open campsites. RVs usually park in the middle of the area, but some shady, isolated tent sites are tucked away on the flanks of the central plateau. It's 3km northeast of Chester off Hwy 3.

Kiwi Café   CAFE $
(☑902-275-1492; 19 Pleasant St; light lunches $4-13; ☺8am-4pm) A New Zealand chef prepares excellent soups, salads, sandwiches and baked goods that you can eat in or take away in recyclable containers. There's also beer, wine and a friendly atmosphere all painted kiwi green.

Rope Loft   PUB $$
(☑902-275-3430; 36 Water St; mains around $15; ☺food served 11:30am-9pm Sun-Thu, to 10pm Fri & Sat, pub open daily to 11pm) You couldn't find a better setting than this bayside pub. Hearty pub food is served indoors or out.

☆ Entertainment

Chester Playhouse   THEATER
(☑902-275-3933; www.chesterplayhouse.ca; 22 Pleasant St; tickets around $25) This older theater space has great acoustics for live performances. Plays or dinner theater are presented most nights, except Mondays in July and August, with occasional concerts during spring and fall.

❶ Information

Tourist office (☑902-275-4616; Hwy 3; ☺10am-4pm Jul & Aug, 10am-6pm Jun & Sep, 10am-5pm May & Oct) In the old train depot near the Chester turnoff.

Mahone Bay

The sun shines more often here than anywhere else along this coast. With more than 100 islands only 100km from Halifax, it's a great base for exploring this section of the South Shore. Take out a kayak or a bike or simply stroll down Main St, which skirts the harbor and is scattered with shops selling antiques, quilts, works by local painters and pottery.

◉ Sights & Activities

FREE **Mahone Bay Settlers' Museum**
          MUSEUM
(☑902-624-6263; 578 Main St; ☺10am-5pm Tue-Sun Jun–mid-Oct) Exhibits on the settlement of this area by 'Foreign Protestants' in 1754 and local architecture.

FREE **Amos Pewter**   DEMONSTRATION
(☑800-565-3369; www.amospewter.com; 589 Main St; ☺9am-6:30pm Mon-Sat, 10am-5:30pm Sun Jul & Aug, 9am-5:30pm Mon-Sat,

Oak Island, near Mahone Bay, is home to a so-called 'money pit' that has cost over $2 million in excavation expenses and six lives. There is still not a shred of information about what the pit is or what might be buried there.

The mystery began in 1795 when three inhabitants of the island came across a depression in the ground. Knowing that pirates had once frequented the area, they decided to dig and see what they could find. Just over half a meter down they hit a layer of neatly placed flagstone; another 2.5m turned up one oak platform, then another. After digging to 9m, the men temporarily gave up but returned eight years later with the Onslow Company, a professional crew.

The Onslow excavation made it down 27.5m; when the crew returned the next morning, the shaft had flooded and they were forced to halt the digging. A year later, the company returned to dig 33.5m down in a parallel shaft, which also flooded. It was confirmed in 1850 that the pit was booby-trapped via five box drains at Smith Cove, 150m from the pit. The beach was found to be artificial.

Ever since, people have come to seek their fortune from far and wide at the 'money pit.' Only a few links of gold chain, some parchment, a cement vault and an inscribed stone have been found.

noon-5:30pm Sun May, Jun, Sep & Oct) Watch demonstrations of the art of pewter-making then buy wares at the attached store.

🔁 Tours

Historic Mahone Bay Walking Tours
WALKING TOURS

(per person $5; ☉1pm Fri, Sat & Sun) In July and August, 1¼-hour walking tours are lead from the VIC to many of Mahone Bay's historic homes. Times change year to year so check with the VIC for times.

South Shore Boat Tours
BOAT TOURS

(☎902-543-5107; www.southshoreboattours. com; ☉Jul-Aug) Offers boatbuilding and nature tours (1¾ hours, adults $35).

🎆 Festivals & Events

Mahone Bay Regatta
REGATTA

(www.mahonebayregatta.wordpress.com) On the weekend prior to the first Monday in August, this regatta features workshops in boatbuilding and daily races.

🛏 Sleeping & Eating

Edgewater B&B
B&B $$

(☎902-624-9382, 866-816-8688; www.bbcanada .com/edgewater; 44 Mader's Cove Rd; r $120-165; ☉Jul-Oct) Overlooking the water on the outskirts of town towards Lunenburg, the three rooms here are decorated in modern yet sea-feeling grays and beiges. There's also a big two-story cottage ($225 per night) – essentially a house – that's perfect for groups or families.

Hammock Inn the Woods B&B
B&B $$

(☎902-624-0891; www.hammockinnthewoods. com; 198 Woodstock Rd; d $75-95) Up a quiet road from Main St, there are two beckoning hammocks nestled in a wooded garden and the house is a restful blend of modern plush and country comfort. The healthy breakfasts are cooked using organic produce and there's free yoga every morning. A loft apartment should be available in 2011.

Three Thistles B&B
B&B $$

(☎902-624-0517; www.three-thistles.com; 389 West Main St; r $90-130) Owner Phyllis Wiseman uses environmentally conscious cleaning agents and cooks with organic foods. Rooms are sparkling and clean and there's a back garden that stretches to a wooded area.

Kiwi Kaboodle Backpackers Hostel
HOSTEL $

(☎902-531-5494, 866-549-4522; www.kiwika boodle.com; Hwy 3; dm $28; 🖥) Three kilometers from the attractions of Mahone Bay and 7km from Lunenburg, this friendly nine-bed hostel is superbly located. Owners offer town pickup as well as economical tours (www.novascotiatoursandtravel. com), shuttle service and excellent area tips. Plans are in the works for bike rentals and tours as well as a private room.

La Have Bakery
BAKERY $

(cnr Edgewater & Main Sts; sandwiches from $4; ☉9am-6pm;🍴) This bakery is famous for its hearty bread, and sandwiches that are made on thick slabs of it. Gluten-free breads are available as well as burgers and pizza.

Gazebo Café RESTAURANT **$$**
(☑902-624-6484; 567 Main St; mains $15-20; ◉lunch & dinner Apr-Oct;☑) This bistro-style eatery has water views and fantastic local favorites prepared with flair rather than a deep-fat fryer. Vegetarian options are available.

ⓘ Information
Biscuit Eater Booktrader & Cafe (☑902-624-2665; 16 Orchard St; internet per hr $5; ◉9am-5pm Wed-Sat, 11am-5pm Sun; ☎) The best place to check email, with a fair trade coffee and a light organic meal. Free wi-fi.

Mahone Bay (www.mahonebay.com) Links to restaurants and accommodations.

VIC (☑902-624-6151; 165 Edgewater St; ◉10am-5pm Sat & Sun May, 9am-6pm Jun & Sep, 9am-7pm Jul & Aug, 10am-5pm Oct) Has do-it-yourself walking-tour brochures.

Lunenburg
The largest of the South Shore fishing villages is historic Lunenburg, the region's only Unesco World Heritage site and the first British settlement outside Halifax. The town is at its most picturesque when viewed from the sea around sunset when the boxy, brightly painted old buildings literally glow behind the ship-filled port. Look for the distinctive 'Lunenburg Bump,' a five-sided dormer window on the 2nd floor that overhangs the 1st floor.

Lunenburg was settled largely by Germans, Swiss and Protestant French who were first recruited by the British as a workforce for Halifax then later became fishermen. Today Nova Scotia has been hard hit by dwindling fish stocks, but Lunenburg's burgeoning tourism trade has helped shore up the local economy.

⊙ Sights & Activities
Fisheries Museum of the Atlantic MUSEUM
(☑902-634-4794; www.fisheries.museum.gov.ns.ca; 68 Bluenose Dr; adult/child $10/3; ◉9:30am-5:30pm May-Oct) The knowledgeable staff at the Fisheries Museum of the Atlantic includes a number of retired fisherfolk who can give firsthand explanations of the fishing industry. A cute aquarium on the 1st floor lets you get eye-to-eye with halibut, a 14lb lobster and other sea creatures.

Film screenings and talks are scheduled throughout the day.

Knaut-Rhuland House MUSEUM
(☑902-634-3498; 125 Pelham St; admission $3; ◉11am-5pm Tue-Sat, 1-5pm Sun Jun-Sep) Knaut-Rhuland House is considered the finest example of Georgian architecture in the province. This 1793 house has costumed guides who point out its features.

Bike Barn CYCLING
(☑902-634-3426; www.bikelunenburg.com; 579 Blue Rocks Rd; hybrid/tandem bikes per day $25/40) About 2km east of town, the Bike Barn rents bikes. On a small peninsula, this area is a cyclist's dream, with few hills, great ocean views and little vehicle traffic. Owners Merrill and Al will gladly help you plan your trip.

Pleasant Paddling KAYAKING
(www.pleasantpaddling.com; 86 Bluenose Dr; rentals 2hr/half-day/full-day $30/50/70, tours half-/full-day $65/110) Offers rentals and tours in double or single kayaks; knowledgeable folks and a beautiful place to paddle.

⌖ Tours
Numerous fishing, sailing and whale-watching tours depart from the wharf adjacent to the Fisheries Museum on Bluenose Dr. Book on the dock or at the VIC.

Bluenose II SAILING
(☑902-634-1963, 800-763-1963; www.bluenose2 .ns.ca; 2hr cruises adult/child $20/10) This classic replica of the *Bluenose* racing schooner is sometimes in Halifax and sometimes in Lunenburg. It was closed in 2010 for refitting but should reopen in 2011. Check the website for details.

Gray Line Lunenburg Town Walking Tours WALKING TOURS
(☑902-634-3848) Enthusiastic and knowledgeable Eric Croft leads leisurely tours during the day or spooky lantern-lit ones at night; call for more information.

Trot in Time CART TOURS
(adult/child $20/8; ◉Jun–mid-Oct) Take a half-hour tour of town in a horse-drawn cart. Leaves from outside the Fisheries Museum of the Atlantic.

✦ Festivals & Events
Boxwood Festival MUSIC
(www.boxwood.org; festival pass $50; ◉last week of Jul) Flautists and pipers from

Lunenburg

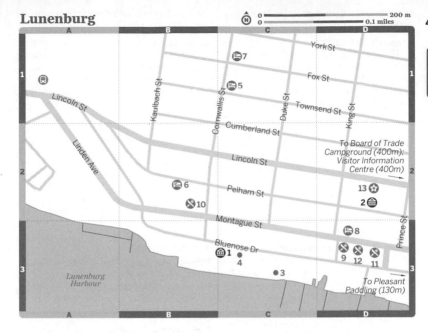

around the world put on stellar public concerts.

Lunenburg Folk Harbour Festival MUSIC
(☏902-634-3180; www.folkharbour.com; ☉Aug)
Singer-songwriters from Canada and beyond, plus traditional music and gospel.

Nova Scotia Folk Art Festival FOLK ART
(www.nsfolkartfestival.com; ☉1st Sun of Aug)

🛏 Sleeping

Make reservations as far ahead as possible, especially during summer festivals. Kiwi Kaboodle Backpackers Hostel (p47), 7km north of town, is the best budget option.

Sail Inn B&B B&B $$
(☏902-634-3537, 877-247-7075; www.sailinn.ca; 99 Montague St; r $80-140; @) Rooms have a view over the waterfront and are bright, airy and modern with an antique twist. You get a free sail on the owner's 48ft ketch with your stay. Don't miss checking out the old well on the ground floor that's been turned into a lighted fish pond.

1775 Solomon House B&B B&B $$
(☏902-634-3477; www.bbcanada.com/5511.html; 69 Townsend St; r $100-125; @) A wonderfully antique place with undulating wooden floors and low door jams (watch

Lunenburg

◎ Sights

1 Fisheries Museum of the
   Atlantic C3
2 Knaut-Rhuland House D2

Activities, Courses & Tours

3 Bluenose II C3
4 Trot in Time C3

🛏 Sleeping

5 1775 Solomon House B&B C1
6 1826 Maplebird House B&B B2
7 Lennox Tavern B&B C1
8 Sail Inn B&B D3

🍴 Eating

9 Fish Cake Café D3
10 Fleur de Sel B2
11 Magnolia's Grill D3
12 Salt Shaker Deli D3

🎭 Entertainment

13 Lunenburg Opera House D2

your head!), this B&B has the nicest and most helpful owner ever. Rooms are cozy amid the ageing walls and you'll be talking about the breakfasts for the rest of your trip. The only drawback is the minuscule bathrooms.

Lennox Tavern B&B B&B $$
(☎902-634-4043, 888-379-7605; www.lennox-inn.com; 69 Fox St; r $85-140) This place feels authentically old, with electric candles lighting the halls and massive plank-wood floors. The inn is the oldest in Canada and you get to eat breakfast in what was once the tavern.

1826 Maplebird House B&B B&B $$
(☎902-634-3863, 888-395-3863; www.maple-birdhouse.ca; 36 Pelham St; d $115; @☒) Decorated country style with teddy bears a-go-go, this house in the heart of town manages to remain cozy, not frilly. The lovely, large rear garden overlooks the harbor and has a barbecue for guests.

Board of Trade Campground CAMPGROUND $
(☎902-634-8100/3656; lbt@aliantzinc.ca; 11 Blockhouse Hill Rd; tent/RV sites $23/$30; @) This campground, beside the VIC, has great views and a lot of gravel RV sites. Grassy tent sites are closely packed together and lack shade.

✗ Eating & Drinking

Try some offbeat Lunenburg specialties. Solomon Gundy is pickled herring with onions. Lunenburg pudding – pork and spices cooked in the intestines of a pig – goes well with Scotch and water.

Fleur de Sel RESTAURANT $$$
(☎902-640-2121; 53 Montague St; mains lunch $8-12, dinner $28-36; ⊙11am-2pm & 5-10pm;☑) This is by far the most elegant eating option in the region. French-inspired seafood, meat and vegetarian dishes use organic produce and are served in the classic, bright dining area.

Fish Cake Café RESTAURANT $$
(☎902-634-9995; 100 Montague St; lunch $10-15; ⊙9am-4pm) Specializing in (surprise!) fish cakes including delicious ones made with salmon and scallops with lime-ginger aioli and red-onion chutney. There are also sandwiches, daily specials, soups, original cocktails and decadent desserts.

Salt Shaker Deli DELI $
(☎902-640-3434; 124 Montague St; meals $8-15; ⊙11am-9pm Tue-Sat, 11am-3pm Sun) With a clean-cut modern atmosphere, a waterfront deck and amazing food, it's no wonder this new deli-restaurant is always packed. Try

the thin-crust pizzas or a pound of mussels cooked to the style of your choosing.

Magnolia's Grill RESTAURANT $
(☎902-634-3287; 128 Montague St; mains $8-16; ⊙lunch & dinner) Try one of the many soups of the day at this diner-style local's favorite. Seafood (including Solomon Gundy) and an extensive wine list are available.

☆ Entertainment

Lunenburg Opera House THEATER
(☎902-634-4010; 290 Lincoln St; tickets $5-20) This rickety old 400-seat theater is rumored to have a resident ghost. Built as an Oddfellows Hall in 1907, it's now a favorite venue for rock and folk musicians. Check the posters in the window for what's coming up.

❶ Information

Explore Lunenburg (www.explorelunenburg.ca) Local history and tourism information.

Lunenburg Public Library (☎902-634-8008; 19 Pelham St; ⊙10am-6pm Tue, Wed & Fri, 10am-8pm Thu, 10am-5pm Sat) Free internet access.

VIC (☎902-634-8100, 888-615-8305; 11 Blockhouse Hill Rd; ⊙9am-6pm May-Oct, 9am-8pm Jul & Aug) Walking-tour maps and help with accommodations.

❶ Getting There & Away

Trius Lines buses serve Lunenburg on their once-daily Halifax–Yarmouth route; the best source of information on Trius' prices and departure locations is **Acadian Lines** (☎902-454-9321, 800-567-5151; www.acadianbus.com). For alternative shuttles, see p43.

Liverpool

There is plenty to do in Liverpool and it's well situated for exploring several gorgeous beaches as well as Kejimkujik National Park (68km north) and its Seaside Adjunct (15km southwest). That said, it lacks the seaside quaintness of the villages north of here.

◉ Sights & Activities

Rossignol Cultural Centre MUSEUM
(☎902-354-3067; www.rossignolculturalcentre.com; 205 Church St; adult/child $5/3; ⊙10am-5:30pm Mon-Sat) Local character Sherman Hines' most fabulous endeavor is a must-see for anyone who enjoys the offbeat. There are lifelike halls of taxidermy ani-

mals, cases of gorgeous aboriginal bead-work, walls of Hines' beautiful photography (including his Mongolian adventures) and a room dedicated to outhouses around the world. If you love it so much you don't want to leave, an authentic Mongolian **yurt** (with en-suite bathroom) is for rent adjacent to the museum for a $100 per night donation. Admission to the museum includes entry to the **Sherman Hines Museum of Photography** (☑902-354-2667; www.shermanhines photographymuseum.com; 219 Main St; ☺10am-5:30pm Mon-Sat).

Perkins House Museum MUSEUM
(☑902-354-4058; www.museum.gov.ns.ca/peh; 105 Main St; adult/child $2/1; ☺9:30am-5.30pm Mon-Sat, 1-5:30pm Sun Jun–mid-Oct) Perkins House Museum displays articles and furniture from the colonial period. Built in 1766, it's the oldest house belonging to the Nova Scotia Museum.

Queen's County Museum MUSEUM
(☑902-354-4058; www.queenscountymuseum. com; 109 Main St; admission $1; ☺9:30am-5:30pm Mon-Sat, 1-5:30pm Sun Jun–mid-Oct, 9am-5pm Mon-Sat mid-Oct–May) This museum has aboriginal artifacts and more materials relating to town history as well as some writings by early citizens.

FREE **Fort Point** LANDMARK
At Fort Point a cairn marks the site where Frenchman Samuel de Champlain landed in 1604. You can blow the hand-pumped foghorn in the **lighthouse** (☑902-354-5260; 21 Fort Lane; ☺10am-6pm mid-May–mid-Oct), at the end of Main St.

Hank Snow Country Music Centre MUSEUM
(☑902-354-4675; www.hanksnow.com; 148 Bristol Ave; admission $3; ☺9am-5pm Mon-Sat, noon-5pm Sun late May-early Oct) The Hank Snow Country Music Centre sheds light on Nova Scotia's status as a northern Nashville. In the old train station, it captures the history of Snow, Wilf Carter and other crooners and yodelers.

🎉 Festivals & Events
Privateer Days HISTORICAL
(www.privateerdays.com; ☺early Jul) A celebration of piracy and history.

🛏 Sleeping & Eating
Geranium House B&B $
(☑902-354-4484; 87 Milton Rd; r $60) This B&B on a large wooded property next to

the Mersey River has three rooms with shared bathroom and is ideal for families.

Lane's Privateer Inn INN $$
(☑902-354-3456, 800-794-3332; www.lanes privateerinn.com; 27 Bristol Ave; r incl breakfast $95-150; @) Originally the home of a swash-buckling privateer, this 211-year-old inn now looks more 1980s than anything else but it's still a clean and pleasant place to stay. There's also a gourmet food store and a dining room (open 7am to 10pm; mains $9 to $25).

Woodpile Carving Cafe CAFE $
(☑902-354 4494; 181 Main St; light meals $4-10; ☺8am-4pm Mon-Sat) This atmospheric cafe, a local favorite, has the owner's wood-carving workshop right in its center. Grab a specialty coffee, soups, sandwiches and salads.

☆ Entertainment
Astor Theatre THEATER
(☑902-354-5250; www.astortheatre.ns.ca; 59 Gorham St) The Astor is the oldest continuously operating performance venue in the province. Built in 1902 as the Liverpool Opera House, it presents films, plays and live music.

ℹ Information
Tourist office (☑902-354-5421; 28 Henry Hensey Dr; ☺9:30am-5:30pm Jul & Aug, 10am-5pm mid-May–Jul & Sep–mid-Oct) Near the river bridge; has a walking-tour pamphlet.

Kejimkujik National Park

Less than 20% of Kejimkujik's 381-sq-km wilderness is accessible by car; the rest is reached either on foot or by canoe. Bird-watchers can hope to see plenty of water fowl, barred owls and pileated woodpeckers, while wildlife ranges from porcupines to black bear. On a less joyful note, biting insects are rampant; watch out for mosquitoes the size of hummingbirds and eel-like leeches in the lakes.

Get an entry permit and reserve back-country sites at the **visitor center** (☑902-682-2772, 800-414-6765; www.parkscanada.gc. ca/keji; Hwy 8; adult/child $5.80/2.90; ☺8:30am-9pm mid-Jun–early Sep, to 4pm rest of year, closed weekends Nov-Mar).

🏃 Activities
The main **hiking** loop is a 60km trek that begins at the east end of George Lake and

ends at the Big Dam Lake trailhead. A shorter loop, ideal for an overnight trek, is the 26km Channel Lake Trail that begins and also ends at Big Dam Lake. September to early October is prime hiking time; the bugs in the spring would drive you mad. More than a dozen lakes are connected by a system of portages, allowing canoe trips of up to seven days. A topographical map ($10) may be required for ambitious multiday trips. Rent canoes and other equipment in the park at **Jakes Landing** (☑902-682-5253; ⊗8am-9pm Jun-Sep). One-hour hire of a double kayak, canoe or rowboat is $8, kayak or bike is $7; 24-hour hire is $35/30 and one-week hire is $130. It's open during the off-season by appointment.

🛏 Sleeping & Eating

Forty-five backcountry sites ($24.50 per person including firewood) are scattered among the lakes of Kejimkujik. You must book them in advance by telephone or stopping at the park's visitor center. There's a 14-day maximum; you can't stay more than two nights at any site.

Mersey River Chalets   CABINS **$$**
(☑902-682-2447, 877-667-2583; www.mersey riverchalets.com; 2537 River Rd; tepees $70, d $110, cabins $150-205; @) Comfy cabins have pine floors, wood-burning stoves and very private porches complete with barbecue; rooms in the lodge have private decks with lake views; and cosy tepees have fully equipped kitchens. Free canoes and kayaks are available for guests.

Caledonia Country Hostel   HOSTEL **$**
(☑902-682-3266, 877-223-0232; www.caledonia countryhostel.com; 9960 Hwy 8, Caledonia; dm/d $25/60; @) In the heart of Caledonia – the only town near the park that has an internet cafe, a VIC, a gas station and a grocery store – this spotless hostel has beds on the 2nd floor of an adorable Victorian-style home. Cozy nooks with TV, books, oldstyle upholstered chairs and country linens abound. The owners also have tours and shuttle services available.

Raven Haven Hostel & Family Park
                    HOSTEL & CAMPGROUND **$**
(☑902-532-7320; www.annapoliscounty.ns.ca; 2239 Virginia Rd, off Hwy 8, South Milford; dm member/nonmember $20/22, tent/RV sites $20/24, cabins $68; ⊗mid-Jun–early Sep) This HI hostel and campground is 25km south of Annapolis Royal and 27km north of the

national park. The four-bed hostel is in a cabin near the white-sand beach and rustic two-bedroom cabins have equipped kitchens but no linens. There are 15 campsites but the camping in the park is better. Canoes and paddleboats can be rented.

Jeremy's Bay Campground   CAMPGROUND **$**
(☑902-682-2772, 800-414-6765; campsites $25.50) Of the 360 campsites within the park, 30% are assigned on a first-come, first-served basis. There is only one shower area for the whole camp so be prepared to wait for a stall. It costs $10 to reserve a site.

M&W Restaurant & Variety Store
                              RESTAURANT **$**
(☑902-682-2189; Hwy 8; mains $4-12; ⊗9am-8pm mid-May–mid-Oct) Only 500m from the park entrance this place serves 'hungry camper' breakfasts ($6) as well as lunch and dinner. It's also a general store stocked with camping supplies (including firewood) and a Laundromat.

Seaside Adjunct (Kejimkujik National Park)

The 'Keji Adjunct' protects angelic landscapes of rolling low brush, wildflowers, white sandy coves and the granite outcrops spreading between Port Joli and Port Mouton (ma-*toon*) Bay. The only access from Hwy 103 is along a 6.5km gravel road. Pay your park fee and grab a trail map at the helpful **Park Office** (adult/child $6/3; ⊗8:30am-8pm mid-Jun–Sep, 8:30am-4pm Oct–mid-Jun) at the parking lot. From there, two mostly flat trails lead to the coast. **Harbour Rocks Trail** (5.2km return) follows an old cart road through mixed forest to a beach where seals are often seen. A loop trail around **Port Joli Head** is 8.7km return.

The Port Joli Basin contains **Point Joli Migratory Bird Sanctuary** with waterfowl and shorebirds in great numbers (*Nova Scotia Birding on the Lighthouse Route* is an excellent resource available at VICs). It's only easily accessible by kayak. The **Rossignol Surf Shop** (☑902-683-2550; www. surfnovascotia.com; White Point Beach Resort) in nearby White Point rents kayaks (half-/fullday $30/45), surfboards and bodyboards ($20/40), and offers kayak tours ($65/110) and surfing lessons ($65).

Thomas Raddall Provincial Park (☑902-683-2664; www.parks.gov.ns.ca; campsites $24;

⊙mid-May–Oct), across Port Joli Harbour from Keji Adjunct, has large, private campsites with eight walk-in ones. The forested campground extends out onto awesome beaches.

Port Mouton International Hostel (☑902-947-3140; www.wqccda.com/PMhostel; 8100 Hwy 3; dm $30; @), only five minutes from Keji Adjunct, is run on a volunteer basis by the community in a former school. There are 30 beds (plus one private room), a good kitchen and a washer and dryer. Call in advance or if you arrive between 10am and 5pm you can check in at the crafts store next door.

Shelburne

Shelburne's beautiful historic waterfront area bobs with sailboats and has 17 pre-1800 homes – it feels like a historical re-creation but it's real. The wonderfully maintained, low-in-the-earth buildings once housed Loyalists who retreated here from the American Revolution. In 1783 Shelburne was the largest community in British North America with 16,000 residents, many from the New York aristocracy, who exploited the labor of Black Loyalists living in nearby Birchtown (see the boxed text, below). Shelburne's history is celebrated with **Founders' Days** during the last weekend of July.

⊙ Sights & Activities

Shelburne has started organizing a slew of activities from mid-June to mid-August in-

cluding daily demonstrations around town by folks in period costumes of old-style cooking, sewing, music, military exercises, carving and more; schedules change daily but start around 1pm. Check at the VIC for more information. Admission to the following museums is $3, but you can buy a pass for all four for $8.

Built in 1784, **Ross-Thomson House** (☑902-875-3141; www.rossthomson.museum.gov. ns.ca; 9 Charlotte Lane; admission free 9:30am-noon Sun; ⊙9:30am-5:30pm Jun–mid-Oct) belonged to well-to-do Loyalist merchants who arrived from Cape Cod. Furniture, paintings and original goods from the store are on display. The house is surrounded by authentic period gardens.

Another c 1787 Loyalist house is now the **Shelburne County Museum** (☑902-875-3219; cnr Maiden Lane & Dock St; ⊙9:30am-5:30pm) with a collection of Loyalist furnishings, displays on the history of the local fishery and a small collection of Mi'kmaq artifacts.

The **Muir-Cox Shipyard** (☑902-875-1114; www.historicshelburne.com/muircox.htm; 18 Dock St; ⊙9:30am-5:30pm Jun-Sep) has been in almost continuous operation since 1820, turning out barques, yachts and fishing boats. It's still active year-round, but the interpretive center is seasonal. Likewise, Shelburne dories (small open boats once used for fishing from a mother schooner) are still made to order at the **Dory Shop Museum** (☑902-875-3219; www.museum.gov. ns.ca/dory; 11 Dock St; ⊙9:30am-5:30pm Jun-Sep) for use as lifeboats.

BLACK LOYALIST BIRCHTOWN

Just as Shelburne was once the largest settlement in British North America, so Birchtown was once the largest settlement of freed African slaves in North America. After the American Revolution, about 3500 Black Loyalists were rewarded by the British with land for settlements near Shelburne, Halifax, Digby and Guysborough. Nine years later, in 1792, after barely surviving harsh winters and unequal treatment, 1200 of them boarded 15 ships bound for Sierra Leone, in West Africa, where they founded Freetown. An additional 2000 from the USA settled in the Maritimes after the War of 1812, and others came from the Caribbean in the 1890s to work in the Cape Breton Island coal mines.

The future was no brighter. Underfunded, segregated schools existed until the 1950s. Birchtown's **Black Loyalist Heritage Society Historical Site & Museum** (☑902-875-1381, 888-354-0722; www.blackloyalist.com; 104 Birchtown Rd; ⊙11am-6pm Tue-Fri, noon-6pm Sat, noon-5pm Sun) includes a museum and a walking trail that leads to a 'pit house' which archaeologists think was once a temporary shelter. There is also a **trail** for hiking or cycling the 6km to Shelburne.

A self-guided tour of African heritage in Nova Scotia is available online (www.gov. ns.ca/nsarm/virtual/africanns/).

There's a **trail** for hiking or biking the 6km to Birchtown across from Spencer's Garden Centre at the far south end of Main St. Historic 1½-hour **walking tours** (per person $10; ☺2pm Tue-Fri, 7pm Tue & Thu) depart from the VIC.

🛏 Sleeping

TOP CHOICE **Cooper's Inn B&B**　　　　B&B $$
(☎902-875-4656, 800-688-2011; www.thecoopersinn.com; 36 Dock St; r $100-150; @) Part of this waterfront building dates to 1784 and was brought here from Boston. Now it's a relatively modern but still charmingly heritage-style inn with six rooms and a flower-filled garden where you can drink your complimentary bottle of Jost wine at sunset.

Water Street Lighthouse B&B　B&B $
(☎902-875-2331; www.shelburnelighthouse.com; 263 Water St; r $60-80; @) Not luxurious, but comfy and friendly, this is a great B&B to shack up your bike for the night. A lighthouse theme runs through the house.

The Islands Provincial Park　CAMPGROUND $
(☎902-875-4304; www.parks.gov.ns.ca; off Hwy 3; campsites $18) Across the harbor from Shelburne are 65 campsites in mature forest and a beach for swimming.

🍴 Eating & Drinking

TOP CHOICE **Charlotte Lane**　　RESTAURANT $$$
(☎902-875-3314; 13 Charlotte Lane; mains $16-35; ☺lunch & dinner Tue-Sat) People drive from Halifax to eat here, and then rave about it; evening reservations are highly recommended. Swiss chef Roland Glauser is constantly revising an extensive annotated wine list to accompany his ever-changing menu of local seafood, meat and pasta dishes.

Bean Dock　　　　　　　CAFE $
(☎902-875-1302; sandwiches from $4; ☺10am-4pm Mon-Fri, to 8pm Wed, 10am-4pm Sat) Snuggle over to a wood table overlooking the bay for coffee, grilled sandwiches and light mains from fish cakes and salad ($9) to sun-dried tomato pasta salad ($7). The giant Adirondack chair out front is worth chatting about.

ℹ Information

VIC (☎902-875-4547; 31 Dock St; ☺8am-8pm Jul & Aug, 11am-5pm mid-May–Jun & Sep) Has copies of a self-guided historic district walking tour.

Barrington to West Pubnico

At Barrington you can choose to take the fast, not-very-scenic Hwy 103 to Yarmouth or meander along about 100km of interesting coastline via Hwy 3. It's worth taking a detour to **Cape Sable Island** (not to be confused with Sable Island, p88), a puddle-flat appendage that is Nova Scotia's southernmost point. Many of the island's windy, white-sand beaches are designated as 'important bird areas,' and a few are piping plover nesting grounds. The whole island tends to get banked in fog which might explain why its lighthouse is 31.1m tall, the tallest in Nova Scotia.

Not to be confused with all the other nearby Pubnicos, West Pubnico is an old Acadian community. **Le Village Historique Acadien** (☎902-762-2530; Old Church Rd; adult/child $16/11; ☺10am-6pm mid-Jun–Sep) re-creates an Acadian village, with a blacksmith shop, a timber-frame house and a fish store.

Yarmouth

Yarmouth is the biggest town in southern Nova Scotia, due mostly to the ferry that has linked the province to Bar Harbor (Maine) since the 1950s. Unfortunately the ferry service stopped in 2010, although there were plans for starting it up again in 2011 with a new boat; if it doesn't, Yarmouth could be in for some tough times. The only really pretty area is out beyond town around the lighthouse, but like anywhere in the province, stay awhile and the people will win you over.

◉ Sights & Activities

First settled by New Englanders from Massachusetts in 1761, Yarmouth reached its peak of growth and prosperity in the 1870s. The Collins Heritage Conservation District protects many fine Victorian homes built around that time. Check at the VIC for a self-guided walking tour.

FREE **Yarmouth Light**　NOTABLE BUILDING
(☎902-742-1433; Hwy 304; ☺9am-9pm) Yarmouth Light is at the end of Cape Forchu, a left on Hwy 304 from Main St. The lighthouse affords spectacular views and there's a tearoom below. On the drive or pedal out, stop at **Stanley Lobster Pound** (Hwy 304; ☺11am-7pm Mon-Sat, 2-7pm Sun),

Yarmouth

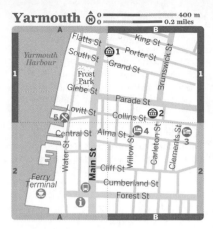

Yarmouth Harbour

400 m
0.2 miles

Sleeping & Eating

TOP CHOICE MacKinnon-Cann House Historic Inn   INN $$

(☑902-742-0042; www.mackinnoncanninn.com; 27 Willow St; r $140-185; ⊜@) Each of the six rooms here represent a decade from the Victorian 1900s to the groovy '60s. Each room depicts the decade at its most stylish while managing to stay calming and comfortable. Two rooms can be joined to create a family suite and the inn is gay friendly.

Clementine's B&B   B&B $$

(☑902-742-0079; 21 Clements St; d $95; @) Open for over 20 years, Clementine's hasn't faded a bit. Rooms with shared bathrooms are unpretentiously decorated and Evelyn's breakfasts are famous throughout Yarmouth. The B&B is only a few minutes' walk to Main St.

Rudder's Brew Pub   PUB $$

(☑902-742-7311; 96 Water St; pub menu $8-14, dinner mains $14-32) The 300 seats at this waterfront pub and restaurant fill fast. A mean ale is brewed on site and there's a wide-ranging menu. Drinks are poured until the wee hours on busy summer nights.

ℹ Information

VIC (☑902-742-5033; 228 Main St; ☺7:30am-9pm Jul & Aug, to 4:30pm May, Jun, Sep & Oct) Also has a money-exchange counter.

Yarmouth Public Library (☑902-742-2486; 405 Main St; ☺10am-8pm Mon-Thu, 10am-5pm Fri, 10am-4pm Sat, 1-4pm Sun) Free internet access.

ℹ Getting There & Away

The **Trius Lines** (☑902-454-9321, 800-567-5151) bus leaves from the Rodd Colony Hotel at 6:20am Mondays to Saturdays or 11:20am Sundays and holidays and travels along the southwestern shore. For information on private shuttles, see p43. If the ferry starts running again, Yarmouth will also be the departure point to Maine.

where you can get a fresh-cooked lobster at market-value price to take and eat on the beach.

Art Gallery of Nova Scotia   ART GALLERY
(☑902-749-2248; www.artgalleryofnovascotia.com; 341 Main St; adult/child $5/1; ☺noon-8pm) Practical Yarmouth is the unexpected home to the refreshingly cosmopolitan Art Gallery of Nova Scotia. The new three-story building has well-selected works from mostly Maritime artists.

Yarmouth County Museum   MUSEUM
(☑902-742-5539; http://yarmouthcountymuseum.ednet.ns.ca; 22 Collins St; adult/student $5/2; ☺9am-5pm Mon-Sat, 2-5pm Sun) This museum, in a former church, contains five period rooms related to the sea. A regular single admission ticket (adult/student $3/0.50) includes **Pelton-Fuller House** (☺9am-5pm Mon-Sat Jun-Oct) next door, which is filled with period artwork, glassware and furniture.

ANNAPOLIS VALLEY & FRENCH SHORE

Heading up the French Shore you'll be regularly waved to by the Stella Maris, the single-starred, tricolored Acadian flag. Admire the many elaborate Catholic churches, stop at a roadside eatery to sample Acadian rappie pie (a type of meat pie topped with grated pastelike potato from which all the starch has been drawn) and take a walk along a fine-sand beach. If you stay longer, don't miss the chance to sample the region's foot-tapping music performances that take place frequently throughout the summer.

Continuing northeast, the Annapolis Valley was once the main breadbasket for colonial Canada and it still produces much of Nova Scotia's fresh produce, especially apples. In more recent years, a number of wineries have taken advantage of the sandy soil. Make sure to get to the Fundy coast at Annapolis Royal and eastwards for tidal vistas over patchwork farmland, red sands and undulating hills.

Cape St Mary to Meteghan

A long, wide arc of fine sand, just 900m off Hwy 1, **Mavillete Beach** is great for collecting seashells, and the marsh behind it is good for bird-watching. At the southern edge of Meteghan, the largest community on the French Shore, **Smuggler's Cove Provincial Park** is named for its popularity with 19th-century pirates. A hundred wooden stairs take you down to a rocky beach and a good cave for hiding treasure. There are picnic sites with barbecue pits at the top of the stairs, with a view across St Mary's Bay to Brier Island.

La Maison D'Amité B&B (🖉902-645-2601; www.houseoffriendship.ca; 169 Baseline Rd; r from $175; 🌐) is perched dramatically on a cliff close to the beach on 6 private hectares. The huge, American-style home has cathedral ceilings and sky-high windows with views on all sides.

Church Point to St Bernard

The villages of Church Point, Grosses-Coques, Belliveau Cove and St Bernard, on the mainland directly across St Mary's Bay from Digby Neck, make up the heart of the French Shore. This is where Acadians settled when, after trekking back to Nova Scotia following the deportation, they found their homesteads in the Annapolis Valley already occupied. Now linked by Hwy 1 – pretty much the only road in town – these are small fishing communities.

The oldest of the annual Acadian cultural festivals, **Festival Acadien de Clare** (www.festivalacadiendeclare.ca), is held during the second week of July at Church Point. In July

and August the musical *Évangéline,* based on Henry Wadsworth Longfellow's romantic poem about the Acadian deportation, is presented in the **Théâtre Marc-Lescarbot** (🖉902-769-2114; adult/child $25/15) also at Church Point. Performances are given in English on Saturday, in French with headset translation Tuesday and Friday, and outdoors in French on Wednesday only.

◉ Sights & Activities

Hinterland Adventures & Gear   KAYAKING
(🖉902-837-4092; www.kayakingnovascotia.com; 54 Gates Lane, Weymouth; rentals per hr/day $7/40, guides per hr $10, half-/full-day tours $45/115) Running tours for over 15 years, this well-respected kayaking outfit specializes in paddling tours of St Mary's Bay and the Sissiboo River.

Église Ste Marie   CHURCH
(🖉902-769-2808; Hwy 1; admission incl guide $2; ⊙9am-5pm mid-May–mid-Oct) The town of Church Point, also commonly known as Pointe de l'Église, takes its name from Église Ste Marie, which towers over the town. Built between 1903 and 1905, the church is said to be the tallest and biggest wooden church in North America. An informative guide will show you around. Adjacent is the **Université Ste Anne**, the only French university in the province and a center for Acadian culture, with 300 students.

Belliveau Beach   BEACH
Belliveau Beach, near the southern end of Belliveau, is reached by turning right onto Major's Point. The beach is made up of masses of sea-polished stones broken only by small clumps of incredibly hardy fir trees. Just behind the beach, a cemetery and monument recall the struggles of the early Acadian settlers of the French Shore.

St Bernard Church   CHURCH
(🖉902-837-5637; Hwy 1; ⊙tours Jun-Sep) St Bernard is also known for its church, a huge granite structure built by locals who added one row of blocks each year between 1910 and 1942. It has incredible acoustics which are showcased each summer through the **Musique Saint-Bernard** (www.musiquesaint-bernard.ca; adult/child $15/5) concert series.

🛏 Sleeping & Eating

Chez Christophe Guesthouse & Restaurant   INN & RESTAURANT **$$**
(🖉902-837-5817; www.chezchristophe.ca; 2655 Hwy 1; breakfast $10, dinner mains $12-36; ⊙6am-

9pm Tue-Sun) Locals drive from Yarmouth and Digby to dine at this restaurant in Grosses-Coques. Master chef Paul Comeau has turned the house that his grandfather built in 1837 into a guesthouse (rooms $70 to $85) and restaurant; this is probably the most renowned Acadian restaurant in Nova Scotia. Live Acadian music is performed from 6pm to 8pm Thursday nights through June and nearly every night of the week in July and August.

Roadside Grill   RESTAURANT **$**
(☑902-837-5047; 3334 Hwy 1; meals $7-15; ☺8am-9pm Jul & Aug, 9am-7pm Sep-Jun) A pleasantly old-fashioned local restaurant in Belliveau Cove – try the steamed clams or the rappie pie. It also rents three small cabins (singles/doubles $55/70) with cable TV and microwaves. There's live Acadian music Tuesday nights from 5:30pm to 7:30pm June through August.

Digby Neck

Craning out to take a peek into the Bay of Fundy, Digby Neck is a giraffe's length strip of land that's a haven for whale- and seabird-watchers. At the far western end of the appendage are Long and Brier Islands, connected by ferry with the rest of the peninsula.

Plankton stirred up by the strong Fundy tides attracts finback, minke and humpback whales and this is the best place in the world to see the endangered North Atlantic right whale. Blue whales, the world's largest animal, are also sighted on occasion plus you're almost certain to see plenty of seals.

Bring plenty of warm clothing (regardless of how hot a day it seems), sunblock and binoculars; motion-sickness pills are highly recommended.

LONG ISLAND

Most people head straight to Brier Island, but Long Island has better deals on whale-watching as well as a livelier community. At the northeastern edge of Long Island, **Tiverton** is an active fishing community.

FREE **Island Museum** (☑902-839-2853; 3083 Hwy 217; ☺9:30am-7:30pm Jul & Aug, to 4:30pm late May-Jun & Sep–mid-Oct), 2km west of the Tiverton ferry dock, has exhibits on local history and a tourist information desk.

One of the best whale-watching tours in the province is found just near the Tiver-

ton ferry dock. **Ocean Explorations Whale Cruises** (☑902-839-2417, 877-654-2341; www. oceanexplorations.ca; half-day tours adult/child $59/40; ☺Jun-Oct), led by biologist Tom Goodwin, has the adventurous approach of getting you low to whale-level in a Zodiac. Shimmy into an orange coastguard-approved flotation suit and hold on tight! Goodwin has been leading whale-watching tours since 1980 and donates part of his proceeds to wildlife conservation and environmental education organizations. Discounts are given for groups of three or more; tour times depend on weather and demand.

A 4km round-trip trail to the **Balancing Rock** starts 2km southwest of the museum. The trail features rope railings, boardwalks and an extensive series of steps down a rock bluff to the bay. At the end there's a viewing platform where you can see a 7m-high stone column perched precariously just above the pounding surf of St Mary's Bay.

Near the center of Long Island, **Central Grove Provincial Park** has a 2km hiking trail to the Bay of Fundy. There's camping at quirky **Whale Cove Campground** (☑902-834-2025; www.whalecovecampground. com; Hwy 217; serviced/unserviced sites $30/25, cabin or trailer $35-62; @) in Tiddville, about 5km before Freeport; there's a cabin and a trailer to rent if you don't have gear.

At the southwestern end of Long Island, **Freeport** is central for exploring both Brier and Long Islands.

Lavena's Catch Café (☑902-839-2517; 15 Hwy 217; mains $5-15; ☺lunch & dinner) is a country-style cafe directly above the wharf at Freeport; it's the perfect spot to enjoy a sunset and you might even see a whale from the balcony. There's occasional live music in the evenings.

BRIER ISLAND

Westport was the home of Joshua Slocum, the first man to sail solo around the world, and is the only community on Brier Island. It's a quaint little fishing village and a good base to explore the numerous excellent, if rugged and windy, hiking trails around the island; don't miss a trip to the West Lighthouse. Columnar basalt rocks are seen all along the coast and agates can be found on the beaches.

The **Brier Island Backpackers Hostel** (☑902-839-2273; www.brierislandhostel.com; 223 Water St; dm adult/child $20/10; ☎) is a tiny, spotless place about 1.5km to the left as you come off the ferry. The common room and kitchen area has big windows with views over the water. There's a general store, gas station and basic **cafe** (mains $5-8; ☺8am-9pm Mon-Sat, 10am-8pm Sun) next door that are owned by the same people. You can also book excellent whale-watching tours here with eco-conscious **Brier Island Whale & Seabird Cruises** (☏902-839-2995, 800-656-3660; www.brierislandwhalewatch.com; adult/child $49/27; ☺Jun-Oct). The trips last anywhere from 2½ to five hours depending on where the whales are.

Atop cliffs 1km east of Westport, **Brier Island Lodge** (☏902-839-2300, 800-662-8355; www.brierisland.com; r $90-150; ☎) has four rooms, most of which have ocean views. Its **restaurant** (mains $14-33; ☺breakfast & dinner) is the island's best dining option, with views on two sides, perfect service and fabulously fresh seafood. Boxed lunches are available.

🛈 Getting There & Away

Two ferries connect Long and Brier Islands to the rest of Digby Neck. The Petit Passage ferry leaves East Ferry (on Digby Neck) 25 minutes after the hour and Tiverton on the hour; ferries are timed so that if you drive directly from Tiverton to Freeport (18km) there is no wait for the Grand Passage ferry to Westport. Both ferries operate hourly, 24 hours a day, year-round. Round-trip passage is $5 for a car and all passengers. Pedestrians ride free.

Digby

Known for its scallops, mild climate and daily ferry to Saint John, New Brunswick (p92), Digby is nestled in a protected inlet off the Bay of Fundy. Settled by United Empire Loyalists in 1783, it's now home to the largest fleet of scallop boats in the world.

Digby has been a tourist mecca for more than a century and it's a good base from which to explore Digby Neck and some lesser-known hiking trails in the area. If you're here in passing, the best things to do are to stroll the waterfront, watch the scallop draggers come and go, and eat as much of their catch as your belly can hold. If you're in town mid-August, reserve even more space in your gut for the delicious **Digby Scallop Days** (www.townofdigby.ns.ca) festival.

The only real sight in town is the **Admiral Digby Museum** (☏902-245-6322; www.

admuseum.ns.ca; 95 Montague Row; admission by donation; ☺9am-5pm Tue-Sat, 1-5pm Sun mid-Jun–Aug, 9am-5pm Tue-Fri Sep–mid-Oct, 9am-5pm Wed & Fri mid-Oct–mid-Jun), a mid-19th century Georgian home which contains exhibits of the town's marine history and early settlement.

🛏 Sleeping & Eating

TOP CHOICE **Digby Backpackers Hostel** HOSTEL $ (☏902-245-4573; www.digbyhostel.com; 168 Queen St; dm/r $28/65; ☺@) Arguably the nicest hostel in Nova Scotia. Saskia and Claude keep their solid four-bed dorm rooms spotless and can be known to spontaneously take the whole hostel out to see the sunset from a hiking trail. The heritage house has plenty of communal areas including a deck with a barbecue, and there's a lively vibe. Internet access, a light breakfast and towels are included in the price.

Bayside Inn B&B B&B $$ (☏902-245-2247, 888-754-0555; www.baysideinn.ca; 115 Montague Row; r $60-100; @) In continuous operation since the late 1800s, the historic 11-room Bayside is Digby's oldest inn. Centrally located in town, it has views over the scallop fleet and Fundy tides. It was remodeled in 2010.

Digby Pines Golf Resort & Spa HOTEL $$$ (☏902-245-2511, 800-667-4637; www.digbypines.ca; 103 Shore Rd; r $160-440; ☺May-Oct; ☺@) At the posh Pines you almost expect Jay Gatsby to come up and slap you on the back with a hearty 'old sport.' Rooms are elegantly furnished with dark woods and lush beds but are small for the price. The family-friendly grounds include everything from a golf course, spa and swimming pool to walking trails and a playground. Ask for a water-view room.

Boardwalk Café CAFE $ (☏902-245-5497; www.boardwalkcafe.netfirms.com; 40 Water St; mains $8-15; ☺lunch daily, dinner Thu & Fri) This little waterfront cafe serves delicious light mains such as chicken rappie pie and salad ($8) or shrimp jambalaya ($9). Dinner is a more upscale experience with mains around $18.

Royal Fundy Seafood Market CAFE $$ (☏902-245-5411; 144 Prince William St; mains $6-14; ☺11am-8pm) Get your seafood from the source at this little fishmonger-cum-cafe. Local seafood is made into all the usual fried suspects as well as soups.

ℹ Information

VIC (☎902-245-2201; Shore Rd; ⏰8:30am-8:30pm mid-Jun–mid-Sep, 9am-5pm mid-Sep–Oct & May–mid-Jun) A large provincial tourist office, 2km from the ferry wharf, with hundreds of brochures.

Western Counties Regional Library (☎902-245-2163; 84 Warwick St; ⏰12:30-5pm & 6-8pm Tue-Thu, 10am-5pm Fri, 10am-2pm Sat) Free internet access.

ℹ Getting There & Away

Acadian Lines (☎902-454-9321, 800-567-5151; www.acadianbus.com) buses from Halifax ($40, four hours, daily) stop at the **Irving gas station** (☎902-245-2048; 77 Montague Row). For ferry information, see p29.

Bear River

This country haven for offbeat artists and quirky characters is only minutes from the coast but enjoys inland, fogless temperatures. There's a strong Mi'kmaq presence here that mixes in with the Scottish, giving Bear River a unique vibe. Some buildings near the river are on stilts while other historic homes nestle on the steep hills of the valley. A few wineries are also starting to pop up just out of town.

◉ Sights & Activities

Bear River Vineyards   WINERY
(☎902-467-4156; www.wine.travel; 133 Chute Rd) All estate-produced, award-winning wines are made at this adorable little winery using solar energy, biodiesel, wind power and the natural slope of the property. Stop by to take a free tour and tasting (July to September) or stay longer at friendly hosts Chris and Peggy's one-room B&B ($130 per night) to enjoy wine-making workshops and retreats.

Annapolis Highland Vineyards   WINERY
(☎902-467-0917; www.novascotiawines.com; 2635 Clementsvale Rd; ⏰10am-5pm Mon-Sat, noon-5pm Sun) A more commercial winery – don't miss the gold-medal-winning White Wedding dessert wine if you come in for a free tasting here. Delicious fruit wines are also available.

Bear River First Nation   CULTURAL CENTER
The Bear River First Nation is a five-minute drive from the heart of town: turn left after crossing the bridge, then take a left where the road forks. In a beautiful building, with a wigwam-shaped foyer, the

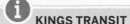
The local **Kings Transit** (☎902-628-7310, 888-546-4442; www.kingstransit.ns.ca) bus line runs every other hour from 6am to around 7pm from Weymouth to Bridgetown stopping in every little town along the way. Tickets cost around $3.50 depending on the distance traveled.

Heritage & Cultural Centre (☎902-467-0301; 194 Reservation Rd; admission $3; ⏰10am-6pm mid-May–mid-Oct) offers demonstrations of traditional crafts and hands-on workshops. A 1km **trail** starts behind the center and highlights plants with traditional medicinal uses.

🛏 Sleeping & Eating

Inn Out of the Fog   INN **$$**
(☎902-467-0268; www.innoutofthefog.com; 1 Wharf Rd; r $75-95) Sparkling tapestries and old kimonos grace the brightly painted walls of this whimsically artistic inn, which is housed in a historic marine warehouse. The sunny gardens that surround the inn are bubbling with flowers and chirping birds. Make sure you don't miss the shop downstairs.

Bear River Cafe   CAFE **$**
(☎902-467-3008; 1870 Clementsvale Rd; mains $7-14; ⏰10am-5pm Tue-Sun) The Bear River Cafe is a great place to drop in for a chat with the locals, drink a cup of coffee over a slice of pie and to enjoy the view of Bear River.

🛍 Shopping

Flight of Fancy   SOUVENIRS
(☎902-467-4171; Main St; ⏰9am-7pm Mon-Sat, 11am-7pm Sun Jul & Aug, 9am-5pm Mon-Sat, 11am-5pm Sun Sep-Jun) An exquisitely curated craft store and gallery with work by more than 200 artists and craftspeople. If you want to buy one unique treasure to take away from Nova Scotia, this is a good place to find it.

Bear Town Baskets   SOUVENIRS
(☎902-467-3060; 44 Maple Ave, Bear River First Nation; ⏰10am-10pm) Baskets sold here are made by a retired chief of the Bear River First Nation. Follow the signs to the studio in his front yard where he makes traditional ash baskets.

Annapolis Royal & Around

The community's efforts of village restoration have made this one of the most delightful places to visit in the region. In fact, Annapolis Royal (population 800) is one of the only well-trodden towns of its size in Nova Scotia without a Tim Hortons (a ubiquitous fast-food franchise).

The site was Canada's first permanent European settlement, Port Royal, founded by French explorer Samuel de Champlain in 1605. As the British and French battled, the settlement often changed hands. In 1710 the British had a decisive victory and changed the town's name to Annapolis Royal in honor of Queen Anne.

Orientation

Most sights are on or near long, curving St George St. A waterfront boardwalk behind King's Theatre on St George St provides views of the village of Granville Ferry across the Annapolis River.

◉ Sights & Activities

Fort Anne National Historic Site
HISTORICAL SITE

(☑902-532-2397; www.parkscanada.gc.ca/fort anne; Upper St George St; adult/child $4/2; ☉9am-6pm) This historic site in the town center preserves the memory of the early Acadian settlement plus the remains of the 1635 French fort. Entry to the extensive grounds is free, but you'll also want to visit the museum where artifacts are contained in various period rooms. An extraordinary four-panel tapestry, crafted in needlepoint by more than 100 volunteers, depicts 400 years of history.

Annapolis Royal Historic Gardens GARDEN
(☑902-532-7018; www.historicgardens.com; 441 St George St; adult/student $8/7; ☉8am-dusk) Annapolis Royal Historic Gardens covers a rambling 6.5 hectares with various themed gardens such as an Acadian kitchen garden one might have seen in the late 1600s and an innovative modern one. Munch on blueberries, ogle the vegetables and look for frogs. The **Secret Garden Café** offers lunches and German-style baked goods.

Delap's Cove Wilderness Trail
NATURE RESERVE

Over the North Mountain from Annapolis Royal, Delap's Cove Wilderness Trail lets you get out on the Fundy shore. It consists of two loop trails connected by an old inland road that used to serve a Black Loyalist community, now just old foundations and apple trees in the woods. Both the loop trails are 9km return.

Port Royal National Historic Site
HISTORICAL SITE

(☑902-532-2898; 53 Historic Lane; adult/child $4/2; ☉9am-6pm) Some 14km northwest of Annapolis Royal, Port Royal National Historic Site is the actual location of the first permanent European settlement north of Florida. The site is a replica of de Champlain's 1605 fur-trading habitation, where costumed workers help tell the story of this early settlement.

FREE **Tidal Power Project** INDUSTRIAL MUSEUM
(☑902-532-5454; ☉10am-6pm) A hydroelectric prototype at the Annapolis River Causeway, Tidal Power has been harnessing power from the Bay of Fundy tides since 1984 (see the boxed text, opposite). An interpretive center includes models, exhibits and a video.

☞ Tours

Be escorted by an undertaker-garbed guide for a tour of the Fort Anne **graveyard** (adult/child $7/1; Fort Anne National Historic Site; ☉9:30pm Tue, Thu & Sun Jun-Sep). Everyone carries a lantern to wind through the headstones and discover this town's history through stories of those who've passed away. Proceeds go to the Annapolis Royal Historical Society.

Starting from the lighthouse on St George St, **daytime tours** (adult/child $7/1; ☉2pm Mon-Fri), run by the same group, focus on the Acadian heritage of Annapolis Royal or the architecture of the historic district.

🛏 Sleeping

TOP CHOICE **Queen Anne B&B** B&B $$
(☑902-532-7850, 877-536-0403; www. queenanneinn.ns.ca; 494 St George St; r $120-180, carriage house $209; ☎) Arguably the most elegant property in Annapolis Royal, this B&B is the perfect balance of period decor and subtle grace. It's so beautiful, with the Tiffany lamp replicas, manicured grounds and sweeping staircases, that it might seem stuffy were it not for the friendly owners who make you feel like you could (almost) kick your feet up on the antique coffee table.

Bailey House B&B B&B $$
(☑902-532-1285, 877-532-1285; www.bailey house.ca; 150 Lower St George St; r $135-145; ☎)

With 14 billion tons of sea water flowing in and out of the Bay of Fundy every day (the equivalent of the flow of every river on Earth combined), it seems only logical to try to convert this power into usable energy. Annapolis Tidal began in 1984 as a pilot project and it employs the largest straight-flow turbine in the world, generating more than 30 million kilowatt-hours of electricity per year – enough for 4500 homes.

Nowadays, the newer instream tidal systems (underwater windmills anchored to the sea floor) are preferred, and Nova Scotia has been chosen to house the first major instream tidal power plant in North America. In collaboration with the Irish company OpenHydro, plans are underway to build one of the world's largest single underwater turbines within the 6km-wide Minas Passage.

Once the first one-megawatt-producing, doughnut-shaped unit has been built and tested, as many as 300 more could be constructed in the Bay of Fundy. The combined efforts of these 300-plus turbines could power over 200,000 homes; about one-fifth of the province's population.

The only B&B on the waterfront, Bailey House is also the oldest inn in the area. The friendly owners have managed to keep the vintage charm (anyone over 6ft might hit their head on the doorways!) while adding all the necessary modern comforts and conveniences. The B&B is gay friendly.

Croft House B&B B&B $
(☑902-532-0584; www.crofthouse.ca; 51 Riverview Lane; r $75; ☎) This farmhouse stands on about 40 hectares of land, across the river and about a five-minute drive from Annapolis Royal. One of the enthusiastic owners is a chef, and he whips up a fine breakfast with organic ingredients.

Dunromin Campground CAMPGROUND $
(☑902-532-2808; www.dunromincampsite.com; Hwy 1, Granville Ferry; serviced/unserviced sites $26/39, tepees/caravans $50/55, cabins $65-110; @☎) This offbeat campground has some secluded riverside sites as well as nifty options such as a tepee (for up to six people) and a gypsy caravan. You can rent canoes for $10 per hour.

✖ Eating

Many of the B&Bs, such as the Queen Anne, are open for elegant lunches and dinners.

Leo's SANDWICH SHOP $
(☑902-532-7424; 222 St George St; mains $6-12; ⊙9am-8pm Mon-Sat, noon-4pm Sun) In a flower-filled garden, Leo's is very popular with locals; be prepared to wait for a delicious sandwich.

Ye Olde Pub PUB $
(☑902-532-2244; 9-11 Church St; mains $5-15; ⊙11am-11pm Mon-Sat, noon-8pm Sun) On sun-

ny days eat gourmet pub fare on the outdoor terrace; when it's cooler slip into the dark and cosy old bar. Try the marinated scallop appetizer ($7).

☆ Entertainment

King's Theatre THEATER
(☑902-532-7704; www.kingstheatre.ca; 209 St George St; movies $6, live shows $14-22) Right on the waterfront, this nonprofit theater presents musicals, dramas and concerts most evenings in July and August, and occasionally during the rest of the year. Hollywood films are screened on most weekends and independent films most Tuesdays, year-round.

🛍 Shopping

Farmers & Traders Market MARKET
(cnr St George & Church Sts; ⊙10am-3pm Wed, 8am-noon Sat) Annapolis Royal's thriving community of artists and artisans offer their wares alongside local farmers at this popular market. There's live entertainment most Saturday mornings.

ℹ Information

Annapolis Royal (www.annapolisroyal.com) Links to history, festivals and everything else.

VIC (☑902-532-5769; 209 St George St; ⊙10am-6pm mid-May–mid-Oct) At the King's Theatre; pick up a historic walking tour pamphlet.

ℹ Getting There & Away

Acadian Lines (☑902-454-9321, 800-567-5151; www.acadianbus.com) buses stops at the **Port Royal Wandlyn Inn** (☑902-532-2323; 3924 Hwy 1) from Halifax (3½ hours, daily), en route to Digby (30 minutes).

Kentville

During the colorful spring bloom of the valley, the **Annapolis Valley Apple Blossom Festival** (www.appleblossom.com) in early June brings folks together with concerts, a parade and art shows. Kentville is the county seat for this area, with a number of government offices and stately old homes.

◉ Sights & Activities

FREE **Agriculture Research Station**
MUSEUM
(☑902-678-1093; off Hwy 1; ⊙8:30am-4:30pm) At the eastern end of town, the Agriculture Research Station includes a museum on the area's farming history and the apple industry in particular. Guided museum tours are offered during summer.

FREE **Old King's County Museum** MUSEUM
(☑902-678-6237; 37 Cornwallis Ave; ⊙9am-4pm Mon-Sat) Local artifacts, history and an art gallery can be seen at the Old King's County Museum.

ℹ Information

Tourist office (☑902-678-7170; 125 Park St; ⊙9:30am-7pm Jul & Aug, to 5:30pm Sep-early Oct & mid-May–Jun) West of the town center.

ℹ Getting There & Away

Acadian Lines (☑902-678-2000; www.acadianbus.com; 66 Cornwallis St) Has an office in the old train station; buses run to Halifax (two hours, twice daily).

North of Highway 1

The North Mountain, which ends at the dramatic Cape Blomidon, defines one edge of the Annapolis Valley. On the other side of the mountain are fishing communities on the Bay of Fundy. The valley floor between Hwy 1 and the North Mountain is crisscrossed with small highways lined with farms and orchards. It's a great place to get out your road map – or throw it out – and explore. To start the adventure, turn north on Hwy 358 just west of Wolfville (at exit 11 of Hwy 101). The historic town of Canning is en route to Scots Bay, where Hwy 358 ends and a dramatic hiking trail leads to views of the Minas Basin and the Bay of Fundy.

PORT WILLIAMS

Only a blink away from Wolfville on Hwy 358 is **Tin Pan** (☑902-691-0020; 978 Main St;

mains $3-9; ⊙breakfast, lunch & dinner Mon-Sat), a favorite for motorbikers who congregate here Saturday mornings for hearty breakfasts.

Prescott House Museum (☑902-542-3984; www.prescott.museum.gov.ns.ca; 1633 Starr's Point Rd; adult/student $3/2; ⊙9:30am-5:30pm Mon-Sat, 1-5:30pm Sun Jun–mid-Oct), c 1814, is one of the the the finest examples of Georgian architecture in Nova Scotia and former home of the horticulturalist who introduced many of the apple varieties grown in the Annapolis Valley. To get here, turn right on Starr's Point Rd at the flashing light in Port Williams, 2km north of Hwy 1, and follow it for 3.25km.

CANNING

From November to March, hundreds of **bald eagles** gather in the Canning area, attracted by local chicken farms – a photographer's and nature-lover's dream. Just west of Canning on Hwy 221 **Blomidon Estate Winery** (☑902-582-7565; www.blomidonwine.com; 10318 Hwy 221; tastings $4; ⊙10am & 6pm Jun-Sep) offers tastings and free tours. Further along Hwy 358, stop at the **Look-Off**. About 200m above the Annapolis Valley, this is the best view of its rows of fruit trees and picturesque farmhouses.

Art Can Gallery & Café (☑902-582-7071; www.artcan.com; 9850 Main St; mains $11; ⊙10am-5pm Tue-Thu, to 10pm Fri & Sat, to 4pm Sun) is an art-store-cum-cafe. Enjoy fair trade coffee and delicious baked goods with views over the valley. Check the website for the availability of art classes and workshops.

SCOTS BAY

The hike to the end of **Cape Split** starts in Scots Bay. This is probably the most popular hiking trail in Nova Scotia. It's about 14km return, taking five hours with little elevation change if you follow the easier inland route. To do that, follow the trail along the fence as you leave the parking area, and then choose the trail on your right when you come to a fork. (The trail on the left leads to a coastal route, which is poorly marked and subject to erosion. Give yourself extra time and consider carrying a compass if you want to explore that route.) The hike ends in a grassy meadow on cliffs high above the Bay of Fundy. Here you can see the tides creating waves called tidal rips. The unique geography of the Bay of Fundy results in the most extreme tides in the world: at its peak, the flow of water between Cape Split and the Parrsboro shore is equal to the combined flow of all the rivers in the world.

Take time before or after the hike to look for agates along the beach at Scots Bay.

Blomidon Provincial Park (☎902-582-7319; www.parks.gov.ns.ca; off Hwy 358; campsites $24) is on the opposite side of Cape Blomidon from Scots Bay. There are a number of routes to get here from Hwy 358, all well signed. One route begins 15km south of Scots Bay and involves driving 10km along the Minas Basin. The campground is set atop high cliffs that overlook the basin. There's a beach and picnic area at the foot of the hill and a 14km system of hiking trails within the park.

HALL'S HARBOUR

Further southeast on the Bay of Fundy (take any route west from Hwy 358 until you hit Hwy 359, then take it over the North Mountain), **Hall's Harbour** is a great spot to spend an afternoon hiking along the beach and in the surrounding hills. It's also the one of the best places in Nova Scotia to eat lobster.

Pick your own lobster at **Hall's Harbour Lobster Pound** (☎902-679-5299; ⊙noon-8pm Jul & Aug, to 7pm May, Jun, Sep & Oct). The price is determined by the market – a whole lobster will rarely cost below $28. Seafood baskets with scallops or clams cost $16.

On the road back towards Kentville in Centreville, stay the night or stop for tea at **Delft Haus B&B Inn & Goodchild's Tea Room** (☎902-678-4333; www.delfthaus.com; 1942 Hwy 359; r $90-145; @), a storybook white Victorian house on an acre of gardens. The tearoom serves light meals (sandwiches from $4.50), free trade tea and coffee, and a great selection of ice cream.

Wolfville

Wolfville is a college town with several wineries nearby so as you'd expect there are plenty of drinking holes, good eating establishments and culture all around. The students and faculty of Acadia University make up about 50% of the town's 7000 residents. Just outside of town you'll find Acadian dikes, scenic drives and enough hiking to keep you here for days. If you're in town early fall, rock out to modern roots music at the annual **Canadian Deep Roots Festival** (www.deeprootsmusic.ca).

◉ Sights

Waterfront Park   PARK
(cnr Gaspereau Ave & Front St) Waterfront Park offers a stunning view of the tidal mudflats, Minas Basin and the red cliffs of Cape Blomidon. Displays explain the tides, dikes, flora and fauna, and history of the area. This is an easy spot to start a walk or cycle on top of the dikes.

Randall House Museum   MUSEUM
(☎902-542-9775; 171 Main St; admission by donation; ⊙10am-5pm Mon-Sat, 2-5pm Sun mid-Jun–mid-Sep) Randall House Museum relates the history of the New England planters and colonists who replaced the expelled Acadians.

L'Acadie Vineyards   WINERY
(☎902-542-8463; www.lacadievineyards.ca; 310 Slayter Rd; ⊙10am-5pm May-Oct) Overlooking Gaspereau Valley just south of Wolfville, this geothermal winery grows certified organic grapes to make unique traditional method sparkling and dried grape wines. You can also stay in one of three country-style two-bedroom, kitchen-equipped cottages ($150 per night), which of course include a free bottle of wine.

Gaspereau Vineyards   WINERY
(☎902-542-1455; www.gaspereauwine.com; 2239 White Rock Rd; ⊙10am-5pm mid-May–Oct, tours noon, 2pm & 4pm daily mid-May–Oct) In Gaspereau, 3km south of Wolfville, this is one of the province's best known wineries with award-winning ice wine.

Muir Murray Winery   WINERY
(☎902-542-0343; www.muirmurraywinery.com; 90 Dyke Rd; ⊙10am-5pm late Jul-Sep, tastings 11am, 1pm & 3pm daily) Three kilometers east of Wolfville, this is the area's newest winery in a barn-like structure overlooking fields. A tearoom is planned that will serve lunch. We particularly liked the Cape Split Leon Millot.

☂ Activities

Locals fought to save the home of hundreds of chimney swifts, birds that migrate annually to Wolfville from Peru. As a result, the chimney of a now-demolished dairy has become the focal point of the **Robie Tufts Nature Centre**, which is located opposite the public library on Front St. Drop by in the late evening in spring or summer to see the birds swooshing down for a good night's rest.

Rent bikes at **Valley Stove & Cycle** (☎902-542-7280; 234 Main St; half-/full-day $25/30).

🛏 Sleeping

TOP CHOICE **Garden House B&B** B&B $$
(☎902-542-1703; www.gardenhouse.ca; 220 Main St; r $65-110; 🐾) This antique house retains its old-time feel in the most comfortable way. Creaky floors, a rustic breakfast table decorated with wildflowers, and the fact that everyone is encouraged to take off their shoes, creates a lived-in vibe you instantly feel a part of. Bathrooms are shared.

Blomidon Inn INN $$
(☎902-542-2291, 800-565-2291; www.theblomidon.net; 195 Main St; d $110-160, ste $160-290; ❄@🐾) Lofty Victorian architecture and old-world extravagance make this a very uppercrust-feeling inn. On 2.5 hectares of gardens, the rooms are just as well groomed. Check the website for package deals.

Gingerbread House Inn INN $$
(☎902-542-1458; www.gingerbreadhouse.ca; 8 Robie Tufts Dr; d $115-135, ste $145-215; 🐾) The exterior of this unique B&B is like a big pink birthday cake with lacy white edging. Rooms, several of which have a hot tub, are like your own candle-lit spa.

🍴 Eating & Drinking

Acton's RESTAURANT $$
(☎902-542-7525; 268 Main St; mains lunch $11-18, dinner $18-32; ☺lunch & dinner) Acton's fame spreads as far as Yarmouth as one of the finest restaurants in the region. Spectacular salads and new twists on old favorites are the house specialties.

Tempest RESTAURANT $$$
(☎902/866-542-0588; 117 Front St; mains lunch $8-18, dinner $22-30; ☺lunch & dinner) Tasty fine dining that borrows from all sorts of cuisines, with dishes such as chicken satay with coconut and daikon or sambuka flambéed prawns served on polenta.

Coffee Merchant & Library Pub
CAFE & PUB $
(☎902-542-4315; 472 Main St; ☺11:30am-midnight Mon-Sat) Downstairs the cafe serves up good fair trade coffee and baked goods, while you can get a pint and a square meal at the cosy upstairs pub.

Ivy Deck RESTAURANT $$
(☎902-542-1868; 8 Elm Ave; mains $9-17; ☺lunch & dinner, closed Mon Nov-Jun) Try a salad with flowers intermingled among the lettuce or salmon and shrimp penne. There's a pleasant outside deck.

ℹ Information

Tourist office (☎902-542-7000; 11 Willow Ave; ☺9am-9pm Jul-Sep, 9am-5pm May, Jun & Oct) A very helpful office at the east end of Main St.

Wolfville (www.wolfville.info) Information on Wolfville, Acadia University and exploring Nova Scotia.

Wolfville Memorial Library (☎902-542-5760; 21 Elm Ave; ☺11am-5pm & 6:30-8:30pm Tue-Thu, 11am-5pm Fri & Sat, 1-5pm Sun) Free internet access.

RAISING A GLASS TO NOVA SCOTIA WINES

The wine-making tradition in Nova Scotia goes back to the early 1600s and it's possible that this was the first place in North America where wine grapes were grown. Today wineries are springing up everywhere (there are six distinct wine-growing regions in the province) although most are found in the Annapolis Valley and on the Malagash Peninsula. These are mellow regions to pop in for some tastings between hikes and sight-seeing.

The French hybrid grape l'Acadie Blanc grows particularly well in Nova Scotia and has become the province's signature grape; it makes a medium-bodied, citrusy white wine that pairs well with scallops or smoked salmon. New York Muscat also grows well and is often used for dry white and ice wines.

Most restaurant wine lists in the province will include several for you to choose from. It's easy to find Jost, Gaspereau and Blomidon wines, but it's worth seeking out the smaller vineyards, some organic, that make excellent and often award-winning blends.

In its fourth year in 2011, the 10-day **Ice Wine Festival** in early February is celebrated through wine pairing and culinary events in Halifax and at wineries around the province.

When the French first settled the area around the Minas Basin, they called the region Arcadia, a Greek and Roman term for 'pastoral paradise.' This became Acadia, and by the 18th century the Acadians felt more connection with the land here than with the distant Loire Valley they'd come from.

To the English, however, they would always be French, with whom rivalry and suspicion was constant. The Acadians refused to take an oath of allegiance to the English king after the Treaty of Utrecht granted Nova Scotia to the British, considering it an affront to their Catholic faith. When hard-line lieutenant governor Charles Lawrence was appointed in 1754, he became fed up with the Acadians and ordered their deportation. The English burned many villages and forced some 14,000 Acadians onto ships.

Many Acadians headed for Louisiana and New Orleans; others went to various Maritime points, New England, Martinique in the Caribbean, Santo Domingo in the Dominican Republic, or back to Europe. Not once were they greeted warmly with open arms. Some hid out and remained in Acadia. In later years many of the deported people returned but found their lands occupied. In Nova Scotia, Acadians resettled the Chéticamp area on Cape Breton Island and the French Shore north of Yarmouth. New Brunswick has a large French population stretching up the east coast past the Acadian Peninsula at Caraquet.

ⓘ Getting There & Away

Acadian Lines (☑902-454-9321, 800-567-5151; www.acadianbus.com) buses stop at Acadia University in front of Wheelock Hall off Highland Ave. **Kings Transit** (☑902-678-7310, 888-546-4442; www.kingstransit.ns.ca) buses run between Cornwallis and Wolfville and stop at 209 Main St.

Grand Pré

Grand Pré, 25km northwest of Windsor at the outskirts of Wolfville, is now a very small English-speaking town. In the 1750s, however, it was the site of one of the most tragic but compelling stories in eastern Canada's history that you learn about at the Grand Pré National Historic Site.

◉ Sights & Activities

Grand Pré National Historic Site

HISTORICAL SITE

(☑902-542-3631; 2205 Grand Pré Rd; adult/child $7.80/3.90; ⊗9am-6pm May-Oct) At Grand Pré National Historic Site a modern interpretive center explains the historical context for the deportation from Acadian, Mi'kmaw and British perspectives and traces the many routes Acadians took from and back to the Maritimes.

Beside the center, a serene **park** contains gardens and an Acadian-style stone church. There's also a bust of American poet Henry Wadsworth Longfellow who chronicled the Acadian saga in *Evangeline: A Tale of Acadie,* and a statue of his fictional Evangeline, now a romantic symbol of her people.

Beyond the park, you can see the farmland created when the Acadians built dikes along the shoreline. There are 12 sq km below sea level here, protected by just over 9km of dike.

Domaine de Grand Pré

WINERY

(☑902-542-1753; www.grandprewines.ns.ca; 11611 Hwy 1; tours $7; ⊗tours 11am, 3pm & 5pm, free tastings 10am-6pm) Many people travel to town to visit Domaine de Grand Pré vineyards and winery. The tours take about 45 minutes or you can do tastings and stroll through the vines by yourself.

🛏 Sleeping & Eating

TOP CHOICE The Olde Lantern Inn & Vineyard

INN **$$**

(☑902-542-1389, 877-965-3845; www.oldlanterninn.com; 11575 Hwy 1; r $100-155; 🐾) Clean lines and attention to every comfort (such as butter-soft sheets) makes this a great place to stay. The vineyard grounds overlook Minas Basin where you can watch the rise and fall of the Fundy tides.

Le Caveau

RESTAURANT **$$**

(☑902-542-1753; 11611 Hwy 1; mains $16-32; ⊗lunch & dinner) Considered to be the finest Northern European style restaurant in the province, this Swiss restaurant is on the grounds of Domaine de Grand Pré. The beautiful outdoor patio is paved with fieldstones and shaded with grapevines.

Evangeline RESTAURANT $
(☑902-542-2703; pie $3-5; ☺8am-7pm) The restaurant on the same grounds as the Evangaline Inn & Motel is famous for its homemade pie and exceptional local fare; it's always packed.

🔒 Shopping

Tangled Garden FOOD & DRINK
(☑902-542-9811; 11827 Hwy 1; ☺10am-6pm) Impossible to classify, this is probably the best-smelling shopping experience in Nova Scotia. Buy a bottle of herb-infused vinegar or jelly to take away, or stroll the gardens and meditative labyrinth while licking herb-flavored ice cream.

Windsor

Windsor was once the only British stronghold in this region but today it's just a graying little town eking out an existence between the highway and the Avon River. Windsor is a place to enjoy bluegrass music – think lots of fast banjo picking. Avon River Park hosts two bluegrass festivals, one in June and one in July, and is a hangout for aficionados all summer long. The **tourist office** (☑902-798-2690; 31 Colonial Rd; ☺8:30am-6:30pm Jul & Aug, 9am-5pm Sat & Sun Jun, Sep & Oct) is located just off exit 6 from Hwy 101, and the dike just beside the tourist office offers a good view of the tidal river flats.

While in town check out **Haliburton House** (☑902-798-2915; 414 Clifton Ave; adult/student $3.60/2.55; ☺10am-5pm Mon-Sat, 1-5pm Sun), once home of Judge Thomas Chandler Haliburton (1796–1865), writer of the Sam Slick stories. Many of Haliburton's expressions, such as 'quick as a wink' and 'city slicker,' are still used.

Stay the night at the **Clockmaker's Inn** (☑902-792-2573, 866-778-3600; www.the clockmakersinn.com; 1399 King St; d $100-190; 🛜), a French-chateau-style mansion with curved bay windows, lots of stained glass and sweeping hardwood staircases. It's gay friendly and afternoon tea is served everyday as is breakfast.

CENTRAL NOVA SCOTIA

Hiking, rafting and rockhounding are the activities of choice around this mildly touristed region. For those traveling overland from the rest of Canada this is your first taster of Nova Scotia – do not let it pass you by on bleak Hwy 104.

Called the 'Glooscap Trail' in provincial tourism literature, the area is named for the figure in Mi'kmaq legend who created the unique geography of the Bay of Fundy region. Unfortunately, stories and representations of Glooscap are easier to come across than genuine acknowledgments of present-day Mi'kmaq people.

Shubenacadie

Shubenacadie, or simply 'Shube,' is best known for the **Shubenacadie Provincial Wildlife Park** (☑902-758-2040; http://wildlifepark.gov.ns.ca; 149 Creighton Rd; adult/child $4.25/$1.75; ☺9am-7pm mid-May–mid-Oct, 9am-3pm Sat & Sun mid-Oct–mid-May), the place to commune with Nova Scotia's wildlife (you can hand-feed the deer and, if you're lucky, pet a moose). The animals were either born in captivity or once kept as 'pets,' and as a result cannot be released into the wild – they live in large enclosures. Turn off Hwy 102 at exit 11 and follow Hwy 2 to the park entrance.

Maitland

Tiny Maitland is the place to go rafting on the white-water that is created by the outflow of the Shubenacadie River meeting the blasting force of the incoming Fundy tides but it's also one of the oldest towns in Canada.

Wave heights are dependant on the phases of the moon (see the boxed text, opposite); get information from your rafting company about the tides for your chosen day since your experience (either mild or exhilarating) will be dictated by this. Outboard-powered Zodiacs plunge right through the white-water for the two to three hours that the rapids exist. Prepare to get very, very wet – no experience is needed.

⊙ Activities

Shubenacadie River Runners RAFTING
(☑902-261-2770, 800-856-5061; www.tidalbore rafting.com; 8681 Hwy 215; half-/full-day adult $55/75, child $50/70) The biggest rafting company is hyper-organized and professional in every way.

The **tidal bore** phenomenon occurs when the first surge of the extreme Bay of Fundy tides flows up river at high tide. Sometimes the advancing wave is only a ripple, but with the right phase of the moon it can be a meter or so in height, giving the impression that the river is flowing backwards. It's not a very thrilling spectacle but you can see it from the lookout on Tidal Bore Rd, off Hwy 236 just west of exit 14 from Hwy 102 on the northwest side of Truro. Staff in the adjacent Palliser Motel **gift shop** (☎902-893-8951) can advise when the next tidal bore will arrive. There's another viewpoint in Moncton, New Brunswick (p122).

Shubenacadie River Adventures   RAFTING
(☎902-261-2222, 800-878-8687; www.shubie.com; 10061 Hwy 15; day rafting with barbecue adult/child $75/70) Also offers mud sliding.

Sleeping

There are a handful of places to sleep in Maitland but the few eating options have unpredictable opening hours – bring your own food or a full belly.

Tidal Life Guesthouse   B&B $
TOP CHOICE (☎902-261-2583; www.thetidallife.ca; 9568 Cedar St; dm $35, r $90-120; ☎) This place is a backpackers-B&B hybrid in an old beauty of a house with grand airy rooms and large windows overlooking grassy fields. Artistically designed communal spaces are everywhere including a hammock on the back porch. All options include a big healthy breakfast and bathrooms are shared.

Cresthaven by the Sea   B&B $$
(☎902-261-2001, 866-870-2001; www.cresthavenbythesea.com; 19 Ferry Lane; r $140-150) Stay here for what is possibly the best view in Canada over the Fundy tides. The immaculate white Victorian sits on a bluff right over the point where the Shubenacadie River meets the bay. All the rooms have river views and the lower ones are wheelchair accessible.

Truro

Several major highways converge here, along with a VIA Rail line so it's no wonder Truro is known as the hub of Nova Scotia. It's also a bus transfer point. While the town does look somewhat like an aging shopping mall, it's exceptionally well serviced and can make a good stop to pick up that nagging item you need or just stock up on food.

Sights & Activities

Victoria Park   PARK
(Park St off Brunswick St) Escape Truro's busy streets at Victoria Park, 400 hectares of green space in the very center of town, which includes a deep gorge and two waterfalls. The park attracts dozens of bird species.

Festivals & Events

Truro International Tulip Festival   CANADIAN
(www.townoftruro.ca; ☉mid-May) A great family gathering with bluegrass concerts and a big antique market.

Millbrook Annual Powwow   CULTURAL
(☎902-897-9199, www.millbrookfirstnation.net; ☉2nd weekend of Aug) The best time to visit Truro is when Millbrook First Nation hosts its annual powwow. Campsites and showers are available; drugs and alcohol are prohibited.

Sleeping & Eating

Baker's Chest B&B   B&B $$
(☎902-893-4824, 877-822-5655; www.bakerschest.ca; 53 Farnham Rd; r/ste $100/125; ☎) A newly restored classic older home with contemporary decor and a fitness room and hot tub. The famous tearoom was closed in 2010 but keep your fingers crossed for a reopening.

Wooden Hog   RESTAURANT $$
(☎902-895-0779; 627 Prince St; mains lunch $8, dinner $11-17; ☉9am-4pm Mon, 9am-9pm Tue-Fri, 11am-9pm Sat) Named for the huge, sculpted Harley that hangs off the back wall, this is a popular restaurant with local and Mexican specialties plus decadent desserts.

Information

Tourist office (☎902-893-2922; Victoria Sq, cnr Prince & Commercial Sts; ☉9am-5pm May & Jun, 8:30am-7:30pm Jul & Aug, 9am-5pm

Sep & Oct) Offers internet access and a great guide to the tree sculptures around town that were carved after the region was hit with Dutch Elm disease over 30 years ago.

ℹ️ Getting There & Away

The **bus station** (☎902-895-3833; 280 Willow St; ⊙8am-10:30pm) is busy with **Acadian Lines** (☎902-454-9321, 800-567-5151; www.acadian bus.com) buses en route to Amherst ($23, two hours, three times daily) and Sydney ($52, five hours, three times daily).

Economy to Five Islands

Highway 2 hugs the shore of the Minas Basin, the northeast arm of the Bay of Fundy, and this is the first sizable community you'll hit. There's great hiking and several interesting sites around Economy.

◉ Sights & Activities

Cobequid Interpretation Centre   MUSEUM
(☎902-647-2600; 3248 Hwy 2, near River Phillip Rd; admission free; ⊙9am-4:30pm Mon-Fri year-round, to 6pm Sat & Sun Jul & Aug) Stop here for good exhibits on the area's ecology and history. Climb a WWII observation tower for a bird's-eye view of the surrounding area and pick up hiking information from the staff.

Hiking
The most challenging hikes are around Economy Falls. The **Devil's Bend Trail** begins 7km up River Phillip Rd toward the Cobequid Mountains. Turn right and park; the 6.5km (one-way) trail follows the river to the falls. The **Kenomee Canyon Trail** begins further up River Phillip Rd, at the top of the falls. A 20km loop, it takes you up the river to its headwaters in a protected wilderness area. Several streams have to be forded. There are designated campsites, making this a good two-day adventurous trek.

The **Thomas Cove Coastal Trail** is actually two 3.5km loops with great views across the Minas Basin and of the Cobequid Mountains. They begin down Economy Point Rd, 500m east of the Cobequid Interpretation Centre. Follow the signs to a parking area. Finally, just 7km west of Economy, there are several hikes in **Five Islands Provincial Park** (☎902-254-2980; parks.gov.ns.ca). The 4.5km **Red Head Trail** is well developed with lookouts, benches and great views.

🛏️ Sleeping & Eating

Four Seasons Retreat   HOTEL $$
(☎902-647-2628, 888-373-0339; www.foursea sonsretreat.ns.ca; 320 Cove Rd, Upper Economy; 1-/2-bedroom cottages $109/210; 🐾🛜) Fully equipped cottages are surrounded by trees and face the Minas Basin. In summer there's a hot tub near the pool; in winter – or on a chilly night – there are woodstoves.

Mo's at Five Islands   HOSTEL & CAFE $
(☎902-254-8088; www.mosatfiveislands.com; 951 Hwy 2, Five Islands; dm $28; 🛜) You can usually count on an interesting crowd at this spotless hostel and at the large homey cafe out front (light meals from $4). The owner also owns one of the five islands (of the synonymous town) and holds a running race each year from the mainland to the island when the tide goes out high enough – the race and the hostel are named after Moses and his parting of the Red Sea.

High Tide B&B   B&B $$
(☎902-647-2788; www.hightidebb.com; 2240 Hwy 2, Lower Economy; d $85-95; 🛜) This friendly, modern bungalow has great views. Janet, one of the owners, will have you down on the beach for a clam boil in no time.

That Dutchman's Farm   CAFE $
(☎902-647-2751; www.thatdutchmansfarm.com; 112 Brown Rd, Upper Economy; lunch $8; ⊙11am-5pm late Jun-early Sep) The yummy cafe here offers sandwiches, soups and plates of the eccentric farmer's own gouda. You can tour the farm for a small fee.

Several takeaway stands selling fried clams pop up along the highway near Five Islands Provincial Park in the summer.

Parrsboro

Rockhounds come from far and wide to forage the shores of Parrsboro, the largest of the towns along the Minas Basin. The Fundy Geological Museum has wonderful exhibits and good programs that take you to the beach areas known as Nova Scotia's 'Jurassic Park.' For more serious rock-lovers, the annual **Gem & Mineral Show** is in mid-August.

◉ Sights & Activities

Fundy Geological Museum   MUSEUM
(☎902-254-3814; www.museum.gov.ns.ca/ fgm; 162 Two Islands Rd; adult/child $6/3.50; ⊙9:30am-5:30pm)This award-winning museum got a $1 million makeover in 2010 and uses interactive exhibits to help its visitors

RODD & HELEN TYSON: GEOLOGISTS & MINERAL DEALERS

Rodd Tyson is considered one of the most successful mineral dealers in Canada. He and his wife Helen moved to Parrsboro several years ago and opened a small shop that displays some of their finest pieces.

Why Parrsboro?

The tides and the rains are moving things all the time so on any given day we could still potentially find something in one of several places suitable for our own private collection.

Where to Go

Partridge Island is the easiest place to go. Just remember to wear good footwear, be careful of the cliffs and be vigilant about checking the tides so you don't get stuck.

What to Look For

You're looking for color. Stilbite is amber-gold, chabazite is orange, agates have banded colors and patterns, and jasper is a deep brick red or forest green. You won't find much amethyst here no matter what anyone tells you, unless it's pretty pale. It's illegal to take fossils.

'time travel' to a time when the animals whose fossils littering Parrsboro's beaches were alive. You can see a lab where dinosaur bones are being cleaned and assembled. Beach tours (dependent on the tides) are included in the admission price and focus on minerals or fossils.

Partridge Island NATURE RESERVE
Steeped in history, Partridge Island is the most popular shoreline to search for gems, semiprecious stones and fossils. The island is 4km south of town on Whitehall Rd. From the end of the beach a 3km **hiking trail** with explanatory panels climbs to the top of the island (connected to the mainland by an isthmus) for superb views of Cape Blomidon and Cape Split.

Ottawa House Museum MUSEUM
(☑902-254-2376; 1155 Whitehall Rd; admission $2; ☉10am-6pm) Just before the beach is Ottawa House Museum, a 21-room mansion that was once the summer home of Sir Charles Tupper (1821–1915), who served as both premier of Nova Scotia and prime minister of Canada. The museum has exhibits on the former settlement on Partridge Island, shipbuilding and rum-running.

🛏 Sleeping & Eating
Riverview Cottages INN $
(☑902-254-2388; www.riverviewcottages.ca; 3575 Eastern Ave; cottages $55-90; ☎) These country-cute, completely equipped cottages are a steal. You can canoe and fish on the border-

ing river and there's a big lawn perfect for a barbecue.

Evangeline's Tower B&B B&B $$
(☑902-254-3383, 866-338-6937; www.evangelinestower.ca; 322 Main St; d $70-150; ☎) This gay-friendly Victorian home has three rooms; one can be a two room suite for families. Mountain bikes are available.

Bare Bones RESTAURANT $$
(☑902-254-3507; 121 Main St; mains $10-22; ☉11am-9pm Mon-Sat, 1-9pm Sun) Bare Bones serves far and away the best food in town. Enjoy steamed mussels, sandwiches such as lobster bacon club or curry apple chicken, and larger mains like baby back ribs or pan-seared scallops.

☆ Entertainment
Ship's Company Theatre THEATER
(☑902-254-3000, 800-565-7469; www.shipscompany.com; 18 Lower Main St; tickets $12-28; ☉Jul–mid-Sep) This innovative theater company performs new Canadian and Maritime works 'on board' the MV *Kipawo,* the last of the Minas Basin ferries, now integrated into a new theater. There's high-quality theater for kids, improv comedy, readings and concerts.

🛍 Shopping
Parrsboro Rock & Mineral Shop
ROCKS & MINERALS
(☑902-254-2981; 39 Whitehall Rd; ☉9am-9pm Mon-Sat, to 5pm Sun May-Nov) Browse the

AGE OF SAIL HERITAGE CENTRE

Stop for tea, baked goods and a tour at the **Age of Sail Heritage Centre** (☑902-348-2030; Rte 209; adult $3; ☺10am-6pm Jun-Sep) in Port Greville, about 20km to the west of Parrsboro on Rte 209. It captures the area's shipbuilding heritage. The site also includes a restored 1857 Methodist church and a working blacksmith shop.

collection of prehistoric reptile fossils, semiprecious stones from Parrsboro and around the world, and even a one-of-a-kind fossilized footprint of the world's smallest dinosaur found by the proprietor, Eldon George. If Eldon is there don't miss the chance to chat with him – he's one of Parrsboro's favorite characters.

Tysons' Fine Minerals   ROCKS & MINERALS (☑902-254-2376; 249 Whitehall Rd; ☺10am-variable) This place is more like a museum than a shop with some of the most sparkling, massive and colorful minerals on display you're likely to see anywhere. Sometimes Helen (see p69) takes visitors in to see the Tysons' private collection which is even more breathtaking.

ℹ Information

Tourist office (☑902-254-3266; 69 Main St; ☺10am-7pm Jun-Oct) Tide information and free internet access.

Cape d'Or

This spectacular cape of sheer cliffs was misnamed Cape d'Or (Cape of Gold) by Samuel de Champlain in 1604 – the glittering veins he saw in the cliffs were actually made of copper. Mining took place between 1897 and 1905 and removed the sparkle.

TOP CHOICE **Lightkeeper's Kitchen & Guest House** (☑902-670-0534; www.capedor.ca; s/d with ocean view $80/110; 🛜) This original lighthouse-keeper's residence is now a laid-back four-room guesthouse in what is perhaps one of the most perfect spots in Nova Scotia (even more so when the sun's out). Take the side road off Hwy 209 to Cape d'Or then hike down the dirt trail. A cosmopolitan **restaurant** (mains lunch $9-16,

dinner $22-28; ☺noon-7pm;☑) pumps out low-volume techno music and serves original seafood, meat and vegetarian creations.

Cape Chignecto Provincial Park & Advocate Harbour

The **Cape Chignecto Coastal Trail** is a rugged 60km loop with backcountry – nay, old-growth – campsites. Allow four days and three nights for the hike. The **Mill Brook Canyon Trail** (15km return) and the hike to **Refugee Cove** (20km return) are other challenging overnight hikes. There are some easier hikes and more are being developed – the newest is the **Eatonville Trail** (5.6km return) that begins at a new 'Phase 2' entrance to the park about 15km north of the main entrance. Some hikers have tried to avoid the ups and downs of the trails by taking shortcuts along the beach at low tide and been cut off by the Bay of Fundy tides. Get a tide table and follow advice from park staff to avoid being trapped on the cliffs.

Park visitors must register and leave an itinerary at the **Visitor Centre** (☑902-392-2085; www.capechignecto.net; 1108 West Advocate Rd; hiking permits day/annual $5/25, campsites $24; ☺8am-7pm Mon-Thu, to 8pm Fri & Sat). Camping in the backcountry requires reservations. In addition to 51 wilderness campsites at six points along the coastal trail and 27 walk-in sites near the visitor center, there is also a bunkhouse ($53.40, up to four people) and a wilderness cabin ($53.40, up to four people).

Advocate Harbour is the nearest town, about 2km southeast of the park entrance. It's a breathtaking place with a 5km-long beach piled high with driftwood that changes dramatically with the tides. Behind the beach, salt marshes reclaimed with dikes by the Acadians are now replete with birds.

Kayak Cape Chignecto Provincial Park with **Nova Shores Adventures** (☑866-638-4118; www.novashores.com; Hwy 33, Advocate Harbour; one-day tours $85, two-day tours incl overnight and food $350; 🛜). You'll often see seals and bears. The outfit also offers a beautiful, sea-view room ($110 per night) in its Victorian home headquarters.

TOP CHOICE **Wild Caraway Restaurant & Cafe** (☑902-392-2889; www.wildcaraway.com; 3721 Hwy 209; meals around $20, r $80; 🛜) Wild Caraway Restaurant is an excellent place to stop or stay in Advocate Harbour. The invitingly cosy, well-tended Victorian overlooks the often foggy harbor.

Joggins

Joggins, between Amherts and Advocate Harbour on Chignecto Bay, is famous for its Unesco World Heritage fossil cliffs, said to be the best place on Earth to see what life was like over 300 million years ago in the late Carboniferous (Coal Age). The wealth of fossils in the 15km of seaside cliffs are preserved in their original setting and include rare land species. The big new **Joggins Fossil Centre** (100 Main St; www.jogginsfossil cliffs.net; adult/child $8/6; ⊙9:30am-5:30pm) is the place to start your visit and explains through displays and film what you can see in the cliffs below. The best time to visit the cliffs is at low tide when all of the beaches can be accessed – otherwise you'll be cut off from some of the more interesting sites by high water. Recommended guided tours are available at the Fossil Centre, starting from $5 and leaving on an irregular schedule depending on the tides; you can reserve in advance on the website.

Amherst

Amherst is the geographic center of the Maritimes and a travel junction for travelers to Nova Scotia, PEI and New Brunswick. There's little reason to dawdle here as you're just a short drive from either the Bay of Fundy shore or the Northumberland Strait (between Nova Scotia and PEI), but the historic downtown does have some stately buildings and there's bird-watching at the 490-hectare **Amherst Point Migratory Bird Sanctuary** nearby (off Exit 3 from the Trans-Canada Hwy). The massive **VIC** (☑902-667-8429; ⊙8:30am-8pm) is at exit 1 off Hwy 104, just as you cross the border from New Brunswick.

Acadian Lines (☑902-454-9321, 800-567-5151; www.acadianbus.com) has bus services to Halifax that leave from the **Irving Mainway gas station** (☑902-667-8435; 213 S Albion St). The Trans-Canada Hwy east of Amherst charges a toll of $4. It's an incentive to use scenic Hwy 2 through Parrsboro instead of dull – but fast – Hwy 104. The Sunrise Trail (Hwy 6) through Pugwash and Tatamagouche to Pictou also avoids the toll.

It's claimed that the Northumberland Strait between Nova Scotia's north shore and PEI has some of the warmest waters north of the US Carolinas, with water temperatures averaging slightly over 20°C during summer. It's prime area for beach-hopping, cycling and exploring friendly countryside towns.

Wallace

Wallace is perfect territory for birding and beachcombing. The tourist information center is at the **Wallace Museum** (☑902-257-2191; Hwy 6; ⊙9am-5pm Mon-Sat, 1-4pm Sun) where collections of baskets woven by the Mi'kmaq, period dresses and shipbuilding memorabilia are displayed.

Wallace Bay Wildlife Bird Sanctuary (1km north of Hwy 6 on Aboiteau Rd) protects 585 hectares, including tidal and freshwater wetlands. In the spring, keep your eyes peeled for bald eagles nesting near the parking lot, which is on the left just before the causeway.

Wentworth

The Wentworth Valley is a detour off the shore, 25km south of Wallace via Hwy 307, and is particularly pretty in fall when the deciduous trees change color. The 24-bed, cabin-like **Wentworth Hostel** (☑902-548-2379; www.hihostels.ca; 249 Wentworth Station Rd; HI member/nonmember dm $20/25, r $40/45) is 1.3km west of Hwy 4 on Valley Rd, then straight up steep, dirt Wentworth Station Rd. The rambling farmhouse, built in 1866, has been used as a hostel for half a century. It's central enough to be a base for both the Sunrise Trail and much of the Minas Bay shore. Trails for hiking and mountain biking start just outside the door. It gets particularly booked-up in winter for the cross-country and downhill skiing nearby.

Tatamagouche

The Malagash Peninsula, which juts out into protected Tatamagouche Bay, is a low-key, bucolic loop for a drive or bike ride. Stop at the local winery for tastings, explore beaches galore or take a peak in some interesting museums found just inland. Tatamagouche is the largest on the Northumberland Shore coast west of Pictou and makes a great base for exploring. The **Fraser Cultural Centre** (☎902-657-3285; 362 Main St; ⊙10am-5pm Mon-Fri, 10am-4pm Sat, 11am-3pm Sun mid-Jun–Sep) has tourist information, internet access and local history displays.

◎ Sights & Activities

Jost Winery
WINERY

(☎902-257-2636; www.jostwine.com; off Hwy 6, Malagash; ⊙tours noon & 3pm mid-Jun–mid-Sep) Take a free tour of the scenically located Jost Winery. While regular wine is free to taste, the ice wine costs $5 – if you want to try all three ice wine varieties, ask to have three small glasses for the price of one large one. Winery signs direct you about 5km off Hwy 6.

Mills

In a gorgeous setting on the stream that once provided it with power, the **Balmoral Grist Mill** (☎902-657-3016; 660 Matheson Brook Rd; adult/child $3/2; ⊙9:30am-5:30pm Mon-Sat, 1-5:30pm Sun) still grinds wheat in summer. From Tatamagouche, turn south on Hwy 311 (at the east edge of town) and then east on Hwy 256.

From the Balmoral Grist Mill, drive further east on Hwy 256, and then north on Hwy 326, to get to the **Sutherland Steam Mill** (☎902-657-3365; off Hwy 326, Denmark; adult/child $3/2; ⊙9:30am-5:30pm Mon-Sat, 1-5:30pm Sun). Built in 1894, it produced lumber, carriages, wagons and windows until 1958.

Beaches

Blue Sea Beach on the Malagash Peninsula has warm water and fine sand, and a marsh area just inland that's ideal for bird-watching. There are picnic tables and shelters to change in. Small cottages crowd around **Rushton's Beach**, just east of Tatamagouche in Brule, but it's worth a visit to look for seals (turn left at the end of the boardwalk and walk toward the end of the beach) and birdlife in the adjoining saltmarsh.

Tatamagouche Centre
RETREAT CENTER

(☎800-218-2220; www.tatacentre.ca; Loop 6) This gay-friendly centre, which is affiliated with the Uniting Church, offers retreats and short courses on everything from organic gardening to yoga (two-day course including lodging $250), plus guided excursions to powwows.

★ Festivals & Events

Oktoberfest
FOOD & DRINK

(☎902-657-2380; tickets $10-20; ⊙Sep) The wildly popular Oktoberfest is held the last weekend in September – yes, September.

⌘ Sleeping & Eating

Train Station Inn
INN $$

(☎902-657-3222, 888-724-5233; www.trainstation.ca; 21 Station Rd; carriages $89-179) It's a museum, it's a kooky gift shop, it's a restaurant, it's a hotel and...it's a stationary train. Each unique carriage suite is an eight-year-old boy's dream decorated with period train posters, toy trains and locomotive books. The dreamer behind the inn, James LeFresne, grew up across the tracks and saved the train station from demolition when he was just 18. Dine on delicious seafood, meat and salads in the c 1928 dining car or have a blueberry pancake breakfast ($6) in the station house. Free self-guided tours are available from the gift shop.

Sugar Moon Farm
CAFE $

(☎902-657-3348, 866-816-2753; www.sugarmoon.ca; Alex Macdonald Rd, off Hwy 311, Earltown; mains $8-13; ⊙9am-5pm Thu-Mon Jul & Aug, 9am-5pm Sat & Sun Sep-Jun) The food – simple, delicious pancakes and locally made sausages served with maple syrup – is the highlight of this working maple farm and woodlot. Check online for dates of the monthly 'Chef's Night', which is one Saturday night where a prix fixe meal ($69) is served.

🔒 Shopping

Lismore Sheep Farm
SOUVENIRS

(☎902-351-2889; 1389 Louisville Rd, off Hwy 6; ⊙9am-5pm) A working farm with more than 300 sheep, this is a fun destination even if you don't buy a rug, blanket or socks. From May to October, the barn is open (adult/child $2/1) for visitors to pat the lambs and learn all about producing wool.

Pictou

Many people stop in Pictou (*pik*-toe) for a side trip or as a stopover via ferry to/from PEI, but it's also an enjoyable base for exploring Northumberland Strait. Water St, the main street, is lined with interesting shops and beautiful old stone buildings but unfortunately the sea views are blighted by a giant smoking mill in the distance. The town is known as the 'Birthplace of New Scotland' because the first Scottish immigrants to Nova Scotia landed here in 1773.

◉ Sights & Activities

You can picnic and swim at Caribou/Munroe's Island Provincial Park (right).

Hector   SHIP

A replica of the ship *Hector* that carried the first 200 Highland Scots to Nova Scotia is tied up for viewing during the summer. **Hector Heritage Quay** (☑902-485-4371; 33 Caladh Ave; adult/student $5/2; ⊘9am-5pm Mon-Sat, noon-5pm Sun mid-May–early Oct) captures the experience of the first Scottish settlers through a re-created blacksmith shop, a collection of shipbuilding artifacts and displays about the *Hector* and its passengers. There are guided tours at 10am and 2pm.

Northumberland Fisheries Museum
                                           MUSEUM

(☑902-485-4972; 71 Front St; adult/student $4/2; ⊘10am-6pm Mon-Sat) In the old train station, this museum explores the area's fishing heritage. Exhibits include strange sea creatures and the spiffy *Silver Bullet*, an early 1930s lobster boat.

✯ Festivals & Events

Pictou Landing First Nation Powwow
                                         CULTURAL

(☑902-752-4912; ⊘1st weekend of Jun) Across the Pictou Harbour (a 25-minute drive through New Glasgow), this annual powwow features sunrise ceremonies, drumming and craft demonstrations. Camping and food are available on site, which is strictly alcohol- and drug-free.

Lobster Carnival   FOOD & DRINK

(☑902-485-5150; www.townofpictou.com; ⊘2nd week of Jul) Begun in 1934 as the Carnival of the Fisherfolk, this four-day event now offers free entertainment, boat races and lots of chances to feast on lobster.

Hector Festival   MUSIC

(☑902-485-8848; www.decostecentre.ca; ⊘mid-Aug) Free daily outdoor concerts, Highland dancing and piping competitions and a *Hector* landing reenactment

🛏 Sleeping & Eating

Pictou Lodge   HOTEL **$$**

(☑902-485-4322, 888-662-7484; www.maritimeinns.com; 172 Lodge Rd, off Braeshore Rd; r/cottages from $139/159; ≋) This atmospheric 1920s resort is on more than 60 hectares of wooded land between Caribou/Munroe's Island Provincial Park and Pictou. Beautifully renovated ocean-side log cabins have original stone fireplaces. Motel rooms are also available. There's a life-sized checkerboard, paddle boats, a private beach and the best restaurant in town.

Customs House Inn   INN **$$**

(☑902-485-4546; www.customshouseinn.ca; 38 Depot St; r incl breakfast $80-170; @🛜) The tall stone walls here are at once imposingly chic and reassuringly solid. The chunky antique decor is as sturdy and elegant as the walls and many rooms have waterfront views. Identical twin brothers run this inn so don't be alarmed if the innkeeper seems to be everywhere at once!

Willow House Inn   B&B **$$**

(☑902-485-5740; www.willowhouseinn.com; 11 Willow St; r with shared/private bathroom $60/120; 🛜) This historic c 1840 home is a labyrinth of staircases and cozy, antique rooms. The owners whip up great breakfasts as well as conversation and tips for what to do around town.

Caribou/Munroe's Island Provincial Park   CAMPGROUND **$**

(☑902-485-6134; www.parks.gov.ns.ca; 2119 Three Brooks Rd; campsites $24) Less than 5km from Pictou, this park is set on a gorgeous beach. Sites 1 to 22 abut the day-use area and are less private; sites 78 to 95 are gravel and suited for RVs. The rest are wooded and private.

Carver's Coffeehouse & Studio   CAFE **$**

(☑902-382-3332; 41 Coleraine St; light meals around $8; ⊘8am-9pm) This bright and inviting cafe is also the carving studio for Keith Matheson, who did the detail work on the *Hector*. Anne, his partner, runs the cafe, which specializes in decadent desserts, traditional Scottish oatcakes, and strong coffee with free refills.

Pressroom Pub & Grill   RESTAURANT **$$**

(☑902-485-4041; 50 Water St; mains $8-15; ⊘11am-midnight) Often so busy that it resembles a pressroom, the Pressroom serves up standard salads, sandwiches, wraps or chowder to enjoy on the big outdoor patio

☆ Entertainment

deCoste Centre   MUSIC & THEATER
(☎902-485-8848; www.decostecentre.ca; 91 Water St; tickets about $18; ☺box office 11:30am-5pm Mon-Fri, 1-5pm Sat & Sun) Opposite the waterfront, this impressive performing arts center stages a range of live shows. Experience some top-notch Scottish music during a summer series of ceilidhs (*kay*-lees) at 2pm from Tuesday to Thursday (adult/child $15/7).

ℹ Information

Pictou Public Library (☎902-485-5021; 40 Water St; ☺noon-9pm Tue & Thu, noon-5pm Wed, 10am-5pm Fri & Sat) Free internet access.

Town of Pictou (www.townofpictou.com) Links to sights and festivals.

VIC (☎902-485-6213; Pictou Rotary; ☺8am-9:30pm Jul & Aug, 9am-7pm May, Jun & Sep–mid-Dec) A large information center situated northwest of town to meet travelers arriving from the PEI ferry.

ℹ Getting There & Away

Ferries to/from PEI leave and arrive from Pictou. For more information, see p29.

New Glasgow

The largest town on the Northumberland Shore, New Glasgow has always been an industrial center; the first mine opened in neighboring Stellarton in 1807. Still, it's a pleasant town with plenty of aging architecture, a river running through the center and some good places to eat. The few major local attractions are in Stellarton, a 5km drive south.

⊙ Sights & Activities

FREE   **Crombie Art Gallery**   ART GALLERY
(☎902-755-4440; 1780 Abercrombie Rd; ☺tours on the hour 9-11am & 1-4pm Wed Jul & Aug) This private gallery in the personal residence of the founder of the Sobey supermarket chain has an excellent collection of 19th- and early-20th-century Canadian art, including works by Cornelius Krieghoff and the Group of Seven.

Museum of Industry   MUSEUM
(☎902-755-5425; www.industry.museum.gov. ns.ca; Hwy 104 at Exit 24; adult/child $7/3; ☺9am-5pm Mon-Sat, 10am-5pm Sun) This is a wonderful place for kids. There's a hands-on water power exhibit and an assembly line to try to keep up with.

✗ Eating

The Bistro   RESTAURANT **$$**
(☎902-752-4988; 216 Archimedes St; mains $18-27; ☺dinner Tue-Sat) The only constant on the menu is creativity in spicing and sauces. The menu changes daily according to what's available and in summer everything is organic. Try the Thai grilled salmon or pork tenderloin with black mission-fig butter. Enjoy the local art on display that's also for sale.

Café Italia   RESTAURANT **$**
(☎902-928-2233; 62 Provost St; pizza & salad $8; ☺7:30am-10pm Mon-Thu, 7:30am-midnight Fri, 11:30am-10pm Sat) Between noon and 1pm you might have to wrestle a local for a booth at this small trattoria. Choose from salads, sandwiches, homemade pasta and thin-crust pizza. Open in the morning for coffee and snacks, but not breakfast.

Antigonish

Beautiful beaches and hiking possibilities north of town could easily keep you busy for a couple of days, but Antigonish (an-tee-guh-*nish*) town is lively enough and has some great places to eat. Catholic Scots settled and established St Francis Xavier University and today the university still dominates the ambience of the town. Antigonish is known for the Scottish Highland Games held each July since 1861.

⊙ Sights & Activities

St Francis Xavier University

     NOTABLE BUILDING
The attractive campus of 125-year-old St Francis Xavier University is behind the Romanesque **St Ninian's Cathedral** (120 St Ninian St; ☺7:30am-8pm). The **Hall of the Clans** is on the 3rd floor of the old wing of the Angus L MacDonald Library, just beyond the St Ninian's Cathedral parking lot. In the hall, crests of all the Scottish clans that settled this area are displayed. Those clans gather each July for the Antigonish Highland Games.

Antigonish Landing   NATURE RESERVE
A 4km hiking/cycling trail to the nature reserve at Antigonish Landing begins just across the train tracks from the museum, then 400m down Adam St. The landing's estuary is a good bird-watching area where you have a chance of seeing eagles, ducks and ospreys.

✦ Festivals & Events

Antigonish Highland Games   CULTURAL
(www.antigonishhighlandgames.ca; ☉mid-Jul)
An extravaganza of dancing, pipe-playing
and heavy-lifting events involving hewn
logs and iron balls.

Evolve   MUSIC
(www.evolvefestival.com; ☉late Jul) Five
stages of funk, bluegrass, hip-hop and
more, plus workshops on everything from
puppetry to media literacy.

🛏 Sleeping & Eating

Antigonish Highland Heart B&B   B&B **$$**
(☎902-863-1858, 800-863-1858; www.bbcan-
ada.com/3241.html; 135 Main St; r $85-95; ☎)
Smiling Shebby, the friendly owner of this
c 1854 house, brightens her centrally locat-
ed home with special touches such as rag
dolls on the beds.

TOP CHOICE **Gabrieau's Bistro**   RESTAURANT **$$**
(☎902-863-1925; 350 Main St; mains
lunch $8-13, dinner $16-30; ☉7:30am-9:30pm
Mon-Sat;✑) Grab a coffee and pastry in the
morning or any of a number of imaginative vegetarian dishes, salads, meats and
seafood for lunch or dinner. Locals credit
chef Mark Gabrieau for setting the culinary
high-watermark in Antigonish. The cedar
roasted salmon with nasturtium butter and
a white wine velouté infused with lemon-
grass and roseberries is divine.

Sunshine on Main Café   CAFE **$**
(☎902-863-5851; 332 Main St; mains $8-13;
☉7am-9pm Sun-Thu, 7am-9:30pm Fri & Sat) A
great place to stop if you're tiring of fried
food, this bright cafe serves healthy breakfasts, lunches and dinners using plenty of
organic ingredients.

ℹ Information

Antigonish Public Library (☎902-863-4276;
274 Main St; ☉10am-9pm Tue & Thu, 10am-
5pm Wed, Fri & Sat) Free internet access. Enter
off College St.

VIC (☎902-863-4921; 56 West St; ☉10am-
6pm mid-Jun–early Oct, to 8pm Jul & Aug)
Brochures, local calls and free internet access.
It's in the Antigonish Mall parking lot at the
junction of Hwys 104 and 7.

ℹ Getting There & Away

Acadian Lines (☎902-454-9321, 800-567-
5151; www.acadianbus.com) bus services
stop at Bloomfield Centre at St Francis Xavier
University.

Around Antigonish

POMQUET

About 16km east of Antigonish, this tiny
Acadian community is on a stunning
beach with 13 dunes that keep growing;
waves dump the equivalent of more than
4000 truckloads of sand on the beach each
year. Many bird species frequent the salt
marshes behind the dunes. Comfortable
Sunflower B&B (☎902-386-2492; www.bb-
canada.com/5382.html; 1572 Monk's Head Rd; r
$85-115; ☎) is right on the water.

Cape George

It's a pleasant day cruising this 72km route
that loops up Hwy 245 from Antigonish to
Malignant Cove and around Cape George.
It's been dubbed a 'mini-Cabot Trail' (see
p77) but really the two routes are quite different; Cape George is much less mountainous and forested but has more beaches.

From a well-marked picnic area close to
Cape George Point Lighthouse, a 1km
walk leads to the lighthouse itself. It's automated and not that big, but there are lovely
views to Cape Breton Island and PEI. Signs
at the picnic area point to longer hikes
through forests and coastal areas, including one 32km loop.

You can also start exploring these trails
from the wharf at **Ballantyne's Cove**, one
of the prettiest communities in Nova Scotia.
To walk from the wharf to the lighthouse
and back again is an 8km trip. Also stop in
at the **Ballantyne's Cove Tuna Interpretive Centre** (☎902-863-8162; 57 Ballantyne's
Cove Wharf Rd; admission free; ☉10am-7:30pm
Jul-Sep) for displays on both the fish and the
fishery. A fish-and-chips van parks nearby.

CAPE BRETON ISLAND

Floating over the rest of Nova Scotia like
an island halo, Cape Breton is a heavenly,
forested realm of bald eagles, migrating
whales, palpable history and foot-tapping
music. Starting up the Ceilidh Trail along
the western coastline, Celtic music vibrates
through the pubs and community centers,
eventually reaching the Cabot Trail where
more eclectic Acadian-style tunes ring out
around Chéticamp.

The 300km Cabot Trail continues
around Cape Breton Highlands National
Park. It winds and climbs around and over

coastal mountains, with heart-stopping ocean views at every turn, moose on the roads (watch out!) and plenty of trails to stop and hike.

Take a side-trip to Glace Bay to learn firsthand about the region's coal mining history, Fortress Louisbourg in the east to get a taste of 18th-century military life or at the Highland Village Museum in Iona to get some visuals of what life was like for early Scottish immigrants. The region around Bras d'Or Lake offers opportunities to explore the past and present of the Mi'kmaq and in Baddeck you can learn everything you ever wanted to know about Alexander Graham Bell.

Most tourists visit in July and August, and many restaurants, accommodations and VICs are only open from mid-June to September. **Celtic Colours** (www.celtic -colours.com; ☺Oct), a wonderful roving music festival that attracts top musicians from Scotland, Spain and other countries with Celtic connections, helps extend the season into the fall – a superb time to visit.

Port Hastings

Cape Breton Island ceased to be a true island when the Canso Causeway was built across the Strait of Canso in 1955. A big and busy **VIC** (✆902-625-4201; 96 Hwy 4; ☺9am-8pm) is on your right as you drive onto Cape Breton Island. This is definitely worth a stop: there are few other information centers on Cape Breton, especially outside of July and August; the staff is very well informed; and one wall is covered with posters advertising square dances and ceilidhs.

Ceilidh Trail

Take a hard left immediately after leaving the Port Hastings VIC to get on the Ceilidh Trail (Hwy 19), which snakes along the western coast of the island. Then get on your dancing shoes: this area was settled by Scots with fiddles in hand and is renowned for its ceilidh music performances, square dances and parties.

For a great introduction to local culture, visit the **Celtic Music Interpretive Centre** (✆902-787-2708; www.celticmusicsite.com; 5473 Hwy 19; admission $12; ☺9am-5pm Mon-Fri Jun-Aug). Half-hour tours (which can be self-guided if you arrive when no guides

are available) include a fiddle lesson and a dance step or two. Square dances are advertised around the admissions desk – try a Saturday dance at the community hall in West Mabou or a Thursday evening dance in Glencoe Mills. Celidhs at the music centre itself are held at 11:30am Monday to Friday during summer.

Creignish B&B (✆902-625-5709; www.bbcanada.com/159.html; 2154 Hwy 19; s/d/f $30/60/75) is a 'recycled school house' that's been turned into a guesthouse/artist's haven. Wildflowers, shells and bones are everywhere and there's even a 1000lb stuffed tuna hanging on the ceiling. 'Improvised' arts and crafts classes are offered and owner Sandra can point you to the best-hidden secrets of Cape Breton Island. Rooms are large and comfortable, and the B&B is only a 10-minute drive from the causeway.

MABOU

Although it looks unlikely at first glance, micro Mabou is the not-so-underground hot spot of Cape Breton's Celtic music scene. Among lush hills and quiet inlets you can hike away your days and dance away your nights – and don't forget to scorch your tonsils with single malt whiskey at the distillery down the road.

◉ Sights & Activities

Mabou is more a place to experience than to see specific sights. Take any turn off Hwy 19 and see where it takes you.

Glenora Inn & Distillery   INN & DISTILLERY
(✆902-258-2662, 800-839-0491; www.glenora distillery.com; Hwy 19; guided tours incl tasting $7; ☺tours on the hour 9am-5pm mid-Jun–mid-Oct) Glenora Inn & Distillery is the only distillery making single malt whiskey in Canada. After a tour and a taste of the rocket fuel, stop for a meal at the gourmet pub (there are daily lunchtime and dinner ceilidhs) or even for the night; cave-like rooms ($125 to $150 per night) are perfect for sleeping it off if you've been drinking the local beverage, but the chalets ($175 to $240) are a better choice if you want brighter surroundings. It's 9km north of Mabou. Tours are held on the hour.

Cape Mabou Highlands   NATURE RESERVE
In the Cape Mabou Highlands an extensive network of hiking trails extends between Mabou and Inverness toward the coast west of Hwy 19. The trails are sometimes closed when fire danger is high but oth-

erwise hikes ranging from 4km to 12km start from three different trailheads. An excellent trail guide ($5) is available at the grocery store across from the Mull Café & Deli when the trails are open. Maps are also posted at the trailheads.

Sleeping & Eating

Clayton Farm B&B   B&B **$$**
(✆902-945-2719; 11247 Hwy 19; s/d $75/90; @) This 1835 farmhouse sits on a working red angus ranch and is run by hard-working Isaac Smith. Paraphernalia of old Cape Breton life and of Isaac's family are casually scattered throughout the common areas and comfortable guest rooms. It's rustically perfect.

Duncreigan Country Inn   INN **$$**
(✆902-945-2207, 800-840-2207; www.duncreigan.ca; Hwy 19; r incl breakfast $120-195; 🐾) Nestled in oak trees on the banks of the river, this inn has private, spacious rooms, some with terraces and water views. Bikes are available to guests and there's a licensed dining room (mains $10 to $23) that serves breakfast to guests or dinner by reservation.

TOP **Red Shoe Pub**   PUB **$$**
CHOICE (✆902-945-2996; www.redshoepub.com; 11533 Hwy 19; mains $9-22; ⊙11:30am-midnight Wed, 11:30am-2am Thu-Sat, noon-midnight Sun) Straddling the spine of the Ceilidh Trail, this pub is the beating heart of Mabou. Gather round a local fiddle player (often from the Rankin family) while enjoying a pint and a superb meal – the desserts, including the gingerbread with rumbutterscotch sauce and fruit compote, are divine. Don't be afraid to stay on after dinner to get to know some locals and maybe a few travelers too. Check the website for performances.

INVERNESS

Row upon row of company housing betrays the history of coal mining in Inverness, the first town of any size on the coast. Its history and people are captured evocatively by writer Alistair MacLeod. His books are for sale at the **Bear Paw** (✆902-258-2528; Hwy 19), next to the Royal Bank.

Beginning near the fishing harbor there are miles of sandy **beach** with comfortable water temperatures in late summer. A **boardwalk** runs 1km along the beach. In the old train station just back from the beach, the **Inverness Miners' Museum**

(✆902-258-3822; 62 Lower Railway St; admission by donation; ⊙9am-5pm Mon-Fri, noon-5pm Sat & Sun) presents local history. **Inverness County Centre for the Arts** (✆902-258-2533; www.invernessarts.ca; 16080 Hwy 19; ⊙10am-5pm) is a beautiful establishment with several galleries and an upmarket gift shop featuring work by local and regional artists. It's also a music venue with a floor built for dancing – of course!

Macleods Inn B&B (✆902-253-3360; www.macleods.com; Broad Cove Rd, off Hwy 19; r $70-125; 🐾) is a high-end B&B for a not-so-high-end price about 5km north of Inverness. The house is big and modern but the decoration is in keeping with Cape Breton heritage.

Cabot Trail & Cape Breton Highlands National Park

One of Canada's most dramatic parks, these lively surrounds are accessible via the famous Cabot Trail. The drive is at its best along the northwestern shore of Cape Breton and then down to Pleasant Bay. Be sure to take advantage of the many pull-offs for scenic views and otherwise keep your eyes on this very circuitous road. Of course it's even better if you can explore on foot, hiking through a tapestry of terrain to reach vistas looking out over an endless, icy ocean.

CHÉTICAMP

While Mabou is the center of Celtic music, lively Chéticamp throws in some folky notes and French phrases to get your feet moving to Acadian tunes. The town owes much of its cultural preservation to its geographical isolation; the road didn't make it this far until 1949. Today it's a gateway to Cape Breton Highlands National Park, and has some top-notch museums and live-music opportunities – there's always something going on. The 1893 **Church of St Pierre** dominates the town with its silver spire and colorful frescoes but the rest of this seaside town is modern and drab.

Chéticamp is also known for its crafts, particularly hooked rugs, and as a pioneer of the cooperative movement. Check out the rug displays at Les Trois Pignons and take notice of all those co-ops around town: the Credit Union, Co-op grocery store, Co-op Artisanale Restaurant.

Visitor information and internet access are available at Les Trois Pignons.

JOE'S SCARECROW THEATRE

About 25km south of Chéticamp, stop at this quasi-macabre outdoor **collection** (☑902-235-2108; 11842 Cabot Trail; admission by donation; ☺8:30am-9pm mid-Jun–early Oct) of life-sized, stuffed figures, from a dead-looking Richard Nixon in a housedress to a cartoon duck head with the body of Michael Jackson. Often the figures are arranged holding hands in a circle as if they're awaiting the mother ship. The area started when Joe Delany made some scarecrows out of Mi-Carême costumes (see below) and folks touring the Cabot Trail began stopping to take pictures.

⊙ Sights & Activities

Whale Cruisers   WHALE WATCHING
(☑902-224-3376, 800-813-3376; www.whale cruisers.com; Government Wharf; adult/child $32/15) Several operators sell tours from the Government Wharf, across and down from the church. Captain Cal is the most experienced and offers three-hour expeditions up to four times daily. It's wise to reserve your trip a day in advance in midsummer.

Les Trois Pignons   MUSEUM
(☑902-224-2642; www.lestroispignons.com; 15584 Cabot Trail; admission $5; ☺9am-5pm) This excellent museum explains how rug hooking went from being a home-based activity to an international business. Artifacts, including hooked rugs, illustrate early life and artisanship in Chéticamp. Almost everything here – from bottles to rugs – was collected by one eccentric local resident.

Centre de la Mi-Carême   MUSEUM
(☑902-224-1016; www.micareme.ca; 12615 Cabot Trail; admission $5; ☺9am-5pm) Mi-Carême, celebrated in the middle of Lent, is Chéticamp's answer to Mardi Gras. Locals wear masks and disguises and visit houses trying to get people to guess who they are. This museum covers the history of the celebration and displays traditional masks.

🛏 Sleeping & Eating

Accommodations are tight throughout July and August. It's advisable to call ahead or arrive early in the afternoon.

Chéticamp Outfitters Inn B&B   B&B $$
(☑902-224-2776; www.cheticampns.com/cheti campoutfitters; 13938 Cabot Trail; r $65-100, chalet with kitchen $110; 🛜) Just 2km south of town, this place offers a range of well-priced choices in Acadian style. Views stretch from the sea to the mountain, wildflowers burst from every corner of the garden, and you might even see a passing moose. Very

full breakfasts are served in the panoramic dining area by energetic hosts.

Laurence Guest House B&B   B&B $$
(☑902-224-2184; 15408 Cabot Trail; r $70-100) This gay-friendly, heritage B&B faces the waterfront and is within walking distance of most attractions. Four rooms furnished with antiques all have private bathrooms.

Co-op Artisanale Restaurant RESTAURANT $$
(☑902-224-2170; 15067 Main St; mains $8-16; ☺9am-9pm) This restaurant specializes in Acadian dishes such as a stewed chicken dinner ($13) and *pâté à la viande* (meat pie) for $8. Delicious potato pancakes ($8) with apple sauce, molasses or sour cream are the only vegetarian option.

All Aboard   RESTAURANT $$
(☑902-224-2288; mains $8-15; ☺11am-midnight) The local's favorite for seafood and more has very reasonable prices. It has a fresh, nautical ambience and some creative extras on the menu such as a maple vinaigrette for the salads. You'll find it at the south entrance to Chéticamp.

☆ Entertainment

Doryman's Beverage Room   BAR
(☑902-224-9909; 15528 Cabot Trail) This drinking establishment hosts 'sessions' (cover $8) with a fiddler and piano players from Mabou each Saturday (2pm to 6pm); an acoustic Acadian group plays at 8pm Sunday, Tuesday, Wednesday and Friday.

CAPE BRETON HIGHLANDS NATIONAL PARK

One-third of the Cabot Trail runs through this extensive park of woodland, tundra, bog and startling sea views. Established in 1936 and encompassing 20% of Cape Breton's landmass, it is the jewel in Nova Scotia's island cap.

There are two park entrances: one at Chéticamp and one at Ingonish. Purchase an **entry permit** (adult/child/up to 7 people in a vehicle $7.80/3.90/19.60) at either park entrance. A one-day pass is good until noon the next day. Wheelchair-accessible trails are indicated on the free park map available at either entrance.

The **Chéticamp Information Centre** (☑902-224-2306; www.parkscanada.gc.ca; 16646 Cabot Trail; ☺8am-8pm Jul & Aug, 9am-5pm mid-May–Jun, Sep & Oct) has displays and a relief map of the park, plus a bookstore. Ask the staff for advice on hiking or camping. It's usually staffed from 8am to 4pm, Monday to Friday November to April.

The **Ingonish Information Centre** (☑902-285-2535; 37677 Cabot Trail; ☺8am-8pm Jul & Aug, 9am-5pm mid-May–Jun, Sep & Oct) on the eastern edge of the park is much smaller than the one at Chéticamp and has no bookstore.

🏃 Activities

HIKING

Two trails on the west coast of the park have spectacular ocean views. **Fishing Cove Trail** gently descends 330m over 8km to the mouth of rugged Fishing Cove River. You can opt for a steeper and shorter hike – 2.8km – from a second trailhead about 5km north of the first. Double the distances if you plan to return the same day. Otherwise, you must preregister for one of eight backcountry sites ($9.80) at the Chéticamp Information Centre. Reviews of trails in and near the park are available at www.cabot trail.com.

Most other trails are shorter and close to the road, many leading to ridge tops for impressive views of the coast. The best of these is **Skyline Trail**, a 7km loop that puts you on the edge of a headland cliff right above the water. The trailhead is about 5.5km north of Corney Brook Campground.

Just south of Neil's Harbour, on the eastern coast of the park, the **Coastal Trail** runs 11km round-trip and covers more gentle coastline.

CYCLING

Don't make this your inaugural trip. The riding is tough, there are no shoulders in many sections and you must be comfortable sharing the incredible scenery with RVs. Alternatively you can mountain bike on four inland trails in the park. Only **Branch Pond Lookoff Trail** offers ocean views.

Sea Spray Outdoor Adventures (☑902-383-2732; www.cabot-trail-outdoors.com; 1141 White Point Rd; rentals per day/week $40/145; ☺9am-5pm Jun–mid-Oct) In Smelt Brook near

Dingwall rents bikes and will do emergency repairs on the road. It also offers help planning trips and leads organized cycling, kayaking and hiking tours.

🛏 Sleeping

Towns around the park offer a variety of accommodations. **Cape Breton Highlands National Park** (tent/RV sites from $17.60/29.40) has six drive-in campgrounds with discounts after three days. Most sites are first-come, first-served, but wheelchair-accessible sites, group campsites and backcountry sites can be reserved for $9.80. In the smaller campgrounds further from the park entrances, just pick a site and self-register. To camp at any of the three larger ones near the park entrances, register at the closest information center.

The 162-site **Chéticamp Campground** is behind the information center. There are no 'radio free' areas, so peace and quiet is not guaranteed.

Corney Brook (20 sites), 10km further north, is a particularly stunning campground high over the ocean. There's a small playground here, but it would be a nerve-racking place to camp with small kids. **MacIntosh Brook** (10 sites) is an open field 3km east of Pleasant Bay. It has wheelchair-accessible sites. **Big Intervale** (10 sites) is near a river 11km west of Cape North.

Near the eastern park entrance, you have a choice of the 256-site **Broad Cove Campground** at Ingonish and the 90-site **Ingonish Campground**, near Keltic Lodge at Ingonish Beach. Both have wheelchair-accessible sites. These large campgrounds near the beach are popular with local families in midsummer.

From late October to early May, you can camp at the Chéticamp and Ingonish campgrounds for $22, including firewood. In truly inclement weather, tenters can take refuge in cooking shelters with woodstoves.

PLEASANT BAY

A perfect base for exploring the park, Pleasant Bay is a carved-out bit of civilization hemmed on all sides by wilderness. It's an active fishing harbor known for its whale-watching tours and Tibetan monastery. If you are in the area on Canada Day (July 1), try to be in the stands for the annual monks versus townspeople baseball game. There are lots of fish-and-chip and burger places around town but no really special places in which to eat.

WILEY COYOTES

Coyote attacks are rare worldwide but in fall 2009 a woman was killed by the wild dogs on the Skyline Trail; in August 2010 a teenage girl was attacked and injured in her sleeping bag. Fifteen trappers are now on-call to deal with complaints about aggressive animals and any found near communities will be killed. There's also a $20 bounty on coyote pelts during trapping season and it's estimated that the population will be halved by 2011 – not good news for the coyotes.

Awareness is the best safety method:

» Don't hike alone

» Sleep in a tent

» Carry a solid walking stick

» Dispose of food properly so animals can't access it

» If you see a coyote back away slowly, act big and make noise

» Report incidents to Parks Canada at ☎877-852-3100

◉ Sights & Activities

Gampo Abbey   MONASTERY
(☎902-224-2752; www.gampoabbey.org; ☺tours 1:30-3:30pm Mon-Fri mid-Jun–mid-Sep) This abbey, 8km north of Pleasant Bay past the village of Red River, is a monastery for followers of Tibetan Buddhism. Ane Pema Chödrön is the founding director of the abbey and a noted Buddhist author, but you aren't likely to see her here as she is often on the road. You can visit the grounds any time during the day but you get a more authentic experience with a tour – a friendly monk escorts you.

Pollett's Cove   HIKING
The popular, challenging 20km-return hiking trail to Pollett's Cove begins at the end of the road to Gampo Abbey. There are great views along the way and perfect spots to camp when you arrive at the abandoned fishing community. This is not a Parks Canada trail, so it can be rough underfoot.

Captain Mark's Whale & Seal Cruise
WHALE WATCHING
(☎902-224-1316, 888-754-5112; www.whaleandsealcruise.com; adult $25-39, child $12-19; ☺mid-May–Sep) Two to five daily tours (depending on the season) can be taken in the lower-priced 'Cruiser' motor boat or closer to the action in a Zodiac. Captain Mark promises not only guaranteed whales but also time to see seabirds and seals as well as Gampo Abbey. There's a discount of 25% if you reserve a spot on the earliest (9:30am) or latest (5pm) tour. Tours leave from the wharf next to the Whale Interpretive Centre.

Whale Interpretive Centre   MUSEUM
(☎902-224-1411; www.whalecentre.ca; 104 Harbour Rd; adult/child $4.75/3.75; ☺9am-5pm Jun–mid-Oct) Stop here before taking a whale-watching tour from the adjacent wharf. Park entrance permits are for sale here, and internet access is available at the C@P site downstairs.

🛏 Sleeping

Scottish Hillside B&B   B&B $$
(☎877-223-8111, 902-224-21156; scottishhill sidebnb@hotmail.com; 23562 Cabot Trail; r $85-135; ☎) Run by a friendly young family, this new Victorian-style home sits right on the Cabot Trail and is a comfortable and convenient base for hiking and whale-watching. Ornately decorated rooms are big and the buffet-style breakfasts feature everything from local fruit to authentic oatcakes.

Cabot Trail Hostel   HOSTEL $
(☎902-224-1976; www.cabottrail.com/hostel; 23349 Cabot Trail; dm/r $27/59; @☎) Bright and basic, this very friendly 18-bed hostel has a common kitchen and barbecue area. The office for Cabot Trail Whale Watching is here.

BAY ST LAWRENCE

Bay St Lawrence is a picturesque little fishing village at the very north edge of Cape Breton Island.

Captain Cox (☎902-383-2981, 888-346-5556; Bay St Lawrence Wharf; adult/child $25/12) has been taking people to see whales aboard the 35ft *Northern Gannet* since 1986. He does trips at 10:30am, 1:30pm and

4:30pm in July and August. Call for spring and fall schedules.

Jumping Mouse Campground (✆902-383-2914; 3360 Bay St Lawrence Rd; jumping-mousecamping@gmail.com; campsites $25, cabin $40; ⊙Jun-Sep) is an ecofriendly campground with 10 oceanfront sites (no cars allowed). Reservations are accepted for multinight stays and for a beautifully built four-bunk cabin. There are hot showers, a cooking shelter, frequent whale sightings and the whole place is nearly bug-free.

To enjoy Aspy Bay and its spectacular beach just for an afternoon, stop at nearby **Cabot's Landing Provincial Park** (www.parks.gov.ns.ca).

MEAT COVE

The northernmost road in Nova Scotia finishes at the steep, emerald coast of Meat Cove, 13km northwest of Bay St Lawrence (the last 7km of the road is gravel). As well as watching for frolicking whales in unbelievably clear water, keep an eye on the earth for orchids – some rare species aren't found anywhere else in Nova Scotia. Stop by the **Meat Cove Welcome Center** (✆902-383-2284; 2296 Meat Cove Rd; ⊙8am-8:30pm Jul-Sep) to get excellent information on hiking trails, check email and grab a bite to eat (sandwiches to lobster suppers). Leave your car here if there's no room at the trailhead.

From Meat Cove, a 16km **hiking trail** continues west to Cape St Lawrence lighthouse and Lowland Cove. Spend an hour gazing over the ocean, and you're guaranteed to see pods of pilot whales. They frolic here all spring, summer, and into the fall. Carry a compass and refrain from exploring side paths; locals have gotten lost in this area.

🛏 Sleeping & Eating

Meat Cove Lodge   B&B $
(✆902-383-2672; 2305 Meat Cove Rd; d/f $40/50; ⊙Jun–mid-Sep) Just across from the welcome center, this flower- and bric-a-brac-surrounded house is so cute and sunken into the landscape that it looks like part of a Hobbit's shire.

Meat Cove Campground   CAMPGROUND $
(✆902-383-2379/2658; 2475 Meat Cove Rd; campsites $25, cabins $60; ⊙Jun-Oct) Meat Cove Campground is spectacular, perched on a grassy bluff high above the ocean out in the middle of nowhere. A few new cabins (bring your own bedding) with no electric-

ity or plumbing share the magnificent view. The adjacent **Chowder Hut** (mains $7-16; ⊙11am-8pm) serves mostly basic seafood dishes. Bring loose change for the coin-operated showers ($1 for 12 minutes), firewood is $3 for nine pieces. Be prepared for high winds.

Hine's Ocean View Lodge   HOSTEL $
(✆902-383-2512; www.hinesoceanviewlodge.ca; r $60; ☎) If there's no room at Meat Cove Lodge, backtrack to this even more isolated spot, high up its own road, that has plain near-dormitory style rooms and a shared kitchen; cash only.

INGONISH

At the eastern entrance to Cape Breton Highlands National Park are Ingonish and Ingonish Beach, small towns lost in the background of motels and cottages. This is a long-standing popular destination, but there are few real attractions other than the **Highlands Links golf course** (✆902-285-2600, 800-441-1118; www.highlandslinksgolf.com; round $91), reputed to be one of the best in the world, and the beach. There are several hiking trails and an information center nearby in the national park (see p78).

Ingonish Beach is a long, wide strip of sand tucked in a bay surrounded by green hills.

🛏 Sleeping & Eating

Keltic Lodge   HOTEL $$$
(✆902-285-2880, 800-565-0444; www.signatureresorts.com; Ingonish Beach; r $155-280, cottages $315-395; P@☎⛵) The finest digs in the area are scattered within this theatrical Tudor-style resort erected in 1940. It shares Middle Head Peninsula with the famous **golf course** and the **Ingonish Campground**. The lodge is worth visiting even if you're not a guest for its setting and the **hiking trail** to the tip of the peninsula just beyond the resort. You must have a valid entry permit to the national park, as the lodge, the golf course and the hiking trail are all within park boundaries.

Driftwood Lodge   INN $
(✆902-285-2558; www.driftwoodlodge.ca; 36125 Cabot Trail, Ingonish; r $50, ste with kitchen $80-95) This funky cabin-meets-hotel establishment, 8km north of the Ingonish park entrance, is a steal. The owner works at the park and is a mine of info about hiking and activities. There's a fine-sand beach just below the lodge.

Main Street Restaurant & Bakery
RESTAURANT $$

(☑902-285-2225; 37764 Cabot Trail, Ingonish Beach; lunch around $10, dinner $10-20; ⊘7am-9pm Tue-Sat) By far the best breakfast stop (from $6) near the park and also a great stop for lunch and dinner. Sandwiches and French toast are made with thick fresh bread and there are very reasonable full-lobster suppers for dinner.

WHITE POINT TO NEIL'S HARBOUR
On your way south to Ingonish, leave the Cabot Trail to follow the rugged, windswept White Point Rd via Smelt Brook to the fishing villages of **White Point** and **Neil's Harbour**. These are gritty, hard-working towns but there is some nice architecture, colorful homes, and illuminated, slightly disorienting views of Cape North to Meat Cove when the sun hits them at the end of the day. These are villages where there are as many fishing boats as houses – the area feels distinctly off the beaten tourist track.

Stay the night at homey **Two Tittle** (☑902-383-2817, 866-231-4087; www.twotittle.com; 2119 White Point Rd; r $60-90; 🛜), which smells like supper and whose grandparent-like proprietors are in most evenings watching *Wheel of Fortune*. Don't miss the short but gorgeous walk out back to the Two Tittle Islands the B&B is named for and look out for whales and eagles.

The perfect stop for lunch or dinner is **Chowder House** (chowder from $6, suppers from $14; ⊘11am-8:30pm), out beyond the lighthouse at Neil's Harbour. It's famous for its chowder but also serves great-value suppers of snow crab, lobster, mussels and more. There are plenty of dining locals who like to chat with folks from away while they splatter themselves with seafood juice.

ST ANN'S LOOP
Settle into the artsy calm of winding roads, serene lakes, eagles soaring overhead and a never-ending collection of artists' workshops that dot the trail like Easter eggs. Although you could skip the drive around St Ann's Bay and take a $5 ferry to Englishtown, you'd be missing a leg of the Cabot Trail that is unique unto itself. If you explore deeper you'll discover walking trails to waterfalls and scenic vistas, Mi'kmaw culture and a decidedly interesting mishmash of characters.

Gaelic College of Celtic Arts & Crafts (☑902-295-3411; www.gaeliccollege.edu; 51779 Cabot Trail; 5-day course incl lodging $705-805;

⊘9am-5pm Jun–mid-Oct), at the end of St Ann's Bay, teaches Scottish Gaelic, bagpipe playing, Highland dancing, weaving and more. The **Great Hall of the Clans Museum** (admission $3) traces Celtic history from ancient times to the Highland clearances.

Don't leave the area without stopping in at an **artist's workshop** or two; you'll find pottery, leather and pewter workers, hat shops and more. The artists are easy to find – just keep an eye out for the signs along the main road.

🛏 Sleeping & Eating

J Kerr's B&B
B&B $$

(☑902-929-2114; 43627 Cabot Trail, Breton Cove; 🛜) For 26 years Joan Kerr has offered her home to travelers for whatever the traveler decides to pay – and so far she's not discouraged. Rainbow paintings grace the walls and Joan cooks up a million-dollar breakfast in the morning.

Chanterelle Country Inn & Cottages
INN $$$

(☑902-929-2263, 866-277-0577; www.chanterelleinn.com; 48678 Cabot Trail, North River; r $145-225; ⊘May-Nov; @🛜🐾) Unparalleled as an environmentally friendly place to stay, the house and cabins are on 60 hectares overlooking rolling pastures and bucolic bliss. Meals (breakfast and dinner) are served on the screened-in porch. If you're not staying here, you can reserve for dinner at the highly reputed **restaurant** (mains $20-28, prix-fixe four courses veg/nonveg $38/45; ⊘6-8pm May-Nov).

Clucking Hen Deli & Bakery
CAFE $

(☑902-929-2501; 45073 Cabot Trail; mains $4-14; ⊘7am-7pm Jul-Sep, to 6pm May, Jun & Oct) A sign reads 'no fowl moods in here.' Listen to the local 'hens' cluck away while you eat a delicious meal of homemade breads, soup and salad.

Bras d'Or Lake Scenic Drive

The highlands meet the lowlands along the shores of this inland saltwater sea where eagles nest and puffins play. At 1099 sq km, it's the biggest lake in Nova Scotia and all but cleaves Cape Breton Island in two.

BADDECK
An old resort town in a pastoral setting, Baddeck is on the north shore of Bras

HIGHLAND VILLAGE MUSEUM

Explore Scottish heritage through the **Highland Village Museum** (☎902-725-2272; www.highlandvillage.museum.gov.ns.ca; 4119 Hwy 223; adult/child $9/4; ⏲9:30am-5:30pm), a living history museum perched on a hilltop overlooking the Bras d'Or lakes. Costumed Scotspeople demonstrate day-to-day activities of early settlers' lives and there are Celtic-inspired workshops from spring through fall – check the website for scheduling.

d'Or Lake, halfway between Sydney and the Canso Causeway. It's the most popular place to stay for those who intend to do the Cabot Trail as a one-day scenic drive.

Sights & Activities

TOP CHOICE Alexander Graham Bell National Historic Site MUSEUM
(☎902-295-2069; www.parkscanada.gc.ca; 559 Chebucto St; adult/child $7.80/3.90; ⏲9am-6pm) The inventor of the telephone is buried near his summer home, Beinn Bhreaghm, which is visible across the bay from Baddeck. The excellent museum of the Alexander Graham Bell National Historic Site, at the eastern edge of town, covers all aspects of his inventions and innovations. See medical and electrical devices, telegraphs, telephones, kites and seaplanes and then learn about how they all work. You'll come out feeling much smarter than when you went in.

Bras d'Or Lakes & Watershed Interpretive Centre MUSEUM
(☎902-295-1675; www.brasdor-conservation.com; 532 Chebucto St; admission by donation; ⏲11am-7pm Jun–mid-Oct) Bras d'Or Lakes & Watershed Interpretive Centre explores the unique ecology of the enormous saltwater lake.

Sleeping & Eating

Broadwater Inn & Cottages INN $$
(☎902-295-1101, 877-818-3474; www.broadwater.baddeck.com; Bay Rd; r $90-140, ste $199, cottages $95-200; 📶) In a tranquil spot 1.5km east of Baddeck, this c 1830 home once belonged to JAD McCurdy, who worked with Alexander Graham Bell on early aircraft designs. The rooms in the inn are full of character, have bay views and are decorated with subtle prints and lots of flair. Modern self-contained cottages are set in the woods and are great for families. Only the B&B rooms include breakfast. It's gay friendly.

Mother Gaelic's B&B $
(☎902-295-2885, 888-770-3970; www.mothergaelics.com; 26 Water St; d $90, with shared bathroom $50-75; 📶) Named for the owner's great-grandmother, who was a bootlegger patronized by Alexander Graham Bell, this sweet cottage opposite the waterfront has the feel of an uncluttered summer home.

Lynwood Inn INN $$
(☎902-295-1995; www.lynwoodinn.com; 441 Shore Rd; r $100-230; P📶) Rooms in this enormous inn go far beyond the hotel standard with Victorian wooden beds, muted color schemes and airy, spacious living spaces. There's a family-style restaurant downstairs that serves breakfast, lunch and dinner (breakfast is not included in room rates).

Highwheeler Cafe & Deli CAFE $
(486 Chebucto St; sandwiches $8; ⏲6am-8pm) This place bakes great bread and goodies (some gluten-free), makes big tasty sandwiches (including vegetarian), quesadillas, soups and more. Finish off on the sunny deck licking an ice-cream cone. Box lunches for hikers are also available.

Baddeck Lobster Suppers SEAFOOD $$$
(☎902-925-3307; 17 Ross St; dinners $30; ⏲4-9pm Jun-Oct) In the former legion hall, this high production, arguably high priced institution gets live lobsters in the pot then fresh to you lickety-split. Meals come with just about everything and, although not spectacularly prepared, could fuel you for days.

Entertainment

Baddeck Gathering Ceilidhs LIVE MUSIC
(☎902-295-2794; www.baddeckgathering.com; St Michael's Parish Hall, 8 Old Margaree Rd; adult/child $10/5; ⏲7:30pm Jul & Aug) Nightly fiddling and dancing. The parish hall is just opposite the VIC right in the middle of town.

Information

VIC (☎902-295-1911; 454 Chebucto St; ⏲9am-7pm Jun-Sep)

Visit Baddeck (www.visitbaddeck.com) Maps, tour operators, golf courses etc.

WAGMATCOOK & AROUND

Stop in the Mi'kmaq community of Wagmatcook just west of Baddeck to visit the **Wagmatcook Culture & Heritage Centre** (☑902-295-2999/2492; www.wagmatcook.com; Hwy 105; ☺9am-8pm May-Oct, call for hours Nov-Apr). This somewhat empty cultural attraction offers an entryway into Mi'kmaq culture and history.

TOP CHOICE **Bear by the Lake Hostel** (☑902-404-3636; www.bearonthelake.com; 10705 Hwy 105; dm/r $30/75; ☜), between Wagmatcook and the next town of Whycocomagh, is a super-fun place overlooking the lake. Everything is set up for backpacker bliss from the drive share board to the big sunny deck and inviting communal areas. This place is so popular another six-bed dorm was being added on when we passed; there are also rooms with private sitting areas on the top level of the house. Everyone falls in love with effervescent Kat who manages the place.

Also on Hwy 105, 12km southwest of Baddeck, is **Herring Choker Deli** (☑902-295-2275; sandwiches around $4; ☺8am-6pm). Arguably the region's best pit stop, the deli serves gourmet sandwiches, soups and salads.

North Sydney

North Sydney itself is nondescript, though there are some fine places to stay nearby.

Reserve accommodations if you're coming in on a late ferry or going out on an early one. Most North Sydney motels and B&Bs are open year-round, and it's understood that guests will arrive and leave at all hours. Most places to stay are located along Queen St about 2km west of the ferry terminal.

🛏 Sleeping

Highland View Organic Farm & Cottages
COTTAGES $$
(☑902-794-1955, 800-440-5251; www.highlandviewcottages.com; 20 Allen Lane, George's River; cottages $150-160) Ten kilometers away in the farming community of George's River, stay in luxurious Nova Scotia pine-wood cabins on an organic farm overlooking the Bras d'Or lakes. Owners Cyril and Loretta are phenomenally knowledgeable about their natural surroundings and will proudly teach you about everything from beekeeping to medicinal plants.

Heritage Home B&B B&B $
(☑902-794-4815, 866-601-4515; www.bbcanada.com/3242.html; 110 Queen St; r $60-95; ☜) This exceptionally well decorated and maintained Victorian home is an extremely elegant place to stay for the price. Most rooms have private bathrooms.

Alexandra Shebib's B&B B&B $
(☑902-794-4876, 866-573-8294; 88 Queen St; r $50-70; ☜) This B&B is simple, friendly and excellent value. Rooms have shared bathrooms.

Black Spoon RESTAURANT $$
(☑902-241-3300; 320 Commercial St; mains $10-17; ☺11am-8pm Mon-Thu, 11am-9pm Fri & Sat) At this amazingly chic black and beige bistro dine on local faves with a twist, like breaded haddock with mango salsa, or colorful salads like the grilled vegetable salad with goat cheese. There's also espresso drinks, cocktails and a reasonable wine list.

❶ Getting There & Away

For information about **Marine Atlantic ferry** (☑800-341-7981; www.marine-atlantic.ca) services to Newfoundland, see p181 and p208.

Acadian Lines (☑902-454-9321, 800-567-5151; www.acadianbus.com) buses to Halifax (adult/child $64/32) and points in between can be picked up at the Ultramar gas station on Blower's St. **Transit Cape Breton** (☑902-539-8124; adult/child $3.75/$3.25) runs bus 5 back and forth between North Sydney's Commercial St and Sydney at 8:40am, 12:40pm, 2:40pm and 5:40pm Monday to Saturday.

Sydney

POP 24,115

The second-biggest city in Nova Scotia and the only real city on Cape Breton Island, Sydney is the embattled core of the island's collapsed industrial belt. The now-closed steel mill and coal mines were the region's largest employers and now the city feels a bit empty. Although Sydney itself is nothing special, it is well serviced and you get more bang for your buck staying here as a base to explore Louisbourg and the Cabot Trail than you would in more scenic areas.

Orientation

Downtown, Charlotte St is lined with stores and restaurants and there's a pleasant boardwalk along Esplanade, while the

North End historic district has a gritty charm.

◎ Sights & Activities

Architecture   NOTABLE BUILDINGS
There are eight buildings older than 1802 in a two-block radius in North End Sydney. Three are open to the public, including **St Patrick's Church Museum** (☑902-562-8237; 87 Esplanade; admission free; ⊗9am-5pm), the oldest Catholic church on Cape Breton Island. The 1787 **Cossit House** (☑902-539-7973; www.cossit.museum.gov.ns.ca; 75 Charlotte St; adult/conc $2/1; ⊗9am-5pm Mon-Sat, 1-5pm Sun Jun–mid-Oct) is the oldest house in Sydney. Just down the road, **Jost Heritage House** (☑902-539-0366; 54 Charlotte St; admission free; ⊗9am-5pm Mon-Sat, 1-5:30pm Sun) features a collection of model ships as well as an assortment of medicines used by an early 20th-century apothecary.

Lyceum   MUSEUM
This building houses the **Cape Breton Centre for Heritage & Science** (☑902-539-1572; 225 George St; admission free; ⊗9am-5pm Mon-Sat) and explores the social and natural history of Cape Breton Island.

Cape Breton Centre for Heritage & Science   MUSEUM
(☑902-539-1572; 225 George St; admission free; ⊗9am-5pm Mon-Sat) In the Lyceum, this center explores the social and natural history of Cape Breton Island.

⛵ Tours

Ghosts & Legends of Historic Sydney
                                        WALKING TOURS
(☑902-539-1572; per person $10; ⊗7pm Jul & Aug) This recommended walking tour leaves from St Patrick's Church, does the loop of historic buildings and finishes with tea and scones at the Lyceum.

🛏 Sleeping & Eating

Most establishments in Sydney are open year-round.

[TOP CHOICE] **Colby House**   B&B **$$**
(☑902-539-4095; www.colbyhousebb.com; 10 Park St; r $100-120; @🤶) It's worth staying in Sydney for the affordable luxe of this exceptional B&B. The owner used to travel around Canada for work and she decided to offer everything she wished she'd had while on the road. The result is a mix of heritage and modern design, the softest sheets you can imagine, guest bathrobes, plenty of delicious smelling soaps, chocolates next to the bed and so many other comfort-giving details we can hardly begin to list them.

Gathering House B&B   B&B **$$**
(☑902-539-7172, 866-539-7172; www.gathering house.com; 148 Crescent St; r $60-150; P @) This welcoming, ramshackle Victorian home is close to the heart of town. Shared bathrooms get awfully busy when the B&B is full.

Flavors   RESTAURANT **$$**
(☑902-562-6611; 6 Pitt St; lunch/dinner around $10/20; ⊗8:30am-8:30pm Mon-Sat; 🗷) What the setting lacks in feng shui (small tables and a strange street-side patio setup), the restaurant makes up for in delicious food prepared from locally sourced ingredients. Start with mains like maple-seared salmon or roast pork loin with wild blueberry sauce then finish with a homemade ice cream sandwich with coconut cookies rolled in toffee bits. Vegan and gluten-free options are also available.

Allegro Grill   RESTAURANT **$$**
(☑902-562-1623; 222 Charlotte St; mains $9-25; ⊗lunch Mon-Sat, dinner Tue-Sat) Seafood and meat lovers, go here. This simple-looking spot serves not-so-simple specialties including their famous, handmade turkey andouille sausages

☆ Entertainment

A lot of touring bands make the trek to Sydney. Fiddlers and other traditional musicians from the west coast of the island also perform here or at the Savoy in Glace Bay. Gigs are about $12.

Upstair's at French Club   NIGHTCLUB
(☑902-371-0329; 44 Ferry St) This groovy little North End club features rock, Celtic, jazz and movie nights.

Chandler's   BAR
(☑902-539-3438; 76 Dorchester St) This standard, cavernous bar has top-end local and Canadian talent on stage.

ℹ Information

VIC (☑902-539-9876; 74 Esplanade; ⊗9am-7pm Jul & Aug, to 5pm Jun, Sep & Oct) On the waterfront just behind the world's largest illuminated fiddle.

ℹ Getting There & Away

The Sydney airport is none too busy. **Air Canada Jazz** (☑902-873-5000, 888-247-2262;

www.aircanada.com) flies between Sydney and Halifax while **Air Saint-Pierre** (☑902-562-3140, 877-277-7765; www.airsaintpierre.com) flies to Saint Pierre ($175 one-way, two hours) from early July to early September, on Thursdays and Sundays.

The **Acadian Lines** (☑902-454-9321, 800-567-5151; www.acadianbus.com) bus depot is at 99 Terminal Dr. There are also a number of shuttle services to Halifax.

Glace Bay

Glace Bay, 6km northeast of Sydney, would be just another fading coal town were it not for its exceptional **Cape Breton Miners' Museum** (☑902-849-4522; www.minersmuseum.com; 42 Birkley St; tour & mine visit adult/child $12/10; ☺10am-6pm); it's off South St less than 2km east from the town center. The highlight of this museum is the adventure under the seafloor to visit closed-down mines with a retired miner as a guide. The museum's **restaurant** (mains $8-14; ☺noon-8pm) is highly recommended and offers seafood, sandwiches and burgers; there's a daily lunch buffet from noon to 2pm.

The town's grand 1920 **Savoy Theatre** (☑902-842-1577; www.savoytheatre.com; 116 Commercial St) is the region's premier entertainment venue.

Louisbourg

Louisbourg, 37km southeast of Sydney, is famous for its historic fortress. The town itself has plenty of soul, with its working fishing docks, old-timers and a friendly vibe.

◉ Sights & Activities

Starting from the trailhead at the lighthouse at the end of Havenside Rd, a rugged 6km **trail** follows the coast over bogs, barrens and pre-Cambrian polished granite. Bring your camera to capture the views back toward the fortress at the national historic site.

Louisbourg National Historic Site

HISTORICAL SITE

(☑902-733-2280; 259 Park Service Rd; adult/child $17.60/8.80; ☺9am-5:30pm) Budget a full day to explore this extraordinary historic site that faithfully re-creates Fortress Louisbourg as it was in 1744 right down to the people – costumed thespians take their characters and run with them. Built to protect French interests in the region, it was

also a base for cod fishing and an administrative capital. Louisbourg was worked on continually from 1719 to about 1745. The British took it in a 46-day siege in 1745 but it would change hands twice more. In 1760, after British troops under the command of General James Wolfe took Québec City, the walls of Louisbourg were destroyed and the city was burned to the ground.

In 1961, with the closing of many Cape Breton Island coal mines, the federal government funded the largest historical reconstruction in Canadian history as a way to generate employment, resulting in 50 buildings open to visitors. Workers in period dress take on the lives of typical fort inhabitants.

Free guided tours around the site are offered throughout the day. Travelers with mobility problems can ask for a pass to drive their car up to the site; there are ramps available to access most buildings. Be prepared for lots of walking, and bring a sweater and raincoat even if it's sunny when you start out.

Though the scale of the reconstruction is massive, three-quarters of Louisbourg is still in ruins. The 2.5km **Ruins Walk** guides you through the untouched terrain and out to the Atlantic coast. A short **interpretive walk** opposite the visitor center discusses the relationship between the French and the Mi'kmaq and offers some great views of the whole site.

Three restaurants serve food typical of the time. **Hotel de la Marine** and the adjacent **L'Épée Royale** (grilled cod with soup $14, 3-course meal $20) are where sea captains and prosperous merchants would dine on fine china with silver cutlery. Servers in period costume also dish out grub at **Grandchamps House** (meals $9-15), a favorite of sailors and soldiers. Wash down beans and sausage with hot buttered rum ($4). Otherwise buy a 1kg ration ($4) of soldiers' bread at the **Destouches Bakery**. There's also a small coffee shop between the restaurants serving hot drinks and a few snacks.

🛏 Sleeping & Eating

TOP CHOICE **Cranberry Cove Inn**   INN $$

(☑902-733-2171, 800-929-0222; www.cranberrycoveinn.com; 12 Wolfe St; r $105-160; ☺May-Nov; 🛜) From the dark pink facade to the period perfect interior of mauves, dusty blues and antique lace, you'll be transported back in time through rose-colored glasses

Fortress Inn 7464 Main St

at this stunning B&B. Each room is unique and several have Jacuzzis and fireplaces.

Stacey House B&B
B&B $

(📞902-733-2317; www.hhcanada.com/thestacey house; 7438 Main St; r $60-90; ⊘Jun–mid-Oct; 📶) Interesting knickknacks such as antique teddy bears, dolls and model ships are harmoniously placed throughout this pretty house.

Spinning Wheel B&B
B&B $

(📞902-733-3332, 866-272-3222; www.spinning wheelbedandbreakfast.com; d with shared bathroom $65-75, d with private bathroom $90; ⊘May-Nov; 📶) Try this place if everything else in town is full (which it will be during high season). It's not a looker but the cleanliness, friendly hosts and made-to-order breakfasts more than make up for it.

TOP CHOICE Beggar's Banquet
RESTAURANT $$$

(📞888-374-8439; Point of View Suites, 15 Commercial St Extension; meals $35; ⊘6-8pm late Jul-Sep) Finally here's a chance for you to get into period costume and gorge on a feast of local seafood in a replicated 18th-century tavern. There's a choice of four delicious and copious mains including crab and lobster.

Grubstake
RESTAURANT $$

(📞902-733-2308; 7499 Main St; mains lunch $7-14, dinner $16-28; ⊘lunch & dinner) This informal restaurant is the best place to eat in town. The menu features burger platters at lunch and pastas and fresh seafood for dinner.

☆ Entertainment

Louisbourg Playhouse
THEATER

(📞902-733-2996; 11 Lower Warren St; tickets $15; ⊘8pm late Jun-early Sep) A cast of young, local musicians entertain all summer long in this 17th-century-style theater.

❶ Information

Tourist information office (📞902-733-2720; 7535 Main St; ⊘9am-7pm) Right in the center of town.

EASTERN SHORE

If you want to escape into the fog, away from summer tourist crowds, this is the place to do it. Running from Cape Canso at the extreme eastern tip of the mainland to the outskirts of Dartmouth, the Eastern Shore has no large towns and the main road is almost as convoluted as the rugged shoreline it follows. If you want to experi-

ence wilderness and are willing to hike or kayak, this is your heaven.

Guysborough

Guysborough was settled by United Empire Loyalists after the American Revolution. The 26km Guysborough Trail, part of the Trans Canada Trail (TCT), is great for biking and hiking. The **Old Court House Museum** (📞902-533-4008; 106 Church St; admission free; ⊘9am-5pm Mon-Fri, 10am-4pm Sat & Sun) displays artifacts related to early farming and housekeeping, and also offers tourist information and guides to hiking trails.

🛏 Sleeping & Eating

TOP CHOICE Desbarres Manor
INN $$$

(📞902-533-2099; www.desbarresmanor. com; 90 Church St; r from $149) This tastefully renovated 1830 grand mansion with massive, opulent rooms is reason enough to come to Guysborough. With extraordinary service, fine dining and a range of activities on offer from canoeing and walking to golfing, it's one of the most luxurious properties in Nova Scotia.

Boylston Provincial Park
CAMPGROUND $

(📞902-533-3326; www.parks.gov.ns.ca; off Hwy 16; campsites $18) The 36 shaded sites here are never all taken. From the picnic area on the highway below the campground, a footbridge leads to a small island on the coast about 12km north of Guysborough.

Rare Bird Pub
RESTAURANT & PUB $$

(📞902-533-2128; www.rarebirdpub.com; 80 Main St; mains $9-17; ⊘11am-2am) The Bird is a quintessential stop for a swig of local ale, a pot of mussels, rockin' live east coast music on weekends and fiddlers on the wharf below on Wednesdays. Check the website for schedules.

Canso

Mainland North America's oldest seaport is a cluster of boxy fishermen's houses on a treeless bank of Chedabucto Bay. Long dependent on the fishery, Canso has been decimated by outward emigration and unemployment since the northern cod stocks collapsed around 1990.

The cape surrounding the village has some very off-the-beaten-track opportunities for hiking, kayaking, bird-watching and surfing. The tourist office is at the

SABLE ISLAND

This ever-shifting, 44km-long spit of sand lies some 300km southeast of Halifax and has caused more than 350 documented shipwrecks. But what makes Sable Island most famous is that it's home to one of the world's only truly wild horse populations.

The first 60 ancestors of today's Sable Island horses were shipped to the island in 1760 when Acadians were being deported from Nova Scotia by the British. The Acadians were forced to abandon their livestock and it appears that Boston merchant ship owner Thomas Hancock helped himself to their horses then put them to pasture on Sable Island to keep it low profile. The horses that survived became wild.

Today the island works as a research center; scientists come every year, mostly to study the birds, seals and horses. Since 2003, natural gas fields run by Exxon have been working only 10km from the island but so far there has been little environmental conflict.

It's complicated and expensive but not impossible to visit Sable Island as a layperson – in fact, about 50 to 100 adventurous souls make it there each year. Contact **Sable Island Station** (☎902-453-9350; gforbes@ca.inter.net), in conjunction with Environment Canada, for information about where to get necessary permissions and independently arrange transport.

1885 **Whitman House Museum** (☎902-366-2170; 1297 Union St; admission free; ⊙9am-5pm late May-Sep), which holds reminders of the town's history and offers a good view from the widow's walk on the roof.

⊙ Sights & Activities

Grassy Island National Historic Site
HISTORICAL SITE
(☎902-366-3136; 1465 Union St; admission $3; ⊙10am-6pm Jun–mid-Sep) An interpretive center on the waterfront tells the story of Grassy Island National Historic Site, which lies just offshore and can be visited by boat until 4pm. In 1720 the British built a small fort to offset the French who had their headquarters in Louisbourg but it was totally destroyed in 1744. Among the ruins today there's a self-guided hiking trail with eight interpretive stops explaining the history of the area. The boat to Grassy Island departs from the center upon demand, weather permitting.

Chapel Gully Trail
NATURE TRAIL
This is a 10km boardwalk and hiking trail along an estuary and out to the coast. It begins near the lighthouse on the hill behind the hospital at the eastern end of Canso. A large map is posted at the trailhead.

✯✯ Festivals & Events

TOP CHOICE Stan Rogers Folk Festival
MUSIC
(www.stanfest.com; ⊙1st weekend of Jul) Most people come to Canso for the Stan Rogers Folk Festival, the biggest festival in Nova Scotia, which quadruples the town's population when six stages showcase folk, blues and traditional musicians from around the world. Accommodations are pretty much impossible to get unless you reserve a year ahead. Locals set up 1000 campsites for the festival; check the website for details and try to get a campsite away from the festival site if sleep is a priority.

🛏 Sleeping

Whitman Wharf House B&B
B&B $$
(☎902-366-2450; www.whitmanwharf.com; 1309 Union St; d $95-105; ⊙mid-May–mid-Oct; 🛜) The only place to stay in town outside of festival times is the excellent, wellness-oriented Whitman Wharf House B&B. There's a seaside cottage feel about this place and a shared bathroom that could almost be considered a spa. The owners will help you organize your preferred activity.

Sherbrooke

The pleasant little town of Sherbrooke, 123km west of Canso and 63km south of Antigonish, is overshadowed by its historic site, which is about the same size.

The local tourist office is at **Sherbrooke Village** (☎902-522-2400; www.museum.gov.ns.ca/sv; Hwy 7; adult/child $9/3.75; ⊙9:30am-5:30pm Jun–mid-Oct), which re-creates everyday life from 125 years ago through buildings, demonstrations and costumed workers. There are 25 buildings to visit in this living museum that effectively helps its visitors step back in time.

On a quiet farm, **Days Ago B&B** (☎902-522-2811, 866-522-2811; www.bbcanada.com/daysago; 15 Cameron Rd; r $65-75; 🛜) will lull you with its slower pace. There's a sunporch for sitting on, or you can take out a kayak. Rooms in the house are shared while the loft-style chalet ($80 to $90) has its own bathroom.

You'll find coffee at Godsend **Village Coffee Grind** (coffees $3.25, sandwiches from $4; ⏱8am-5pm Mon-Fri, 9am-4pm Sat & Sun) on the town's minuscule main drag.

Taylor Head Provincial Park

A little-known scenic highlight of Nova Scotia, this spectacular **park** (☎902-772-2218; 20140 Hwy 7; www.parks.gov.ns.ca; ⏱mid-May–mid-Oct) encompasses a peninsula jutting 6.5km into the Atlantic. On one side is a long, very fine, sandy beach fronting a protected bay. Some 17km of hiking trails cut through the spruce and fir forests. The **Headland Trail** is the longest at 8km round-trip and follows the rugged coastline to scenic views at Taylor Head. The shorter **Bob Bluff Trail** is a 3km round-trip hike to a bluff with good views. In spring you'll see colorful wildflowers, and this is a great bird-watching venue. Pack the picnic cooler and plan on spending a full day hiking, lounging and (if you can brave the cool water) swimming here.

Tangier

About 10km southwest of Taylor Head Provincial Park, Tangier is one of the best settings for kayaking in the Maritimes. Highly recommended **Coastal Adventures Sea**

Kayaking (☎902-772-2774; www.coastaladventures.com; off Hwy 7; ⏱mid-Jun–early Oct) offers introductions to sea-kayaking (half-/full-day $75/110), rentals (half-/full-day $35/50) and guided trips. The establishment also has a cozy, excellent-value B&B, **Paddlers Retreat** (s $50, d $60-80).

Murphy's Camping on the Ocean (☎902-772-2700; www.murphyscampingontheocean.ca; 291 Murphy's Rd; tent/RV sites $22/33, trailer rental $65-85; 🛜) gets you out of your tent and into the water to collect mussels; you eat your labors at a beach barbecue to the music of yarns told by Brian the owner. There are RV sites, an RV rental, secluded tent sites and a very rudimentary room above the dock that can sleep four people. Boat rental is $75 per hour and there's also drop-off and pick-up services for camping on the islands.

Don't miss a snack stop at **J Willy Krauch & Sons Ltd** (☎902-772-2188; 35 Old Mooseland Rd off Hwy 7; ⏱10am-5pm Mon-Fri, 9am-5pm Sat & Sun), famed for making the tastiest smoked fish in the province. Choose from a variety of salmon, eel, mackerel and more – don't forget to bring some crackers.

Jedore Oyster Pond

The tiny **Fisherman's Life Museum** (☎902-889-2053; www.museum.gov.ns.ca/flm; 58 Navy Pool Loop; adult/child $3/1.50; ⏱9:30am-5:30pm Mon-Sat, 1-5:30pm Sun), 45km toward Halifax from Tangier, should really be renamed. The man of the house used to row 16km to get to his fishing grounds, leaving his wife and 13 daughters at home. The museum really captures women's domestic life of the early 20th century. Costumed local guides offer tea and hospitality.

New Brunswick

Why Go?

In the early 20th century, New Brunswick was a Very Big Deal. Millionaire businessmen, major league baseball players and US presidents journeyed here to fish salmon from its silver rivers and camp at rustic lodges in its deep primeval forests. But over the decades, New Brunswick slipped back into relative obscurity. Today, some joke that it's the 'drive-thru province,' as vacationers tend to hotfoot it to its better-known neighbors Prince Edward Island (PEI) and Nova Scotia.

But why? The unspoiled wilderness is still here. There are rivers for fly-fishing, coastal islands for kayaking, snowy mountains for skiing, quaint Acadian villages for exploring. So do yourself a favor, and don't just drive through. Prince Edward Island will still be there when you're done, we promise.

Best Places to Eat

» Rossmount Inn
Restaurant (p107)

» North Head Bakery (p113)

» Saint John's Old City
Market (p116)

Best Places to
Stay

» Carriage House Inn (p96)

» Bear's Lair (p102)

» Rossmount Inn (p105)

» Fairmont Algonquin
(p105)

When to Go
Fredericton

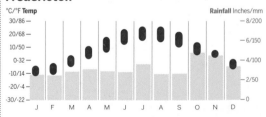

July–September	August	November–March
St Andrews By-The-Sea bustles with crowds of whale-watchers	Acadians unleash their Franco-Canadian spirit for the Festival Acadien in Caraquet	Cross-country skiers hit the groomed trails of Fundy National Park.

Highlights

❶ Feel the power of the highest tides in the world from **Cape Enrage** (p121)

❷ Browse the streets in the picturesque villages of **St Andrews By-The-Sea** (p104), **Gagetown** (p99) and **Sussex** (p118)

❸ Dip your canoe paddle into the lakes of **Chiputneticook** (p104) and **Nictau** (p100)

❹ Breathe in the fresh sea air and unwind on peaceful, isolated **Grand Manan Island** (p110)

❺ Stretch out on the sandy beach at **Kouchibouguac National Park** (p127) or **Parlee Beach** (p126)

❻ Live Loyalist and Acadian history at **King's Landing Historical Settlement** (p98) and **Acadian Historic Village** (p130)

❼ Taste the first strawberries of the season and other delicacies at weekly farmers markets in **Fredericton** (p96) and **Dioppe** (p122)

REGIONAL DRIVING DISTANCES

» Edmundston to Saint John: 375km
» Fredericton to Miramichi: 180km
» St Andrews By-The-Sea to Moncton: 254km

History

What is now New Brunswick was originally the land of the Mi'kmaq and, in the western and southern areas, the Maliseet Aboriginals. Many places still bear their aboriginal names, although the Aboriginal people (who today number around 17,000) are now concentrated on small pockets of land.

Following in the wake of explorer Samuel de Champlain, French colonists arrived in the 1600s. The Acadians, as they came to be known, farmed the area around the Bay of Fundy. In 1755 they were expelled by the English, many returning to settle along the Bay of Chaleur. In the years following, the outbreak of the American Revolution brought an influx of British Loyalists from Boston and New York seeking refuge in the wilds of New Brunswick. These refugees settled the valleys of the St John and St Croix Rivers, established the city of Saint John and bolstered the garrison town at Fredericton.

Through the 1800s lumbering and ship-building boomed and by the start of the 20th century other industries, including fishing, had developed. That era of prosperity ended with the Great Depression. Today, pulp and paper, oil refining and potato farming are the major industries.

Land & Climate

The province encompasses a varied geography of moist, rocky coastal areas, temperate inland river valleys and a heavily forested and mountainous interior. There are four distinct seasons. Summers are generally mild with occasional hot days. The Fundy shore is prone to fog, particularly in the spring and early summer. The primary tourist season lasts from late June to early September. Many tourist facilities (beaches, organized tours and some accommodations in resort areas) shut down for the remainder of the year.

Language

New Brunswick is Canada's only officially bilingual province, although only about one third of the population speaks both French and English (compared to 17% nationwide). Around 34% of the population is of French ancestry, concentrated around Edmundston, the Acadian Peninsula, along the east coast and Moncton. You will rarely have a problem being understood in English or French.

ℹ Getting There & Around

There are tourist information centers at all border crossings and in most towns. These are open from mid-May to mid-October only.

Air

Air Canada has several daily flights from Halifax, Montréal and Toronto into Moncton, Saint John and Fredericton. Moncton has service from Toronto on WestJet; and a daily direct flight from Newark on Continental. WestJet also flies into Saint John from Toronto. See p261 for airline contact details.

Boat

The Bay Ferries' **Princess of Acadia** (☑506-649-7777, 888-249-7245; www.bayferries.com; adult/child 0-5yr/child 6-13yr/senior $40/5/25/30, car/bicycle $80/10) sails between Saint John and Digby, Nova Scotia, year-round. The three-hour crossing can save a lot of driving.

From Saint John between late June and early September, ferries depart twice a day, usually around noon and 11pm. From Digby, twice daily departures are usually in the morning and mid-afternoon. During the rest of the year, ferries run once or twice daily in both directions.

Arrive early or call ahead for vehicle reservations, as the ferry is very busy in July and August. Even with a reservation, arrive an hour

NEW BRUNSWICK FAST FACTS

» Population: 730,000
» Area: 73,400 sq km
» Capital: Fredericton
» Quirky Fact: Home to the world's biggest fake lobster (Shediac), axe (Nackawic) and fiddlehead (Plaster Rock)

Four Days

Spend your first day at **King's Landing Historical Settlement**. Land in **Fredericton** on a Saturday morning – peruse the stalls at the lively **WW Boyce Farmers' Market**, and nip into the **Beaverbrook Art Gallery** to see a few old masters and contemporary Canadian art. Follow the **Old River Road** through Gagetown to the port city of **Saint John**, stopping at a few pottery studios along the way. Hit Saint John on a Saturday night – catch some live Maritime music at **O'Leary's pub** or a play at the **Imperial Theatre**. The next morning, head west to catch the ferry to **Grand Manan Island**. Take your pick of whale-watching tours, hiking, cycling or relaxing on the veranda with a book.

One Week

Back on the mainland from Grand Manan, take the scenic route east through **St Martins**, **Sussex** and **Fundy National Park**. Stop for a dip in the ocean at **Parlee Beach** near Shediac, then head north toward Bouctouche. Get a taster of Acadian culture at **Le Pays de la Sagouine**, then round out the experience with a visit to the modern village of **Caraquet** and a time trip to the early 19th century at **Acadian Historic Village**. Alternatively, head up to the **Miramichi** for a few days of salmon fishing and tubing on the famed river.

Outdoor Adventures

Start with a couple of days camping by the ocean, kayaking along the dunes and exploring the cycling and hiking trails at **Kouchibouguac National Park**. Spend a day or a week hiking the northern end of the **International Appalachian Trail** up over Mt Carleton, around **Grand Manan** or along the **Fundy Trail Parkway**. Take a sea-kayaking expedition in **Passamaquoddy Bay**, then spend a week canoe-tripping through the **Chiputneticook Lakes**. Do a weeklong cycling trip up the **St John River Valley** or day trips around Grand Manan, **Fredericton** and **Sussex**. Leave a couple of days for whale-watching and a boat excursion to **Machias Seal Island** to see the puffins.

Canoe maps for the Nepisiquit, Restigouche, Southwest Miramichi, St Croix and Tobique Rivers are available from **Service New Brunswick** (www.snb.ca; each $7). It also distributes a guide to the New Brunswick Trail ($13) and a snowmobile trail map (free).

before departure. Walk-ons and cyclists should be OK any time. There's a restaurant and a bar.

For Fundy Isles ferries, see the section dedicated to the islands (p108). Book ahead where possible and/or arrive early.

Bus

Acadian Lines (☏800-567-5151; www.acadianbus.com) services the major transportation routes in New Brunswick, with service to Nova Scotia, PEI and into Québec as far as Rivière-du-Loup where they connect with **Orléans Express** (☏888-999-3977; www.orleansexpress.com) buses for points west.

Acadian also runs south to Bangor, Maine, from Saint John ($55, 3½ hours) with onward service to Boston and New York. For information on the daily bus service between Bangor and Calais, see p103.

Car & Motorcycle

For drivers, the main access points into New Brunswick are through Edmundston, Maine

at Calais and Houlton, Nova Scotia or PEI. If you're going to PEI, there's no charge to use the Confederation Bridge eastbound from Cape Jourmain – you pay on the way back. Traffic is generally light, although crossing the Maine border usually means a delay at customs.

Train

VIA Rail (☏888-842-7245; www.viarail.ca) operates passenger services between Montréal and Halifax six times a week. Main New Brunswick stops are Campbellton, Miramichi and Moncton. Fares from Montréal to Moncton for a coach/sleeper are $211/449 (15½ hours).

FREDERICTON

POP 50,500

This sleepy provincial capital does quaint very well. The St John River curves lazily through Fredericton, past the stately

Fredericton

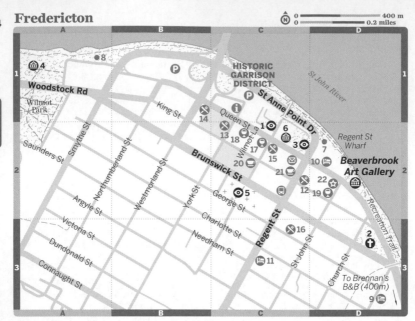

government buildings on the waterfront and the university on the hill. Its neatly mown, tree-lined banks are dotted with fountains, walking paths and playing fields. On warm weekends, 'The Green,' as it's known, looks like something out of a watercolor painting – families strolling, kids kicking soccer balls, couples picnicking.

On a flat, broad curve in the riverbank, the small downtown commercial district is a neat grid of redbrick storefronts. Surrounding it are quiet residential streets lined with tall, graceful elms shading beautifully maintained Georgian and Victorian houses and abundant flower beds. A canopy of trees spreads over the downtown, pierced here and there by church spires.

◎ Sights

The two-block strip along Queen St between York and Regent Sts is known as the Historic Garrison District. In 1875, Fredericton became the capital of the newly formed province of New Brunswick and the garrison housed British soldiers for much of the late 18th and early 19th centuries. It's now a lively multiuse area.

Old Government House   HISTORICAL BUILDING
(www.gnb.ca/lg/ogh; 51 Woodstock Rd; admission free; ☺10am-4pm Mon-Sat, from noon Sun

mid-May–Aug) This magnificent sandstone palace was erected for the British governor in 1826. The representative of the queen moved out in 1893 after the province refused to continue paying his expenses, and during most of the 20th century the complex was a Royal Canadian Mounted Police (RCMP) headquarters. It now evocatively captures a moment in time with tours led by staff in period costume. New Brunswick's current lieutenant governor (Graydon Nicholas, who is a member of the Maliseet Nation as well as the first aboriginal lawyer in Atlantic Canada) lives on the 3rd floor.

Beaverbrook Art Gallery   MUSEUM
(www.beaverbrookartgallery.org; 703 Queen St; adult/student/senior/family $8/3/6/18, pay as you wish Thu after 5:30pm; ☺9am-5:30pm, until 9pm Thu, noon-5pm Sun Sep-Jun, closed Mon in winter) This relatively small but excellent gallery was one of Lord Beaverbrook's gifts to the town. The exceptional collection includes works by international heavyweights and is well worth an hour or so. Among others you will see Constable, Dali, Gainsborough and Turner, Canadian artists Tom Thompson, Emily Carr and Cornelius Kreighoff as well as changing contemporary exhibits of Atlantic art.

Fredericton

NEW BRUNSWICK FREDERICTON

Officers' Square HISTORICAL SITE
(www.downtownfredericton.ca; btwn Carleton & Regent Sts; ceremonies 11am & 4pm mid-July–3rd week Aug, additional performances 7pm Tue & Thu) Once the military parade ground, the Garrison District's Officers' Square now hosts a full-uniform changing of the guard ceremony in summertime. Also in summer the Calithumpians Outdoor Summer Theatre performs daily at 12:15pm weekdays and 2:30pm weekends. The free historical skits are laced with humor. Summer evenings bring jazz, Celtic and rock concerts – see the website for schedules.

York Sunbury Historical Museum MUSEUM
(www.yorksunburymuseum.com; Officers' Sq; adult/child/student $3/free/1; 10am-5pm mid-Jun–Aug, 1-4pm Tue-Sat Apr–mid-Dec) Housed in the 19th-century officers' quarters on the west side of Officers' Sq, this museum's collection preserves the city's past. Displays feature military pieces used by local regiments and by British and German armies from the Boer War and both world wars, furniture from a Loyalist sitting room and a Victorian bedroom, and aboriginal and Acadian artifacts. Don't miss the Coleman Frog, a 42lb creature of Fredericton legend. Real or plaster? Decide for yourself.

Soldiers' Barracks HISTORICAL BUILDING
(cnr Queen & Carleton Sts; admission free; Jun-Sep) See how the common soldier lived in the 1820s (lousy food, too much drink) at this grim stone barracks in the Garrison District. The adjacent 1828 Guard House was also unpleasant (plank beds, thin straw mattresses), but the conditions for those held in cells were truly nasty. Threaten your kids! The lower section of the barracks is now used as artisan studios.

Old Loyalist Burial Ground CEMETERY
(Brunswick St at Carleton St; 8am-9pm) The Loyalist cemetery, dating back to 1784, is an atmospheric, thought-provoking history lesson of its own, revealing large families and kids dying tragically young. The Loyalists arrived from the 13 colonies after the American Revolution of 1776.

Christ Church Cathedral CHURCH
(www.christchurchcathedral.com; off Queen St at Church St; admission free) This cathedral is a fine early example of the 19th-century revival of decorated Gothic architecture and has exquisite stained glass. It was modeled after St Mary's in Snettisham, Norfolk.

Activities

Small Craft Aquatic Centre BOATING
(off Woodstock Rd; mid-May–early Oct) This small center, on the St John River beside Old Government House, rents out canoes, kayaks and rowboats at $10 an hour. On offer are weekly passes, guided canoe and kayak tours, one-hour to three-day river ecology trips, and instruction in either canoeing or kayaking.

Lighthouse on the Green HIKING, BIKING, YOGA
(cnr Regent St & St Anne Point Dr) There are 70km of recreational trails around town and along the river that either begin or intersect at this riverfront lighthouse, which doubles as an info center and small museum. Pick up a map inside. In summer, enjoy weekend concerts and Wednesday night yoga on the lighthouse deck.

☞ Tours

Heritage Walking Tours (free; ⊙10am, 2:30pm & 5pm daily Jul-Oct) Enthusiastic young people wearing historic costumes lead good, free hour-long tours of the river, the government district or the Historic Garrison District, departing from City Hall.

Haunted Hikes (adult/child $13/8; ⊙9:15pm Mon-Sat Jul & Aug) Given by the same, suddenly ghoulish, thespians, and depart from the Coach House at 796a Queen St.

✷ Festivals & Events

NotaBle Acts Summer Theatre Festival (www.nbacts.com; ⊙end Jul-early Aug) Showcases new and noted playwrights with street and theater presentations.

Harvest Jazz & Blues Festival (www.harvestjazzandblues.com; ⊙early Sep) Weeklong event transforms the downtown area into the 'New Orleans of the North' when jazz, blues and Dixieland performers arrive from across North America.

Silver Wave Film Festival (www.swfilmfest.com; ⊙early Nov) Three days of New Brunswick, Canadian and international films and lectures organized by the NB Filmmaker's Cooperative.

⌖ Sleeping

There are a number of budget and midrange motels on the Fredericton Bypass and parallel Prospect St.

TOP CHOICE **Carriage House Inn** B&B $$
(☎506-452-9924, 800-267-6068; www.carriagehouse-inn.net; 230 University Ave; r incl breakfast $99-129; ᴘ⊖❉⊛) In a shady Victorian neighborhood near the Green, this beautifully restored 1875 Queen Anne was built for a lumber baron and former Fredericton mayor. The grand common room has polished hardwood floors, antiques, comfy sofas, fireplaces and a grand piano. Upstairs, the guest rooms have high ceilings, four-posters, period wallpapers and vintage

artwork. There is a deep veranda for lounging. The friendly owners are happy to give local tips.

Brennan's B&B B&B $$
(☎506-455-7346; www.bbcanada.com/3892.html; 146 Waterloo St; r incl breakfast $95-135; ᴘ⊖❉⊛) Built for a wealthy merchant family in 1885, this turreted white riverfront mansion is now a handsome four-room B&B. The better rooms have hardwood floors and water views.

Crowne Plaza Lord Beaverbrook
HOTEL $$$
(☎506-455-3371; www.cpfredericton.com; 659 Queen St; r $120-260; ᴘ❉⊛⊛) Always bustling with weddings, conventions and business travelers, this 1948 downtown hotel is another one of Lord Beaverbrook's legacies to the city. The lobby has a touch of vintage glamour, and the 168 rooms are modern and comfortable. Check out the beaver mosaics on the facade.

Town and Country Motel MOTEL $
(☎506-454-4223; 967 Woodstock Rd; s & d $90, tw $100; ᴘ❉) In a quiet riverside setting, you'll find sparkling clean and bright modern rooms with kitchenettes and big picture windows framing a gorgeous view of the river. It's on the walking/cycling path 3km west from the city center.

Fredericton International Hostel HOSTEL $
(☎506-450-4417; fredericton@hihostels.ca; 621 Churchill Row; r HI members/nonmembers $25/30; ⊙office 7am-noon & 6-10pm; ᴘ⊖⊛) This dark, rambling residence hall is part university student housing, part travelers' lodging. The big, slightly creepy basement has a laundry and pool tables.

✗ Eating

For a small city, Fredericton offers a wide, cosmopolitan cross-section of restaurants, most in the walkable downtown.

WW Boyce Farmers' Market
FARMERS MARKET $
(www.boycefarmersmarket.com; 665 George St; ⊙6am-1pm Sat) This Fredericton institution is great for picking up fresh fruit, vegetables, meat, cheese, handicrafts, dessert and flowers. Many of the 150 or so stalls recall the city's European heritage, with everything from German-style sausage to French duck pâtés to British marmalade. There is also a restaurant where Frederictonians queue to chat and people-watch.

Racine's
FUSION $$$
(www.racinesrestaurant.ca; 536 Queen St; mains $17-33; ☺dinner) Faux leather tablecloths and touches of neon green lend an urban mod look to this trendy downtown bistro. The internationally influenced menu is heavy on seafood and grilled meats – Malpec oysters on the half-shell, curried crab cakes, Szechuan-spiced duck, filet mignon with herb butter – all artfully displayed on white plates like abstract paintings.

Schnitzel Parlour
GERMAN $$$
(☎506-450-2520; www.facklemanschocolate heaven.com; 3136 Woodstock Rd; mains $19-22; ☺dinner Tue, Wed, Fri & Sat, chocolate shop open from 11am) Specializing in hearty, old-fashioned German fare, this cozy countryside restaurant has richly spiced goulash (the secret ingredient is chocolate), wild boar stew and six kinds of schnitzel on homemade spätzle (soft egg noodles). BYOB wine. The on-site Chocolaterie Fackleman sells truffles and traditional central European tortes. The restaurant is about 8km west of town on Woodstock Rd.

Blue Door
FUSION $$$
(☎506-455-2583; www.thebluedoor.ca; 100 Regent St; mains $8-20; ☺11:30am-10pm) This local hot spot serves upscale fusion dishes like gorgonzola bruschetta, maple-miso cod and chicken curry in a dim, urban-chic dining room. Retro cocktails like Singapore slings and Harvey Wallbangers are favorites.

Caribbean Flavas
CARIBBEAN $$
(www.caribbeanflavas.ca; 123 York St; mains $16-23; ☺lunch Mon-Fri, dinner Mon-Sat) A bright nook dishing up the tastes and colors of the Caribbean. Great for a casual, flavorful meal. No alcohol.

Chez Riz
INDIAN $$
(☎506-454-9996; 366 Queen St; mains $16-20; ☺lunch Mon-Fri, dinner Mon-Sat) Delicious Indian and Pakistani cuisine in a darkly stylish, romantically lit cave of a place.

🍷 Drinking
Fredericton has embraced coffee culture in several appealing venues. In the evenings, the bars, pubs and rooftop patios of King and Queen Sts come alive.

Garrison District Ale House
PUB
(www.thegarrison.ca; 426 Queen St; ☺Mon-Sat) Dim lighting and a leather-and-wood decor make this popular Queen St pub feel like an old-school British hunting club. Preppy

crowds munch burgers and sip a wide variety of craft brews.

Lunar Rogue Pub
PUB
(www.lunarrogue.com; 625 King St; ☺daily) This jolly locals' joint has a good beer selection and a fine assortment of single malts. The patio is wildly popular in warm weather.

Second Cup
CAFE
(440 King St in Kings Place Mall; ☺6:30am-10pm Mon-Sat, 9am-10pm Sun) Warm lighting, world beat music and the aroma of fresh-roasted coffee beans draw a loyal clientele of office workers, passersby and aspiring novelists toiling away on their laptops.

Boom! Nightclub
NIGHTCLUB
(www.boomnightclub.ca; 474 Queen St; cover charge $5; ☺Wed-Sun) A hip gay bar and dance club welcoming folks of all stripes.

Trinitea's Cup
CAFE
(www.theatreinthecup.ca; 87 Regent St; ☺8am-5:30pm Mon-Wed, to 8pm Thu-Sat, noon-5pm Sun) It's always 1955 inside this storefront tea parlor, serving traditional English cream teas, soups and sandwiches.

☆ Entertainment
For the scoop on concerts, art gallery openings and other happenings around town, pick up a copy of *here* (www.herenb.com), a free entertainment weekly available all over town.

Outdoor Summer Concerts
LIVE MUSIC
(www.tourismfredericton.ca; admission free; ☺Tue-Fri & Sun) In summer, downtown venues from Officers' Sq to the Lighthouse on the Green feature live local music ranging from highland bagpipes and drums to country and blues. Check the website for schedules.

Playhouse
THEATER
(www.theplayhouse.nb.ca; 686 Queen St) The Playhouse stages concerts, theater, ballet and shows throughout the year.

ℹ Information
Dr Everett Chalmers Hospital (☎506-452-5400; 700 Priestman St)

Fredericton Public Library (12 Carleton St; ☺10am-5pm Mon, Tue, Thu & Sat, to 9pm Wed & Fri) Free internet access is first-come, first-served.

Main Post Office (☎506-444-8602; 570 Queen St; ☺8am-5pm Mon-Fri) General delivery mail addressed to Fredericton, NB E3B 4Y1, is kept here.

Police, Ambulance & Fire (☑911) For emergencies.

Visitors Center (☑506-460-2129, 888-888-4768; www.tourismfredericton.ca; City Hall, 397 Queen St; ☺8am-4:15pm Mon-Fri Oct-May, longer hr in summer) Free city-parking passes provided here.

❶ Getting There & Away

Air Fredericton International Airport (www.yfcmobile.ca) is on Hwy 102, 14km southeast of town. See p92 for flight details.

Bus The new **Acadian Lines Terminal** (www.acadianbus.com; 150 Woodside Lane) is a few kilometers southwest of downtown. Schedules and fares to some destinations include Moncton ($44, 2¼ hours, two daily), Charlottetown, PEI ($68, 5½ hours, two daily), Bangor, Maine ($55, 7½ hours, one daily) and Saint John ($29, 1½ hours, two daily).

Car & Motorcycle Cars with out-of-province license plates are eligible for a free three-day parking pass for downtown Fredericton from May to October, available at the Fredericton Tourism Office at 11 Carleton St. In-province visitors can get a one-day pass. Avis, Budget, Hertz and National car-rental agencies (see p265) all have desks at the airport.

❶ Getting Around

A taxi to the airport costs $16. Bicycle rentals are available at **Radical Edge** (☑506-459-3478; www.radicaledge.ca; 386 Queen St; per hr/day $7.50/25).

The city has a decent bus system, **Fredericton Transit** (☑506-460-2200); tickets cost $2 and include free transfers. Service runs Monday through Saturday from 6:15am to 11pm. Most city bus routes commence at King's Place Mall, just on King St between York and Carleton.

MOOSE ON THE LOOSE

Every year, there are around 300 collisions involving moose on the roads in New Brunswick. These accidents are almost always fatal for the animal and about five people a year die this way. Eighty-five percent of moose-vehicle collisions happen between May and October and the majority occurs at night. Ensure that you slow down when driving after dusk and scan the verges for animals, and use your high-beam lights when there is no oncoming traffic. High-risk zones are posted.

UPPER ST JOHN RIVER VALLEY

The St John River rises in the US state of Maine, then winds along the western border of the province past forests and beautiful lush farmland, drifts through Fredericton between tree-lined banks and flows around flat islands between rolling hills before emptying into the Bay of Fundy 700km later. The broad river is the province's dominant feature and for centuries has been its major thoroughfare. The valley's soft, eye-pleasing landscape makes for scenic touring by car, or by bicycle on the Trans Canada Trail (see p236), which follows the river for most of its length.

Two automobile routes carve through the valley: the quicker Trans-Canada Hwy (Hwy 2), mostly on the west side of the river, and the more scenic old Hwy 105 on the east side, which meanders through many villages. Branching off from the valley are Hwy 17 (at St Léonard) and Rte 385 (at Perth-Andover), which cut northeast through the Appalachian highlands and lead to rugged Mt Carleton Provincial Park.

King's Landing Historical Settlement

One of the province's best sites is this worthwhile recreation of an early-19th-century Loyalist village (☑506-363-4999; www.kingslanding.nb.ca; adult/child/family $16/11/38; ☺10am-5pm mid-Jun–mid-Oct), 36km west of Fredericton. A community of 100 costumed staff create a living museum by role-playing in 11 houses, a school, church, store and sawmill typical of those used a century ago, providing a glimpse and taste of pioneer life in the Maritimes. Demonstrations and events are staged throughout the day and horse-drawn carts shunt visitors around. The prosperous Loyalist life reflected here can be tellingly compared to that at the Acadian Historic Village in Caraquet (p130). The King's Head Inn, a mid-1800s pub, serves traditional food and beverages, with a nice authentic touch – candlelight. The children's programs make King's Landing ideal for families, and special events occur regularly. It's not hard to while away a good half-day or more here.

About 10km south, busy, resortlike **Mactaquac Provincial Park** (day use per vehicle $7) has swimming, fishing, hiking, pic-

The main Hwy (Rte 7) between the capital and the port city of Saint John barrels south through a vast expanse of trees, trees and more trees. A far more scenic route (albeit about twice as long) follows the gentle, meandering St John River through rolling farmland and a couple of historic villages down to the Fundy coast.

Start on the north side of the river in Fredericton, and follow Rte 105 south through Maugerville to Jemseg. At Exit 339, pick up Rte 715 South which will take you to the **Gagetown ferry landing** (admission free; ⊘24hr year-round). This is the first of a system of eight free cable ferries that crisscross the majestic St John River en route to the city of Saint John. You will never have to wait more than a few minutes for the crossing, which generally takes five to 10 minutes.

When you reach the opposite bank, head north a couple of miles to visit the pretty 18th-century village of **Gagetown** – well worth a look-see. Front St is lined with craft studios and shops and a couple of inviting cafes. Stop into the excellent **Queen's County Museum** (69 Front St; admission $2; ⊘10am-5pm mid-May–mid-Jun) housed in Sir Leonard Tilley's childhood home, built in 1736. The top-notch staff will show you through the exhibits spanning pre-colonial aboriginal history in the area, 18th-century settler life, and up to WWII. **Gagetown Cider Company** (☑506-488-2147; 127 Fox Rd; ⊘1-6pm) offers tours by appointment.

Explore scenic Gagetown Creek by boat. **Village Boatique** (☑877-488-1992; 50 Front St) has canoe/kayak rentals for $10/15 per hour, $50/75 per day. Homey **Step-Aside Inn** (☑506-488-1808; stepamau@nbnet.nb.ca; 58 Front St; s/d incl breakfast $80/95; ⊘May-Dec; ⊖✳🐾) has four bright rooms with views of the river. To eat, grab a smoked-meat sandwich and a beer at the **Old Boot Pub** (48 Front St; ⊘lunch & dinner) on the riverfront.

From Gagetown, head south on Rte 102, known locally as 'the Old River Road,' denoting its status as the major thoroughfare up the valley in the kinder, simpler era between the decline of the river steamboats and the construction of the modern, divided highway. The grand old farmhouses and weathered hay barns dotted at intervals along the valley belong to that earlier age. The hilly 42km piece of road between Gagetown and the ferry landing at **Evandale** (admission free; ⊘24hr year-round) is especially picturesque, with glorious panoramic views of fields full of wildflowers, white farmhouses and clots of green and gold islands set in the intensely blue water of the river.

A hundred years ago, tiny Evandale was a bustling little place, where a dance band would entertain riverboat passengers stopping off for the night at the **Evandale Resort** (☑506-468-2222; ferry landing; r $139-199), now restored to its Victorian grandeur with six rooms and a fine-dining restaurant. On the other side of the water, Rte 124 takes you the short distance to the **Belleisle ferry** (admission free; ⊘24hr year-round). The ferry deposits you on the rural Kingston Peninsula, where you can cross the peninsula to catch the **Gondola Point Ferry** (admission free; ⊘24hr year-round) and head directly into Saint John.

nic sites, camping, boat rentals and a huge **campground** (☑506-363-4747; 1256 Hwy 105; tent/RV sites $22/24; ⊘late May–mid-Oct).

Hartland

This tiny country hamlet has the granddaddy of New Brunswick's many wooden covered bridges. The photogenic 390m-long **Hartland covered bridge** over the St John River was erected in 1897 and is a national historic site. The picnic tables overlooking the river and the bridge at the tourist information center are five-star lunch spots (fixings at the grocery store across the road). Otherwise, the village has a rather forlorn atmosphere.

Rebecca Farm B&B (☑506-375-1699; 656 Rockland Rd; d incl breakfast $100-130; P⊖✳🐾) About 4km from the town center, this scrupulously maintained 19th-century farmhouse sits in the midst of gorgeously hilly potato fields.

Florenceville & Around

The tidy and green riverside village of Florenceville is ground zero of the global french-fry industry. It's home to the McCain Foods frozen foods empire, which is sustained by the thousands of hectares of potato farms that surround it in every direction. Started by the McCain brothers in 1957, the company produces one-third of the world's french fry supply at its Florenceville factory and 54 like it worldwide. That adds up to 500,000kg of chips churned out every hour and $5.8 billion in annual net sales.

Worth a stop is the **Potato World Museum** (www.potatoworld.ca; Rte 110; regular tour adult/child $5/4, experiential tour $10/8; ⊗9am-6pm Mon-Fri, to 5pm Sat & Sun Jun-Aug, 9am-5pm Mon-Fri Sep & Oct). It's a cheesy name, but the museum is a tasteful, top-class interactive exposition of the history of the humble potato in these parts and its continuing centrality to the provincial economy. In this area, school kids are still given two weeks off in the autumn to help bring in the harvest. The museums' new experiential tour lets you get your hands dirty – literally – by planting potato seeds and cutting your own french fries. If all the spud talk leaves you peckish, slip into a potato barrel chair at the on-site **Harvest Cafe** (lunch $5-7; ⊗11am-4pm Mon-Fri). The museum is 2km off Hwy 2 at Exit 152 toward Centreville on Rte 110.

Just outside Florenceville is the **Tannaghtyn B&B** (☑506-392-6966, 866-399-6966; www.tannaghtyn.ca; 4169 Rte 103, off Rte 110, Connell; r incl breakfast $95-140; P❄☎), set high on a ridge with a spectacular view of the St John River and the green and gold patchwork of farms on the opposite side. Both stylish and cozy, the house is furnished with dramatic Canadian art, comfy sofas, beds made up with linens dried in the fresh country air, and there's a hot tub under the stars. Besides the Harvest Cafe, Florenceville has a half-dozen middle-of-the-road restaurants serving three meals a day.

Acadian Lines (www.acadianbus.com; 8738 Main St) buses stop at the Irving gas station in Florenceville.

Mt Carleton & the Tobique Valley

From his workshop on the forested banks of the Tobique River at the foot of Mt Carleton, Nictau canoe-maker Bill Miller rhapsodizes that 'If you telephone heaven, it's a local call.' He may be right.

The 174-sq-km provincial park offers visitors a wilderness of mountains, valleys, rivers and wildlife including moose, deer, bear and, potentially, the 'extinct' but regularly seen eastern cougar. The main feature of the park is a series of rounded glaciated peaks and ridges, including Mt Carleton, which at 820m is the Maritimes' highest. This range is an extension of the Appalachian Mountains, which begin in the US state of Georgia and end in Québec. Mt Carleton is little known and relatively unvisited, even in midsummer. It could be the province's best-kept secret.

The park is open from mid-May to October; entry is free. Hunting and logging are prohibited in the park, and all roads are gravel-surfaced. The nearest town is Riley Brook, 30km away, so bring all food and a full tank of gas.

🏃 Activities

Canoeing

The Mt Carleton area boasts superb wilderness canoeing. In the park itself, the Nictau and Nepisiguit chains of lakes offer easy day-tripping through a landscape of tree-clad mountains. For experienced canoeists, the shallow and swift Little Tobique River rises at Big Nictau Lake, winding in tight curls through dense woods until it joins the Tobique itself at Nictau. The more remote Nepisiguit River flows out of the Nepisiguit Lakes through the wilderness until it empties into the Bay of Chaleur at Bathurst, over 100km away.

The lower reaches of the Tobique, from Nictau, through minute Riley Brook and down to Plaster Rock is a straight, easy paddle through forest and meadow that gives way to farmland as the valley broadens, with a couple of waterfront campgrounds along the way. The easy 10km between Nictau and the Bear's Lair landing in Riley Brook makes for a relaxing afternoon paddle.

Don McAskill at **Bear's Lair** (☑506-356-8351; www.bearslairhunting.com; 3349 Rte 385, Riley Brook) has boats for $40 a day and can provide expert knowledge on canoeing in these parts. He also offers a shuttle service between your put-in and take-out point (eg boat delivery to Mt Carleton Provincial Park and transport of your vehicle down

As anyone who has been in the country for more than five minutes knows, Canadians love their hockey. For many, this affection (obsession?) is wrapped up in happy child-hood memories of bright winter afternoons chasing a puck up and down a frozen pond or backyard rink.

Every February, the small forest town of Plaster Rock (population 1200), 84km from Mt Carleton, hosts the **World Pond Hockey Tournament** (www.worldpondhockey.com; Rte 109, Plaster Rock; admission free; ⊙2nd week Feb). Twenty rinks are plowed on Roulston Lake, which is ringed by tall evergreens, hot-chocolate stands and straw-bale seating for the 8000-odd spectators drawn to the four-day event. The tourna-ment is wildly popular, with 120 amateur four-person teams traveling in from places as far flung as England, Egypt and the Cayman Islands. Anyone can register to play, but they will have to defeat the Boston Danglers, who scrambled over squads like the Skateful Dead, the Raggedy Ass River Boys and the Boiled Owls to put a lock on the championship trophy several years running.

If you want to play, register early. If you want to watch, pack your long johns and a toque (wool hat) and book your accommodations early. If the motels are full, the or-ganizers keep a list of local folks willing to billet out-of-towners in their homes for the weekend.

to Riley Brook is $45). In the park, **Guildo Martel** (☑506-235-2499) rents canoes and kayaks for the day on the edge of Big Nictau Lake at Armstrong Campground.

Fiddles on the Tobique (☑506-356-2409; ⊙late Jun) is a weekend festival held annual-ly in Nictau and Riley Brook. It is a magical idea: a round of community hall suppers, jam sessions and concerts culminating in a Sunday afternoon floating concert down the Tobique River from Nictau to Riley Brook. Upward of 800 canoes and kayaks join the flotilla each year – some stocked with musicians, some just with paddlers – and 8000 spectators line the river banks to watch. By some accounts, the event has been damaged by its own popularity, de-volving into a boisterous booze cruise. Oth-ers call it a grand party and good fun.

On land, **Bill Miller** (☑506-356-2409; www.millercanoes.com; 4160 Rte 385, Nictau) welcomes visitors to his cluttered canoe-making workshop in Nictau (population 12), where he and his father and grandfa-ther before him have handcrafted wooden canoes since 1922. Also worth a stop is the **Tobique Salmon Barrier** (admission free; ⊙9am-5pm), signposted from the road at Nictau, located at the confluence of the Lit-tle Tobique and Campbell Rivers. There is a spectacular view from the Department of Fisheries office situated on a bluff overlook-ing the water. From here, officers keep a 24-hour watch on the Atlantic salmon, which are trucked up by road from below the Mac-

taquac Dam at Fredericton and held here until spawning time, in order to protect their dwindling numbers from poachers.

Hiking

The best way to explore Mt Carleton is on foot. The park has a 62km network of trails, most of them are loops winding to the handful of rocky knobs that are the peaks. The International Appalachian Trail (IAT) passes through here.

The easiest peak to climb is Mt Bailey; a 7.5km loop trail to the 564m hillock be-gins near the day-use area. Most hikers can walk this route in three hours. The highest peak is reached via the Mt Carleton Trail, a 10km route that skirts over the 820m knob, where there's a fire tower. Plan on three to four hours for the trek and pack your parka; the wind above the tree line can be brutal.

The most challenging hike is the Saga-mook Trail, a 6km loop to a 777m peak with superlative vistas of Nictau Lake and the highlands area to the north of it; allow three hours for this trek. The Mountain Head Trail connects the Mt Carleton and Sagamook Trails, making a long transit of the range possible.

All hikers intending to follow any long trails must register at the visitors center or park headquarters before hitting the trail. Outside the camping season (mid-May to mid-September), you should call ahead to make sure the main gate will be open, as the Mt Carleton trailhead is 13.5km from the park entrance. Otherwise park your car at the entrance and walk in – the Mt Bailey trailhead is only 2.5km from the gate.

🛏 Sleeping & Eating

There is lodging, a general store, gas station and restaurant in Riley Brook. The park has four public-use **campgrounds** (☑506-235-0793; www.friendsofmountcarleton.ca). In addition to Armstrong Brook (p102), there are the semiwilderness campgrounds of Franquelin and Williams Brook, with outhouses and fire pits (bring your own water), and the ultraremote Headwaters campground on the slopes of Mt Carleton.

TOP CHOICE **Bear's Lair** INN $
(☑506-356-8351; www.bearslairhunting.com; 3349 Rte 385, Riley Brook; r $60; 🅿😊) If any place in the province captures the essence of life in the north woods, this is it. A cozy log hunting lodge set on the banks of the Tobique River, it is busiest during fall hunting season, but is also a supremely relaxing base for hikers, canoeists and wildlife enthusiasts. The high-ceilinged main lodge is adorned with numerous taxidermied specimens and photographs of happy hunters and fishers with the one that didn't get away. There is also a pool table, big-screen TV, floor-to-ceiling stone fireplace, a few dining tables and huge picture windows framing a serene view of the river slipping by just a few meters away. The cozy log-walled guest rooms are spick and span and nicely accented with plaid fabrics. A long, deep veranda invites lounging after dinner. The lodge's friendly owners offer meals (great homemade pie for dessert), canoe/kayak rentals and guided hunting trips.

The town of Plaster Rock, situated 54km downriver toward the Trans-Canada Hwy (Rte 385), also has several serviceable motels and a couple of casual restaurants.

Armstrong Brook Campground
CAMPGROUND $
(☑506-235-0793; tent & RV sites $9-14; 😊mid-May–Oct) The park's largest campground has 89 sites nestled among the pines on the north side of Nictau Lake, 3km from the entrance. It has toilets, showers and a kitchen shelter, but no sites with hookups. RV drivers often have their noisy generators running, so tenters should check out the eight tent-only sites along Armstrong Brook on the north side of the campground.

ℹ Information

At the entrance to the park is a **visitors center** (☑506-235-0793; www.friendsofmountcarleton.ca; off Rte 385; 😊8am-8pm daily May-Oct) for maps and information. There is also another **office** (☑506-235-6040; dnr.Mt.carleton@gnb.ca; 11 Gagnon St), the park headquarters, in St Quentin.

Grand Falls

With a drop of around 25m and a 1.6km-long gorge with walls as high as 80m, the falls merit a stop in this otherwise un-scenic town. The **Grand Falls** are best in spring or after heavy rain. In summer, much of the water is diverted for generating hydroelectricity, yet the gorge is appealing any time.

In the middle of town, overlooking the falls, the **Malabeam Reception Centre** (25 Madawaska Rd; admission free; 😊10am-6pm May, Jun & Sep, 9am-9pm Jul & Aug) doubles as a tourist office. Among the displays is a scale model of the gorge showing its extensive trail system.

A 253-step stairway down into the gorge begins at **La Rochelle** (1 Chapel St; tour adult/child $4/2, self-guided tour per family $5; 😊mid-May–mid-Oct), across the bridge from the Malabeam Reception Centre and left on Victoria St. Boats maneuver for 45-minute trips (adult/family $11/27) up the gorge. These run up to eight times a day but only in midsummer when water levels are low (it's too dangerous when the river is in full flood). Buy the boat ticket at La Rochelle first, as it includes the stairway to the base of the gorge.

There are dramatically situated tent and RV sites at the **Falls and Gorge Campground** (☑877-475-7769; 1 Chapel St; unserviced/serviced sites $18/25; 😊Jun–mid-Sep). **Côté's** (☑877-444-2683; www.cotebb-inn.com; 575 Broadway Blvd West; r incl breakfast $95-175) is a homey, five-room B&B with a patio and hot tub. **Le Grand Saut** (www.legrandsautristorante.com; 155 Broadway Blvd; mains $11-22; 😊lunch & dinner), a popular, two-tiered spot with an inviting deck out front, serves up salads, pastas, pizzas and steaks.

Acadian Lines (www.acadianbus.com; 555 Madawaska Rd) buses stop at the Esso station, just west of downtown. Hwy 108 (known locally as the Renous Hwy) cuts across the province through Plaster Rock to the east coast, slicing through forest for nearly its entirety. It is most tedious, but fast. Watch out for deer and moose.

Almost the entire southern edge of New Brunswick is presided over by the ever-present, constantly rising and falling, always impressive waters of the Bay of Fundy.

The resort town of St Andrews By-The-Sea, the serene Fundy Isles, fine seaside scenery and rich history make this easily one of the most appealing regions of the province. Whale watching is a thrilling area activity. Most commonly seen are the fin, humpback and minke, and less so, the increasingly rare right whale. Porpoises and dolphins are plentiful. And let's not overlook the seafood – it's bountiful and delicious.

Edmundston

Working-class Edmundston, with a large paper mill, a utilitarian town center and a mainly bilingual French citizenry, doesn't bother much with tourism. Nevertheless, it makes a convenient stopover for those traveling east from Québec. The first port of call for most folks is the **Provincial Tourist Office** (Hwy 2; ⊘10am-6pm late May–early Oct, 8am-9pm Jul & Aug) about 20km north at the Québec border. Halfway between the border and Edmundston in the small community of St Jacques is the **New Brunswick Botanical Garden** (www.jardinbotaniquenb.com; off Rte 2; adult/child $14/7; ⊘9am-6pm May, Jun & Sep, to 8pm Jul & Aug). Here there are 80,000 plants to brighten your day, all accompanied by classical music! Kids might prefer the neat temporary exhibitions, such as a butterfly garden. Edmundston is the eastern terminus of the **Petis Témis Interprovincial Linear Park** (www.petit-temis.com, in French), a 134km cycling/hiking trail between Edmundston and Rivière-du-Loup, Québec. It follows an old railbed along the Madawaska River and the shores of Lake Témiscouata, passing by several small villages and campgrounds along the way.

Get out of gritty Edmundston and sleep next to the botanical gardens at **Auberge Les Jardins** (⊡506-739-5514; www.lesjardinsinn.com; 60 Rue Principale, St Jacques; r $79-180; ☞⊠), a gracious inn whose 17 rooms are each decorated with a different Canadian flower or tree theme. There's also a modern motel in back, and a wood-and-stained-glass dining room that's considered one of the best restaurants in the province (check out the fabulous wine list). Several motels line the highway and old Hwy 2 (Blvd Acadie). For eats, head to **Bel Air** (⊡506-735-3329; 174 Victoria St, cnr Blvd Hébert; mains $6-14; ⊘24hr). A city landmark since the 1950s, this is a total classic right down to the seasoned, uniformed waitresses. The you-name-it menu includes acceptable Italian, Chinese, seafood and basic Canadian fare.

Acadian Lines (www.acadianbus.com; 191 Victoria St) buses depart from the downtown Edmundston bus terminal.

St Stephen

Right on the US border across the river from Calais, Maine, St Stephen is a busy entry point with small-town charm and one tasty attraction. It is home to Ganong, a family-run chocolate business operating since 1873, whose products are known around eastern Canada. The 5-cent chocolate nut bar was invented by the Ganong brothers in 1910, and they are also credited with developing the heart-shaped box of chocolates seen everywhere on Valentine's Day.

The **tourist office** (cnr Milltown Blvd & King St; ⊘10am-6pm Jun & Sep, 8am-9pm Jul & Aug) is in the former train station. The old Ganong chocolate factory on the town's main street is now the **Chocolate Museum** (www.chocolatemuseum.ca; 73 Milltown Blvd; adult/child/family $7/6/22; ⊘9:30am-6:30pm Mon-Sat, 11am-3pm Sun Jul-early Sep, 10am-5pm Mon-Fri Mar-Jun, 10am-4pm Mon-Fri Sep-Nov), with tasteful (and tasty) interactive displays of everything from antique chocolate boxes to manufacturing equipment. The adjacent shop (open daily year-round) sells boxes of Ganong hand-dipped chocolates and is free to visit. Try the iconic chicken bone (chocolate-filled cinnamon sticks) or the old-fashioned Pal-O-Mine candy bar. The museum also offers a **guided heritage walking tour** (adult/child/family $13/10/40) of St Stephen from mid-May to mid-October. Once a year, during **Chocolate Fest** (www.chocolate-fest.ca; ⊘1st week Aug), the town celebrates all things chocolate with a parade, tours of the factory with unlimited sampling of the goods, and games for the kids.

NEW BRUNSWICK WESTERN FUNDY SHORE

CHIPUTNETICOOK LAKES

Tucked away on New Brunswick's southwest border with the US state of Maine is a little-known but spectacular chain of wilderness lakes. Stretching for 180km along the international border, the forest-ringed Chiputneticook Lakes offer canoeing enthusiasts the chance to slip away into the wild for a few weeks. The nonprofit **St Croix International Waterway Commission** (www.stcroix.org; 5 Rte 1, St Stephen) maintains a network of backcountry campsites on the islands and lakeshores along the chain and publishes a detailed map of the waterway ($10). It includes the St Croix River, a popular three- to four-day paddling route beginning south of the lakes. There are a couple of fishing lodges on Palfrey Lake accessible via Rte 630. Day-trippers can use the scenic lakeshore campsites at **Spednik Lake Provincial Park** (free; maintained by volunteers) where there is a hiking trail through the woods, primitive toilets and fire rings. Bring your own water. Take Rte 3 north from St Stephen then bear left on Rte 630 to reach the park gate. Canoe rentals are available in Saint John and Fredericton. Note: the lakes are not patrolled by the park service, and paddlers should be experienced and well equipped.

There are five very comfortable rooms complemented by a quiet garden at **Blair House** (506-466-2233, 888-972-5247; www.blairhouseinn.nb.ca; 38 Prince William St; s incl breakfast $75-100, d $80-109; P⊗✿🕸), a fabulous Victorian home. You can walk the main street easily from here. There are also a few run-down motels on the outskirts of town if you are desperate.

Home cooking is served up at **Carman's Diner** (506-466-3528; 164 King St; mains $4-16; ⊙7am-10pm), a 1960s throwback with counter stools and jukeboxes (that sometimes work) at the tables.

The Red Rooster Country Store doubles as the **Acadian Lines** (www.acadianbus.com; Hwy 1 at 5 Old Bay Rd) bus stop, 4km east of town. There's daily service to Saint John ($29), which connects to Moncton ($55) and Halifax ($88). There's also a daily bus to Bangor ($38), but you have to purchase tickets in person. In Bangor, immediate connections are available to Boston and New York.

Across the border in Calais, Maine, **West's Coastal Connection** (800-596-2823) buses connect to Bangor. They usually leave from Carmen's Hometown Pizzeria on Main Street, but call ahead to confirm. In Bangor, buses use the Greyhound terminal and connect to Bangor airport. Greyhound passes cannot be used from Calais.

St Andrews By-The-Sea

St Andrews is a genteel summer resort town. Blessed with a fine climate and pic-turesque beauty, it also has a colorful history. Founded by Loyalists in 1783, it's one of the oldest towns in the province. Busy with holidaymakers and summer residents in July and August, the rest of the year there are more seagulls than people.

The town sits on a peninsula pointing southward into the Bay of Fundy. Its main drag, Water St, is lined with restaurants, souvenir and craft shops.

⊙ Sights

Huntsman Aquarium   AQUARIUM
(www.huntsmanmarine.ca; 1 Lower Campus Rd; adult/child $5/3; ⊙10am-5pm mid-May–late Sep) Part of the independent not-for-profit Huntsman Marine Science Research Centre, this popular aquarium was in temporary digs at the time of research while a newer, bigger aquatic center was being built. The aquarium features most specimens found in local waters, including seals (feedings at 11am and 4pm) and sharks. Kids love the touch pool. The research center also offers weeklong summer field courses for amateur enthusiasts (both students and adults).

Minister's Island   HISTORICAL BUILDING
(www.ministersisland.ca; adult/child $15/10; ⊙May-Oct) This picturesque tidal island was once used as a summer retreat by William Cornelius Van Horne, builder of the Canadian Pacific Railway and one of Canada's wealthiest men. Covenhoven, his splendid 50-room Edwardian cottage, is now open to visitors – check out the towerlike stone bathhouse, the tidal swimming pool and the chateau-like barn. The island can be visited

at low tide, when you can drive (or walk, or bike) on the hard-packed sea floor. A few hours later it's 3m under water. Be careful! During high tide, a ferry departs from Bar Rd. To get to Minister's Island from downtown St Andrews, follow 127 north for about 1km and turn right on Bar Rd.

Kingsbrae Garden   GARDEN
(www.kingsbraegarden.com; 220 King St; adult/senior & student/family $12/9/28, per person for a personal guided tour extra $2; ⊗9am-6pm mid-May–mid-Oct) Extensive, multihued Kingsbrae Garden is considered one of the best horticultural displays in Canada. Check out the wollemi pine, one of the world's oldest and rarest trees.

Sunbury Shores Arts & Nature Centre
                               ART GALLERY, ART CLASSES
(www.sunburyshores.org; 139 Water St; admission free; ⊗9am-4:30pm Mon-Fri, noon-4pm Sat year-round, plus noon-4pm Sun May-Sep) This nonprofit educational and cultural center offers courses in painting, weaving, pottery and other crafts for a day, weekend or week, as well as natural science seminars. Various changing exhibits run through summer.

St Andrews Blockhouse   HISTORICAL BUILDING
(Joe's Point Rd; admission free; ⊗9am-8pm Jun-Aug, 9am 5pm early Sep) The restored wooden Blockhouse Historic Site is the only one left of several that were built here for protection in the war of 1812. If the tide is out, there's a path that extends from the blockhouse out across the tidal flats.

Sheriff Andrew House   HISTORICAL BUILDING
(cnr King & Queen Sts; admission by donation; ⊗9:30am-4:30pm Mon-Sat, 1-4:30pm Sun Jul-Sep) This 1820 neoclassical home has been restored to look like a middle-class home in the 1800s, attended by costumed guides.

Atlantic Salmon Interpretive Centre
                               MUSEUM, AQUARIUM
(www.salarstream.ca; Chamcook Lake No 1 Rd off Rte 127; adult/child/student $5/3/4; ⊗9am-5pm) This handsome lodge has an in-stream aquarium, guided tours and displays devoted to the life and trials of the endangered wild Atlantic salmon, once so plentiful in provincial rivers and bays.

🏃 Activities

Eastern Outdoors   BIKING, KAYAKING
(☎506-529-4662; www.easternoutdoors.com; 165 Water St; mountain bike rentals per hr/day $20/35, kayak rentals per day $55; ⊗mid-May–

Oct) This St Andrews–based outfitter offers sea-kayak trips ranging from two-hour sunset paddles ($39) to multiday camping expeditions ($99 per day).

Twin Meadows Walking Trail   WALKING
The 800m Twin Meadows Walking Trail, a boardwalk and footpath through fields and woodlands, begins opposite No 165 Joe's Point Rd beyond the blockhouse.

🧭 Tours

Several companies offering boat trips and whale-watching cruises have offices by the wharf at the foot of King St. They're open from mid-June to early September. The cruises, which cost about $55, do take in the lovely coast, seabirds are commonplace and seeing whales is the norm. The ideal waters for watching these beasts are further out in the bay, however, so if you're heading for the Fundy Isles, do your trip there.

Jolly Breeze (☎506-529-8116; www.jollybreeze.com; adult/child $53/38; ⊗tours 9am, 12:45pm, 4:30pm mid-Jun–Oct) Antique-style tall ship that sails around Passamaquoddy Bay on the lookout for seals and whales.

Quoddy Link Marine (☎506-529-2600; adult/child $55/35; ⊗tours 1-3 times daily late Jun-Oct) Serious whale-watchers should hop aboard this catamaran, staffed by trained marine biologists.

🛏 Sleeping

TOP CHOICE **Rossmount Inn**   INN $$
(☎506-529-3351; www.rossmountinn.com; 4599 Rte 127; r with breakfast $112-138; ⊗Apr-Dec; 🐾) Flags flap in the breeze in front of this stately yellow summer cottage, perched atop a manicured slope overlooking Passamaquoddy Bay. Inside, the 18 rooms have a stylish mix of antiques and modern decor, with hand-carved wooden furniture and snowy white linens. Many consider the hotel restaurant the town's best. Rossmount Inn is about 3km north of downtown St Andrews on 127.

Fairmont Algonquin Hotel   HOTEL $$$
(☎506-529-8823, 888-270-1189; www.fairmont.com/algonquin; 184 Adolphus St; r $159-459; ✳🐾🏊]) The doyenne of New Brunswick hotels, this Tudor-style 'Castle-by-the-Sea' has sat on a hill overlooking the town since 1889. With its elegant veranda, gardens, rooftop terrace, golf course, spa and tennis courts, it's worth a look even if you're

NEW BRUNSWICK WESTERN FUNDY SHORE

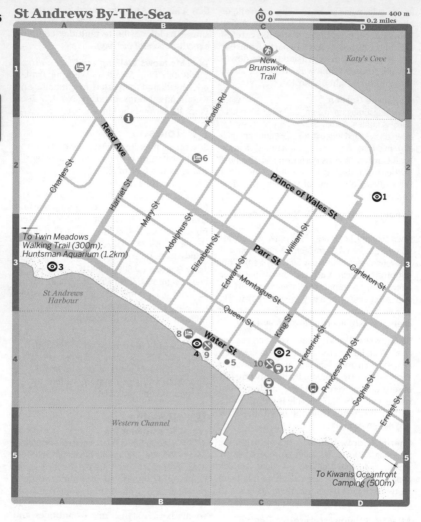

not spending the night. Note the doormen dressed in kilts. There are a couple of places for a drink, be it high tea or gin.

Picket Fence Motel   MOTEL **$**
(☎506-529-8985; www.picketfencenb.com; 102 Reed Ave; s/d $75/85; ❄🖘) Modern, neat-as-a-pin motel rooms within walking distance of the main drag. Ultrafriendly management to boot.

Treadwell Inn   B&B **$$$**
(☎506-529-1011, 888-529-1011; www.treadwellinn.com; 129 Water St; r incl breakfast $145-250; 🚽❄🖘) Big, handsome rooms in an 1820

ship chandler's house, some with private decks and ocean views.

Kiwanis Oceanfront Camping

        CAMPGROUND **$**
(☎877-393-7070; www.kiwanisoceanfrontcamping.com; 550 Water St; tent/RV sites $31/38; ☻early Apr–mid-Oct) At the far east end of town on Indian Point, this is mainly a gravel parking area for trailers, although some grassy spots do exist.

🍴 Eating

In keeping with its genteel atmosphere, St Andrews has embraced the custom of af-

St Andrews By-The-Sea

ternoon cream tea. For lunch and dinner, there are a range of nice choices, mostly clustered around Water St.

Rossmount Inn Restaurant
NEW CANADIAN **$$$**
(☑506-529-3351; www.rossmountinn.com; 4599 Rte 127; mains $16-28; ☺dinner) The Swiss chef-owner makes wonderful use of local bounty in this warm, art-filled dining room. The ever-changing menu might include foraged goose tongue greens and wild mushrooms, periwinkles (a small shellfish) and New Brunswick lobster, each playing a part in complex, exquisite dishes. Imagine, say, lobster with nasturtium flower dumplings and vanilla bisque, or foie gras with cocoa nibs and bee-balm-poached peach. Reservations crucial.

Clam Digger
SEAFOOD **$**
(4468 Hwy 127, Chamcook; mains $6-15; ☺lunch & dinner) Cars park three-deep outside this teeny red-and-white seafood shack, a summertime tradition in these parts. Order your clam platter or juicy, dripping cheeseburger, and claim one of the red-painted picnic tables. Don't forget an ice-cream cone! It's in Chamcook, about 9km north of St Andrews.

Garden Cafe
CAFE **$$**
(www.kingsbraegarden.com; 220 King St; lunch $9-15; cream tea $13, plus admission to Kings-

brae Garden; ☺10am-6pm mid-May–mid-Oct) At Kingsbrae Garden (p105), the terrace cafe serves high tea and sandwiches and salads for lunch with a glass of wine or local ale.

Gables
SEAFOOD **$$$**
(☑506-529-3440; 143 Water St; mains $10-20; ☺8am-11pm Jul & Aug, 11am-9pm Sep & Jun) Seafood and views of the ocean through a row of tall windows dominate this comfortable place. To enter, head down the alley onto a gardenlike patio on the water's edge.

Sweet Harvest Market
CAFE **$**
(182 Water St; all items under $11; ☺8am-5pm Mon-Sat, 9am-3pm Sun) Cheerful counter staff create wholesome soups, salads, sandwiches and sweets that are way beyond average standard, and chowder that is truly outstanding. The coffee's good, too.

▼ Drinking

Afternoon cocktails at the Fairmont Algonquin are a must. In the evenings, several downtown pubs serve up beer, music and camaraderie.

Shiretown Pub
PUB
(www.kennedyinn.ca; 218 Water St; ☺11am-2am daily) On the ground floor of the delightfully creaky Kennedy Inn, this old-school English pub draws a mixed-age crowd of partiers. Early afternoons mean sipping New Brunswick–brewed Picaroon's bitter on the porch, while late nights bring live music and raucous karaoke.

Red Herring Pub
PUB
(211 Water St; ☺noon-2am daily) A fun, slightly dive-y downtown bar with pool tables, live music and frosty Canadian beers.

❶ Information

The main **tourist office** (www.townofstandrews. ca; 46 Reed Ave; ☺8am-8pm Jul & Aug, 9am-5pm mid-May–Jun & Sep-early Oct) has free walking-tour brochures that include a map and brief description of 34 noteworthy places, and free internet access.

❶ Getting There & Around

Acadian Lines (www.acadianbus.com) buses depart from the **HMS Transportation** (www. hmstrans.com; 260 Water St) building once daily for Saint John ($28) and once daily for Bangor, Maine ($38). HMS Transportation also rents cars ($60 per day with 200 free kilometers; you must arrange your own collision insurance coverage).

FUNDY ISLES

The thinly populated, unspoiled Fundy Isles are ideal for a tranquil, nature-based escape. With grand scenery, colorful fishing wharves tucked into coves, supreme whale watching, uncluttered walking trails and steaming dishes of seafood, everyday stresses fade away and blood pressure eases. Each of the three main islands has a distinct personality. They offer a memorable, gradually absorbed peace. Out of the summer season, all are nearly devoid of visitors and most services are shut.

Deer Island

Deer Island, the closest of the three main Fundy Isles, is a modest fishing settlement with a lived-in look. The 16km-by-5km island has been inhabited since 1770, and 1000 people live here year-round. It's well forested and deer are still plentiful. Lobster

Fundy Isles

is the main catch and there are half a dozen wharves around the island.

Deer Island can be easily explored on a day trip. Narrow, winding roads run south down each side toward Campobello Island and the ferry (drive defensively).

Sights & Activities

At Lamberts Cove is a huge lobster pound used to hold live lobsters (it could well be the world's largest). Another massive pound squirms at Northern Harbor.

At the other end of the island is the 16-hectare Deer Island Point Park where Old Sow, the world's second-largest natural tidal whirlpool, is seen offshore a few hours before high tide. Whales pass occasionally.

At the end of Cranberry Head Rd is a deserted beach. Most land on the island is privately owned, so there are no hiking trails.

Tours

Whales usually arrive in mid-June and stay until October. Ask at any motel or restaurant about seasonal whale-watching tours.

Seascape Kayak Tours KAYAKING
(506-747-1884, 866-747-1884; www.seascapekayaktours.com; 40 NW Harbour Branch Rd, Richardson; half-/full-day trips $75/150) Guided paddling excursions around Deer Island and Passamaquoddy Bay. Multiday island-jumping camping trips also available.

Sleeping & Eating

Sunset Beach Cottage & Suites INN $$
(506-747-2972; www.cottageandsuites.com; 21 Cedar Grove Rd, Fairhaven; r from $80, cottage from $120; May-Oct) On a secluded cove, this two-story unit has five tidy, basic suites with carpet and unstylish plaid bedding. Upper floors have better views. The private barbecues and the pool and hot tub overlooking the bay are major draws. The furnished cottage is nice for families.

45th Parallel Motel & Restaurant
MOTEL, SEAFOOD $
(506-747-2222; www.45thparallel.ca; 941 Hwy 772, Fairhaven; mains $6-25; 7:30am-9pm Jul & Aug, 11am-7pm May, Jun & Sep, weekends only Oct-Apr) The specialty is seafood at this small, rustic, country classic with a homey feel and great food. Ask to see Herman, the monster lobster. The creaky-but-clean motel rooms are a fine bargain, too, with singles at $48 and doubles for $62.

Deer Island Point Park CAMPGROUND $
(☑506-747-2423; www.deerislandpointpark.com; 195 Deer Island Point Rd; tent sites $22; ☻Jun-Sep) Set up your tent on the high bluff and spend an evening watching the Old Sow whirlpool. The campground is directly above the Campobello ferry landing.

ⓘ Information

There's a summertime **tourist information kiosk** (www.deerisland.nb.ca; ☻daily in summer) at the ferry landing.

ⓘ Getting There & Away

A free government-run ferry (25 minutes) runs to Deer Island from Letete, which is 14.5km south of St George on Hwy 172 via Back Bay. The ferries run year-round every half-hour from 6am to 7pm, and hourly from 7pm to 10pm. Get in line early on a busy day.

East Coast Ferries (www.eastcoastferries. nb.ca; ☻end Jun–mid-Sep), a private company, links Deer Island Point to Eastport, Maine, an attractive seaside town. It leaves for Eastport every hour on the hour from 9am to 6pm; it costs $13 per car and driver, plus $3 for each additional passenger.

For service to Campobello, see p110.

Campobello Island

The atmosphere on Campobello is remarkably different from that on Deer Island. It's a gentler and more prosperous island, with straight roads and better facilities. The wealthy have long been enjoying Campobello as a summer retreat. Due to its accessibility and proximity to New England, it feels as much a part of the USA as of Canada, and most of the tourists here are Americans.

Like many moneyed families, the Roosevelts bought property in this peaceful coastal area at the end of the 1800s and it is for this that the island is best known. The southern half of Campobello is almost all park and a golf course occupies still more.

Come to the island prepared. There's just a single grocery store, two ATMs, a liquor store and a pharmacy, but no gas station – the 1200 residents of Campobello must cross the bridge to Lubec, Maine when they wish to fill their tanks. They generally use the same bridge to go elsewhere in New Brunswick, as the Deer Island ferry only runs in summer.

☉ Sights & Activities

Roosevelt Campobello International Park PARK
(www.fdr.net; Hwy 774; admission free; ☻sunrise-sunset year-round) The southernmost green area of Campobello Island is the 12-sq-km Roosevelt Campobello International Park. The park's biggest visitor attraction is the **Roosevelt Cottage** (tours late May-early Oct), the 34-room lodge where Franklin D Roosevelt grew up (between 1905 and 1921) and visited periodically throughout his time as US president (1933–45). The tomato-red Arts and Crafts–style structure is furnished with original Roosevelt furniture and artifacts. Adjacent **Hubbard House**, built in 1898, is also open to visitors. The grounds around all of these buildings are open all the time, and you can peek through the windows when the doors are closed.

The park is just 2.5km from the Lubec bridge, and from the Roosevelt mansion's front porch you can look directly across to Eastport, Maine. You'd hardly know you were in Canada.

Unlike the manicured museum area, most of the international park has been left in its natural state to preserve the flora and fauna that Roosevelt appreciated so much. A couple of gravel roads meander through it, leading to beaches and 7.5km of nature trails. It's a surprisingly wild, little-visited part of Campobello Island. Deer, moose and coyote call it home and seals can sometimes be seen offshore on the ledges near Lower Duck Pond, 6km from the visitors center. Look for eagles, ospreys and loons.

Herring Cove Provincial Park PARK
(admission free) Along the international park's northern boundary is Herring Cove Provincial Park. This park has another 10km of walking trails as well as a campground and a picnic area on an arching 1.5km beach. It makes a fine, picturesque place for lunch.

Wilson's Beach BEACH
Ten kilometers north of Roosevelt Park, Wilson's Beach has a large pier with fish for sale, and a sardine-processing plant with an adjacent store. There are various services and shops here in the island's biggest community.

East Quoddy Head Lighthouse LIGHTHOUSE
Four kilometers north of Wilson's Beach is East Quoddy Head Lighthouse. Whales browse offshore and many people sit along

the rocky shoreline with a pair of binoculars enjoying the sea breezes.

☞ Tours

Island Cruises   WHALE-WATCHING
(☎506-752-1107, 888-249-4400; www.bayof
fundywhales.com; 62 Harbour Head Rd, Wilson's
Beach; adult/child $49/39; ⊗Jul-Oct) Offers
2½-hour whale-watching cruises.

🛏 Sleeping & Eating

There are very few restaurants on Campobello, and the pickings across the bridge in Lubec, Maine aren't much better. For self-catering, there's a Valufoods supermarket in Welshpool.

Herring Cove Provincial Park   CAMPING $
(☎506-752-7010; www.tourismnewbrunswick.ca;
136 Herring Cove Rd; tent/RV sites $22/24; ⊗late
May-late Sep) This 76-site park on the east side of the island, 3km from the Deer Island ferry, has some nice secluded sites in a forest setting, plus there's a sandy beach and ample hiking.

Pollock Cove Cottages   COTTAGES $$
(☎506-752-2300; senewman@nbnet.nb.ca; 2455
Rte 774, Wilson's Beach; r $75-175; P@) Simple, clean one- and two-bedroom cottages with million-dollar views.

Owen House B&B   B&B $$
(☎506-752-2977; www.owenhouse.ca; 11 Welshpool St, Welshpool; d incl breakfast with shared
bathroom $107-112, with private bathroom $121-
210) A classic seaside vacation home of yesteryear, complete with antique spool beds made up with quilts, cozy reading nooks and lots of windows on the ocean.

Family Fisheries Restaurant   SEAFOOD $
(Hwy 774, Wilson's Beach; mains $5-23; ⊗8am-
7:30pm, later in summer) Part of a fresh-fish market, this ultracasual seafood shack specializes in fish and chips, lip-smacking chowders and lobster rolls.

❶ Information

For further information try the **Campobello Island Tourism website** (www.campobellois landtourism.com). There's a visitors center at Roosevelt Campobello International Park.

❶ Getting There & Away

East Coast Ferries (www.eastcoastferries.
nb.ca) connects Deer Island to Campobello Island, costing $16 per car and driver plus $3 per additional passenger. The ferry departs every half-hour between 9am and 7pm. It's a scenic 25-minute trip from Deer Island past numerous islands, arriving at Welshpool, halfway up the 16km-long island.

Grand Manan Island

Cue the Maritime fiddle music. As the ferry from the mainland rounds the northern tip of Grand Manan Island (population 2700), Swallowtail Lighthouse looms into view, poised atop a rocky, moss-covered cliff. Brightly painted fishing boats bob in the harbor. Up from the ferry dock, the tidy village of North Head spreads out along the shore; a scattering of clapboard houses and shops surrounded by well-tended flower gardens and tall, leafy trees.

Grand Manan is a peaceful, unspoiled place. There are no fast-food restaurants, no trendy coffeehouses or nightclubs, no traffic lights and no traffic. Just a ruggedly beautiful coastline of high cliffs and sandy coves interspersed with spruce forest and fields of long grass. Along the eastern shore and joined by a meandering coastal road sit a string of pretty and prosperous fishing villages. There is plenty of fresh sea air and that rare and precious commodity in the modern world: silence, broken only by the rhythmic ocean surf. Some people make it a day trip, but lingering is recommended.

The ferry disembarks at the village of North Head at the north end of the island. The main road, Rte 776, runs 28.5km down the length of the island along the eastern shore. It connects all of Grand Manan's settlements en route to the lighthouse perched atop a bluff at South Head. You can drive from end to end in about 45 minutes. The western side of Grand Manan is uninhabited and more or less impenetrable: a sheer rock wall rising out the sea, backed by dense forest and bog, broken only at Dark Harbour where a steep road drops down to the water's edge. A hiking trail provides access to this wilderness.

◉ Sights

Swallowtail Lighthouse   LIGHTHOUSE
Whitewashed Swallowtail Lighthouse (1860) is the island's signature vista, cleaving to a rocky promontory about 1km north of the ferry wharf. Access is via steep stairs and a slightly swaying suspension bridge. Since the light was automated in 1986, the site has been left to the elements. Nevertheless, the grassy bluff is a stupendous setting

for a picnic. It has a wraparound view of the horizon and seals raiding the heart-shaped fishing weirs (an ancient type of fishing trap made from wood posts) below.

All of the approximately 30 weirs dotting the waters around Grand Manan are named, some dating back to the 19th century. They bear labels such as 'Ruin,' 'Winner,' 'Outside Chance' and 'Spite,' evoking the heartbreak of relying on an indifferent sea for a living. A tear made by a marauding seal in a net can free an entire catch of herring in a single night.

Grand Manan Historical Museum MUSEUM
(www.grandmananmuseum.ca; 1141 Rte 776, Grand Harbour; adult/student & senior $5/3; ⊙9am-5:30pm Mon-Sat) This museum makes a good destination on a foggy day. Its diverse collection of local artifacts provides a quick primer on island history. Here you can see a display on shipwreck lore and the original kerosene lamp from nearby Gannet Rock lighthouse (1904). There is also a room stuffed with 200-plus taxidermied birds (including the now-extinct passenger pigeon). The museum hosts a number of evening lectures and community classes and activities.

Seal Cove HISTORICAL SITE
Seal Cove is the island's prettiest village. Much of its charm comes from the fishing boats, wharves and herring smoking sheds clustered around the tidal creek mouth. For a century, smoked herring was king on Grand Manan. A thousand men and women worked splitting, stringing and drying fish in 300 smokehouses up and down the island. The last smokehouse shut down in 1996. Although herrings are still big business around here, they're now processed at a modern cannery. Today, the sheds house an informal **Sardine Museum** (admission by donation; ⊙most days). On display are the world's largest sardine can (alleged) and an authentically smelly exhibit on the smoking process.

Roland's Sea Vegetables MARKET
(www.rolandsdulse.com; 174 Hill Rd; ⊙9am-6pm daily) Grand Manan is one of the few remaining producers of dulse, a type of seaweed that is used as a snack food or seasoning in Atlantic Canada and around the world. Dark Harbour, on the west side of the island, is said to produce the world's best. Dulse gatherers wade among the rocks at low tide to pick the seaweed, then lay it out on beds of rocks to dry just as they've been doing for hundreds of years. Buy some at this little roadside market, which sells various types of edible local seaweeds from nori to sea lettuce to Irish moss. Sandy, Roland's son, recommends sprinkling powdered dulse on fried eggs or baked fish.

🏃 Activities

Sea Watch Tours PUFFIN-WATCHING
(☎506-662-8552, 877-662-8552; www.seawatch tours.com; Seal Cove fisherman's wharf; adult/child $85/45; Mon-Sat late Jun–mid-Aug) Make the pilgrimage out to isolated Machias Seal Island to see the Atlantic puffins waddle and play on their home turf. Access is limited to 15 visitors a day, so reserve well in advance. Getting onto the island can be tricky, as the waves are high and the rocks slippery. Wear sturdy shoes.

Whales-n-Sails Adventures WHALE-WATCHING
(☎506-662-1999, 888-994-4044; www.whales-n -sails.com; North Head fisherman's wharf; adult/child $65/45; ⊙late Jun-late Sep) A marine biologist narrates these exhilarating whale-watching tours aboard the sailboat *Elsie Menota*. You'll often see puffins, razorbills, murre and other seabirds.

Hiking Trails HIKING
Seventy kilometers of hiking trails crisscross and circle the island. Grab the comprehensive guide to the *Heritage Trails and Footpaths on Grand Manan* ($5), available at most island shops. Stay well away from the cliff edges! Unstable, undercut ground can give way beneath your feet. For an easy hike, try the shoreline path from Long Pond to Red Point (1.6km, one-hour round-trip; suitable for children). In Whale Cove, the Hole-in-the-Wall is an often photographed natural arch jutting into the sea. It's a short hike from the parking area.

Adventure High KAYAKING
(☎506-662-3563; www.adventurehigh.com; 83 Rte 776, North Head; tours $45-975; ⊙daily May-Oct) This outfitter offers tours of the Grand Manan coastline ranging from two-hour sunset paddles to multiday Bay of Fundy adventures.

🛏 Sleeping

TOP CHOICE Inn at Whale Cove INN $$
(☎506-662-3181; www.whalecovecot tages.ca; Whistle Rd, North Head; s/d $120/130; ⊙May-Oct) 'Serving rusticators since 1910,' including writer Willa Cather, who wrote

WHOSE ROCK IS IT ANYWAY?

Though Canada and the US share nearly 9000km of border, they manage to play nicely most of the time. So nicely, in fact, that today the sole remaining land dispute between the two countries is over an uninhabited 8-hectare chunk of rock called Machias Seal Island, and a neighboring (and even smaller) island so undistinguished it's referred to only as 'North Rock.' Foggy, barren and treeless, Machias Seal Island is best known as a nesting site for Atlantic puffins. North Rock is best known for...being a rock. Yet the two tiny islands are part of a dispute that dates back to the 1783 Treaty of Paris, which attempted to draw a border between the newly formed USA and what was then called 'British North America.' Machias Seal Island, approximately equidistant between Maine and New Brunswick's Grand Manan Island, was not directly addressed in the treaty (imagine that!), and has remained part of a 'gray zone' ever since. Canada operates a lighthouse on the island and attempts to maintain it as a bird sanctuary, while some American puffin boat-tour operators challenge Canadian sovereignty. One, the late Captain Barna Nelson of Jonesport, Maine, would parade around the island once a year, waving an American flag. Canada and the US have had the opportunity to resolve the border dispute in international courts, but have declined.

several of her novels here in the 1920s and '30s. The main lodge (built in 1816) and half a dozen vine-covered and shingled cottages retain the charm of that earlier era. They are fitted with polished pine floors and stone fireplaces, antiques, chintz curtains and well-stocked bookshelves. Some have kitchens.

Shorecrest Lodge   INN $

(☎506-662-3216; www.shorecrestlodge.com; 100 Rte 776, Seal Cove; r $65-89; ☺May-Oct; 🛜🐾) Near the ferry landing, this big comfy farmhouse has 10 sunny rooms with quilts and antique furniture. A rec room has a TV and a toy train set for the kids. The Austrian owners cook up fresh seafood dinners (mains $18 to $28) and takeout lunches – nonguests can call ahead to order.

Anchorage Provincial Park   CAMPGROUND $

(☎506-662-7022; Rte 776 btwn Grand Harbour & Seal Cove; tent/RV sites $22/24; ☺mid-May–mid-Sep) Family-friendly camping in a large field surrounded by tall evergreens, located 16km from the ferry. There's a kitchen shelter for rainy days, a playground, laundry and long pebbly beach. Get down by the trees to block the wind. Anchorage adjoins some marshes, which comprise a migratory bird sanctuary, and there are several short hiking trails.

Hole-in-the-Wall Campground

                                       CAMPGROUND $
(☎506-662-3152, 866-662-4489; www.grand manancamping.com; 42 Old Airport Rd, North Head; tent sites $25; ☺early May-late Oct) These spectacular cliff-top campsites are secluded

among the rocks and trees, with fire pits, picnic tables and breathtaking views. Choose an inland site if you sleepwalk or suffer from vertigo. Showers and laundry facilities are available, as well as a couple of spotless, simple cabins, furnished with bunk beds and a microwave.

Compass Rose   B&B $$

(☎506-662-8570, off-season 613-471-1772; www.compassroseinn.com; 65 Rte 776, North Head; r incl breakfast $99-139; ☺1 Jun-30 Sep) Cheerful, comfortable guest rooms with a seashore motif and harbor views. Within walking distance of the ferry dock, it has one of the island's most atmospheric restaurants attached.

🍴 Eating

The never abundant options are nearly nonexistent in the off-season (from October to early June). That said, there is some fine eating on Grand Manan. Reservations are essential for dinner due to limited table space island-wide.

TOP CHOICE Inn at Whale Cove   NEW CANADIAN $$$

(☎506-662-3181; www.whalecovecot tages.ca; Whistle Rd, North Head; mains $22-28; ☺dinner late Jun–mid-Oct, weekends only May & Jun) Absolutely wonderful food in a relaxed country setting on the cove. The menu changes daily, but includes mouth-watering upscale meals such as Provençal-style rack of lamb, scallop ravioli and a to-die-for hazelnut crème caramel for dessert. Come early and have a cocktail by the fire in the cozy, old-fashioned parlor.

North Head Bakery   BAKERY $
(www.northheadbakery.ca; 199 Rte 776, North
Head; items $1-5; ⊘6:30am-5:30pm Tue-Sat May-
Oct) Scrumptious Danish pastries, fruit pies
and artisanal breads made with organic
flour make this cheerful red and white bakery the first stop for many folks just off the
ferry. Sit at the lunch counter with a coffee
and sandwich and watch the parade.

Wharf Restaurant   CANADIAN $
(1 Ferry Wharf Rd, North Head; mains $5-10;
⊘breakfast, lunch & dinner) In a hangarlike
corrugated metal building by the ferry
dock, this no-frills restaurant offers three
squares, plus ice cream, candy bars and
other snacks.

ⓘ Information

For further information on the area try the **tourist information office** (www.grandmanannb.
com; 130 Rte 776, North Head; ⊘8am-4pm
Mon-Fri, 9am-noon Sat).

ⓘ Getting There & Away

The only way to get on and off the island from
Blacks Harbour on the mainland to North Head
on Grand Manan is by the **government ferry**
(⌨506-662-3724; www.coastaltransport.
ca; ticket office at North Head ferry terminal).
Service (adult/child $10.50/5.40, automobiles
$32.55, bicycles $3.70, seven departures daily
in summer) is first-come, first-served at Blacks
Harbour; plan on arriving at least 45 minutes
before departure. In July and August especially
there can be long queues for vehicles to board,
but cyclists and pedestrians can walk on at any
time. No ticket is required for the trip over; book
and pay for your return trip in North Head the
day before you plan to leave for the mainland.
The crossing takes 1½ hours. Watch for harbor
porpoises and whales en route.

The ferry dock is within walking distance of
several hotels, restaurants, shops and tour
operators. To explore the whole of the island,
you should bring your own car, as there is no
rental company on Grand Manan. Alternatively,
Leighton Spicer (⌨506-662-4904) drives
the island's only taxi and meets most ferries,
and **Adventure High** (⌨506-662-3563; www.
adventurehigh.com; 83 Rte 776, North Head;
⊘8am-9pm) rents bicycles for $16$22/99 per
half-day/day/week.

New River Provincial Park

Just off Hwy 1, about 35km west of Saint
John on the way to St Stephen, this large
park has one of the best beaches along the
Fundy shore, a wide stretch of sand bor-
dered on one side by the rugged coastline
of Barnaby Head. During camping season
the park charges a $7 fee per vehicle for day
use, which includes parking at the beach
and Barnaby Head trailhead.

You can spend an enjoyable few hours
hiking Barnaby Head along a 6km network
of nature trails. The Chittick's Beach Trail
leads through coastal forest and past four
coves, where you can check the catch in a
herring weir or examine tidal pools for marine life. Extending from this loop is the
2.5km Barnaby Head Trail, which hugs the
shoreline most of the way and rises to the
edge of a cliff 15m above the Bay of Fundy.

The park's **campground** (⌨506-755-
4042; newriver@gnb.ca; 78 New River Beach Rd;
tent/RV sites $22/24.50; ⊘mid-May–early Oct)
is across the road from the beach and features 100 secluded sites, both rustic and
with hookups, in a wooded setting. Draw-
backs are the gravel emplacements and
traffic noise.

SAINT JOHN

POP 68,000
Saint John is the economic engine room
of the province, a gritty port city with a
dynamism missing from the demure capital. The setting is spectacular – a ring of
rocky bluffs, sheer cliffs, coves and peninsulas surrounding a deep natural harbor
where the mighty St John and Kennebeca-
sis Rivers empty into the Bay of Fundy. It
can take a bit of imagination to appreciate
this natural beauty, obscured as it is by the
smokestacks of a pulp mill, oil refinery and
garden-variety urban blight. The city is surrounded by an ugly scurf of industrial detritus and a tangle of concrete overpasses. But
those who push their way through all this
to the historic core are rewarded with beautifully preserved redbrick and sandstone
19th-century architecture and glimpses of
the sea down steep, narrow side streets.

Originally a French colony, the city was
incorporated by British Loyalists in 1785 to
become Canada's first legal city. Thousands
of Irish immigrants arrived during the potato famine of the mid-1800s and helped
build the city into a prosperous industrial
town, important particularly for its wooden
shipbuilding. Today, a large percentage of
the population works in heavy industry,

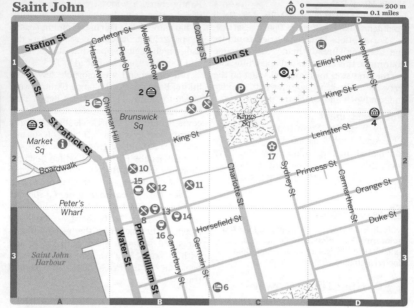

including pulp mills, refineries and the Moosehead Brewery.

Downtown (known as Uptown) Saint John sits on a square hilly peninsula between the mouth of the St John River and Courtenay Bay. Kings Sq marks the nucleus of town, and its pathways duplicate the pattern of the Union Jack.

West over the Harbour Bridge (50¢ toll) is Saint John West. Many of the street names in this section of the city are identical to those of Saint John proper, and to avoid confusion, they end in a west designation, such as Charlotte St W. Saint John West has the ferries to Digby, Nova Scotia.

◉ Sights

New Brunswick Museum   MUSEUM
(www.nbm-mnb.ca; 1 Market Sq; adult/student/family $6/3.25/13; ⊙9am-5pm Mon-Wed & Fri, to 9pm Thu, 10am-5pm Sat, noon-5pm Sun, closed Mon Nov–mid-May) This is a quality museum with a varied collection. There's a captivating section on marine wildlife with an outstanding section on whales including a life-sized specimen. There are also hands-on exhibits, models of old sailing ships and an original copy of *The Night Before Christmas* written in author Clement Clarke Moore's own hand, which was sent to his

godfather Jonathan Odell's family in New Brunswick.

Reversing Rapids   OVERLOOK
The Bay of Fundy tides and their effects (p121) are a predominant regional characteristic. The falls here are part of that and are one of the best-known sites in the province. However, 'reversing falls' is a bit of a misnomer. When the high Bay of Fundy tides rise, the current in the river reverses, causing the water to flow upstream. When the tides go down, the water flows in the normal way. Generally, it looks like rapids. **Reversing Rapids Visitors Centre** (200 Bridge Rd; ⊙8am-7pm mid-May–mid-Oct), next to the bridge over the falls, can supply a 'Reversing Falls Tide Table' brochure that explains where in the cycle you are.

Loyalist House   HISTORIC BUILDING
(120 Union St; adult/child/family $5/2/7; ⊙10am-5pm Mon-Fri May-Jun, daily Jul–mid-Sep) Dating from 1810, the Georgian-style Loyalist House is one of the city's oldest unchanged buildings. It's now a museum, depicting the Loyalist period, and contains some fine carpentry.

Loyalist Burial Ground   CEMETERY
This mood-inducing cemetery, with fading tombstones from as early as 1784, is just

off Kings Sq, in a park-style setting in the center of town.

Carleton Martello Tower HISTORICAL BUILDING
(454 Whipple St; adult/child $3.90/1.90; ⊙10am-5:30pm Jun-early Oct) Built during the War of 1812, this round stone fort features a restored barracks and other historical displays, but the real reason to go is the panoramic view over Saint John and the Bay of Fundy from the hilltop locale.

Saint John Jewish Historical Museum
MUSEUM
(91 Leinster St; admission by donation; ⊙10am-4pm Mon-Fri May-Oct, plus 1-4pm Sun Jul & Aug) This modest museum traces the history of Saint John's once-thriving Jewish community, whose members included Louis B Mayer of Metro-Goldwyn-Mayer (MGM) Hollywood fame.

🏃 Activities

Reversing Falls Jet Boat Rides BOAT TOUR
(☑506-634-8987; www.jetboatrides.com; Fallsview Ave; adult/child $37/27; ⊙Jun–mid-Oct) Offers two types of boat trips. One is a leisurely one-hour sightseeing tour to the Reversing Falls and around the harbor. The other is a 20-minute 'thrill ride' through the white water at Reversing Rapids. Count on getting soaked.

Irving Nature Park PARK
(admission free; ⊙8am-dusk early May-early Nov) For those with vehicles and an appreciation of nature, Irving Nature Park is a must for its rugged, unspoiled coastal topography. It's also a remarkable place for bird-watching, with hundreds of species

regularly reported. Seals may be seen on the rocks offshore. Seven trails of varying lengths lead around beaches, cliffs, woods, mudflats, marsh and rocks. Good footwear is recommended. It's well worth the 5km drive southwest from downtown to get here. Take Hwy 1 west from town and turn south at Exit 107, Bleury St. Then turn right on Sand Cove Rd and continue for 2km to the entrance.

Harbour Passage WALKING
Beginning on a boardwalk at Market Sq (behind the Hilton Hotel), Harbour Passage is a red-paved walk and cycle trail that leads around the harbor, up Bennett St and down Douglas Ave to the Reversing Falls bridge and lookout. Informative plaques line the route and it's about an hour's walk one-way. Much of the path is slated to be under construction through 2012. Ask ahead about its progress before setting out for a stroll.

Gibson Creek Canoeing CANOEING
(☑506-672-8964; www.gibsoncreek.ca; tours per day $65) Guided canoe trips through the numerous intertidal marshes and peaceful rivers close to the city.

☞ Tours

As a popular stop for cruise-ship travelers, Saint John has a surprisingly large range of tour options. Whale watching, unfortunately, is not an attraction in Saint John, save for the very occasional, very wayward minke.

Saint John Transit Commission BUS TOUR
(☑506-658-2855; www.saintjohntransit.com) Runs two-hour bus tours (adult/child

$20/5) around the city from mid-June to early October. Departures and tickets from Reversing Rapids Visitors Centre, Barbour's General Store at Market Sq and Rockwood Park Campground. Two tours daily.

Words, Walks & Workshops WALKING TOUR
(☎506-672-8601; walks free-$5; ☺7pm Tue Jun-Sep) For nearly 30 years David Goss, travel and outdoor columnist, has led themed walks throughout city and natural environments. The walks have so much flair that locals as well as visitors frequent the fun. Departure locations and hours vary; check with the visitors center.

Roy's Tour TAXI TOUR
(www.roystours.webs.com; tours per group per hr $50) Knowledgeable local Roy Flowers narrates personalized five- to six-hour taxi tours of the city and surrounds.

🛏 Sleeping

Saint John motels sit primarily along Manawagonish Rd, 7km west of uptown. There are also a couple of upscale chain hotels uptown.

TOP CHOICE **Mahogany Manor** B&B $$
(☎506-636-8000, 800-796-7755; www.sjnow.com/mm; 220 Germain St; d incl breakfast $95-110; P☺@☎) On the loveliest street in Saint John, this gay-friendly, antique-filled Victorian is a wonderful place to temporarily call home. Five rooms are a comfy mix of antiques and plush, modern bedding. The upbeat owners know more about the city than you'll absorb – even which meal to order at which restaurant!

Homeport B&B $$
(☎506-672-7255, 888-678-7678; www.homeport.nb.ca; 60 Douglas Ave; r with breakfast $95-175; P☺❄☎) Perched above once-grand Douglas Ave, this imposing Italianate-style B&B was once two separate mansions belonging to shipbuilder brothers. It has a boutique hotel vibe, with a stately parlor, a full bar and 10 sunny guest rooms. Try to snag one with a clawfoot tub. It's about 1km west of the uptown peninsula.

Chipman Hill Suites APARTMENTS $$
(☎506-693-1171; www.chipmanhill.com; 9 Chipman Hill; ste $49-299; P☺❄☎) What a great concept! Chipman has taken historic properties around downtown, renovated them into mini-apartments with kitchens while retaining all the character, and rents them

out by the day, week or month. Size and features determine price, but all are a steal.

Rockwood Park CAMPING $
(☎506-652-4050; www.rockwoodparkcampground.com; Lake Dr S; tent/RV sites $22/32; ☺mid-May–early Oct; ☎) A couple of kilometers north of the downtown area is huge Rockwood Park, with small lakes, a woodland crisscrossed by walking paths, and a campground in a small open field. Bus 6 to Mt Pleasant from Kings Sq goes within a few blocks Monday to Saturday.

University of New Brunswick Summer Residences RESIDENCE HALL $
(☎506-648-5755; www.unbsj.ca/hfs; off Sandy Point Rd near Rockwood Park; s/d $34/47, ste $72; ☎) From May to August, the University of New Brunswick's Saint John campus offers simple rooms and rather Spartan kitchenette suites in two residence halls. The university is 6km north of the city center (take bus 15 from Kings Sq).

🍴 Eating

TOP CHOICE **Old City Market** MARKET $
(www.sjcitymarket.ca; 47 Charlotte St; ☺7:30am-6pm Mon-Fri, to 5pm Sat) Wedged between North and South Market Sts, this sense-stunning food hall has been home to wheeling and dealing since 1876. The interior of the impressive brick building is packed with produce stalls, bakeries, fishmongers and butcher shops, as well as numerous counters selling a range of delectable prepared meals. Locals head to the lunch counter at Slocum and Ferris (lunch under $6). Look out for bags of dulse, a dried Atlantic seaweed that's eaten like potato chips in these parts.

Opera Bistro FUSION $$$
(☎506-642-2822; 60 Prince William St; mains $23-33; ☺lunch & dinner) One of Saint John's trendiest spots, this European-run bistro puts an international spin on Maritime ingredients. Ambitious dishes – local halibut with blueberry salsa, New Brunswick cheese soup with sesame croutons – can be a bit hit or miss, so try ordering small plates to share. Lunch means fancy sandwiches (including a Bay of Fundy lobster BLT!) and salads. The dining room, all exposed brick and minimalist plastic chairs, is stylish but unpretentious.

Thandi INDIAN $$$
(☎506-648-2377; www.singhdining.com; 33 Canterbury St; mains $17-33; ☺lunch & dinner

Mon-Fri, dinner Sat & Sun) A+ for atmosphere – exposed brick, heavy timbers and warm lighting with a stylish backlit bar downstairs and cozy fireplaces upstairs. The food is good, too – try Indian classics like lamb korma or shrimp vindaloo, or fusion specialties like tandoori strip loin or snapper with mango salsa.

Bourbon Quarter & Magnolia Cafe
CAJUN $$
(☎506-214-3618; Prince William St; mains $8-30; ☺dinner (Bourbon Quarter), breakfast & lunch (Magnolia Cafe) Cajun food in Canada? Hip young Saint Johners don't seem to find anything odd about the idea, flocking to eat fried oysters and muffuletta sandwiches at this recently opened pair of adjacent New Orleans–style restaurants. Bourbon Quarter is more formal, Magnolia a casual lunch spot. Both have live music.

Taco Pica
MEXICAN, GUATEMALAN $$
(96 Germain St; mains $10-17; ☺lunch & dinner Mon-Sat) A fusion of authentic Guatemalan and Mexican fare is served in this colorful cantina. An economical introduction to the cuisine is *pepian,* a simple but spicy beef stew that is as good as you'll find in any Guatemalan household.

Billy's Seafood Company
SEAFOOD $$$
(www.billysseafood.com; 49 Charlotte St; mains $16-30; ☺lunch & dinner) Since we are on the east coast after all...this popular casual restaurant at the top of the City Market does seafood with flair.

🍺 Drinking & Entertainment
There isn't much of a nightclub scene here, but pub culture and live music thrive in a handful of atmospheric waterfront bars in the uptown core. For weekly goings on, pick up the free *here* (www.herenb.canada east.com) entertainment paper, available around town.

Big Tide Brewing Company
BREWERY
(www.bigtidebrew.com; 47 Princess St; ☺Mon-Sat) This subterranean brewpub is a cozy spot for a pint (try the Confederation Cream Ale or the Whistlepig Stout), a plate of beer-steamed mussels or a friendly game of trivia.

Java Moose
CAFE
(www.javamoose.com; 84 Prince William St; ☎) Get your caffeine fix at this home-grown coffeehouse with a groovy North Woods vibe.

Infusion
CAFE
(www.infusiontearoom.ca; Old City Market; ☎) In the Old City Market, this warmly lit urbanchic cafe offers dozens of rare and exceptional teas, along with sandwiches and other light fare.

Happinez Wine Bar
BAR
(www.happinezwinebar.com; 42 Princess St; ☺Wed-Sat) For a quiet tipple in a sleek urban environment, duck into this intimate little wine bar.

O'Leary's
PUB
(www.olearyspub.com; 46 Princess St) Shoot the breeze with local barflies at this pleasantly divey downtown institution.

Imperial Theatre
THEATER
(☎506-674-4100; www.imperialtheatre.nb.ca; 24 Kings Sq S) Now restored to its original 1913 splendor, this is the city's premier venue for performances ranging from classical music to live theater.

ℹ Information
Main Post Office (41 Church Ave West, Postal Station B, E2M 4X6) In Saint John West, send general delivery mail here.

Police, Fire & Ambulance (☎911) For emergencies.

Saint John Library (1 Market Sq; ☺9am-5pm Mon & Sat, 10am-5pm Tue & Wed, 10am-9pm Thu & Fri) Free internet access.

Saint John Regional Hospital (☎506-648-6000; 400 University Ave; ☺24hr) Emergency room.

Visitor & Convention Bureau (☎506-658-2990, 888-364-4444; www.tourismsaintjohn. com; Market Sq; ☺9:30am-8pm mid-Jun–Aug, to 6pm Sep–mid-Jun) Knowledgeable, friendly staff. Ask for the self-guided walking-tour pamphlets.

ℹ Getting There & Away
Air The airport is east of town on Loch Lomond Rd toward St Martins. See p92 for flight information.

Boat There's a daily ferry service between Saint John and Digby, Nova Scotia (for more information, see p92).

Bus The **bus station** (300 Union St; ☺7:30am-9pm Mon-Fri, 8am-9pm Sat & Sun) is a five-minute walk from town. There are multiple daily Acadian Lines services to Fredericton ($29, 1½ hours) and Moncton ($33, two hours). There's a daily direct bus to Bangor, Maine ($55, 3½ hours), but you'll need to buy your ticket in person.

SCENIC DRIVE: KENNEBECASIS RIVER VALLEY

On a Saturday in summer, do what loads of Saint Johners do and take the **Gondola Point Ferry** (signposted off Hwy 1 at Exit 141; admission free) to the bucolic Kingston Peninsula, then follow Rte 845 east to the **Kingston Farmers' Market** (Rte 845, Kingston; ☻8am-1pm Sat). Sample the fresh fruits and vegetables and various ethnic foods on offer or stop for lunch at the restored 1810 **Carter House Tea Room** (874 Rte 845; cakes & tea $4-8; ☻9:30am-4:30pm Tue-Sat) which is, of course, haunted – by a ghost who likes to tidy up and rearrange the books. Leave the city folk behind, continuing on Rte 845 into the bustling community of Hampton, where you pick up Rte 121, which follows the north side of the Kennebecasis River through farm country and the villages of Norton and Apohaqui into Sussex (population 4200).

Sussex is a working farming community nestled in a green valley dotted with dairy farms. The old-fashioned main street could be a movie set for a heartwarming 1950s coming-of-age story (but please, enough with the outdoor murals!). The well-preserved railway station houses the tourist information center, a small museum devoted to the area's military regiment, and Sully's Ice Cream Parlour.

If you stick around until evening, keep up the 1950s time trip with a double-bill at the **Sussex Drive-In** (www.sussexdrivein.com; Rte 2; adult/child $10/6; ☻show time dusk Fri-Sun May-Sep). You can pitch your tent at the attached **Town & Country Campark** (tent/RV site $24/31). You can also bed down at **Jonah Place B&B** (☎506-433-6978, 866-448-8800; www.jonahplace.com; 977 Main St; r incl breakfast $89-195; ☻@☎).

The classy and cozy **Broadway Cafe** (☎506-433-5414; 73 Broad St; mains lunch $8, dinner $18-35; ☻10am-3pm Mon & Tue, 10am-9pm Wed-Sat) is the place to eat in town.

Gasthof Old Bavarian (☎506-433-4735; 1130 Knightville Rd; mains $10-24; ☻noon-10pm Fri-Sun Jun-Sep, noon-8pm the rest of the year, closed Jan) is the place for a truly memorable meal in the countryside. On a country road in a quiet valley settled by German and Dutch farmers, this place could have been transported – beer steins and all – from the Black Forest. The decor is Bavarian hunting lodge, with low timbered ceilings, heavy wooden furniture and cheerful blue and white checked tablecloths. The plates of schnitzel and sausages made on the family farm are plain beautiful, decorated with purple cabbage, fresh-picked greens and creamy white dumplings, with hearty flavors to match. Despite being more or less in the middle of nowhere, this place is always packed for dinner, so reservations are recommended. It's cash only.

Hang a left out of Gasthof's back onto the Knightville Rd, then left again onto Country View Rd at Anagance Ridge, then right onto Rte 890 into Petitcodiac. This stretch of road affords breathtaking vistas of rolling green countryside that'll make you want to sell up, move here and raise chickens. If you can work up an appetite, stroll through the greenhouses and have a healthy organic lunch or tea and cake at **Cornhill Nursery and Cedar Cafe** (www.cornhillnursery.com; 2700 Rte 890; mains $8-12; ☻lunch Jun-Sep). From Petitcodiac you can rejoin Hwy 1, heading east to Moncton or west back to Fundy Park and Saint John. The views of the valley from Hwy 1 between Hampton and Sussex are also lovely.

❶ Getting Around

To/From the Airport City bus 22 links the airport and Kings Sq. A taxi costs around $35.

Bus Saint John Transit (☎506-658-4700) charges $2.50. The most important route is the east–west bus service, which is either bus 1 or 2 eastbound to McAllister Dr and bus 3 or 4 westbound to Saint John West near the ferry terminal. It stops at Kings Sq in the city center.

Another frequent service is bus 15 or 16 to the university.

Car & Motorcycle Discount Car Rentals (☎506-633-4440; www.discountcar.com; 255 Rothesay Ave) is opposite the Park Plaza Motel. Avis, Budget, Hertz and National all have car-rental desks at the airport.

Parking meters in Saint John cost $1 an hour from 8am to 6pm weekdays only. You can park free at meters on weekends, holidays and in the evening.

Park free any time on back streets such as Leinster and Princess Sts, east of Kings Sq. The **city parking lot** (11 Sydney St) is free on weekends.

EASTERN FUNDY SHORE

Much of the rugged, unspoiled Eastern Fundy Shore from Saint John to Hopewell Cape remains essentially untouched. Indeed, hikers, cyclists, kayakers and all nature lovers will be enchanted by this marvelous coast, edged by dramatic cliffs and tides. It's not possible to drive directly along the coastline from St Martins to Fundy National Park; a detour inland by Sussex is necessary, unless you're prepared to hike.

St Martins

A 40km drive east of Saint John, St Martins is a winsome seaside hamlet surrounded by steep cliffs and flower-studded pastureland. Once a sleepy wooden shipbuilding center, it now draws hikers, bikers and scenic-drive takers to the 11km **Fundy Trail Parkway** (www.fundytrailparkway.com), which winds along a jaw-dropping stretch of coastline. In town, check out the impressive red sandstone sea caves of Mac's Beach, accessible by foot when the tide is low. The village's twin covered bridges are a popular photo op, so bring your camera.

River Bay Adventures (506-663-9530; www.riverbayadventures.com; tours from $45) runs two- to three-hour guided sea-kayaking trips to the caves and islands along the coast. It also rents kayaks (half-/full day $30/50).

Count on simple, homey rooms and a warm welcome at **Minihorse Farm B&B** (506-833-6240; www.stayatminihorsefarm.com; 280 West Quaco Rd; r incl breakfast $70; May-Oct; @), an old farmhouse by the sea. Yes, there are miniature horses to pet. Ask the owners how to get to the nearby hidden beach.

St Martin's Country Inn (506-833-4534, 800-566-5257; www.stmartinscountryinn.com; 303 Main St; r $95-165;), the towering mansion overlooking the bay, is the most deluxe place in town and also offers delectable meals in its delightful, caught-in-time dining room.

Right on Mac's Beach, the resort-style **Seaside Restaurant** (81 Mac's Beach; mains $8-13; lunch & dinner) serves fish and chips, scallops, chowder and more. Now you know you are on holiday.

Fundy National Park

This **national park** (www.pc.gc.ca/fundy; daily permit adult/child/family $7.80/3.90/19.60) is one of the country's most popular. Highlights are the world's highest tides, the

---

SCENIC DRIVE: FUNDY TRAIL PARKWAY

This magnificent **parkway** (www.fundytrailparkway.com; adult/child/family $4/2.50/13; 6am-8pm mid-May–Oct) traverses a rugged section of what has been called the only remaining coastal wilderness between Florida and Newfoundland. The 11km-long parkway to Big Salmon River put an end to the unspoiled wilderness part. There is now a lovely stretch of pavement with numerous viewpoints, picnic areas and parking lots. Eventually, it will extend to Fundy National Park. Nova Scotia is visible across the bay. There is also a separate 16km-long very steep and hilly hiking/biking trail.

On Saturday, Sunday and holidays a free hourly shuttle bus operates from noon to 6pm ferrying hikers up and down the trail between the parkway entrance and Big Salmon River. In the off-season, the main gate is closed, but you can park at the entrance and hike or pedal in.

At Big Salmon River is a superfluous **interpretive center** (8am-8pm mid-May–mid-Oct) with exhibits and a 10-minute video presentation. A suspension bridge leads to a vast wilderness hiking area beyond the end of the road. Hikers can make it from Big Salmon River to Goose River in Fundy National Park in three to five days. At last report, no permits or permissions were required to do so. But beyond Big Salmon River, be prepared for wilderness, rocky scree and even a rope ladder or two.

You can spend the night here too, at **Hearst Lodge** (r per person incl breakfast & dinner $99; mid-Jun–Sep), a cabin-on-steroids built by newspaper magnate J Randolph Hearst.

irregularly eroded sandstone cliffs and the wide beach at low tide that makes exploring the shore for small marine life and debris such a treat. The park features an extensive network of hiking trails.

✷ Activities

Cycling

Mountain biking is permitted on six trails: Goose River, Marven Lake, Black Hole, East Branch, Bennett Brook (partially open) and Maple Grove. Surprisingly, at last report there were no bicycle rentals in Fundy National Park or in nearby Alma. Contact the visitors centers to find current information on this.

Hiking

Fundy features 120km of walking trails where it's possible to enjoy anything from a short stroll to a three-day trek. Several trails require hikers to ford rivers, so be prepared.

The most popular backpacking route is the **Fundy Circuit**, a three-day trek of 45km through the heart of the park. Hikers generally spend their first night at Marven Lake and their second at Bruin Lake, returning via the Upper Salmon River. First, stop at the visitors center to reserve your wilderness campsites ($10 per night; call ahead for reservations).

Another overnight trek is the **Goose River Trail**. It joins the Fundy Trail, accessible by road from St Martins. This undeveloped three-day trek is one of the most difficult in the province. While you can cycle to Goose River, the trail beyond can only be done on foot.

Enjoyable day hikes in Fundy National Park include the **Coppermine Trail**, a 4.4km loop which goes to an old mine site; and the **Third Vault Falls Trail**, a challenging one-way hike of 3.7km to the park's tallest falls. In summer, rangers lead a variety of family-friendly educational programs, including night hikes.

Skiing

In the winter, 25km of park trails are groomed for fantastic cross-country skiing, with additional snowshoeing tracks through the forest.

Swimming

The ocean is pretty bracing here; luckily, there's a heated saltwater **swimming pool** (adult/child $3/1.50; ⊙11am-6:30pm late Jun-early Sep) not far from the park's southern entrance.

🛏 Sleeping

The park has three campgrounds and 13 wilderness sites. **Camping reservations** (☑877-737-3783; www.pccamping.ca; reservation fee $10.80) must be made at least three days in advance. The park entry fee is extra and is paid upon arrival.

With bathhouses and showers, **Chignecto North** (tent/RV sites $25/35) is a good pick for families. The 131-site **Headquarters Campground** (tent/RV sites $23/35) is near the visitors center. It's the only area open for winter camping. Along the coast, 8km southwest of the visitors center, is **Point Wolfe Campground** (tent sites $25) and its 181 sites with sea breezes and cooler temperatures. To reserve a backcountry site ($10), call either of the visitors centers.

Fundy Highlands Inn & Chalets

CABINS, MOTEL **$$**

(☑506-887-2930, 888-883-8639; www.fundyhighlandchalets.com; 8714 Hwy 114; motel $69-89, cabins $79-105; ⊙May-Oct) Simple but charming little cabins, all with decks, kitchenettes and superlative views, and a small, well-kept motel.

ⓘ Information

Headquarters Visitors Centre (☑506-887-6000; ⊙10am-6pm mid-Jun–early Sep, 9am-4pm early Sep–mid-Jun) At the south entrance.

Wolfe Lake Information Centre (☑506-432-6026; Hwy 114; ⊙10am-6pm late Jun-early Sep) North entrance.

Alma

The tiny village of Alma is a supply center for the park. It has accommodations, restaurants, a small gas station, grocery store, liquor outlet and laundry. Most facilities close in winter, when it becomes a ghost town. Down on the beach is a statue of Molly Kool, the first female sea captain on the continent.

Fresh Air Adventure (☑506-887-2249, 800-545-0020; www.freshairadventure.com; 16 Fundy View Dr; tours from $50; ⊙late May–mid-Sep) offers myriad kayaking tours in and around Fundy, from two-hour trips to multiday excursions.

For accommodations, **Parkland Village Inn** (☑506-887-2313; www.parklandvillageinn.

com; 8601 Hwy 114; r incl breakfast $95-140) is a busy 60-year-old inn with comfy, newly renovated rooms, some with killer Bay of Fundy views. At the inn, **Tides Restaurant** (8601 Hwy 114; mains $12-21; ☺lunch & dinner mid-May–Oct) is a beachy, fine-dining place that does top-rate seafood and excellent ribs. The casual take-out patio has fish and chips and cold beer.

Cape Enrage & Mary's Point

From Alma, old Rte 915 yields two sensational, yet relatively isolated, promontories high over the bay.

See the 150-year-old lighthouse at the windblown, suitably named **Cape Enrage** (www.capenrage.org; off Rte 905; adult/child $4/2.50; ☺9am-5pm late May–mid-Oct, to 8pm Jul & Aug). The cape was restored and is still expertly run by local high-school students and volunteer mentors from the area. On-site guides offer **climbing** (per 2hr $65) and **rappelling** (per 2hr $65) off the steep rock faces. Or you can simply wander the beach looking for fossils (low tide only!). When all that activity gets you hungry, head to the **Cape House Restaurant** (☺lunch & dinner) in the original lighthouse-keeper's house, where you can enjoy the dramatic view while dining on pan-seared local scallops, foraged fiddlehead ferns and lobster mac 'n' cheese.

At Mary's Point, 22km east, is the **Shepody Bay Shorebird Reserve** (Mary's Point Rd, off Hwy 915; admission free). From mid-July to mid-August hundreds of thousands of shorebirds, primarily sandpipers, gather here. Nature trails and boardwalks lead through the dikes and marsh. The interpretive center is open from late June to early September, but you can use the 6.5km of trails any time.

Hopewell Rocks

At Hopewell Cape, where the Petitcodiac River empties into Shepody Bay, are the **Hopewell Rocks** (www.thehopewellrocks.ca; off Hwy 114; adult/child/family $8.50/6.25/23, shuttle extra $2; ☺9am-5pm mid-May–mid-Oct, later hr in summer; ♿). The 'rocks' are bizarre sandstone erosion formations known as 'flowerpots,' rising several stories from the ocean floor. Some look like arches, others like massive stone mushrooms, still others like enormous ice-cream cones. Crowds come from all over the world to marvel at their Dr Seussian vibe, making the rocks New Brunswick's top attraction (and certainly one of its most crowded). Visitors can only walk amid the rocks at low tide, so check the tide tables at any tourist office or area hotel before setting out. At high tide, the rock towers are still visible from the trails that wind their way through the woods above.

The park features a large interpretive center with educational displays, two cafes, several picnic areas and a few kilometers of well-trafficked trails. Be warned though: in high season, the massive parking lot is choked with cars, while the staircases that lead down to the beaches suffer human traffic jams.

Another way to visit the rocks is by kayak. **Baymount Outdoor Adventures** (☎877-601-2660; www.baymountadventures.com; tours adult/child $59/49; ☺Jun-Sep) offers two-hour paddling tours.

There are several motels in the Hopewell Rocks vicinity, including the family-run **Hopewell Rocks Motel** (☎506-734-2975; www.hopewellrocksmotel.com; 4135 Hwy 114; r incl breakfast high season $105, low season $55; ☎♨), which features 39 tidy rooms and a heated pool, as well as an adjacent lobster restaurant.

THE TIDES OF FUNDY

The tides of the Bay of Fundy are the highest in the world. A Mi'kmaq legend explains the tide as the effect of a whale's thrashing tail sending the water forever sloshing back and forth. A more prosaic explanation is in the length, depth and gradual funnel shape of the bay itself.

The contrasts between the high and ebb tide are most pronounced at the eastern end of the bay and around the Minas Basin, with tides of between 10m and 15m twice daily, roughly 12½ hours apart. The highest tide ever recorded anywhere was 16.6m, which is the height of a four-story building, at Burncoat Head near Noel in Nova Scotia.

SOUTHEASTERN NEW BRUNSWICK

The southeastern corner of New Brunswick Province is a flat coastal plain sliced by tidal rivers and salt marshes. Moncton, known as 'Hub City,' is a major crossroads with two well-known attractions where nature appears to defy gravity. Southeast, toward Nova Scotia, are significant historical and birdlife attractions.

Moncton

POP 64,100

Moncton is like that fun-loving friend you'd love to introduce to the cute German exchange student you know. You think they'd have some good times together, but you're concerned your European friend might be put off by Moncton's dowdy strip-mall wardrobe and well, let's face it, unmemorable physical features. So, you emphasize the town's vivacious personality, appreciation of music and fine food and the fact that he speaks two languages.

Once a major wooden shipbuilding port, Moncton is now the fastest-growing city in the Maritimes with an economy built upon transportation and call centers drawn here by the bilingual workforce. It's a pleasant, suburban city, with a small redbrick downtown along the muddy banks of the Petitcodiac River. There are some decent restaurants, bars and a bustling Acadian farmers market. Apart from that, there is little to detain the visitor.

◉ Sights

TOP CHOICE **Dieppe Farmers' Market**   MARKET
(www.marchedieppemarket.com; cnr Acadie Ave & Gauvin Rd, Dieppe; ⊘7am-1pm Sat) A great place to get a taste of New Brunswick's vibrant Acadian culture is the weekly market. Stalls overflow with locally made cheeses, cottage wines and homemade preserves as well as Acadian dishes such as *tourtière* (a meat pie), *fricot à la poule* (home-style chicken stew) and rabbit pie. Nibble sweet pastries such as *plogues* and *guaffres* while browsing the craft stalls. To get there from downtown, head 2km east on Main St, which becomes Champlain, to Acadie Ave. Look for the yellow roof.

Magnetic Hill   AMUSEMENT PARK
(www.magnetichill.com; cnr Mountain Rd & Hwy 2; per car $5; ⊘8am-8pm mid-May–mid-Sep) At Magnetic Hill, incredibly one of Canada's best-known (though not best-loved) attractions, gravity appears to work in reverse. Start at the bottom of the hill in a car and you'll drift upward. You figure it out. After hours and in low season, it's free. It's a goofy novelty, worth the head-scratching laugh, but all the money-generating, spin-off hoopla now surrounding the hill is nothing special. Family-oriented attractions include a zoo, a faux village hawking ice cream and souvenirs, and a water park. Magnetic Hill is about 10km northwest of downtown, off Mountain Rd.

Tidal Bore Park   PARK
(east end of Main St; admission free; ⊘24hr) The tourist literature talks up the twice-daily return of the waters of the tidal Petitcodiac River. In theory, the tide comes in as one solid wave, unfurled like a carpet across the muddy riverbed in one dramatic gesture. As the tide advances up the narrowing bay it starts to build up on itself, pushed from behind by the powerful tides in the Bay of Fundy, the world's highest. The height of this oncoming rush can allegedly vary from just a few centimeters to about 1m. In reality, it usually just looks like a big mud seep, and well...boring.

Casino New Brunswick   CASINO
(www.casinonb.ca; 21 Casino Dr; ⊘slots 10am-3am daily) The province's first full-service casino, this 7300-sq-meter gambling palace brings a touch of Vegas to Moncton. Since opening in 2010, it's been packing in crowds with its 500 slot machines, poker room, numerous bars and buffets, and an entertainment venue boasting big-name performers such as the Beach Boys and Bill Cosby. The casino is about 9km northwest of the town center off Mountain Rd.

⛟ Tours

Roads to Sea   BUS TOUR
(☏506-850-7623; www.roadstosea.com; ⊘May-Oct) Roads to Sea offers 3½-hour bus tours ($85) to Hopewell Rocks, an eight-hour guided trip that takes in the Rocks, Fundy National Park, Cape Enrage and a few covered bridges and lighthouses ($160), as well as a 1½-hour tour of the Moncton sights ($45).

🛏 Sleeping

Reservations are a good idea as the city is a major conference destination and often

Moncton

Moncton

gets packed solid. Most of the chain hotels are clustered around Magnetic Hill.

Hotel St James BOUTIQUE HOTEL $$$
(☎888-782-1414; www.hotelstjames.ca; 14 Church St; r $159-289; ☎) On the 2nd floor of a 19th-century brick shop building, this downtown boutique hotel has 10 stylish, urban-chic guest rooms that wouldn't look a bit out of place in Montréal or New York. Swank design touches include mod tile walls, crisp white linens, huge flat-screen TVs and iPod docks. There's a popular pub and restaurant downstairs.

C'mon Inn HOSTEL $
(☎506-854-8155, 506-530-0905; moncton hostel@yahoo.ca; 47 Fleet St; dm $33, r $70; ☎) Moncton's only hostel is housed in a rambling Victorian two blocks from the bus station. The five-bunk dorm rooms and private singles and doubles with shared bathroom are nothing fancy, but they are clean and

comfortable. There is a kitchen for guest use and lots of space for lounging on the verandas.

Auberge au Bois Dormant Inn B&B **$$**
(☎506-855-6767, 866-856-6767; www.auberge -auboisdormant.com; 67 John St; s incl breakfast $85-110, d $95-120; ❹❄@🔊) A gracious Victorian renovated with crisp modern flair. Some rooms have private balconies. This gay-friendly establishment is on a quiet, tree-lined residential street and puts on a three-course breakfast spread.

🍴 Eating

Little Louis' FRENCH, NEW CANADIAN **$$$**
(☎506-855-2022; www.littlelouis.ca; 245 Collishaw St; mains $22-28; ☺dinner nightly) The odd location of this nouvelle-cuisine bistro – upstairs in a faceless industrial strip mall – only adds to its speakeasy vibe. The atmosphere is cozy, with low lights, white tablecloths and jazzy live music. Local foodies rave about dishes like foie gras with apple-wine jelly, or crispy steelhead trout with shiitake and saffron-vanilla butter. Whatever you do, always start with raw local oysters on the half shell with fresh horseradish. The wine list racks up awards on a regular basis.

Bogart's ITALIAN **$$$**
(www.bogartsmoncton.com; 589 Main St; mains $20-32; ☺lunch & dinner Mon-Fri, dinner Sat & Sun) A local favorite, this chic downtown joint specializes in modern, Italian-accented dishes like lobster risotto and rosemary-glazed beef tenderloin. The decor is a smart and snappy mix of tomato orange, dark chocolate-brown wood and fresh creamy linens. Settle in for live after-dinner music on summer weekends.

Calactus VEGETARIAN **$$**
(☎506-388-4833; 125 Church St; mains $10-13; ☺lunch & dinner daily) This is Shangri-la for vegetarians! Enjoy the freedom to order anything off the globally inspired menu, with everything from falafel plates, to tofu cheese pizza, to fried Indian pakoras. The natural wood, warm earth colors and burbling fountain create a soothing atmosphere.

Cafe Archibald FRENCH, CANADIAN **$$**
(221 Mountain Rd; mains $8-12; ☺lunch & dinner daily) At this stylish bistro, crepes are the house specialty, whipped up in the open stainless-steel kitchen and served at red-wood and zebra-print banquettes or on the inviting screened-in porch. Alternatively, feast on the wild mushroom and basil pizza with a leafy salad.

Pump House BREWERY **$$**
(www.pumphousebrewery.ca; 5 Orange Lane; mains $8-15; ☺lunch & dinner) The Pump is where the locals unwind and you can get a good burger, steak-based meal or wood-fired pizza. Of the brews made on the premises, the Muddy River stout is tasty, or try the beer sample tray.

🍷 Drinking & Entertainment

Moncton has a lively little rock and indie music scene, with several bars and clubs clustered around central Main St. The free *here* (www.herenb.canadaeast.com) has the rundown on the city's vibrant (read: raucous) nightlife. Try **Paramount Lounge** (www.paramountlounge.com; 800 Main St) for cheap, fun local punk and indie shows, or the **Old Cosmo** (700 Main St) for Molson-fueled partying on a packed outdoor patio. You can also sip a glass of wine during the interval at the grand **Capitol Theatre** (www. capitol.nb.ca; 811 Main St), a 1922 vaudeville house that has been restored to its original glory. It is the venue for concerts and live theater throughout the year. Get your morning Joe at downtown's **Café Cognito** (www.cafecognito.ca; 700 Main St; ☺7:30am-5:30pm Mon-Fri, 9am-4pm Sat), a tiny European-style cafe with exposed brick walls and a handful of bistro tables.

ℹ Information

Moncton Hospital (☎506-857-5111; 135 MacBeath Ave) Emergency room and trauma center.

Moncton Public Library (644 Main St; ☺9am-8:30pm Tue-Thu, 9am-5pm Fri & Sat) Free internet access.

St George St After Hours Medical Clinic (☎506-856-6122; 404 St George Blvd; ☺5:30-8pm Mon-Fri, noon-3pm Sat, Sun & holidays) No appointment is required to see a doctor. Adjacent to Jean Coutu Pharmacy.

Visitors Information Center (www.gomon cton.com; Bore Park, Main St E; ☺8:30am-6:30pm daily May-Sep, 9am-5pm Mon-Fri Oct-Apr)

ℹ Getting There & Away

Air Greater Moncton International Airport (www.gmia.ca) is about 6km east of Champlain Place Shopping Centre via Champlain St. For flight information see p92.

Bus Acadian Lines stops at the **bus station** (www.acadianbus.com; 92 Lester St), walking distance from downtown. Buses go multiple times a day to Fredericton ($44, two hours), Saint John ($33, two hours), Charlottetown, PEI ($40, three hours) and Halifax ($55, four hours).

Car & Motorcycle If you need wheels, Avis, Budget, Hertz and National all have car-rental desks at the airport, or try **Discount Car Rentals** (📞506-857-2323; www.discountcar.com; 1543 Mountain Rd).

Parking can be a hassle in Moncton: the parking meters ($1 per hour) and 'no parking' signs extend far out from downtown. The municipal parking lot at Moncton Market on Westmorland St charges $1/8 per hour/day and is free on Saturday, Sunday and evenings after 6pm. Highfield Sq Mall on Main St provides free parking for its clients, and who's to say you aren't one?

Train The **train station** (www.viarail.ca; 1240 Main St) is just west of central downtown. With VIA Rail, the *Ocean* goes through northern New Brunswick, including Miramichi and Campbellton, and into Québec, on its way to Montréal (from $129). The train to Halifax departs six days a week (from $38).

ℹ Getting Around

The airport is served by bus 20 Champlain from Champlain Pl nine times on weekdays. A taxi to the center of town costs about $15.

Codiac Transit (www.codiactranspo.ca) is the local bus system, with 40 wi-fi equipped buses going all over town. Single tickets are $2.

Sackville

Sackville is a small university town that's in the right place for a pit stop – for birds and people. The **Sackville Waterfowl Park**, across the road from the university off East Main St, is on a major bird migration route. Boardwalks with interpretive signs rise over portions of it. The **Wildlife Service** (17 Waterfowl Lane, off E Main St; admission free; ⊙8am-4pm Mon-Fri) has information and a wetlands display at one of the entrances. Enthusiasts should also see the **Tantramar Wetlands Centre** (www.weted.com; 223 Main St; admission free; ⊙8am-4pm Mon-Fri) with its walking trail and educational office, behind the high school.

Mel's Tea Room (17 Bridge St; mains $4-10; ⊙breakfast, lunch & dinner) has been operating in the center of town since 1919, now with the charm of a 1950s diner, including a jukebox and prices to match.

Fort Beauséjour National Historic Site

Right by the Nova Scotia border, this **national historic site** (www.pc.gc.ca/fortbeausejour; adult/child/family $3.90/1.90/9.50; ⊙interpretive center 9am-5pm Jun–mid-Oct) 1.5km west of the visitors center preserves the remains of a French fort built in 1751 to hold the British back. It didn't work. Later it was used as a stronghold during the American Revolution and the War of 1812. Only earthworks and stone foundations remain, but the view is excellent, vividly illustrating why these crossroads of the Maritimes were fortified by two empires.

To find out more, visit the **New Brunswick Visitor Centre** (📞506-364-4090; 158 Aulac Rd; ⊙9am-9pm Jul & Aug, 10am-6pm mid-May–early Oct), off Hwy 2 in Aulac, at the junction of roads leading to all three Maritime provinces.

NORTHUMBERLAND SHORE

New Brunswick's Northumberland Shore stretches from the Confederation Bridge to Kouchibouguac National Park, dotted with fishing villages and summer cottages. Shediac, on lobster lovers' itineraries, is a popular resort town in a strip of summer seaside and beach playgrounds. A good part of the population along this coast is French-speaking, and Bouctouche is an Acadian stronghold. Further north, Kouchibouguac National Park protects a large swath of scenic coastal ecosystems.

Cape Jourimain

Near the bridge to PEI, the **Cape Jourimain Nature Centre** (www.capejourimain.ca; Rte 16; admission free; ⊙8am-8pm May-Oct) sits in a 675-hectare national wildlife area that protects this undeveloped shoreline and its migratory birds. Seventeen kilometers of trails wind through salt marshes, dunes, woods and beach. A four-story lookout provides views of the surroundings and Confederation Bridge.

There's a **New Brunswick Visitor Centre** (Hwy 16; ⊙8am-9pm Jul & Aug, 9am-6pm mid-May–Jun & Sep-early Oct) by the bridge.

For information on crossing the Confederation Bridge into PEI, see p93.

Shediac

Shediac, a self-proclaimed lobster capital, is a busy summer beach town and home of the annual July lobster fest. The many white lights sprinkled around town all summer lend a festive air. Don't fail to have your picture taken with the 'World's Largest Lobster' sculpture – you can't miss it!

It seems that on any hot weekend that half the province is flaked out on the sand at Parlee Beach, turning the color of cooked lobster. South at Cap Pelé are vast stretches of more sandy shorelines. Terrific **Aboiteau Beach** is over 5km of unsupervised sand, while others have all amenities and lifeguards.

Shediac Bay Cruises (☑506-532-2175, 888-894-2002; www.lobstertales.ca; adult/child $59/39; Pointe-du-Chene wharf) has a unique concept. They take passengers out on the water, pull up lobster traps, then show you how to cook and eat 'em.

Shediac is ringed with shantytown-like RV campgrounds whose only appeal is their proximity to Parlee Beach. More upscale lodgings are found at **Maison Tait** (☑506-532-4233; www.maisontaithouse.com; 293 Main St; r incl breakfast $179-219; 🛜), a luxurious 1911 mansion with nine sun-drenched rooms, and **Auberge Gabriele Inn** (☑506-532-8007, 877-982-7222; www.aubergegabriele inn.com; 296 Main St; r $99-169; 🖰🌣), with simple, country-chic rooms above a popular restaurant.

Tops for dining out are **Paturel's Shore House** (☑506-532-4774; Rte 133; mains $18-23; 4-10pm) for fresh seafood, or the restaurant at Maison Tait for fine dining and romantic ambience. Grab fresh seafood and strawberry daiquiris at always-packed **Captain Dan's** (www.captaindans.ca; mains $10-24; lunch & dinner) at the busy Pointe-du-Chene wharf. After dinner, catch a flick at the wonderfully retro **Neptune Drive-In** (www.neptunedrivein.ca; 691 Main St).

Bouctouche

This small, surprisingly busy waterside town is an Acadian cultural focal point with several unique attractions. The **visitor information center** (Hwy 134; 9am-5pm Jun-Sep) at the town's south entrance features a boardwalk out over the salt marsh.

⊙ Sights & Activities

Le Pays de la Sagouine   HISTORICAL VILLAGE
(www.sagouine.com; 57 Acadie St; adult/child/family $16/10/37; 9:30am-5:30pm last week Jun-1st week Sep) Sitting on a small island in the Bouctouche River, this reconstructed Acadian village has daily programs in English and French. There are interactive cooking and craft demos, historical house tours and live music, as well as several cafes in which to sample old-fashioned Acadian cuisine. In July and August there's a supper theater at 7pm Monday to Saturday ($53).

Irving Eco Centre   PARK
(www.irvingecocentre.com; 1932 Hwy 475; admission free; interpretive center 10am-8pm Jul & Aug, shorter hr May, Jun, Sep & Oct) On the coast 9km northeast of Bouctouche, this nature center protects and makes accessible 'La Dune de Bouctouche,' a beautiful, long sandspit jutting into the strait. The interpretive center has displays on the flora and fauna, but the highlight is the boardwalk that snakes above the sea grass along the dunes for 2km. The peninsula itself is 12km long, taking four to six hours to hike over the loose sand and back. There are several naturalist-led tours daily. There's a 12km hiking/cycling trail through mixed forest to Bouctouche town, which begins at the Eco Centre parking lot ($4).

KC Irving (1899–1992), founder of the Irving empire, was from Bouctouche, and there's a large bronze statue of him in the town park.

Olivier Soapery   INDUSTRIAL MUSEUM
(www.oliviersoaps.com; 831 Rte 505, St-Anne-de-Kent) This old-fashioned soap factory advertizes its 'museum' on what seems like every highway in New Brunswick. It's really more

---

MR BIG

Kenneth Colin (KC) Irving was born in Bouctouche in 1899. From a modest beginning selling cars, he built up a business Goliath spanning oil refining, shipyards, mass media, transportation, pulp and paper, gas stations, convenience stores and more. The name is everywhere. At least 8% of the province's workforce is employed by an Irving endeavor. KC died in 1992, leaving his three sons to carry on the vast Irving Group empire.

of a store, with tons of luscious-smelling hand-molded soaps, but it does have regular talks on the soap-making process and a few interesting historical displays.

🛏 Sleeping & Eating

Le Vieux Presbytère   INN **$$**
(📞506-743-5568; www.vieuxpresbytere.nb.ca; 157 Chemin du Couvent; s $90-130; 📶) This former priest's residence was once a popular religious retreat for Acadians from across the province. The best rooms are in the older part of the building, with high molded ceilings and simple, sunny decor.

Chez les Maury   CAMPING **$**
(📞506-743-5347; fermemaury@hotmail.com; 2021 Rte 475; ⊗May-Oct) On the grounds of a family-run vineyard, this small basic campground has toilets, showers and a tiny private beach across the way.

Restaurant La Sagouine   ACADIAN **$**
(43 Blvd Irving; mains $8-17; ⊗breakfast, lunch & dinner) For a plate of fried clams or a traditional Acadian dinner, grab a seat on the outdoor patio here.

Kouchibouguac National Park

Beaches, lagoons and offshore sand dunes extend for 25km, inviting strolling, birdwatching and clam-digging. The park also encompasses hectares of forest and salt marshes, crisscrossed or skirted by biking paths, hiking trails and groomed cross-country ski tracks. Kouchibouguac (*koosh-e-boo-gwack*), a Mi'kmaq word meaning 'river of long tides,' also has populations of moose, deer and black bear. For more information try the **visitors center** (www.pc.gc.ca/kouchibouguac; 186 Hwy 117; park daily admission adult/child/family $7.80/3.90/19.60; ⊗9am-5pm mid-May–mid-Oct, 8am-8pm Jun-Sep).

🏃 Activities

Cycling & Kayaking

Kouchibouguac has 60km of bikeways – crushed gravel paths that wind through the heart of the park's backcountry. **Ryan's Rental Centre** (📞506-876-3733), near the South Kouchibouguac campground, rents out bicycles at $6/28 per hour/day and canoes/kayaks at $30/50 per day. From Ryan's it's possible to cycle a 23km loop and never be on the park road. The calm, shallow wa-

ter between the shore and the dunes, which run for 25km north and south, makes for a serene morning paddle.

Hiking

The park has 10 trails, mostly short and flat. The excellent **Bog Trail** (1.9km) is a boardwalk beyond the observation tower, and only the first few hundred meters are crushed gravel. The **Cedars Trail** (1.3km) is less used. The **Osprey Trail** (5.1km) is a loop trail through the forest. **Kelly's Beach Boardwalk** (600m one way) floats above the grass-covered dunes. When you reach the beach, turn right and hike 6km to the end of the dune. Take drinking water.

Swimming

For swimming, the lagoon area is shallow, warm and safe for children, while adults will find the deep water on the ocean side invigorating.

🛏 Sleeping & Eating

Kouchibouguac has two drive-in campgrounds and three primitive camping areas totaling 359 sites. The camping season is from mid-May to mid-October and the park is very busy throughout July and August, especially on weekends. **Camping reservations** (📞877-737-3783; www.pccamping.ca; reservation fee $10.80) are taken for 60% of the sites. Otherwise, get on the lengthy 'roll call' waiting list – it can take two or three days to get a site. The park entry fee is extra.

South Kouchibouguac (with electricity/without in summer $27/32) is the largest campground, 13km inside the park near the beaches in a large open field ringed by trees, with sites for tents and RVs, showers and a kitchen shelter. On the north side of Kouchibouguac River, **Cote-a-Fabien** (campsites $16, first-come first-served only) is the best choice for those seeking a bit of peace and privacy. There is water and vault toilets, but no showers. Some sites are on the shore, others nestled among the trees, with a dozen walk-in sites (100m; wheelbarrows provided for luggage) for those who want a car-free environment. The Osprey hiking trail starts from here.

The three primitive campgrounds have only vault toilets. **Sipu** and **Petit-Large** have water pumps. All cost $10 per person per night. Note that **Pointe-a-Maxime** is the most difficult to get to (access by water only), but this does not translate into remote seclusion. There is a constant stream of passing motorized boat traffic from the fishing wharf nearby.

There are a couple of snack bars and a restaurant in the park, but you should stock up on groceries in nearby St-Louis de Kent.

ℹ Getting There & Away

It is difficult to get to and around the park without a car or bicycle. The distance from the park gate to the campgrounds and beaches is at least 10km. The nearest bus stop is in Rexton, 16km south of the park, where the **Acadian Lines** (www.acadianbus.com; 126 Main St) bus stops at the Circle K gas station. There is one bus a day that heads south to Moncton ($16), and one a day heading north to Miramichi ($23).

MIRAMICHI AREA

In New Brunswick, the word Miramichi connotes both the city and the river, but even more: an intangible, captivating mystique. The spell the region casts emanates partially from the Acadian and Irish mix of folklore, legends, superstitions and tales of ghosts. It also seeps from the dense forests and wilderness of the area and from the character of the residents who wrestle a livelihood from these natural resources. The fabled river adds its serpentine cross-country course, crystal tributaries and world-renowned salmon fishing. The region produces some wonderful rootsy music and provides inspiration for artists including noted writer David Adams Richards, whose work skillfully mines the temper of the region.

Miramichi

The working-class river city of Miramichi is an amalgam of the towns of Chatham, Newcastle, Douglastown, Loggieville, Nelson and several others along a 12km stretch of the Miramichi River near its mouth. Miramichi, with its Irish background, is an English-speaking enclave in the middle of a predominantly French-speaking region. The **tourist information center** (199 King St; ⊘Jun-Sep) is downtown at Ritchie's Wharf, a down-at-heel riverfront boardwalk park.

Though surrounded by two paper mills and sawmills, central Newcastle is pleasant enough. In the central square is a statue to Lord Beaverbrook (1879–1964), one of the most powerful press barons in British history and a major benefactor of his home province. His ashes lie under the statue presented as a memorial to him by the town. Beaverbrook's boyhood home, **Beaverbrook House** (www.beaverbrookhouse .com; 518 King George Hwy; admission free; ⊘9am-5pm Mon-Fri, 10am-5pm Sat, 1-5pm Sun mid-Jun–Aug), built in 1879, now houses a museum.

Miramichi is a mill town, not a tourist center, but traditional folk-music enthusiasts might want to pay a visit for the **Irish Festival** (www.canadasirishfest.com; ⊘mid-Jul) and the **Miramichi Folksong Festival** (www. miramichifolksongfestival.com; ⊘early Aug), the oldest of its kind in North America.

🛏 Sleeping & Eating

Enclosure Campground　　　CAMPGROUND **$**
(☏506-622-8638, 800-363-1733; 8 Enclosure Rd; tent/RV sites $26/30; ⊘May-Oct) Southwest of Newcastle off Hwy 8 is another of Lord Beaverbrook's gifts, a former provincial park called The Enclosure. This riverside park includes a nice wooded area featuring spacious quasi-wilderness sites for tenters.

Governor's Mansion　　　B&B **$$**
(☏506-622-3036, 877-647-2642; www.gover norsmansion.ca; 62 St Patrick's St, Nelson; r incl breakfast $69-109) On the south side of the river overlooking Beaubears Island is the creaky-but-elegant Victorian Governor's Mansion (1860), onetime home of the first Irish lieutenant governor of the province.

Cunard　　　CHINESE **$$**
(www.cunardrestaurant.com; 32 Cunard St, Chatham; mains $9-15; ⊘lunch & dinner daily) Surprisingly decent Canadianized Chinese food like chicken chow mein and honey-garlic spareribs in a classic, lacquer-and-dragon-print dining room.

Saddler's Cafe　　　FUSION **$$**
(www.saddlerscafe.com; 1729 Water St, Chatham; mains $9-18; ⊘lunch & dinner Tue-Sat) Creative sandwiches and international-inspired mains like pineapple rice in a cute downtown storefront.

ℹ Getting There & Away

Acadian Lines (www.acadianbus.com; 201 Edward St) buses depart from the Best Value Inn. Daily buses leave for Fredericton ($38, 2½ hours), Saint John ($55, five hours) and Campbellton ($44, three hours).

The **VIA Rail station** (www.viarail.ca; 251 Station St at George St) is in Newcastle. Trains from Montréal and Halifax stop here.

Miramichi River Valley

The Miramichi is actually a complex web of rivers and tributaries draining much of central New Brunswick. The main branch, the 217km-long Southwest Miramichi River, flows from near Hartland through forest to Miramichi where it meets the other main fork, the Northwest Miramichi. For over a hundred years, the entire system has inspired reverent awe for its tranquil beauty and incredible Atlantic salmon flyfishing. Famous business tycoons, international politicians, sports and entertainment stars and Prince Charles have all wet lines here. Even Marilyn Monroe is said to have dipped her legs. The legendary fishery has had some ups and downs with overfishing, poaching and unknown causes (perhaps global warming) affecting stocks, but they now seem back at sustainable levels. The **tourist office** (www.doaktown.com) is in the Salmon Museum in Doaktown, the center of most valley activity.

◎ Sights

Atlantic Salmon Museum   MUSEUM
(www.atlanticsalmonmuseum.com; 263 Main St; adult/child $5/3; ⊙9am-5pm mid-Apr–mid-Oct) Learn about Historic Doaktown's storied fishing history and check out the salmon and trout aquarium at this lodgelike museum.

**Metepenagiag First Nation Heritage
Park**   HISTORICAL SITE
(☑506-836-6118, 800-570-1344; www.mete penagiag.com; 2202 Hwy 420, Redbank) On the Esk River, the new Metepenagiag First Nation Heritage Park is beginning to offer interpretive tours of Mi'kmaq culture and history on a 3000-year-old archaeological site. Call ahead for info.

☈ Activities

Sport fishing remains the main activity, but is tightly controlled for conservation. Licenses are required and all anglers must employ a registered guide. A three-day license for nonresidents is $60. All fish over 63cm must be released. Salmon fishing on the Miramichi is primarily hook and re

lease, to preserve the precious and endangered species. Most of the salmon served up in the province is, in fact, salmon farmed in the Bay of Fundy.

WW Doak & Sons (www.doak.com; 331 Main St) is one of Canada's best fly-fishing shops. It sells a staggering number of flies annually, some made on the premises. A wander through here will certainly get an angler pumped.

Despite the presence of the king of freshwaters, there are other pastimes to enjoy. The Miramichi Trail, a walking and cycling path along an abandoned rail line, is now partially complete, with 75km of the projected 200km useable. At McNamee, the pedestrian Priceville Suspension Bridge spans the river. It's a popular put-in spot for canoeists and kayakers spending half a day paddling downriver to Doaktown. Several outfitters in Doaktown and Blackville offer equipment rentals, shuttle services and guided trips for leisurely canoe, kayak or even tubing trips along the river. Try **Gaston Adventure Tours** (bgaston@nbnet. nb.ca; falls tour $180, canoe tours $60-180), with personalized fishing trips and falls tours run by Bev Gaston of the Atlantic Salmon Museum.

🛏 Sleeping & Eating

Beautiful rustic lodges and camps abound, many replicating the halcyon days of the 1930s and '40s. Check out www.miramichi rivertourism.com for links to more accommodations and fishing outfitters. Restaurants are few and far between – plan to pack in your own supplies.

O'Donnell's Cottages & Expeditions
    MOTEL, COTTAGES **$$**
(☑506-365-7636, 800-563-8724; www.odon nellscottages.com; 439 Storeytown Rd; r $99-169) Cozy log cabins on the riverbank, with a variety of outdoor activities on offer.

NORTHEASTERN NEW BRUNSWICK

The North Shore, as it is known to New Brunswickers, is the heartland of Acadian culture in the province. The region was settled 250 years ago by French farmers and fishers, starting from scratch again after the upheaval of the Expulsion, frequently intermarrying with the original Mi'kmaq inhabitants. The coastal road north from

GOT POTATOES? AN ACADIAN CUISINE PRIMER

Acadian cuisine is rib-sticking stuff, created out of necessity by settlers braving harsh winters in a new country – potatoes figure prominently. While young francophone New Brunswickers prefer their PFK (Poulet Frit Kentucky) these days, you can still find some old-fashioned Acadian cooking if you look, especially around Caraquet and the Acadian Peninsula. Here are some dishes to look out for:

» *Poutine râpée:* Baseball-sized grated potato dumplings filled with pork and drizzled with molasses or brown sugar. They're gelatinous, and a bit of an acquired taste.

» *Fricot à la poule:* Home-style chicken stew seasoned with summer savory.

» *Pets de soeur:* 'Nun's farts' in English – don't even ask. They're crunchy cinnamon rolls, better than their name might indicate.

» *Pâté à la rapure:* A grated potato and pork casserole known in English as 'Rappie pie.'

» *Tourtière:* A meat pie often served at Christmas.

» *Pot-en-pot:* Another type of meat pie, often served for Sunday supper.

» *Morue:* Cod. Served fried, salted, creamed, tossed with potatoes, or baked into pies.

» *Tire à la mélasse:* Molasses taffy. Maple taffy is also popular.

Miramichi, around the Acadian Peninsula and along Chaleurs Bay to Campbellton passes through small fishing settlements and peaceful ocean vistas. At Sugarloaf Provincial Park, the Appalachian Mountain Range comes down to the edge of the sea. Behind it, stretching hundreds of kilometers into the interior of the province, is a vast, trackless wilderness of rivers and dense forest, rarely explored.

Tracadie-Sheila

Unmasking a little known but gripping story, the **Historical Museum of Tracadie** (Rue du Couvent; adult/child $3/1; ⊘9am-6pm Mon-Fri, noon-6pm Sat & Sun in summer) focuses on the leprosy colony, based here from 1868 to as late as 1965. It's the only place in Canada providing details on a leprosarium. The nearby cemetery has the graves of 60 victims of Hansen's Disease (leprosy).

Caraquet

The oldest of the Acadian villages, Caraquet, was founded in 1757 by refugees from forcibly abandoned homesteads further south. It's now the quiet, working-class center of the peninsula's French community. Caraquet's colorful, bustling fishing port, off Blvd St Pierre Est, has an assortment of moored vessels splashing at the dock. East and west Blvd St Pierre are divided at Rue le Portage.

The **tourist office** (www.ville.caraquet.nb .ca; 51 Blvd St Pierre Est; ⊘9am-5pm mid-Jun–mid-Sep) and all of the local tour operators are found at the **Carrefour de la Mer** complex, with its Day Adventure Centre, restaurant and views down on the waterfront near the fishing harbor.

◎ Sights & Activities

Acadian Historic Village   HISTORIC PARK
(www.villagehistoriqueacadien.com; 14311 Hwy 11; adult/child/senior/family $16/11/14/38; ⊘10am-6pm early Jun-Sep) Acadian Historic Village, 15km west of Caraquet, is a major historic reconstruction set up like a village of old. Thirty-three original buildings relocated to the site and animators in period costumes reflect life from 1780 to 1880. A good three to four hours is required to see the site, and then you'll definitely want to eat. For that, there are old-fashioned sit-down Acadian meals at La Table des Ancêtres, the 1910 historical menu at the Château Albert dining room, and several snack bars. The village has a program for kids ($35), which provides them with a costume and seven hours of supervised historical activities.

✦ Festivals & Events

The largest annual Acadian cultural festival, **Festival Acadien** (www.festivalacadien.

ca), is held here the first two weeks of August. It draws 100,000 visitors; over 200 performers including singers, musicians, actors, dancers from Acadia and other French regions (some from overseas) entertain. Especially picturesque is the annual blessing of the fleet, when a flotilla of fishing vessels cruises the harbor with ribbons and flags streaming from their rigging. The culminating Tintamarre Parade is a real blowout.

🛏 Sleeping & Eating

TOP CHOICE **Hotel Paulin** HOTEL $$
(📞506-727-9981, 866-727-9981; www. hotelpaulin.com; 143 Blvd St Pierre W; r incl breakfast $128, incl breakfast & 4-course dinner for 2 from $195) Scrimp elsewhere and splurge on a night at the exquisite Hotel Paulin. This vintage seaside hotel overlooking the bay was built in 1891 and has been run by the Paulin family since 1907. The rooms are sunny and polished, done up in crisp white linens, lace and antiques. If you are staying elsewhere, make reservations for dinner; the hotel has earned a reputation for fine cuisine. An example: fiddlehead (a green, immature fern) soup followed by Acadian chicken fricot with herb dumplings (table d'hôte $45).

Château Albert INN $$$
(www.villagehistoriqueacadien.com/chateauan glais.htm; Acadian Historic Village; r incl dinner & theater package for 2 $257) For complete immersion in the Acadian Historic Village, spend the night in early-20th-century style – no TV, no phone, but a charming, quiet room restored to its original 1909 splendor (with a modern bath). The original Albert stood on the main street in Caraquet until it was destroyed by fire in 1955. Packages are available including dinner in the period dining room downstairs and a tool around in a model T Ford.

Maison Touristique Dugas
INN, CAMPGROUND $
(📞506-727-3195; www.maisontouristiquedugas. ca; 683 Blvd St Pierre W; campsites $20-28, r with shared bathroom $55, d with private bathroom & cooking facilities $70, cabins $70-100) A few kilometers west of Caraquet, five generations of the friendly Dugas family have run this rambling, something-for-everyone property. The homey, antique-filled 1926 house has 11 rooms with shared bathrooms. There are five clean, cozy cabins with private bathrooms and cooking facilities in the backyard, a small field for RVs beyond that, and a quiet, tree-shaded campground for tenters.

Le Caraquette CANADIAN $$
(89 Blvd St-Pierre; mains $8-14) Overlooking the harbor, this casual family-run restaurant serves Maritime standards like fried clams and mayonnaise shrimp salad along with French-Canadian specialties like *poutine* (French fries topped with gravy and cheese) and smoked meat sandwiches.

ℹ Getting There & Away
Public transportation around this part of the province is very limited as Acadian Lines buses don't pass this way. Local residents wishing to connect with the bus or train in Miramichi or Bathurst use a couple of van shuttles. Ask for details at the tourist office.

Campbellton
Campbellton is a pleasant but unremarkable mill town on the Québec border. There are really only two reasons to come here: transiting to or from Québec; or to hike, ski and camp at Sugarloaf Provincial Park. The

---

SCENIC DRIVE: THE ACADIAN PENINSULA

Take a run out to the very northeastern tip of the province – a chain of low, flat islands pointing across the Gulf of St Lawrence to Labrador. Rte 113 cuts across salt marsh and scrub arriving first in Shippagan, home of the province's largest fishing fleet, where crab is king. Visit the sea creatures at the **Aquarium & Marine Centre** (www. aquariumnb.ca; 100 Aquarium St; adult/child $8/5; ⊙10am-6pm late May-Sep). Kids will love the touch tanks full of sea creatures, and the seals (fed at 11am and 4pm). Hop the bridge to **Lamèque**, a tidy fishing village that has hosted the **Lamèque International Baroque Festival** (📞506-344-5846, 800-320-2276; www.festivalbaroque.com; ⊙last week Jul) for over 30 years. Note the red, white and blue Acadian flags flying from nearly every porch. Rte 113 continues north to Miscou Island. Stop to walk the boardwalk trail over a cranberry bog before the road dead-ends at the lighthouse.

lengthy Restigouche River, which winds through northern New Brunswick and then forms the border with Québec, empties to the sea here. The Bay of Chaleur is on one side and dramatic rolling hills surround the town on the remaining sides. Across the border is Matapédia and Hwy 132 leading to Mont Joli, 148km into Québec.

Dominated by Sugarloaf Mountain, which rises nearly 400m above sea level and looks vaguely like one of its other namesakes in Rio, **Sugarloaf Provincial Park** (www.sugarloafpark.ca; 596 Val d'Amours Rd; admission free) is off Hwy 11 at Exit 415. From the base, it's just a half-hour walk to the top – well worth the extensive views of the town and part of the Restigouche River. Another trail leads around the bottom of the hill.

The last naval engagement of the Seven Years' War was fought in the waters off this coast in 1760. The Battle of Restigouche marked the conclusion of the long struggle for Canada by Britain and France. The helpful provincial **tourist office** (☎506-789-2367; 56 Salmon Blvd; ☺10am-6pm mid-May–Jun & Sep-early Oct, 8am-9pm Jul & Aug) is next to City Centre Mall.

Sugarloaf Provincial Park (☎506-789-2366; www.sugarloafpark.ca; 596 Val d'Amours Rd; tent/RV sites $22/29; ☺mid-May–early Oct) has 76 campsites in a pleasant wooded setting 4km from downtown Campbellton. You can also crash comfortably at **Campbellton Lighthouse Hostel** (☎506-759-7044; campbellton@hihostels.ca; 1 Ritchie St; dm $21; ☺mid-Jun–Aug; 🛜). This clean, recently renovated hostel is in a converted lighthouse by the Restigouche River, near the Acadian bus stop and Campbellton's 8.5m **salmon sculpture**. Alternatively, **Maison McKenzie House B&B** (☎506-753-3133; www.bbcanada.com/4384.html; 31 Andrew St; r incl breakfast with shared bathroom $75-100; P☺🛜) is a 1910 house handy to downtown. For $60, they'll rent you a kayak and drop you off upriver.

ℹ Getting There & Away

Acadian Lines (www.acadianbus.com; 46 Water St) stops at the Pik-Quik convenience store, near Prince William St. The bus departs daily for Fredericton ($71, six hours) and Moncton ($65, six hours). Twice a day (once in the morning and once in the afternoon), an **Orléans Express** (www.orleansexpress.com) bus leaves from the Pik-Quick for Gaspé ($38, six hours) and Québec City ($89, seven hours).

The **VIA Rail station** (www.viarail.ca; 99c Roseberry St) is conveniently central. There's one train daily, except Wednesday, going south to Moncton ($50, four hours) and Halifax ($64, 10 hours), and one daily, except Tuesday, heading the other way to Montréal ($146, 12 hours).

Prince Edward Island

Best Places to Eat

» Lot 30 (p141)
» Lobster Suppers at town halls and churches around the province
» Shipwright's Café (p156)
» Ship to Shore (p156)
» The Pearl (p155)

Best Places to Stay

» Fairholm Inn (p140)
» Barachois Inn (p152)
» Great George (p140)
» Maplehurst Properties (p145)
» Willow Green Farm B&B (p157)

Why Go?

Move over Mounties, Canada's got a spunky, red-headed feminine side. In Prince Edward Island (PEI) little Anne Shirley, Lucy Maud Montgomery's immortal heroine of the *Anne of Green Gables* series, is larger than her fictional britches. Ironically, the island itself is a red-head – from tip to tip sienna-colored soil peeks out from under potato plants, and the shores are lined with rose and golden sand. Meanwhile the Green Gables-esque landscape is a pastoral green patchwork of rolling fields, tidy gabled farmhouses and seaside villages.

Yet despite the pervasive splendor of the province, the first thing most visitors notice, and fall in love with, is PEI's charm and relaxed atmosphere. The 'Gentle Island' really lives up to its nickname and the least authentic things you'll find here are the orange nylon braids of little girls in tourist spots dressed up as 'Anne.'

When to Go
Charlottetown

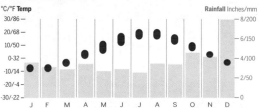

June Enjoy the spring calm before the crowds hit; the rolling hillsides are abloom with wildflowers.

July & August The entire island is in festival mode with live music and lobster suppers nightly.

September Traditional music and food mark Charlottetown's PEI International Shellfish Festival

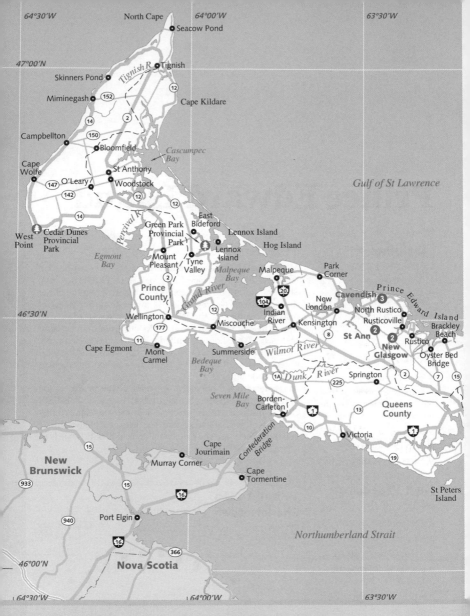

Highlights

① Wiggle your feet and hear a squeak at the 'singing sands' of **Basin Head Provincial Park** (boxed text, p146)

② Eat your fill of fresh island lobster with all the fixings in **New Glasgow** (p152) or **St Ann** (p153)

③ Be taken away into the pages of *Anne of Green Gables* while visiting the House of Green Gables in **Cavendish** (p154)

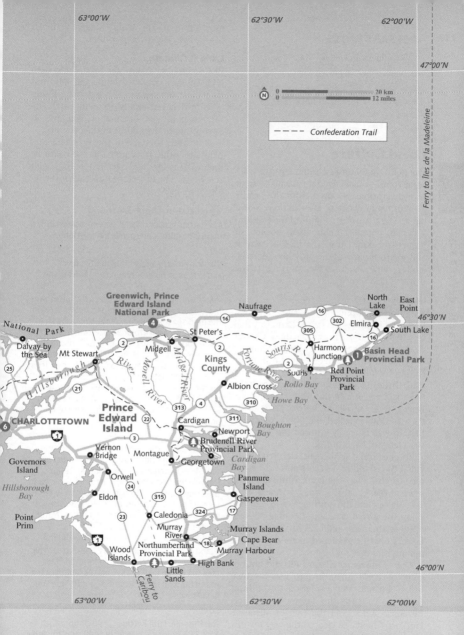

4 Follow the floating boardwalk across the salt marsh and over the sand dunes onto the empty beach at **Greenwich** (boxed text, p148)

5 Work up an appetite peddling through the countryside on the **Confederation Trail** (boxed text, p143)

6 Kick up your heels at the Benevolent Irish Society's weekly ceilidh in **Charlottetown** (p137)

PEI FAST FACTS

» Population: 141,000

» Area: 5700 sq km

» Capital: Charlottetown

» Quirky Fact: Kilos of potatoes produced per year: 1.3 billion

Local Culture

The defining feature of island culture is its rural roots – most islanders are just one or two generations removed from the family farm or fishing boat, or are still there working it. There are descendants of the original Mi'kmaq population and small pockets of French-speaking Acadians in the eastern and western parts of the province. Most islanders, however, trace their heritage to the British Isles.

History

Its Aboriginal inhabitants, the Mi'kmaq, knew the island as Abegeit – 'Land Cradled on the Waves.' Although Jacques Cartier of France first recorded PEI's existence in 1534, settlement didn't begin until 1603. Initially small, the French colony grew only after Britain's expulsion of the Acadians from Nova Scotia in the 1750s. In 1758 the British took the island, known then as Île St Jean, and expelled the 3000 Acadians. Britain was officially granted the island in the Treaty of Paris of 1763.

To encourage settlement, the British divided the island into 67 lots and held a lottery to give away the land. Unfortunately, most of the 'Great Giveaway' winners were speculators and did nothing to settle or develop the island. The questionable actions of these absentee landlords hindered population growth and caused incredible unrest among islanders.

One of the major reasons PEI did not become part of Canada in 1867 was because union did not offer a solution to the land problem. In 1873 the Compulsory Land Purchase Act forced the sale of absentee landlords' land and cleared the way for PEI to join Canada later that year. But foreign land ownership is still a sensitive issue in the province. The population has remained stable, at around 140,000, since the 1930s.

In 1997, after much debate, PEI was linked to New Brunswick and the mainland by the Confederation Bridge – at almost 13km, it's the world's longest artificial bridge over ice-covered waters.

Land & Climate

PEI stretches 224km tip to tip; it's 6km wide at its narrowest point, and 64km at its widest. The island is a low-lying hump of iron-rich red sandstone and earth. Its highest point rises 152m above sea level, at Springton, in the middle of the province.

July and August are the warmest and driest months. In winter the snow can be meters deep, but it rarely hinders the major roadways. The last of the white stuff is usually gone by May.

ℹ Getting There & Around

Apart from a couple of shuttle services (see p137), there is no intra-island public transportation.

AIR

Charlottetown's airport is 8km from town and serves all flights entering and leaving the province.

Air Canada has daily flights to Charlottetown from Halifax and Toronto, and from Montréal in the high season (June to September). WestJet offers direct flights to Charlottetown from Toronto and Montréal. From June to September, Northwestern Airlines and Delta Airlines each run one daily direct flight to Charlottetown from Detroit and Boston, respectively. See p261 for these airlines' contact details. **Sunwing** (☎877-786-9464; www.flysunwing.com) flies to the island from Toronto during the summer only.

BICYCLE

Cyclists and pedestrians are banned from the Confederation Bridge (see p137) and must use the 24-hour, demand-driven shuttle service (bicycle/pedestrian $8/4). On the PEI side, go to the bridge operations building at Gateway Village in Borden-Carleton; on the New Brunswick side, the pickup is at the Cape Jourimain Nature Centre at exit 51 on Rte 16 (p125).

While your easiest option to get around the island is by car, bicycle is also a fine choice. The flat and well-maintained Confederation Trail (see the boxed text, p143) runs the length of the island through some beautiful countryside and small towns.

BOAT

Northumberland Ferries (☎902-566-3838, 888-249-7245; www.peiferry.com) runs the ferry service that links PEI's Wood Islands to Caribou, Nova Scotia, from May to December. There are up to nine daily sailings in each direction during the summer, and five in the fall and spring (car/pedestrian/motorcycle $69/18/45). Note that vehicle fees include all passengers for the

1¼-hour trip. You only pay as you're leaving PEI; the trip over from Nova Scotia is free. The ferry operates on a first-come, first-served basis.

BUS

Acadian Coach Lines (☎800-567-5151; www. acadianbus.com; 156 Belvedere Ave, Charlottetown) has service to Charlottetown three times per day from Moncton, New Brunswick ($38 one way, three hours), with stops at Borden-Carleton and Summerside en route. There is one bus per day to Halifax ($64 one way, 5½ hours), with a transfer in Amherst, Nova Scotia.

Advanced Shuttle (☎877-886-3322; Nassau St, University Ave, Charlottetown) is a convenient service from Charlottetown or Summerside to Halifax or any point along the way (adult/ student $52/47). The van has a bicycle carrier.

Beach Shuttle (☎902-566-5259; www. princeedwardtours.com; Founders' Hall, 6 Prince St, Charlottetown), running between Charlottetown and Cavendish several times per day (one way $15, same-day return $25, June to September), also makes a daily run from Charlottetown to the evening stage show in Summerside.

East Connection (☎902-892-6760, 902-393-5132) departs Charlottetown daily around noon for Souris, arriving at 1pm in time for the 2pm ferry. The shuttle van leaves Souris at 1:30pm, arriving at Charlottetown an hour later.

CAR & MOTORCYCLE

The **Confederation Bridge** (☎902-437-7300, 888-437-6565; www.confederationbridge.com; car/motorcycle $43/17; ☺24hr) is the quickest way to get to PEI from New Brunswick and East Central Nova Scotia. Unfortunately, the 1.1m-high guardrails rob you of any hoped-for view. The toll is only charged on departure from PEI, and includes all passengers.

If you're planning to travel one way on the bridge and the other by ferry, it's cheaper to take the ferry to PEI and return via the bridge.

See p143 for car rental information.

CHARLOTTETOWN

POP 38,114

It's been said that Charlottetown is too small to be grand and too big to be quaint. In fact, PEI's capital is just about the per-fect size with a collection of stylish eateries and a lively cultural scene. Couple this with quiet streets for strolling, abundant greenery and a well-preserved historical core, and you have plenty of small-town appeal.

History

Charlottetown is named after the exotic consort of King George III. Her African roots, dating back to Margarita de Castro Y Sousa and the Portuguese royal house, are as legendary as they are controversial.

While many believe the city's splendid harbor was the reason Charlottetown became the capital, the reality was less glamorous. In 1765 the surveyor-general decided on Charlottetown because he thought it prudent to bestow the poor side of the island with some privileges. Thanks to the celebrated 1864 conference, however, Charlottetown is etched in Canadian history as the country's birthplace.

⊙ Sights

All of the major sights are within the confines of Old Charlottetown, which makes wandering between them as rewarding as wandering through them.

Province House National Historic Site

HISTORICAL SITE

(☎902-566-7626; 165 Richmond St; admission $3.40; ☺8:30am-5pm) Charlottetown's centerpiece is the imposing, yet welcoming, neoclassical Province House. The symmetry of design is carried throughout, including two brilliant skylights reaching up through the massive sandstone structure. It was here in 1864, within the Confederation Chamber, that 23 representatives of Britain's North American colonies first discussed the creation of Canada. Along with being the 'birthplace of Canada,' the site is home to Canada's second-oldest active legislature.

Several rooms have been restored, and in July and August you may find yourself face to face with Canada's first prime minister: actors in period garb wander the halls and regularly coalesce to perform reenactments of the famous conference. Enjoy the *Great Dream*, a 17-minute film about the monumental 1864 conference.

Founders' Hall

MUSEUM

(☎902-368-1864, 800-955-1864; 6 Prince St; adult/child $7/3.75; ☺8:30am-8pm) Opened in 2001, this high-tech multimedia exhibit, housed in an old train station, deluges your

Charlottetown

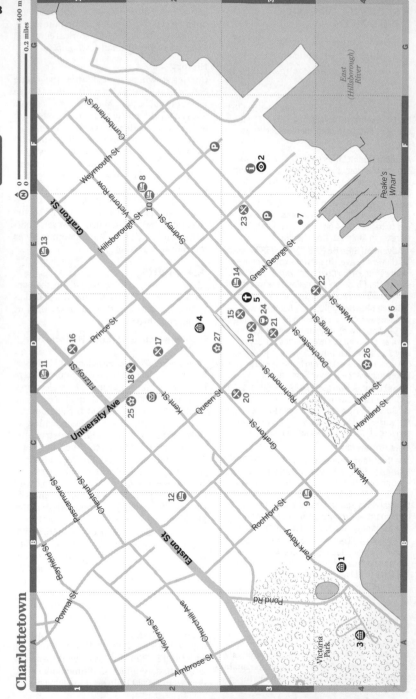

400 m
0.2 miles

East
(Hillsborough)
River

Peake's
Wharf

Cumberland St
Weymouth St
Victoria Row
Hillsborough St
Sydney St
Grafton St
Great George St
Prince St
Fitzroy St
University Ave
Kent St
Queen St
Grafton St
Richmond St
Dorchester St
King St
Water St
Union St
Haviland St
West St
Rochford St
Park Rdwy
Pond Rd
Euston St
Chestnut St
Passmore St
Bellfield St
Pownal St
Victoria St
Churchill Ave
Ambrose St

Victoria
Park

Charlottetown

Sights
1 Beaconsfield House ... B4
2 Founders' Hall ... F3
3 Government House ... A4
4 Province House National Historic Site ... D2
5 St Dunstan's Basilica ... D3

Activities, Courses & Tours
Confederation Players ... (see 2)
6 Harbour Hippo Hippopotabus ... D4
7 Peake's Wharf Boat Cruises ... E3

Sleeping
8 Aloha Tourist Home ... F2
9 Charlotte's Rose Inn ... B3
10 Charlottetown Backpackers ... E2
11 Fairholm Inn ... D1
12 Fitzroy Hall B&B ... B2
13 Spillet House B&B ... E1
14 The Great George ... E3

Eating
15 Claddagh Room ... D3
16 Formosa Tea House ... D1
17 Leonard's ... D2
18 Lot 30 ... D2
19 Off Broadway ... D3
20 Pilot House ... C3
21 Sim's Corner ... D3
22 Sirenella ... E4
23 Water Prince Corner Shop ... E3

Drinking
42nd St Lounge ... (see 19)
24 Gahan House ... D3

Entertainment
25 Baba's Lounge ... C2
26 City Cinema ... D4
27 Confederation Centre of the Arts ... D2
Olde Dublin Pub ... (see 15)

senses with facts and fun about Canada's history since 1864. It's sure to entertain children and the child in you.

Beaconsfield House NOTABLE BUILDING
(902-368-6603; 2 Kent St; adult/student/family $4.25/3.25/14; 10am-5pm) With its crowning belvedere, intricate gingerbread trim and elegant 19th-century furnishings, Beaconsfield House is the finest Victorian mansion in Charlottetown. Have a wander or sit on the verandah and be stunned by the view.

Government House NOTABLE BUILDING
(902-368-5480; admission free; 10am-4pm Mon-Fri Jul & Aug) Within the sprawling gardens of Victoria Park is Government House. This striking colonial mansion, with its grand hall, Palladian window and Doric columns, has been home to PEI's lieutenant governors since 1835. In 2003 the Hon JL Bernard broke with an almost 170-year-old tradition and opened its doors to the public.

St Dunstan's Basilica NOTABLE BUILDING
(902-894-3486; 45 Great George St; admission free; 9am-5pm) Rising from the ashes of a 1913 fire, the three towering stone spires of this neo-Gothic basilica are now a Charlottetown landmark. The marble floors, Italianate carvings and decoratively embossed ribbed ceiling are surprisingly ornate.

Tours

Self-guided walking tour booklets are available for just a Loonie ($1) at the tourist office.

Confederation Players WALKING TOURS
(902-368-1864; 6 Prince St; adult/child $10/5) There is no better way to tour Charlottetown. Playing the fathers and ladies of Confederation, actors garbed in 19th-century dress educate and entertain through the town's historic streets. Tours leave from Founders' Hall, and there are three variations on the theme: historic Great George St, island settlers and the haunts of local ghosts.

Peake's Wharf Boat Cruises BOAT CRUISES
(902-566-4458; 1 Great George St; 70min cruise $20; 2:30pm, 6:30pm & 8pm Jun-Aug) Observe sea life, hear interesting stories and witness a wonderfully different perspective of Charlottetown from the waters of its harbor. An excellent seal-watching trip ($28) departs at 2:30pm, returning at 5pm.

Harbour Hippo Hippopotabus
BUS & BOAT TOURS
(902-628-8687; Lower Prince St Wharf; 1hr tour adult/child $24/16) Want to explore historic Charlottetown, but afraid the kids will get bored? Hop on this amphibious bus that takes you to all the sights on land, then floats in the water.

Abegweit Tours
BUS TOURS

(📞902-894-9966; 157 Nassau St; adult/child $11/2) One-hour double-decker bus tours through Charlottetown leave from the Confederation Centre. The six-hour north shore tour (adult/child $80/40) will pick you up if you're staying in town. It also does a pilgrimage to the home turf of Anne of Green Gables (adult/child $65/32.50).

✯✯ Festivals & Events

Charlottetown Festival
THEATER

(📞902-566-1267; www.confederationcentre. com/festival.asp; ⊘mid-May–mid-Oct) This theatrical festival features free outdoor performances, a children's theater and dance programs.

Old Home Week
CULTURAL

(📞902-629-6623; www.peiprovincialexhibition. com; ⊘mid-Aug) Held at the Provincial Exhibition grounds, this event features carnival rides, musical entertainment, games of chance, harness racing and traditional livestock shows.

PEI International Shellfish Festival
FOOD

(📞866-955-2003; www.peishellfish.com; ⊘3rd weekend Sep) Now one of the island's largest festivals, this massive kitchen party, set on the Charlottetown waterfront, merges great traditional music with incredible seafood. Don't miss the oyster-shucking championships or the chowder challenge.

🛏 Sleeping

Old Charlottetown's charms and proximity to major sights and restaurants makes it the most enviable area to rest your head. During summer, Charlottetown hums with activity, so it's wise to book ahead. In the off-season, accommodations are plentiful and most places reduce their rates. Parking is freely available at or close to all accommodations.

TOP CHOICE Fairholm Inn
B&B $$$

(📞902-892-5022, 888-573-5022; www. fairholm.pe.ca; 230 Prince St; ste incl breakfast $129-289) This historic inn was built in 1838 and is a superb example of the picturesque movement in British architecture. Take tea while enjoying the morning sun in the beautiful conservatory, wander the gardens or hole up with a book in the library. Luxurious English fabrics, beautiful PEI artwork and grand antiques fill each suite. Light a fire, soak in your tub and sink back into the elegant days of the 19th century.

TOP CHOICE Great George
INN $$$

(📞902-892-0606, 800-361-1118; www. innsongreatgeorge.com; 58 Great George St; d incl breakfast $175-219, ste $269-899; 🅿❄@🛜) A colorful collage of celebrated buildings along Charlottetown's most famous street has rooms ranging from plush and historic to bold and contemporary – but all are simply stunning. It's both gay- and family-friendly. A babysitting service is available, as is a fitness room.

Fitzroy Hall B&B
B&B $$$

(📞902-368-2077; www.fitzroyhall.com; 45 Fitzroy St; d $110-190, ste $225-300) A perfect blend of elegance and comfort, this house is as grand as they come, while the welcome is warm and down to earth. The innkeepers have put some serious thought into how to make their guests comfortable: the answer is found with refined antiques, muted color schemes, and details like hidden alcoves with fridges and hot pots for guests to keep cold drinks or make tea.

Charlotte's Rose Inn
INN $$

(📞902-892-3699, 888-237-3699; www.charlot tesrose.ca; 11 Grafton St; r incl breakfast $155-205, apt $180; 🅿➡❄@🛜) Miss Marple must be around here somewhere. This decadent Victorian has true English flair with bodacious rose-printed wallpaper, lace canopies, big fluffy beds and grand bathrooms. There's a fire in the parlor for guests to enjoy along with complimentary tea and cakes. A modern loft apartment can accommodate five and has its own private rooftop deck.

TOP CHOICE Spillett House B&B
B&B $

(📞902-892-5494; www.spilletthouse.pe. ca; 157 Weymouth St; s/d with shared bathroom incl breakfast $50/60) This lovely heritage home is scrupulously clean, with polished hardwood floors and antique furnishings, homemade quilts on the beds and lace curtains on the windows. Kids are welcome and there are storage facilities for bicycles.

Charlottetown Backpackers
B&B $

(📞902-367-5749; www.charlottetownbackpack ers.com; 60 Hillsborough St; dm/r incl break-fast $32/79; 🛜) Impossible to miss with its bright red-and-white paint job and happy hostellers milling about on the lawn. This superbly happening backpackers has cozy single-sex and mixed dorms, a good kitchen, plus a quirky common room with a turntable and a rather epic vinyl collection. Be prepared for spontaneous barbecues and pub outings.

Aloha Tourist Home
B&B $$

(☑902-892-9944, 866-892-9944; www.aloha amigo.com; 234 Sydney St; r incl breakfast $40-150; ☎) A welcoming choice that's really a heritage B&B complete with antiques and comfy beds, but without the hefty price tag. The serve-yourself breakfasts are gourmet, the location central and the owner is sweet and helpful. Lower-end rooms have shared bathrooms.

✗ Eating

Thanks largely to the Culinary Institute at Charlottetown's Holland College, which keeps churning out talented chefs, the city has a heaping helping of fine eateries. During summer, Victoria Row's pedestrian mall and the waterfront are hot spots for diners and drinkers. Pubs are also a great place to go for good-value eating.

TOP CHOICE Lot 30
RESTAURANT $$$

(☑902-629-3030; 151 Kent St; lunch mains $22-55; ☺from 5pm Tue-Sun) Anyone who's anyone goes to Lot 30, but show up unknown and in jeans and you'll be treated just as well. Tables are in view of each other so you can see the ecstatic expressions of food bliss on the merry diners' faces; dishes from beurre blanc to curry are spiced to perfection. For a treat, try the excellent-value five-course tasting menu ($55) – small servings of a starter, three mains and a dessert sampler. Servers are wine-pairing masters, the eclectic ever-changing menu is made with local seasonal ingredients, and the chef is happy to cater to food allergies and special needs. A Charlottetown highlight.

TOP CHOICE Leonard's
CAFE $

(University Ave; sandwiches from $5; ☺9am-5pm Tue-Sat) Find absolute comfort in this little cafe full of cushioned seating and soothing country-style muted hues. Treat yourself to excellent German pastries, salads and creative sandwiches as well as all-day breakfasts made with free-range eggs, a great cheese selection, and cold cuts like Black Forest ham. Wash it down with farmers market teas and espresso.

Water Prince Corner Shop
RESTAURANT $$

(☑902-368-3212; 141 Water St; meals $10-17; ☺9:30am-8pm) When locals want seafood they head to this inconspicuous, sea-blue eatery near the wharf. It is deservedly famous for its scallop burgers but it's also the best place in town for fresh lobster. You'll

probably have to line up for a seat or order takeout lobster, which gets you a significant discount.

Sirinella
RESTAURANT $$

(☑902-628-2271; 83 Water St; lunch mains $8-17, dinner $15-28; ☺lunch & dinner Mon-Fri, dinner Sat) Cross the threshold of this diner-looking restaurant and you are transported to seaside Italy. It's nothing fancy, just little round, white-clothed tables, some Mediterranean oil paintings and incredibly authentic Italian fare.

Off Broadway
RESTAURANT $$

(☑902-566-4620; 125 Sydney St; lunch mains $9-14, dinner $15-28; ☺11am-11pm Mon-Sat, to 10pm Sun) Slip into an art-deco booth, draw the burgundy curtains and pretend you're escaping the paparazzi. The dark yet chic ambience is matched by fine entrées such as lobster crepes or seafood coconut curry. Don't leave without taking a cocktail or dessert in the even more elaborate upstairs lounge.

Sim's Corner
RESTAURANT $$

(☑902-894-7467; 86 Queen St; mains $12-40; ☺4-9pm Sun-Thu, to 10pm Fri & Sat) Feeling successful, hip and carnivorous? Head to this urban-chic spot where plush lounge-style seating spills onto the sidewalk. Food is of the steak-house and seafood variety and you're un-cool without a glass in hand from the wine bar.

Claddagh Room
RESTAURANT $$$

(☑902-892-6992; 131 Sydney St; mains $19-45; ☺5-10pm Mon-Thu, to 10:30pm Fri & Sat) Locals herald the Claddagh Room as one of the best seafood restaurants in Charlottetown. Trust 'em! The Irish-inspired Galway Bay Delight features a coating of fresh cream and seasonings over scallops and shrimp that have been sautéed with mushrooms and onions, then flambéed with Irish Mist liqueur.

Pilot House
RESTAURANT $$

(☑902-894-4800; 70 Grafton St; mains $19-37; ☺11am-10pm Mon-Sat) The oversized wood beams and brick columns of the historic Roger's Hardware building provide a bold setting for fine dining or light pub fare. A loyal clientele tucks into lobster stuffed chicken, vegetarian pizza or seafood torte. Lunch specials start at $10.

Formosa Tea House
RESTAURANT $

(☑902-566-4991; 186 Prince St; mains $6-7; ☺11:30am-3pm & 5-8pm) Savory Taiwanese vegetarian dishes are served in this cozy Victorian, fitted out with warm wood paneling and intimate booths upholstered in red, green and gold and accented with Chinese art. Recommended are the spicy vegetables and fried rice chased with a steaming mug of hot almond milk.

Farmers' Market MARKET **$**
(☑902-626-3373; 100 Belvedere Ave; ☺9am-2pm Sat, also Wed Jul & Aug) Come hungry and empty-handed. Enjoy some prepared island foods or peruse the cornucopia of fresh organic fruit and vegetables. The market is north of the town center off University Ave.

🍷 Drinking

Charlottetown has an established and burgeoning drinking scene. Historic pubs dot the old part of town. Most bars and pubs have a small cover charge (about $5) on weekends, or when there is live music. People spill into the streets at 2am when things wrap up.

Gahan House TOP CHOICE PUB
(☑902-626-2337; 126 Sydney St; ☺11am-10pm or 11pm Sun-Thu, to midnight or 1am Fri & Sat) Within these historic walls the pub owners brew PEI's only homegrown ales. Sir John A's Honey Wheat Ale is well worth introducing to your insides, as is the medium- to full-bodied Sydney Street Stout. The food here is also great – enjoy with friends old and new.

42nd St Lounge BAR
(☑902-566-4620; 125 Sydney St; ☺4:30pm-midnight) Climb the stairs for a cocktail or a nightcap. Above Off Broadway (p141), the 42nd St Lounge sets the same glamorous tone, with lots of richly colored velvet, gilt-framed mirrors and deep, cozily grouped sofas set against exposed brick walls.It usually closes around midnight but will stay open until the crowd thins out.

☆ Entertainment

From early evening to the morning hours, Charlottetown serves up a great mix of theater, music, island culture and fun. To tap into the entertainment scene, pick up a free monthly copy of *Buzz*.

Cinemas

City Cinema (☑902-368-3669; 64 King St) A small independent theater featuring Canadian and foreign-language films.

Theater
Confederation Centre of the Arts THEATER
(☑902-566-1267, 800-565-0278; www.confederationcentre.com; 145 Richmond St) This modern complex's large theater and outdoor amphitheater host concerts, comedic performances and elaborate musicals. *Anne of Green Gables – The Musical* has been entertaining audiences here as part of the Charlottetown Festival since 1964, making it Canada's longest-running musical. You'll enjoy it, and your friends will never have to know.

Live Music
Throughout Charlottetown and PEI various venues host traditional ceilidhs (*kay*-lees). They are sometimes referred to as 'kitchen parties' and usually embrace gleeful Celtic music and dance. If you have the chance to attend one, don't miss it. The Friday edition of the *Guardian* newspaper lists times and locations of upcoming ceilidhs.

Olde Dublin Pub PUB
(☑902-892-6992; 131 Sydney St; cover $8) A traditional Irish pub with a jovial spirit and live entertainment nightly during the summer. Celtic bands and local notables take the stage and make for an engaging night out.

Baba's Lounge BAR
(☑902-892-7377; 81 University Ave; cover $8) Located above Cedar's Eatery, this welcoming, intimate venue hosts great local bands playing their own tunes. Occasionally there are poetry readings.

Benevolent Irish Society LIVE MUSIC
(☑902-963-3156; 582 North River Rd; admission $10; ☺8pm Fri mid-May–Oct) On the north side of town, this is a great place to catch a ceilidh. Come early, as seating is limited.

ℹ Information
Main Post Office (☑902-628-4400; 135 Kent St)

Police, Ambulance & Fire (☑911)

Polyclinic Professional Centre (☑902-629-8810; 199 Grafton St; ☺5:30-8pm Mon-Fri, 9:30am-noon Sat) Charlottetown's after-hours, walk-in medical clinic. Non-Canadians must pay a $40 fee.

Queen Elizabeth Hospital (☑902-8894-2111; 60 Riverside Dr) Twenty-four-hour emergency room.

Royal Canadian Mounted Police (☑902-368-9300; 450 University Ave) For non-emergencies.

Visit Charlottetown (www.visitcharlottetown. com) A helpful website which features upcoming festival information, city history and visitor information.

Visitors Centre (☑902-368-4444, 888-734-7529; www.peiplay.com; ☺9am-8pm Jun, to 10pm Jul & Aug, 8:30am-6pm Sep–mid-Oct, 9am-4:30pm Mon-Fri mid-Oct–May; @) Located in Founders' Hall, this visitors center is the island's main tourist office. It has all the answers, a plethora of brochures and maps, and free internet access.

❶ Getting There & Away

Air

Charlottetown Airport is 8km north of the city center at Brackley Point and Sherwood Rds. A taxi to/from town costs $12, plus $4 for each additional person.

Bus

For information, see p137.

Car & Motorcycle

With next to no public transportation available, rental cars are the preferred method for most travelers going to/from Charlottetown. During the summer cars are in short supply, so book ahead.

Nationwide companies such as Avis, Budget, National and Hertz have offices in town and at the airport. Note that the airport desks are strictly for people with reservations.

❶ Getting Around

Bicycle

Riding is a great way to get around this quaint town. **MacQueen's Bicycles** (☑902-368-2453; www.macqueens.com; 430 Queen St; per day/ week $25/125) rents a variety of quality bikes.

Children's models are half price. **Smooth Cycle** (☑902-566-5530; www.smoothcycle.com; 330 University Ave; per day/week $25/110) also provides super service. Both of these operators also offer excellent customized island-wide tours of the Confederation Trail.

Car & Motorcycle

The municipal parking lots near the tourist office and Peak's Wharf charge $6 per day. One Loonie gets you two hours at any of the town's parking meters, which operate between 8am and 6pm on weekdays.

Public Transportation

Trius Tours (☑902-566-5664) operates the anemic city transit within Charlottetown (one-way fare $1.80). One bus makes various loops through the city, stopping sporadically at the Confederation Centre between 9:20am and 2:40pm.

Taxi

Fares are standardized and priced by zones. Between the waterfront and Hwy 1 there are three zones. Travel within this area is about $11, plus $3 per extra person. **City Taxi** (☑902-892-6567) and **Yellow Cab PEI** (☑902-566-6666) provide good service.

EASTERN PEI

You can make your own tracks across Kings County, the eastern third of the province and PEI's most under-touristed region. From stretches of neatly tended homesteads to the sinuous eastern shore with protected harbors and beaches, natural spaces and country inns, majestic tree canopies seem to stretch endlessly over the

---

CYCLING THE CONFEDERATION TRAIL

Following the rail-bed of Prince Edward Island's erstwhile railway, the 357km-long Confederation Trail is almost entirely flat as it meanders around hills and valleys. There are some sections of the trail that are completely canopied in lush foliage, and in late June and the early weeks of July the trail is lined with bright, flowering lupines. There's perhaps no better way to enjoy the fall's change of colors than by riding the trail.

The 279km tip-to-tip route from Tignish (p160), near North Cape, to Elmira, near East Point (p147), is a rewarding workout, passing through idyllic villages, where riders can stop for meals or rest for the night. Note that the prevailing winds on PEI blow from the west and southwest, so cycling in this direction is easier. Branches connect the trail to the Confederation Bridge (p137), Charlottetown (p137), Souris (p146) and Montague (p145).

Provincial **tourist offices** (www.gov.pe.ca/visitorsguide) have excellent route maps and their website offers a plethora of planning and trail information. The bicycle rental shops in Charlottetown (above) also run superb island-wide tours.

scenic heritage roads. The 338km Points East Coastal Drive winds along the shore, hitting the highlights, but the best thing to do is to hop on a bike: these sections of the Confederation Trail are some of the most beautiful on the island.

Orwell

Found 28km east of Charlottetown, via Hwy 1, is **Orwell Corner Historic Village** (☎902-651-8510; off Hwy 1; adult/under 12yr $7.50/free; ☺9am-5pm Jul-early Sep, 9am-5pm Mon-Fri mid-May–Jun & early Sep-Oct), a living recreation of a 19th-century farming community, complete with bonneted school teacher and a blacksmith. Come on a Wednesday and take part in a traditional **ceilidh** (admission $10; ☺8pm). The **Sir Andrew MacPhail Homestead**, a further 1km down the road, is open for tea on summer afternoons.

Point Prim

This skinny bucolic spit of land is covered in wild rose, Queen Anne's lace and wheat fields through summer and has views of red sand shores on either side. At the tip is the province's oldest **lighthouse** (adult/child $7/2; ☺9am-6pm); we think it's one of the prettiest spots on the island. Climb up the steep lighthouse steps to pump the foghorn and for panoramas over the south coast on sunny days.

Many folks come out this way for the **Seaweed Experience** (☎866-887-3238; adult/child $60/30, minimum 4, maximum 8; ☺Mon, Tue, Thu & Fri) where you can harvest seaweed and learn about which types are edible or have medicinal qualities, all led by a local family who have been in the industry for generations, plus a knowledgeable marine botanist.

There are lots of cottages for rent by the week but the only one offering shorter-term stays is **Gerritson's Cottage** (☎902-659-2418; 1993 Point Prim Rd; cottage $130), with one modern, fully equipped cottage right on the coast that's set up with a barbecue and a swing set for the kids. Inside are a TV and microwave. It's perfect for families.

Eat at **Chowder House** (chowder with a biscuit $8; ☺11am-7pm), a homey cafe near the lighthouse, reminiscent of Cape Cod circa 1950; they serve a mean chowder and homemade pie.

Wood Islands

Wood Islands is the jumping-off point for ferries to Nova Scotia. A **visitor information center** (☎902-962-7411; Plough Waves Centre, cnr Hwy 1 & Rte 4; ☺10:30am-9pm) is up the hill from the terminal.

If you'll be waiting a while at the terminal, **Wood Islands Provincial Park** and its 1876 lighthouse are well worth the short walk. Munch a rock crab sandwich or a lobster roll at **Crabby's Seafood** (snacks $4-7; ☺noon-6pm Jun-Sep) near the ferry terminal.

Murray River & Around

From Wood Islands, Rte 4 heads east along the Northumberland Strait, veering inland at High Bank toward the lively and surprisingly artsy fishing settlement of Murray River. The coastal road becomes Rte 18, keeping the sea in view as it rounds Cape Bear, passing the lighthouse before looping back through the village of Murray Harbour and into Murray River. This stretch of flat, empty road offers superbly serene scenery and excellent cycling possibilities. Cyclists can follow the coastal road from Murray River, then loop back on the extension of the Confederation Trail at Wood Islands.

Alternatively, feel the wind in your hair aboard **Cruise Manada** (☎902-838-3444, 800-986-3444; www.cruisemanada.com; adult/under 13yr $22/11.50; ☺mid-May–Sep). It offers two-hour boat tours on the Murray River, passing mussel farms to the Murray Islands, home to hundreds of seals.

At Little Sands, 9km from the Wood Island Ferry, **Rossignol Estate Winery** (☎902-962-4193; Rte 4; ☺10am-5pm Mon-Sat, 1-5pm Sun May-Oct) has free tastings and specializes in fruit wines. The Blackberry Mead has won a string of gold medals and the Wild Rose Liquor is also worth a try; call ahead for winter hours.

For an excellent hearty meal, head to **Brehaut's Restaurant** (☎902-962-3141; Murray Harbour; dinner under $8; ☺8am-9pm Mon-Sat, 11am-9pm Sun). There are cozy booths in this big, red wooden house. The seafood chowder gets rave reviews.

Panmure Island

Duck off Hwy 17 and ride the tarmac to the tip of Panmure Island, known for its variety of beaches: white sand and cold water line the ocean side while pink sands and warmer water run along the St Mary's Bay side. Joined to the main island by a causeway, the island offers sweeping vistas of sand dunes and ocean surf, grazing horses and a gaily painted **lighthouse** (☑902-838-3568; tours $5; ☺9:30am-5pm Jul & Aug, hours vary Jun & Sep). You can climb the tower for $4. There's an annual **Powwow** (☑902-892-5314; www.ncpei.com/powwow-trail.html; ☺mid-Aug) held each year with drumming, crafts and a sweat tent – it attracts around 5000 visitors, so don't expect any secluded beaches!

Bring a picnic for the supervised beach at **Panmure Island Provincial Park** (☑902-838-0668; Hwy 347; campsites $21; ☺Jun–mid-Sep). The park campground has every amenity for its 44 sites (most unserviced) tucked under the trees and along the shore. For something more luxurious stay at the grand **Maplehurst Properties** (☑902-838-3959; www.maplehurstproperties.com; Rte 347; d $109-190, cottage $125-190; ☺May-Nov). Marsha Leftwich has mustered every glimmer of her native Southern hospitality to create this exceptional B&B that drips with gorgeous chandeliers as well as fresh baked muffins and treats.

Montague & Around

The fact that Montague isn't flat gives it a unique, inland feel. Perched on either side of the Montague River, the busy little town is the service center for Kings County; its streets lead from the breezy, heritage marina area to modern shopping malls, supermarkets and fast-food outlets.

In the old train station on the riverbank there's an **Island Welcome Center** (☑902-838-0670; cnr Rtes 3 & 4; ☺9am-4:30pm late May-late Jun & late Aug–mid-Oct, 8am-7pm late Jun-late Aug). Here, you can hop on the Confederation Trail, which follows the former rail line; rent bikes at **Pines Bicycle Rentals** (☑902-838-3650; 31 Riverside Dr; rentals half/full day $20/30; ☺8am-8pm). Alternatively, buy a ticket for **Cruise Manada** (☑902-838-3444, 800-986-3444; www.cruisemanada.com; adult/under 13yr $22/11.50; ☺mid-May-Sep), at their second location, which offers popular two-hour boat tours to PEI's largest seal colony.

On the other side of the river, the statuesque former post office and customs house

(1888) overlooks the marina, and houses the **Garden of the Gulf Museum** (☑902-838-2467; 564 Main St S; adult/under 12yr $3/free; ☺9am-5pm Mon-Fri early Jun-late Sep). Inside are several artifacts illustrating local history.

Just north of town, development meets nature at **Brudenell River Provincial Park** (☑902-652-8966; off Rte 3; tent sites $21, RV sites $24-28; ☺late May–mid-Oct), which is a park and resort complex. Options range from kayaking with **Outside Expeditions** (☑902-652-2434; www.getoutside.com; half-/full-day tours $55/100) to nature walks and, as Winston Churchill put it, 'a good walk ruined' – ie golf – on two championship courses. You can also take a one-hour horseback trail ride through the sun-dappled forest and onto the beach with **Brudenell Riding Stables** (☑902-652-2396; 1hr ride $25; ☺Jun-Sep).

🍴 Sleeping & Eating

TOP CHOICE **Knox's Dam B&B**   B&B **$$**
(☑902-838-4234, 866-245-0037; knox dambandb@hotmail.com; cnr Rtes 353 & 320; r incl breakfast $85-100; ☺mid-May–Oct; ☎) This cheerful, red Victorian country home is constantly serenaded by the babble and flow of Knox's dam on the Montague River. Guest rooms are thoughtfully appointed with soft linens, the old-fashioned elegance of a claw-foot tub and modern amenities such as satellite TV. Rooms overlook the prize-winning flower gardens or the bountiful vegetable patch, there's good trout fishing at the dam and your hosts couldn't be kinder.

Boudreault's White House   B&B **$**
(☑902-838-2560, 800-436-3220; 342 Lower Montague Rte 17; r incl breakfast $50-65; ☺May-Oct; ☎) Three small, cozy rooms heaped with fresh towels and country quilts share a bathroom in friendly Zita's homey abode. You're given maps, menus and activity ideas for the area, then are pretty much left on your own. There's bicycle storage and kids are welcome.

Windows on the Water Café   RESTAURANT **$$**
(☑902-838-2080; cnr Sackville & Main Sts; dinner mains $15-27; ☺11:30am-9:30pm May-Oct) Enjoy a flavorful array of seafood, chicken and vegetarian dishes on the deck overlooking the water and, sort of, the road. Try the sole stuffed with lobster and scallops ($15) and leave room for a freshly baked dessert,

Georgetown

The many heritage buildings in Georgetown are testament to the town's importance as a shipbuilding center in the Victorian era. Today it's a sleepy place that's gaining popularity as a tourist spot thanks to its great places to eat and waterfront setting. It's also the site of **Tranquility Cove Adventures** (☑902-969-7184; www.tranquility coveadventures.com; Fisherman's Wharf, 1 Kent St; full/half-day tours $90/50) that leads excellent lobstering, fishing and clamming trips and promises to let you live the life of a fisherperson for a day. Be prepared for physical work, getting wet, and then filling up on your fresh catch. Check out the website for details on even more worthwhile packages.

🛏 Sleeping & Eating

Georgetown Inn & Dining Room

INN & RESTAURANT **$$**

(☑902-652-2511, 877-641-2414; www.georgetown historicinn.com; 62 Richmond St; r incl breakfast $85-155; 🛜) Right in the center of Georgetown, this place is as equally well-known for its PEI-themed rooms (including a Green Gables room) as for its fine casual island-fare dining.

Clamdigger's Beach House & Restaurant

RESTAURANT **$$**

(☑902-652-2466; 7 West St; mains $12-40; ⏲11am-9pm) Some claim this place serves PEI's best chowder but no matter what your opinion, you can't help but ooh and aah about the water view from the deck or through the dining room's giant windows.

Cardigan Lobster Suppers

SEAFOOD **$$**

(☑902-583-2020; Rte 311; adult/child $34/20; ⏲5-9pm Jun-Oct) In nearby Cardigan, enjoy a five-course lobster supper in a heritage building on Cardigan Harbor.

Souris

Wrapped around the waters of Colville Bay is the bustling fishing community of Souris (*sur*-rey). It owes its name to the French Acadians and the gluttonous mice who repeatedly ravaged their crops. It's now known more for its joyous annual music festival than for the hungry field rodents of old. The **PEI Bluegrass & Old Time Music Festival** (☑902-569-3153; www.bluegrasspei. com/rollobay.htm; Rte 2; ⏲early Jul) draws acts from as far away as Nashville. Come for just a day, or camp out for all three.

This is a working town that's a friendly jumping-off point for cycling the coastal road (Rte 16) and the Confederation Trail, which comes into town. The town is also the launching point for ferries to the Îles de la Madeleine in Québec.

🛏 Sleeping & Eating

Inn At Bay Fortune

INN & RESTAURANT **$$**

(☑902-687-3745; www.innatbayfortune.com; 758 Rte 310; r from $135, ste $200-335; meals from $60; ❋🛜) Find some of PEI's most upscale rooms at this waterside inn about 12km south of Souris, as well as one of the island's best restaurants. Chef Warren Barr (who plans to hand his whisk to a new chef in 2011) has created a menu that captures the essence of PEI flavors; highlights include tartar of PEI scallops with strawberry and balsamic salsa or crispy beef short ribs with roasted organic shiitake mushrooms. Rooms are modern with country flair; the most fun rooms, tiny units in a tower with nearly 360-degree views, are the least expensive. The price goes up with size, culminating in private cottages.

McLean House Inn

INN **$$**

(☑902-687-1875; www.mcleanhouseinn.com; 16 Washington St; r $105-120, ste $190, incl breakfast; 🛜) The view from, and the atmosphere of,

---

DON'T MISS

BASIN HEAD PROVINCIAL PARK

While this **park** (off Rte 16; admission free) is home to the **Basin Head Fisheries Museum** (☑902-357-7233; adult/student $4.50/2; ⏲9am-5pm Jun & Sep, to 6pm Jul & Aug), its star attraction is the sweeping sand of golden **Basin Head Beach**. Many islanders rank this as their favorite beach and we have to agree. The sand is also famous for its singing – well, squeaking – when you walk on it. Unfortunately, the sand only performs when dry so if it's been raining, it's no show. Five minutes of joyous 'musical' footsteps south from the museum and you have secluded bliss – enjoy!

WORTH A TRIP

DISTILLERIES

In the last few years two distinctly different distilleries have opened on PEI, echoing the province's fame for bootlegging during prohibition. Even today many families distill their own moonshine and this is what is often mixed in punch and cocktails at country weddings and parties.

Prince Edward Distillery (☎902-687-2586; www.princeedwarddistillery.com; Rte 16, Hermanville; �11am-6pm) specializes in potato vodka that even in its first year of production turned international heads that have called it among the finest of its class. Stop in for tours (with/without tasting $10/2) of the immaculate distillery and to taste the different vodkas (potato, grain and blueberry) as well as the newer products such as bourbon, rum and a very interesting and aromatic gin.

Myriad View Distillery (☎902-687-1281; www.straightshine.com; 1336 Rte 2, Rollo Bay; �11am-6pm Mon-Sat, 1-5pm Sun) produces Canada's first and only legal moonshine. The hardcore Straight Lightning Shine is 75% alcohol and so potent it feels like liquid heat before it evaporates on your tongue. Take our advice and start with a micro-sip! A gulp could knock the wind out of you. The 50% alcohol Straight Shine lets you enjoy the flavor a bit more. Tours and tastings are free and the owner is happy to answer any questions.

It's about a 10-minute drive on Hwy 307 between the two places.

this beautiful mansard-roofed house make it perfect for a lazy afternoon. Head to the sunroom, grab some wicker and sink into a book. Ask for the Colville Bay room (No 303).

Dockside B&B B&B $$
(☎902-687-2829, 877-687-2829; www.colvillebay.ca; 37 Breakwater St; d $70; ☀) Simple but large and airy double rooms are in a modern house situated steps from the ferry dock. Breakfast is served in a bright, glassed-in porch with a view of the harbor.

Bluefin Restaurant RESTAURANT $
(☎902-687-3271; 10 Federal Ave; meals $10-14; ☀6:30am-7pm Mon-Sat, 6am-8pm Sun from 7am) Near McLean House Inn, this place is a local favorite known for its heaped servings of traditional island food. Its lunch special runs from 11am to 1pm.

East Point & Around

Built the same year Canada was unified, the **East Point Lighthouse** (☎902-357-2106; adult/child $5/4; ☀10am-6pm mid-Jun–Aug) still stands guard over the northeastern shore of PEI. After being blamed for the 1882 wreck of the British *Phoenix,* the lighthouse was moved closer to shore. The eroding shoreline is now chasing it back. There's a gift shop and a little **cafe** next to the lighthouse that serves good-value lobster rolls ($5), hearty chowder and sandwiches.

The wooded coast and lilting accents of the north shore make for an interesting change of pace. Giant white windmills march across the landscape. **North Lake** and **Naufrage** harbors are intriguing places to stop and, if you feel so inclined, join a charter boat in search of a 450kg tuna.

The **railway museum** (☎902-357-7234; Rte 16A; adult/student/family $3/2/10; ☀10am-6pm Jul & Aug, to 5pm Fri-Wed mid-Jun–late Jun & early Sep–mid-Sep) in Elmira includes a quirky miniature train ride (adult/student/family $7/4/15) that winds through the surrounding forest. The station marks the eastern end of the Confederation Trail (see boxed text, p143).

St Peter's to Mt Stewart

The area between these two villages is a hotbed for cycling. The section of the Confederation Trail (see boxed text, p143) closest to St Peter's flirts with the shoreline and rewards riders with an eyeful of the coast. In Mt Stewart three riverside sections of the Confederation Trail converge, giving riders and hikers plenty of attractive options within a relatively compact area. Both the Confederation Trail and a **provincial tourist office** (☎902-961-3540; Rte 2; ☀8am-7pm late Jun-late Aug, 9am-4:30pm mid-Jun–late Jun & late Aug-Oct) are found next to the bridge in St Peter's.

WORTH A TRIP

GREENWICH

Massive, dramatic and ever-shifting sand dunes epitomize the amazing area west of Greenwich. These rare parabolic giants are fronted by an awesome beach – a visit here is a must. Preserved by Parks Canada in 1998, this 6km section of shore is now part of Prince Edward Island National Park.

Avant-garde meets barn at the **Greenwich Interpretation Centre** (☎902-961-2514; Hwy 13; ☉9:30am-4:30pm mid-May–late Jun & Sep–mid-Oct, to 7pm late Jun-Aug) where an innovative audio-visual presentation details the ecology of the dune system and the archaeological history of the site. The highlight though is getting out into the tree-eating dunes. Four walking trails traverse the park; the **Greenwich Dunes Trail** (4.5km return, 1½ hours) is especially scenic.

Sleeping & Eating

Inn at St Peters INN & RESTAURANT **$$$**
(☎902-961-2135, 800-818-0925; www.innatstpeters.com; 1168 Greenwich Rd; d $220-265; lunch mains from $17, dinner mains from $22; ☉breakfast, lunch & dinner; ☎) Even with its luxurious rooms and stunning water views, the main reason to come to this inn is to dine on some of PEI's finest fare at the sunset-facing restaurant. Rooms are simply and elegantly decorated with antique furniture, but even if you don't stay here we highly recommend stopping in for a meal (even you, sweaty bikers).

Tir na Nog Inn INN **$$**
(☎902-961-3004, 866-961-3004; www.tirnanoginn.com; 5749 Hwy 2; r incl breakfast $65-115; P☎) In a beautifully restored Victorian home in St Peter's, enjoy gracious lodgings and gourmet breakfasts, and a deep verandah facing the bay.

Midgell Centre HOSTEL **$**
(☎902-961-2963; 6553 Rte 2, Midgell; dm & s with shared bathroom $20; ☉mid-Jun–mid-Sep) Although designed for guests of the Christian center, the austere rooms are available to visitors. Depending on the set-up, you may be in a dorm or private room. Communal kitchens in each building add value to this

great budget option, near St Peter's and Greenwich.

Rick's Fish 'n' Chips & Seafood House
RESTAURANT **$**
(☎902-961-3438; Rte 2, St Peter's; meals $5-15; ☉11am-10pm) Make a beeline for the lip-smacking battered fish and fresh-cut fries. For variety, try the vegetarian burgers, mussels done several ways, or fine pizza.

CENTRAL PEI

Central PEI contains a bit of all that's best about the island – verdant fields, quaint villages and forests undulating north to the dramatic sand-dune-backed beaches of Prince Edward Island National Park. Anne of Green Gables, the engaging heroine of Lucy Maud Montgomery's 1908 novel, has spawned a huge global industry focused on the formerly bucolic hamlet of Cavendish. However, this being PEI, even its most savagely developed patch of tourist traps and commercial detritus is almost quaint – freshly painted and flower bedecked.

For those entering central PEI via the Confederation Bridge, it's worth stopping at the **Gateway Village Visitor Information Centre** (☎902-437-8570; Hwy 1; ☉8:30am-8pm), just off the bridge on the PEI side, for its free maps, brochures, restrooms and an excellent introductory exhibit called 'Our Island Home' (open May to November). Staff can point you to the Confederation Trail (see boxed text, p143), which lurks nearby.

Victoria

A place to wander and experience more than 'see,' the shaded, tree-laden lanes of this charming little fishing village scream out character and charm. The entire village still fits neatly in the four blocks laid out when the town was formed in 1819. Colorful clapboard and shingled houses are home to more than one visitor who was so enthralled by the place they decided to stay. There's a profusion of art, cafes and eateries, as well as an excellent summer theater festival.

Sights & Activities

By the Sea Kayaking SEA KAYAKING
(☎902-658-2572, 877-879-2572; www.bythesea kayaking.ca; kayak rentals per hr/day $25/50)

Paddle round the bay on your own or on a guided tour, then take a dip off the beach at **Victoria Harbour Provincial Park** (admission free), where there are change rooms available. The outfit also runs popular 'I Dig Therefore I Clam' clamming expeditions ($70) and bike rentals (hour/day $15/30).

Victoria Playhouse   THEATER
(☑902-658-2025, 800-925-2025; www.victoria playhouse.com; 20 Howard St; tickets $26; ⊙8pm Jun-Sep) The ornate red velvet and gold theater at Victoria Playhouse presents a series of plays over the summer, with concerts from some of the region's finest musicians on Monday nights.

Lighthouse Museum   MUSEUM
(admission by donation; ⊙9am-5:30pm late Jun-Aug) The Lighthouse Museum holds an interesting exhibit on local history. If it's closed, get the key from the shop across the road.

🛏 Sleeping & Eating

Orient Hotel B&B   B&B $$
(☑902-658-2503, 800-565-6743; www.theorien thotel.com; 34 Main St; r $85-105, ste $125-160, incl breakfast; 🐾) A delightful Victorian confection of buttercup yellow, red and blue, this historic seaside inn is a perfect jewel. Mrs Proffitt's Tea Room (open 11:30am to 4pm Wednesday to Monday) serves afternoon cream tea and light lunches.

Victoria Village Inn   INN & RESTAURANT $$
(☑902-658-2483; www.victoriavillageinn.com; 22 Howard St; r incl breakfast $80-150; 🐾) Next to the theater, this inn has relaxed rooms in a slightly disheveled heritage home with one great family suite. The restaurant (mains $19 to $27, open 5pm to 10pm) has a deliciously decadent menu including creative delicacies like lobster and asparagus risotto. Vegetarian selections and theater packages are also available.

TOP **Landmark Café**   CAFE $$
CHOICE (☑902-658-2286; 12 Main St; mains $12-25; ⊙11:30am-10pm mid-May–Sep) People come from miles around for the wonderful imaginative food at this family-run cafe. Prepared with wholesome ingredients, every colorful menu item from lasagne and homemade soups to Cajun stir-fries and feta-stuffed vine leaves is a winner. Enjoy the photos on the wall of the family's annual exotic trips and their equally multicultural music selection, softly pumping through the cafe.

Island Chocolates   CHOCOLATE $
(☑902-658-2320; 13 Main St; chocolates $1.25 each; ⊙10am-8pm Mon-Sat, noon-8pm Sun) We dare you to eat only one of the sublime handmade Belgian chocolates at this place! Cafe tables on the front porch and inside the warmly lit, old-fashioned shop are inviting for morning coffee or a sumptuous chocolate dessert. Also offers two-hour chocolate-making workshops ($45) by reservation.

Prince Edward Island National Park

Heaving dunes and red sandstone bluffs provide startling backdrops for some of the island's finest stretches of sand; welcome to **Prince Edward Island National Park** (☑902-672-6350; www.pc.gc.ca/pei; day pass adult/child $7.80/3.90). This dramatic coast, and the narrow sections of wetland and forests behind it, is home to diverse plants and animals, including the red fox and endangered piping plover.

The park is open year-round, but most services only operate between late June and the end of August. Entrance fees are charged between mid-June and mid-September, and admit you to all park sites except the House of Green Gables (p154). If you're planning to stay longer than five days, look into a seasonal pass. The park maintains an information desk at the Cavendish Visitor Centre (p155).

The following sights and sleeping and eating options are organized from east to west, first covering the park-run facilities, then the private operations inside and out of the park.

◉ Sights & Activities

Beaches lined with marram grasses and wild rose span almost the entire length of the park's 42km coastline. In most Canadians' minds, the park is almost synonymous with the beaches. **Dalvay Beach** sits to the east, and has some short hiking trails through the woods. The landscape flattens and the sand sprawls outward at **Stanhope Beach**. Here, a boardwalk leads from the campground to the shore. Backed by dunes, and slightly west, is the expansive and popular **Brackley Beach**. On the western side of the park, the sheer size of **Cavendish Beach** makes it the granddaddy of them all. During summer this beach sees copious

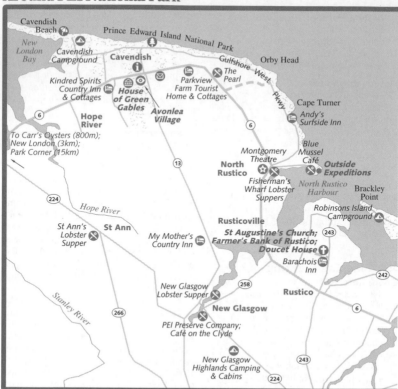

numbers of visitors beneath its hefty dunes. If crowds aren't your thing, there are always the pristine sections of sand to the east. Lifeguards are on duty at Cavendish, Brackley and Stanhope Beaches in midsummer. A new bike lane now runs all the way along this coast.

🛏 Sleeping

Parks Canada operates three highly sought-after **campgrounds** (☑800-414-6765; www.pccamping.ca; tent/RV sites $28/36; ☺early Jun-late Aug), which are spread along the park's length. They all have kitchen shelters and showers. For an additional fee of $10, you can reserve a campsite, but you must do so at least three days in advance by phone or via their website. You can request a campground, but not a specific site; you must accept whatever is available when you arrive. While 80% of sites can be booked in advance, the remaining sites

are first-come, first-served, so it's wise to arrive early.

Stanhope Campground, on Gulfshore East Pkwy, is nestled nicely in the woods behind the beach of the same name. There is a well-stocked store on-site.

Robinsons Island Campground, also on Gulfshore East Pkwy, is open to the public from late June. The most isolated of the three sites, it's set at the end of Brackley Point. It's not too much fun if the wind gets up.

The proximity of **Cavendish Campground**, located just off Rte 6, to the sights makes it the most popular option. It has exposed oceanfront sites and ones within the shelter and shade of the trees. Don't be lured by the view – it's nice, but sleep is better.

The following communities also provide excellent options for accommodations in or around the park.

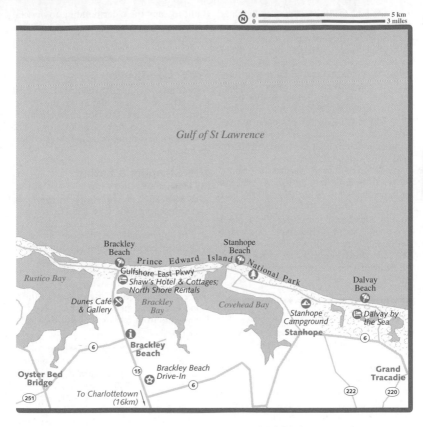

Dalvay by the Sea

Standing proudly near the east end of the park, and overlooking the beach named after it, is Dalvay, an historic mansion. Built in 1895 this majestic building is now owned by Parks Canada, and operated as an **inn** (902-672-2048, 888-366-2955; www.dalvaybythesea.com; Gulfshore East Pkwy; r $174-344, cottages $404-444, incl breakfast; ❄🛜♿). It's easily the most luxurious and stunning accommodations on the north shore. Each plush room's view and antique furnishings are refreshingly unique. The majestic dining room (dinner mains $18 to $36, open breakfast, lunch and dinner July and August) prepares remarkable dishes ranging from hazelnut- and sage-crusted rack of lamb to fresh island lobster. It is open to nonguests, and both lunch and afternoon tea (from 2pm to 4pm) are reasonably priced. The inn also rents bicycles (per hour/day $9/26).

Brackley Beach

There's a **Welcome Centre** (902-672-7474; cnr Rtes 6 & 15; ⊙8am-9pm) 4km before the park entrance. **North Shore Rentals** (902-672-2022; Shaw's Hotel, Rte 15, 99 Apple Tree Rd; bikes per hr/day $7/22) rents bicycles, kayaks and canoes for exploring the area. For some evening variety, catch a movie at **Brackley Beach Drive-In** (902-672-3333; www.drivein.ca; 3164 Rte 15; adult/child $9/6; ⊙May-Sep). Check the website for what's playing.

Shaw's Hotel & Cottages (902-672-2022; www.shawshotel.ca; Rte 15, 99 Apple Tree Rd; d $75-170, cottages $120; ⊙cottages year-round, inn Jun-Oct; ❄♿), open since 1860, is Canada's oldest family-operated inn; it hearkens back to an earlier era, when families of sufficient means decamped to the seaside for the summer. The hotel occupies 30 hectares of the family farm, with a private lane leading to Brackley Beach, a 600m walk away. Rooms in the inn have old-fashioned simplicity and elegance. One-to four-bedroom cottages, ranging from rustic to modern, are scattered around the property. A children's program runs in July and August, with hay rides, games, trips to the beach and a supervised supper hour. The **dining room** (☑902-672-2022; mains $22-33; ⊘8-10am & 5:45-9:30pm) is open to outside guests; reservations are recommended for the popular Sunday evening buffet ($40; held in July and August).

While over-the-top springs to mind, **Dunes Café & Gallery** (☑902-672-2586; Rte 15; dinner mains $16-25; ⊘11:30am-10pm) is a nice change of pace. Honestly, where else on the island can you enjoy Vietnamese rice-noodle salad in the shade of a giant Buddha? Come in for a coffee, a meal or just to roam the eclectic mix of Asian and island art in the sprawling glass gallery and garden.

Rustico

The seafront Acadian settlement at Rustico dates back to 1700, and several fine historic buildings speak of this tiny village's former importance. Most prominent is **St Augustine's Church** (1830), the oldest Catholic church on PEI. The old cemetery is on one side of the church, the solid red-stone **Farmer's Bank of Rustico** is on the other. The bank operated here from 1864 to 1894; it was a forerunner of the credit-union movement in Canada. Beside the bank is **Doucet House**, an old Acadian dwelling that was relocated here. A **museum** (☑902-963-2194; adult/student $4/2; ⊘9:30am-5:30pm Mon-Sat, 1-5pm Sun) describing the settlement of the community and the establishment of the bank is now housed in the two secular buildings.

In a prime location just across the street from the towering old church, **Barachois Inn** (☑902-963-2906, 800-963-2194; www.barachoisinn.com; 2193 Church Rd; d incl breakfast $125-399; ❋⊛) is one of the finest B&Bs on PEI. The grand Acadian-style mansion is decorated not only with the standard sublime selection of antiques, but also very eclectic paintings, which makes walking around the many common areas like touring an art museum. Bathrooms are nearly equal in size to the enormous rooms, and hidden in the basement of the newer annex

(built to copy the older building to perfection) is an exercise room, sauna and conference area.

New Glasgow

New Glasgow is a quiet town that spreads elegantly across the shores of the River Clyde. This is the favorite lobster supper getaway for folks from Charlottetown, although it's becoming equally respected for its luscious preserves.

🛏 Sleeping & Eating

My Mother's Country Inn   B&B **$$**
(☑902-964-2508, 800-278-2071; www.mymotherscountryinn.com; Rte 13; d $85-225, cottages $125-250, incl breakfast) Here is another reason to linger in New Glasgow: an oasis within 20 hectares of rolling hills, brisk streams and enchanting woodlands, this is pure, rural delight. The house is the essence of country style with sea green and ochre painted walls, bright pastel quilts, wood floors and plenty of light. A big red barn waits to be photographed by a storybook brook.

New Glasgow Highlands Camping &
Cabins   CAMPING **$**
(☑902-964-3232; www.campcabinpei.com; Rte 224; tent/RV sites $30/35, cabins $55; ⊘May-Oct; ⚟) The 20-odd sites here are properly spaced in the forest, each with its own fire pit. For rainy days there are light cooking facilities in the lodge. Add a laundry, a small store, a heated swimming pool and a mystifying absence of bugs, and you're laughing. There are also bright cabins, each with two bunks, a double bed, a sofa and a picnic table but no linen or pillows; bathrooms are shared. Book ahead and don't even think about making late-night noise – peace is the word.

Café on the Clyde   RESTAURANT **$$**
(☑902-964-4300; dinner mains $13-20; ⊘9am-8pm) This is one of the better casual dining options near the national park, as long as the tour buses haven't arrived before you have. Sun reflects in off the River Clyde and makes this place glow. The vegetarian wraps with a hint of feta truly hit the spot and finish the meal with the house specialty, raspberry cream cheese pie. The cafe is an addition to the famous **PEI Preserve Company** (⊘9am-5pm, to 9pm mid-Jun–late Sep). While the preserves are a tad

pricey, we think they're worth every penny; if you're not going to buy, at least come in to browse the free samples. Don't pass the orange ginger curd or the raspberry champagne preserves.

New Glasgow Lobster Supper

LOBSTER SUPPER **$$**

(☑902-964-2870; Rte 258; lobster dinners $26-35; ◷4-8:30pm) You can make a right mess with the lobster here, while also gorging on an endless supply of great chowder, mussels, salads, breads and homemade desserts.

St Ann

St Ann is so small you hardly even know you've arrived. Yet on a summer evening, follow the traffic and wafts of lobster steam to **St Ann's Lobster Supper** (☑902-621-0635; Rte 224; supper $26-34; ◷4:30-8:30pm), which rivals New Glasgow as PEI islanders' favorite lobster supper.

North Rustico

Within a few minutes of arrival, it is obvious that this is not simply a tourist town. Rickety, boxy fishermen's houses painted in navies, brick reds and beiges, line a deep harbor that is simply packed with fishing vessels. A walk east from the pier along the boardwalk, and out to North Rustico Harbour, is an excellent way to take in the sights, sounds and smells of this little village.

✷ Activities

If your idea of ocean activity is reeling in a big one, look for the plethora of **deep-sea fishing operators** (3-3½hr trip adult/child $38/24) along Harbourview Dr.

Outside Expeditions   BIKING & KAYAKING
(☑902-963-3366, 800-207-3899; www.getout side.com; 374 Harbourview Dr) Situated at the far end of the harbor in a bright-yellow fishing shed, the 1½-hour introductory 'Beginner Bay' tour ($39) begins with a lesson in kayaking techniques. The most popular trip is the three-hour 'Harbour Passage' tour ($59), which operates three times daily (9am, 2pm and 6pm). It also offers guided 'Land of Anne' bicycle tours ($65), and bike rentals (per half/full day $20/35). Trips are run in the off-season, whenever at least four people want to go.

Montgomery Theatre   THEATER

(☑902-963-3963; www.themontgomerytheatre .com; North Rustico Village; tickets $25-32) Opened in 2008 in honor of the 100th anniversary of the publication of *Anne of Green Gables,* this theater presents plays from the life and times of Lucy Maud Montgomery. Performances are in a renovated 19th-century church that Montgomery herself attended. Seats sell out fast, so book in advance!

🛏 Sleeping & Eating

Andy's Surfside Inn   INN **$**

(☑902-963-2405; Gulfshore West Pkwy; d with shared bathroom incl light breakfast $45-75; 🛜) Inside the national park, 2.7km toward Orby Head from North Rustico, is this large rambling house overlooking Doyle's Cove. It has been an inn since the 1930s, and the kitchen is open to those who want to bring home a few live lobsters. Sit back on the porch, put your feet up and thank your lucky stars.

Blue Mussel Café   CAFE **$$**

(☑902-963-2152; Harbourview Dr; mains $18-45, burgers from $14; ◷11:30am-8pm) This place is relatively small and expensive, but its bayside location, pan-fried scallops and steamed mussels will leave a big impression. Grab a table on the covered deck facing the bay. It's en route to Outside Expeditions.

Fisherman's Wharf Lobster Suppers

SEAFOOD **$$$**

(☑902-963-2669; 7230 Main St; lobster dinners $30; ◷noon-9pm) During the dinner rush in July and August this huge place has lines of people out the door. It's a fun, casual, holiday-style restaurant offering good value – that is if you don't wreck your shirt! Come hungry, as there are copious servings of chowder, tasty local mussels, rolls and a variety of desserts to go with your pound of messy crustacean. If things go your way, you may get a table with an ocean view.

Cavendish

Anyone familiar with *Anne of Green Gables* might have lofty ideas of finding Cavendish as a quaint village bedecked in flowers and country charm; guess again. While the Anne and Lucy Maud Montgomery sites are right out of the imagination-inspiring book pages, Cavendish itself is a mishmash of

Cuter than Pokémon and able to leap cultures in a single bound, *Akage no An* (Red-haired Anne) has secured her place in Japanese pop culture. The novel was introduced to Japan in the 1950s and quickly found its way into the school curriculum with the idea that its wholesomeness and positive themes would build hope after the devastation of WWII. Anne remained steadfast in Japanese culture by capturing their hearts with her courage and free spirit. Today, visiting PEI is many a Japanese girl's dream.

Japanese homage to Anne has appeared in many forms. She became an animated character in 1979 and a musical version of *Akage no An* toured Japan in the '80s and '90s. In 1981 23 Anne enthusiasts visited PEI and later established the 'Buttercups,' an Anne fan club; today the club has over 200 members. 'Philosophy of Anne' books are available to young Japanese readers wanting to get more understanding of Anne and the 'School of Green Gables,' a social work and nursing college in Okayama, tries to instill Anne ideology in its students. But the biggest Anne shrine of them all was 'Canadian World,' a PEI theme park that recreated Green Gables down to the patch-work quilts and a little red-haired Canadian girl. Unfortunately the park, located in an out-of-the-way collapsed mining town, became too much like Canada – lots of open spaces and too few people – and went bankrupt.

manufactured attractions with no particular town center. The junction of Rte 6 and Hwy 13 is the tourist center and the area's commercial hub. When you see the service station, wax museum, church, cemetery and assorted restaurants, you know you're there. This is the most-visited community on PEI outside of Charlottetown and, although an eyesore in this scenic region, it is kiddie wonderland. To get out of the world of fabricated and fictional free-for-all, head to beautiful **Cavendish Beach**; it gets crowded during summer months but with perfect sand and a warm (ish) ocean in front, you wont really care.

If you haven't read the 1908 novel, this is the place to do it – not just to enjoy it, but to try and understand all the hype. The story revolves around Anne Shirley, a spirited 11-year-old orphan with red pigtails and a creative wit, who was mistakenly sent from Nova Scotia to PEI. The aging Cuthberts (who were brother and sister) were expecting a strapping boy to help them with farm chores. In the end, Anne's strength of character wins over everyone in her path.

Sights

House of Green Gables   HISTORICAL SITE
(902-672-7874; Rte 6; adult/under 17yr/family $5.75/3/14.50; 9am-8pm) Cavendish is the home town of Lucy Maud Montgomery (1874–1942), author of *Anne of Green Gables*. Here she is simply known as Lucy Maud or LM. Owned by her grandfather's cousins, the now-famous House of Green

Gables and its Victorian surrounds inspired the setting for her fictional tale. In 1937 the house became part of the national park and it's now administered as a national heritage site.

The site celebrates Lucy Maud and Anne with exhibits and audio-visual displays. The trails leading from the house through the green, gentle creek-crossed woods are worthwhile. The 'Haunted Wood' and 'Lover's Lane' have maintained their idealistic childhood ambience.

Avonlea Village   THEME PARK
(902-963-3050; www.avonlea.ca; Rte 6; adult/child/family $19/15/65; 9am-5pm) Delve deeper into Anne fantasy at this theme park where costumed actors portray characters from the book and perform dramatic moments and scenes from Green Gable chapters. Beyond the theatrical exploits, the park offers you cow-milking demonstrations, a ride in horse-drawn wagon and other period farm activities. Check the website for the day's schedule.

Site of Lucy Maud Montgomery's Cavendish Home   HISTORICAL SITE
(902-963-2231; Rte 6; adult/child $4/2; 9am-6pm) This is considered hallowed ground to Anne fans worldwide. Raised by her grandparents, Lucy Maud lived in this house from 1876 to 1911 and it is here that she wrote *Anne of Green Gables*. The land is now owned and tended to by Lucy Maud's grandson who also runs a small on-site museum and bookshop.

🛏 Sleeping & Eating

While accommodations are numerous, remember that this is the busiest and most expensive area you can stay. There are more bargains and more bucolic settings east, toward North Rustico.

Kindred Spirits Country Inn & Cottages
INN $$

(☎902-963-2434, 800-461-1755; www.kindred spirits.ca; Rte 6; d $55-285, ste $125-285; P❄🐾🖥) A huge, immaculate complex, this place has something for everyone from a storybook-quality inn-style B&B to deluxe suites. Rooms are every Anne fan's dream with dotty floral prints, glossy wood floors and fluffy, dreamlike beds. Downstairs the lounge has a fireplace that'll make you wish it would snow and couches perfect for snuggling up with a mug of cocoa.

Parkview Farm Tourist Home & Cottages
B&B $$

(☎902-963-2027, 800-237-9890; www.peionline.com/al/parkview; 8214 Rte 6; r with shared bathroom incl light breakfast $60-65, 2-bedroom cottages $160-225; 🖥) This fine choice is set on a working dairy farm, 2km east of Cavendish. Ocean views, bathrooms and the prerequisite flowered wallpaper and frills abound in this comfortable and roomy tourist home. Each of the seven cottages (available May to mid-October; B&B open year-round) has a kitchen and a barbecue, as well as a balcony to catch the comings and goings of the sun.

TOP CHOICE The Pearl
RESTAURANT $$

(☎902-963-2111; 7792 Cavendish Rd; mains $22-32, brunch $8-12; ⊙from 4:30pm daily, 10am-2pm Sun) This shingled house surrounded by flowers just outside Cavendish is an absolutely lovely place to eat. There are plenty of unusual and seasonally changing options like ice wine–infused chicken liver pâté on a Gouda brioche for starters and locally inspired mains like butter-poached scallops.

Carr's Oysters
RESTAURANT $$

(☎902-886-3355; Stanley Bridge Wharf, Rte 6; mains $14-32; ⊙10am-7pm) Dine on oysters straight from Malpeque Bay, or lobster, mussels and seafood you've never even heard of like quahogs from this place's saltwater tanks. There are also plenty of fish on the offer from salmon to trout. The setting over the bay is sociable and bright and there's also on on-site market selling fresh and smoked sea critters.

ⓘ Information

Cavendish Visitor Centre (☎902-963-7830; cnr Rte 6 & Hwy 13; ⊙9am-9pm)

ⓘ Getting Around

The **Cavendish Red Trolley** (⊙10am-6pm late Jun-Aug) runs hourly along Hwy 6 and through Cavendish, making various stops, including the Cavendish Visitor Centre, Cavendish Beach and the House of Green Gables (all-day ticket $3).

New London & Park Corner

New London and Park Corner both have strong ties to Lucy Maud Montgomery, and

JOHN BIL: CHEF & OYSTER SHUCKING CHAMPION

Three-time oyster shucking champion of Canada and chef and owner of Ship to Shore restaurant in Darnley, John Bil has been called 'one of the island's shellfish shamans' by the *New York Times*.

Tell us about the local oysters. I think of oysters like wine. Our oysters here are the best in the world because of the species, the climate, water salinity and the fact that people really give a shit about quality and how they raise them. Oysters from different areas even around the island taste different. For example North shore oysters are saltier because they grow in the open Atlantic where there's more salinity; South shore oysters are sweeter. Which type you prefer depends on your preference but I like them salty.

Any other types of seafood visitors should try? Soft-shell clams, also called seamer clams, although they aren't served many places any more. Locals know about them and love them but they are scarcer and more expensive since they're seasonal and hand dug from the wild.

are thus caught up in the everything-Anne pandemonium.

In New London, 10km southwest of Cavendish, is the **Lucy Maud Montgomery Birthplace** (902-886-2099; cnr Rtes 6 & 20; admission $3; 9am-5pm). The house is now a museum that contains some of her personal belongings, including her wedding dress.

Almost 10km northwest of New London is the village of Park Corner and the **Lucy Maud Montgomery Heritage Museum** (902-886-2807; 4605 Rte 20; admission $4; 9:30am-6pm). It's believed to be the home of Lucy Maud's grandfather and there's a lot of Anne paraphernalia. Take a guided tour; there's a guarantee that if you're not absolutely fascinated, you don't pay the admission.

Almost 500m down the hill from here, surrounded by a luscious 44-hectare property, is the charming home Lucy Maud liked to call **Silver Bush**. It was always dear to her and she chose the parlor for her 1911 wedding. Silver Bush hosts the **Anne of Green Gables Museum** (902-886-2884; 4542 Rte 20; adult/under 17yr $3/1; 9am-5pm mid-May–Jun & Sep-early Oct, to 6pm Jul & Aug). It contains such items as her writing desk and autographed first-edition books.

✕ Eating

TOP CHOICE **Ship to Shore**　　　　RESTAURANT **$$**
(902-836-5475; 2684 Rte 20, Darnley; mains $9-29; noon-11pm) If you love shell-fish, you'd be doing yourself a disservice not eating here. The menu is simple and straight-forward, focusing on the flavors of the best and freshest seafood you're likely to find anywhere. Some you simply won't find elsewhere. Be warned: this place looks like a regular old roadhouse from the outside but open the door and you're in for a treat.

Blue Winds Tea Room　　　RESTAURANT **$$**
(902-886-2860; 10746 Rte 6, New London; meals under $14; 11am-6pm Mon-Thu, to 8pm Fri-Sun) Just 500m southwest of Lucy Maud's birthplace, this is a pretty tearoom surrounded by English gardens. Of course like everything else in this region, they've got to be 'Anne,' so order a raspberry cordial or some New Moon Pudding, both recipes have been taken from Lucy Maud's journals.

Kensington & Around

Kensington is a busy market town about halfway between Cavendish and Summerside. It's a good place to replenish supplies and the closest service center for those attending the **Indian River Festival** (www.indianriverfestival.com) when some of Canada's finest musicians (from Celtic to choral) play in the wonderfully acoustic St Mary's Church, from June through September.

Home Place Inn & Restaurant (902-836-5686, 866-522-9900; www.thehomeplace.ca; 21 Victoria St East; d incl breakfast $89-109, ste $149;) exudes country elegance at its finest. In the morning you may be awakened with scents of freshly baking cinnamon rolls and there's a licensed pub and restaurant on the premises.

In nearby Margate, **Shipwright's Café** (902-836-3403; cnr Rtes 6 & 233; dinner mains $25-35; 11:30am-3:30pm Mon-Fri, from 5pm daily) is housed in an 1880s farmhouse overlooking rolling fields and flower gardens. It earns rave reviews for its seafood dishes and vegetarian fare concocted from organic herbs and vegetables from the gardens. Try the 'Salute to Our Greenhouse' salad, a paella endowed with the island's best seafood and creations with PEI beef.

WESTERN PEI

Malpeque and Bedeque Bays converge to almost separate the western third of PEI from the rest of the province. This region

---

WORTH A TRIP

MALPEQUE

So where is this place where all the oysters come from? You might ask. The tiny hamlet of Malpeque takes you off the beaten path, past shadeless, rolling farmland to a tiny bay simply jammed-packed with fishing boats and their colorfully painted storage barns. Don't miss lunch at **Malpeque Oyster Barn** (Malpeque Wharf; half-dozen oysters $14; 11am-9pm Mon-Sat, noon-9pm Sun), one of PEI's more authentically ambient cafes, in the top of a fisherman's barn and overlooking the bay and its oyster-filled action. Downstairs is a seafood monger where you can pick up fresh local sea critters to take away (a dozen oysters are around $6).

sits entirely within the larger Prince County, and it combines the sparse pastoral scenery of Kings County's interior with some of Queens County's rugged coastal beauty.

The cultural history here stands out more than elsewhere on the island. On Lennox Island a proud Mi'kmaq community is working to foster knowledge of its past, while French Acadians are doing the same in the south, along Egmont and Bedeque Bays.

Summerside

While it lacks the elegance and cosmopolitan vibe of Charlottetown, Summerside is a simpler, seaside-oriented place with everything you need in one small, tidy package. Recessed deep within Bedeque Bay and PEI's second-largest 'city,' this tiny seaside village possesses a modern waterfront and quiet streets lined with leafy trees and grand old homes. The two largest economic booms in the province's history, shipbuilding and fox breeding, shaped the city's development in the 19th and early 20th centuries. Like Charlottetown, its outskirts are plagued by unsightly development – you'll find most of Summerside's interesting bits along, or near to, Water St, which runs parallel to the waterfront.

◎ Sights & Activities

The Confederation Trail (see boxed text, p143) makes its way right through town and passes behind the library on Water St.

Spinnaker's Landing   BOARDWALK
This redeveloped waterfront is the highlight of Summerside. A continually expanding boardwalk allows you to wander and enjoy the harbor and its scenic surrounds. There are some nice eateries, a stage for live music in the summer and numerous shops. A mock lighthouse provides adults with a nice lookout and some local information, while a large model ship is a dream playground for kids. Backing all of this is the modern **Eptek Exhibition Centre** (☑902-888-8373; 130 Harbour Dr; admission by donation; ⊙10am-4pm), which features local and traveling art exhibitions.

College of Piping & Celtic Performing Arts   MUSIC
(☑902-436-5377; 619 Water St E; ⊙9am-9pm late Jun-Aug) In celebration of Celtic dance and music, this school provides visitors with free 20-minute miniconcerts from Monday

to Friday at 11:30am, 1:30pm and 3:30pm – expect bagpipes, singing and dancing. Inspired? Put on some warm clothes and enjoy the two-hour **ceilidhs** (adult/student $12/7; ⊙7pm) that take place every night in the covered amphitheater.

🛏 Sleeping

[TOP CHOICE] **Willow Green Farm B&B**   B&B $$
(☑902-436-4420, 888-436-4420; www.willowgreenfarm.com; 117 Bishop Dr; d incl breakfast $50-115; 🕸) With the Confederation Trail at its back door, and the College of Piping & Celtic Performing Arts out its front door, this rambling farmhouse is an incredibly great-value place to stay; you feel like you're in the country but actually you're in the central Summerside. Rooms are bright, and the bold country interior is a refreshing change from busy period decors. Read by the wood stove or check out some of the more interesting farm animals.

Comme Chez Nous B&B   B&B $$
(☑902-436-8600; anwe@pei.sympatico.com; 161 Fitzroy St; r incl breakfast $90-115; 🕸) This lovingly restored early-20th-century house sits on a quiet residential street within easy walking distance of restaurants and attractions. The guest rooms feature crisp, sumptuous fabrics and richly polished antiques, as well as big windows and flatscreen TVs with headphones. The easygoing hosts serve a gourmet breakfast in the wood-paneled dining room, and will also prepare a four-course dinner feast for guests by reservation.

Silver Fox Inn   B&B $$
(☑902-436-1664, 800-565-4033; www.silverfoxinn.net; 61 Granville St; d $80-155; 🕸) Featuring opulent details such as antique lace curtains and navy and gold striped wall paper, this Queen Anne revival B&B feels like a stylish 1920s and '30s recreation of the Victorian era.

🍴 Eating

Deckhouse Pub & Restaurant
                                   RESTAURANT $$
(☑902-436-0660; 150 Harbour Dr; mains $7-17; ⊙11am-11pm Jun–mid-Sep) Step off the Spinnaker's Landing boardwalk and onto one of the Deckhouse's two outdoor decks for a great meal in harborfront surroundings. Live music adds to the atmosphere on weekends. It's well known for its hand-battered fish and chips.

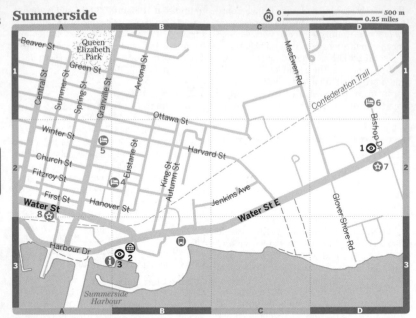

Summerside

⊙ Sights

⊟ Sleeping

Eating

☆ Entertainment

Brothers Two Restaurant   RESTAURANT **$$**
(📞902-436-9654; 618 Water St E; mains $11-26;
⊙11:30am-9pm Mon-Thu, 11:30am-9pm Mon-Fri,
4-10pm Sat, 4-8pm Sun) Brothers Two's ser-
vice, pasta, steak and fresh seafood have
made it a local favorite for more than 30
years. The vegetarian stir-fry and island
blue mussels steamed in garlic and white
wine are both excellent. If you want in on
the laughter coming from below, check out
Feast Dinner Theatres (below).

🍷 Drinking & Entertainment

Jubilee Theatre   THEATER
(📞902-888-2500, 800-708-6505; www.jubilee
theatre.com; 124 Harbour Dr) This modern the-
ater is in the same complex as the Eptek
Exhibition Centre and is the venue for *Anne
and Gilbert* (adult from $29, child $15; runs
July to September), a musical that picks
up where the ever-popular *Anne of Green
Gables* musical in Charlottetown leaves
off, and will likely be playing for the next
hundred years. The Jubilee also hosts the
Summer on the Waterfront Festival
(July to mid-September), which has local
and well-known Canadian musical acts.

Feast Dinner Theatres   THEATER
(📞902-888-2200, 888-748-1010; 618 Water St E;
dinner & show $36; ⊙6:30pm Mon-Sat Jun-Dec)
Most locals start to giggle when they speak
of their last time at Feast Dinner Theatres.
It's found below Brothers Two Restaurant
and is the longest-running theater restau-
rant in Atlantic Canada. Music, script and
improvisation combine with audience par-
ticipation to make a memorable evening.
The food's not too shabby, either.

Heritage Pub & Restaurant   PUB
(☑902-436-8484; 250 Water St) This traditional pub is the only live-music venue in town
(no cover charge). Local bands play on Friday, and occasionally on Saturday.

ℹ Information

Provincial Tourist Office (☑902-888-8364;
Hwy 1A; ☺9am-4:30pm late May-late Jun &
late Aug–mid-Oct, to 7pm late Jun-late Aug)
Grab the walking-tour pamphlet, which details
the town's finer 19th-century buildings.

ℹ Getting There & Away

Acadian Coach Lines (p137) stops at the **Irving
gas station** (☑902-436-2420; 96 Water St) in
the center of town and has services to Charlottetown ($12, one hour), Moncton ($33, two hours)
and Halifax ($60, 3½ hours). On request, bus
shuttles pick up at the Esso station on Hwy 1A at
the end of Water St E.

Région Évangéline

The strongest French Acadian ancestry on
the island is found here, between Miscouche
and Mont Carmel. Some 6000 residents
still speak French as their first language,
although you'll have trouble discerning this
region from others in the province. There is
one notable exception: the red, white, blue
and yellow star of the Acadian flag hangs
proudly from many homes. It was in Miscouche, on August 15, 1884, that the Acadian flag was unfurled for the very first time.
The yellow star represents the patron saint
of the Acadians, the Virgin Mary. Renewed
efforts are under way to preserve the unique
Acadian culture on the island. See the Nova
Scotia (p65) and New Brunswick (p90)
chapters for more information on Acadians.

A favorite stop on this stretch is **The
Bottle Houses** (☑902-854-2987; Rte 11, Cape
Egmont; adult/child $5/2; ☺9am-8pm), the art-
ful and monumental recycling project of
Edouard Arsenault. Over 25,000 bottles of
all shapes and sizes (that Edouard collected
from the community) are stacked in white
cement to create a handful of buildings
with light-filled mosaic walls.

The worthwhile **Acadian Museum**
(☑902-432-2880; 23 Maine Dr E; admission $5;
☺9:30am-7pm), in Miscouche, uses 18th-
century Acadian artifacts, texts, visuals
and music to enlighten visitors about the
tragic and compelling history of the Acadians on PEI since 1720. The introspective

video introduces a fascinating theory that
the brutal treatment of the Acadians by the
British may have backhandedly helped preserve a vestige of Acadian culture on PEI.

Tyne Valley

This area, famous for its Malpeque oysters,
is one of the most scenic in the province.
The village, with its cluster of ornate houses, gentle river and art studios, is definitely
worth a visit.

Green Park Provincial Park, 6km north
of the village, hosts the **Green Park Shipbuilding Museum & Historic Yeo House**
(☑902-831-7947; Rte 12; adult $5; ☺9am-5pm).
The museum and restored Victorian home,
along with a recreated shipyard and partially constructed 200-tonne brigantine,
combine to tell the story of the booming
shipbuilding industry in the glory days of
the 19th century.

The park has 58 **campsites** (☑902-831-
7912; off Rte 12; campsites $23-25, with hookups
$30, cabins with shared bathroom $45; ☺mid-
Jun–mid-Sep) spread within a mixed forest.
The dozen cabins just beyond the campground are a steal.

Doctor's Inn (☑902 831 3057; www.peis
land.com/doctorsinn; 32 Allen Rd; d with shared
bathroom incl breakfast $60-75) is an old coun-
try home that makes for a comfortable stay,
but when we passed the owners were considering stopping the B&B and focusing on
the restaurant; call first. The dining room
(three-course meal guests/nonguests $45/55,
open by reservation, closed Friday) is known
to prepare the finest meals in the region.
Cooked over a wood stove, the *tournedos
rossini* (beef tenderloin and liver pâté with
a red-wine sauce), *sole almandine* (fillet of
sole coated with white wine and toasted al-
monds) and organic vegetables from the garden are all superb. You can also take a tour of
the gardens and buy fresh produce.

Not surprisingly, the specialty at **Landing Oyster House & Pub** (☑902-831-3138;
1327 Port Hill Station Rd; mains $8-13; ☺lunch &
dinner) is 15 deep-fried oysters – definitely
indulge. Live bands (cover $3 to $5) play
here on Friday night, and also on Saturday
during July and August.

Lennox Island

Set in the mouth of Malpeque Bay, sheltered
behind Hog Island, is Lennox Island and

its 250 Mi'kmaq Aboriginal people. While working hard to promote awareness and understanding of their past, both in and out of their own community, they are also making renewed efforts to preserve their culture. The island is connected by a causeway, making it accessible from the town of East Bideford off Rte 12.

The **Lennox Island Aboriginal Ecotourism Complex** (☑866-831-2702; 2 Eagle Feather Trail; adult/student $4/3; ☺10am-6pm Mon-Sat Jul & Aug, noon-6pm Mon-Sat late Jun & early Sep) opened its doors in June 2004. Inside there are small, changing exhibits and information about the two excellent **interpretive trails** around the island. These trails consist of two loops, forming a total of 13km, with the shorter one (3km) being accessible to people in wheelchairs – for $4 a local will guide you, explaining the medicinal qualities of the plants, and lead you to a beaver dam. Also ask at the center if anything else is on offer, since it seems to change frequently: when we passed a local was offering **boat tours** around the island including a pass by sacred Hog Island, for $40 for up to four people.

Tignish

Tignish is a quiet town tucked up near the North Cape; it sees only a fraction of PEI's visitors. The towering **Church of St Simon & St Jude** (1859) was the first brick church built on the island. Have a peek inside – its ceiling has been restored to its gorgeous but humble beginnings, and the organ (1882) is of gargantuan proportions. Of its 1118 pipes, the shortest is 15cm, while the longest is nearly 5m!

The Confederation Trail begins (or ends!) two blocks south of the church on School St. The **Tignish Cultural Centre** (☑902-882-1999; 305 School St; admission free; ☺8am-4pm Mon-Fri), near the church, has a good exhibition of old maps and photos, tourist information and a library with internet access.

North Cape

The drive toward North Cape seems stereotypically bucolic, until the moment your eyes rise above the quaint farmhouses to see the heavens being churned by dozens of sleek behemoth-sized white blades. Strangely, expecting the surreal sight takes nothing away from it.

The narrow, windblown North Cape is not only home to the **Atlantic Wind Test**, but also to the longest **natural rock reef** on the continent. At low tide, it's possible to walk out almost 800m, exploring tide pools and searching for seals along the way. The newly expanded **interpretive center** (☑902-882-2991; admission $6; ☺9:30am-8pm), at the northern end of Rte 12, provides high-tech displays dedicated to wind energy, and informative displays on the history of the area. The aquarium is always a hit with kids. The **Black Marsh Nature Trail** (2.7km) leaves the interpretive center and takes you to the west side of the cape – at sunset these crimson cliffs simply glow against the deep-blue waters.

Located above the interpretive center, the atmospheric **Wind & Reef Restaurant & Lounge** (☑902-882-3535; mains $9-29; ☺lunch & dinner) attracts visitors and locals out for a treat. The menu and view are equally vast and pleasing.

West Coast

Along the west coast, you may be puzzled at the sight of horseback riders dragging rakes in the shallows offshore. They are collecting Irish moss, a valuable purplish seaweed used in everything from toothpaste to automobile tires, that gets uprooted and blown to shore in storms.

In Miminegash, stop into the **Seaweed Cafe** (meals $5-12) that serves a special seaweed pie ($4.50), although nothing about this fluffy, creamy creation reeks of the beach.

A little inland at O'Leary is the **Prince Edward Island Potato Museum** (☑902-859-2039; 1 Dewar Lane; admission $6; ☺9am-5pm Mon-Sat, 1-5pm Sun). It's a bit like a giant school science fair project with hallways of information panels and pictures on the walls, but there are also rooms filled with farming equipment and a cafe serving samples of treats made from potatoes (the fudge is awesome).

Between Miminegash and West Point, Rte 14 hugs the shore and provides stunning vistas. It's perhaps the finest drive on the island. Off Hwy 14, the striking black-and-white-striped **West Point Lighthouse** (☑902-859-3605, 800-764-6854; www.westpointlighthouse.com; ☺8am-9:30pm), dating from 1875, has been restored. Between 1875 and 1955 there were only two lighthouse keepers. Today the staff is made up of their direct descendants. There's a small **museum** (admission $4; ⊙9am-9pm), where you can climb the tower for a breathtaking view. Part of the former lighthouse keepers' quarters have been converted into a nine-room **inn** (d $100-145); the Tower Room ($145) is actually in the old lighthouse tower. The **restaurant** (meals $8-18; ⊙8am-8pm mid-May–Sep) is locally famous for its clam chowder.

Cedar Dunes Provincial Park (☑902-859-8785; tent sites $23-25, RV sites $26-27) has tent space in an open grassy field adjacent to West Point Lighthouse. Its red-sand beach is an island gem.

Newfoundland & Labrador

Best Places to Eat

» Lighthouse Picnics (p179)

» Norseman Restaurant (p201)

» Nicole's Cafe (p193)

» Bacalao (p173)

Best Places to Stay

» Tuckamore Lodge (p203)

» Artisan Inn (p183)

» Tickle Inn (p200)

» The Cliffhouse (p182)

Why Go?

Canada's easternmost province floats in a world of its own. Blue icebergs drift by. Puffins flap along the coast. Whales spout close to shore. The island even ticks in its own off-beat time zone (a half-hour ahead of the mainland) and speaks its own dialect (the *Dictionary of Newfoundland English* provides translation, me old cock).

Outside the good-time capital St John's, it's mostly wee fishing villages that freckle the coast, some so isolated they're reached only by boat. They offer plenty of hiking and kayaking escapes where it will just be you, the local family who's putting you up for the night and the lonely howl of the wind.

If you're looking to get off the beaten path – to see Viking vestiges, eat meals of cod tongue and partridgeberry pie, and share fish tales over shots of rum – set a course for this remote hunk of rock.

When to Go

St John's

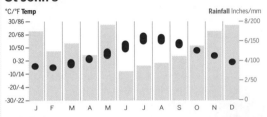

June Icebergs glisten offshore, though the weather can be wet and foggy.

July & August Whales swim by, festivals rock most weekends, and the province is at its sunniest.

December & January Skiers hit the slopes as Marble Mountain receives most of its 5m of snow.

Map labels

60°W · 58°W · 56°W · 54°W · 52°W

510 Port Hope Simpson

Labrador

Mary's Harbour

52°N

Québec

Belle Isle

Red Bay 6

Strait of Belle Isle

Cape Onion

L'Anse aux Meadows 3 National Historic Site

St Lunaire-Griquet

Pinware

Forteau

Old Fort Bay

Blanc Sablon

St Anthony

430

St Barbe

Hare Bay

Main Brook

Plum Point

432

Conche

Port au Choix

Roddickton

Grey Islands

ATLANTIC OCEAN

Northern Peninsula

Hawke's Bay

430

Portland Creek

Fleur de Lys

La Scie

Change Islands

50°N

Cow Head

The Arches

Baie Verte

Twillingate Island

Gros Morne National Park 4

Baie Verte Peninsula

Notre Dame Bay

Sally's Cove

Rocky Harbour

Norris Point

Moreton's Harbour

Fogo Island 5

Farewell

Boyd's Cove

Trout River

Woody Point

410 Springdale

Glenburnie

Lewisporte

340

Deer Lake

Grand Lake

330

320 Gander

Bonavista Bay

Lark Harbour

Corner Brook

Marble Mountain

1

Grand Falls-Windsor

Burnside

Bonavista

Port au Port Peninsula

Red Indian Lake

Terra Nova National Park

Salvage

Elliston

Lourdes

Stephenville

Newfoundland

Trinity

Port au Port West

Trans-Canada Hwy

Maelpaeg Lake

Bonavista Peninsula

Trinity Bay

48°N

St George's Bay

Barachois Pond Provincial Park

480

Head of Bay d'Espoir

360

Bay du Nord Wilderness Reserve

Clarenville

Conception Bay

Heart's Content

70

Cape Anguille

Isle aux Morts

Rose Blanche

Burgeo

Grey River

St Alban's

McCallum

Pool's Cove

Heart's Delight

Cupids

Harbour Grace

ST JOHN'S 2

Cape Ray

Port aux Basques

Sandbanks Provincial Park

Ramea

François

Hermitage

210

Harbour Breton

Dildo 8

Brigus

Witless Bay 1 Ecological Reserve

Argentia

Placentia

91

Avalon Peninsula

South Coast Outports Ferry

Port aux Basques-North Sydney (NS) Ferry

Cabot Strait

Ile de Miquelon

Fortune Bay

Grand Bank

Fortune

Marystown

Burin

Cape St Mary's

100

Avalon Wilderness Reserve

La Manche PP

Ferryland

St-Pierre & Miquelon (FRANCE) 7

Burin Peninsula

St Lawrence

St Mary's Ecological Reserve

St Mary's

Chance Cove PP

Ile St-Pierre

Argentia-North Sydney (NS) Ferry

St Vincent's

Mistaken Point Ecological Reserve

58°W · 56°W · 54°W · 52°W

Highlights

① Share the waves with whales and puffins at **Witless Bay Ecological Reserve** (p178)

② Hoist a drink, hear live music, take a ghost tour and soak up the history of North America's oldest city, **St John's** (p166)

③ Explore Leif Eriksson's 1000-year-old Viking pad at the sublime **L'Anse aux Meadows National Historic Site** (p199)

④ Hike the mountains and kayak the fjordlike lakes at **Gros Morne National Park** (p195)

⑤ Try out the outport life in **Fogo** (p192)

⑥ Learn Basque whaling history then walk alongside ancient whale bones at **Red Bay** (p213)

⑦ Get your French fix – wine, chocolate éclairs and baguettes – in **St-Pierre** (p187)

⑧ Snap a photo with the captain in **Dildo** (p181)

NEWFOUNDLAND FAST FACTS

» Population: 510,900

» Area: 405,720 sq km

» Capital: St John's

» Quirky Fact: Newfoundland has 82 places called Long Pond, 42 called White Point and one called Jerry's Nose

History

The Paleoindians walked into Labrador 9000 years ago. They hunted seals, fished for salmon and tried to stay warm. The Vikings, led by Leif Eriksson, washed ashore further south at L'Anse aux Meadows in Newfoundland in AD 1000. They established North America's first European settlement – 500 years ahead of Columbus – but conflicts with natives and harsh conditions eventually sent them back to Iceland.

John Cabot (Italian-born Giovanni Caboto) sailed around the shores of Newfoundland next. It was 1497, and he was employed by England's Henry VII. He returned to Bristol a hero, with news of finding a new and shorter route to Asia. While Cabot was badly mistaken, his stories of cod stocks so prolific that one could nearly walk on water spread quickly throughout Europe.

Soon the French, Portuguese, Spanish and Basques were also fishing off Newfoundland's coast. There were no permanent settlements on the island, and the fishing crews returned to Europe with their bounties at the end of each season. The English fishers' primary base was St John's, while the French congregated around Placentia and the Port au Port Peninsula. In the end it was the 1713 Treaty of Utrecht that ceded all of Newfoundland to England.

The land remained a British colony for most of the next two centuries, with life revolving around the booming fishing industry. Newfoundland's Aboriginal people, the Beothuk, did not fare well after settlement began. Diseases and land conflicts contributed to their demise by 1829.

Ever true to its independent spirit, Newfoundland was the last province to join Canada, doing so in 1949. While Labrador was always part of the package, it wasn't until 2001 that it became part of the provincial name.

Language

One recent visitor described the local accent as Irish meets Canadian while chewing a mouthful of cod. Well said.

Two hundred years ago, coastal fishing families from Ireland and England made up almost the entire population. Since then, as a result of living in isolated outposts, their language has evolved into almost 60 different dialects. Strong, lilting inflections, unique slang and colorful idioms pepper the language, sometimes confounding even residents.

The authoritative source is the **Dictionary of Newfoundland English** (www.heri

NEWFOUNDLAND ITINERARIES

Five Days

Start in St John's by visiting **Signal Hill** and **Cape Spear**. Both are historic sites, but they also offer walking trails and views where you just may see an iceberg, whale or both. At night sample St John's eateries, funky shops and music-filled pubs.

After a couple of days of 'big city' life, move onward through the Avalon Peninsula. Cruise to see whales and puffins at **Witless Bay Ecological Reserve**, plan a picnic in **Ferryland** or visit the birds at **Cape St Mary's**.

Spend the last day or two soaking up the historic eastern communities of **Trinity** and **Bonavista** and the cliffside hikes in between.

Ten Days

Do the five-day itinerary and then go west, possibly via a quick flight to **Deer Lake**, and reap the reward of viewing the mighty fjords of **Gros Morne National Park** and the monumental Viking history at **L'Anse aux Meadows**. With a few extra days you could sail across the Strait of Belle Isle and slow waaay down among the wee towns and bold granite cliffs of the **Labrador Straits**.

tage.nf.ca/dictionary). In the meantime, here are a few translations:

Long may yer big jib draw. Good luck.

Newfoundland Pronounced 'new-fun-*land*' (emphasized the same way as 'understand').

Oweshegettinonbys? Pronounced 'how's she getting on, boys?' ie how are you?

Where you longs to? Where are you from?

Land & Climate

They don't call it The Rock for nothing. Glaciers tore through, leaving behind a rugged landscape of boulders, lakes and bogs. The interior remains barren, while the island's cities and towns congregate at its edges near the sea.

Newfoundland's most significant landscape feature is actually offshore. The Grand Banks, which swing around the southeast coast, are an incredibly fertile marine feeding ground. The continental shelf here sticks out like a thumb to intercept the south-flowing waters of the frigid Labrador Current right at the point where it mingles with the warm north-flowing waters of the Gulf Stream. The mix of warmth and nutrient-rich arctic waters creates an explosion of plankton that feeds everything from the smallest fish to the biggest humpback. This is why the fishing was supreme here for so many years, and why it remains a top place to view whales and seabirds.

Labrador is more sparse than Newfoundland, puddled and tundralike, with mountains thrown in for good measure.

Temperatures peak in July and August, when daytime highs average 20°C. These are also the driest months; it rains or snows about 15 days out of every 30. Wintertime temperatures hover at 0°C. Fog and wind plague the coast much of the year (which makes for a lot of canceled flights).

Parks & Wildlife

Whales, moose and puffins are Newfoundland's wildlife stars, and most visitors see them all. Whale-watching tours depart from all around the province and will take you close to the sea mammals (usually humpback and minke). Puffins – the funny-looking love child of the penguin and parrot – flap around Witless Bay (p178) and Elliston (see the boxed text, p185). Moose nibble shrubs near roadsides throughout the province, so keep an eye out while driving. Some

» Book ahead for rental cars and accommodations. If you're arriving during the mid-July to early August peak, secure a car by April or May and don't wait much longer to book a room. **Newfoundland & Labrador Tourism** (www.newfoundlandlabrador. com) has listings.

» Driving distances are lengthy so have realistic expectations of what you can cover. For instance, it's 708km between St John's and Gros Morne National Park. The **Road Distance Database** (www.stats.gov. nl.ca/datatools/roaddb/distance) is a good reference.

» Know your seasons for puffins (May to August), icebergs (June to early July) and whales (July to August). Icebergs, in particular, can be tricky to predict. Check **Iceberg Finder** (www.icebergfinder.com) to get the drift.

visitors also glimpse caribou near the Avalon Wilderness Reserve (p179), which is special because usually these beasts can only be seen in the High Arctic. Large caribou herds also roam in Labrador.

ⓘ Getting There & Around

AIR

St John's Airport (YYT; www.stjohnsairport. com) is the main hub for the region, though **Deer Lake Airport** (YDF; www.deerlakeairport.com) is an excellent option for visitors focusing on the Northern Peninsula. Airlines flying in include **Air Canada** (www.aircanada.com), **Provincial** (www.provincialairlines.com), **Porter** (www. flyporter.com) and **Continental** (www.continental.com).

BOAT

Marine Atlantic (☑800-341-7981; www. marine-atlantic.ca) operates two massive car/ passenger ferries between North Sydney, Nova Scotia and Newfoundland. There's a daily, six-hour crossing to Port aux Basques (western Newfoundland) year-round, and a thrice-weekly, 14-hour crossing to Argentia (on the Avalon Peninsula) in summer. Reservations are recommended, especially to Argentia.

Provincial Ferry Service (www.gov.nl.ca/ ferryservices) runs the smaller boats that travel within the province to various islands and

REGIONAL DRIVING DISTANCES

» St John's to Port aux Basques: 905km

» St John's to Gros Morne: 708km

» Gros Morne to St Anthony: 372km

coastal towns. Each service has its own phone number with up-to-the-minute information; it's wise to call before embarking.

BUS

DRL (☑709-263-2171; www.drl-lr.com) sends one bus daily each way between St John's and Port aux Basques (13½ hours), making 25 stops en route. Other than DRL, public transportation consists of small, regional shuttle vans that connect with one or more major towns. Although not extensive, the system works pretty well and will get most people where they want to go.

CAR

The Trans-Canada Hwy (Hwy 1) is the main cross-island roadway. Driving distances are deceptive, as travel is often slow-going on heavily contorted, single-lane roads. Watch out for moose, especially at dusk. High-risk zones are signposted (the yellow-and-black graphic of an antlered beast crumpling a car is a Newfoundland photo op).

ST JOHN'S

POP 100,600

Encamped on the steep slopes of a harbor, with jelly-bean-colored row houses popping up from hilly streets, St John's is often described as looking like a mini San Francisco. And like its American counterpart, it's home to artists, musicians, inflated real-estate prices and young, iPhone-using denizens. Yet the vibe of Newfoundland's largest

city and capital remains refreshingly small-town, with locals happy to share conversation and a sudsy drink with newcomers. At some point, they'll be sure to let you know St John's is North America's oldest city.

Highlights include view-gaping from Signal Hill, walking the seaside North Head Trail and listening to live music and hoisting a pint (or shot of rum) in George St's pubs. Many visitors take advantage of the city's beyond-the-norm eating and lodging options by making St John's their base camp for explorations elsewhere on the Avalon Peninsula. Cape Spear, Witless Bay Ecological Reserve and Ferryland are among the easy day trips.

History

St John's excellent natural harbor, leading out to what were once seething seas of cod, prompted the first European settlement here in 1528. Sir Humphrey Gilbert landed in town 55 years later, and proudly claimed the land for Queen Elizabeth I. The many Spanish, French and Portuguese settlers living around the harbor were not amused. During the late 1600s and much of the 1700s, St John's was razed and taken over several times as the French, English and Dutch fought for it tooth and nail. After Britain's ultimate victory on Signal Hill in 1762, things finally settled down and St John's started to take shape throughout the 1800s.

Since then four fires have ripped through the city, the last in 1892. Each time locals rebuilt with their pride and, more importantly, their sense of humor, intact.

Despite the centuries of turmoil, the harbor steadfastly maintained its position as the world trade center for salted cod well into the 20th century. By mid-century, warehouses lined Water St, and the merchants who owned them made a fortune. Come the early 1960s, St John's had more millionaires per capita than any other city in North America. Many called it the Codfish Republic, a riff on Central America's Banana Republics, and said these merchants got rich off the backs of the outport fishing communities, which only seemed to get poorer.

Today the city's wharves still act as service stations to fishing vessels from around the world and the occasional cruise ship, though the cod industry suffered mightily after the 1992 fishing moratorium (see the boxed text, p186). The offshore oil industry now drives the economy.

ℹ️ **THE RENTAL CAR CRUNCH**

Be warned: rental car fleets are small (thanks to the island's remoteness and short tourist season), which means loads of visitors vie for limited vehicles in midsummer. Costs can rack up to $100 per day (including taxes and mileage fees). Reserve well in advance – April or May is recommended if you're traveling during the mid-July to early August peak – and confirm the booking before you arrive.

⊙ Sights

Most sights are downtown or within a few kilometers, though prepare for some serious uphill walking.

Signal Hill National Historic Site

HISTORIC PARK

(🏛/709-772-5367; www.pc.gc.ca/signalhill; Signal Hill Rd; grounds free; ☺grounds 24hr) A trip up Signal Hill, the city's most famous landmark, is worth it for the glorious view alone, though there's much more to see.

An **interpretive center** (adult/child $3.90/1.90; ☺10am-6pm, reduced hr mid-Oct–mid-May) features interactive displays on the site's history. The last North American battle of the Seven Years' War took place here in 1762, and Britain's victory ended France's renewed aspirations for control of eastern North America.

You can see cannons and the remains of the late-18th-century British battery at **Queen's Battery & Barracks** further up the hill. The tiny castle topping the hill is **Cabot Tower** (admission free; ☺9am-9pm Jun-early Sep, to 5pm rest of year, closed mid-Jan–Mar), built in 1900 to honor both John Cabot's arrival in 1497 and Queen Victoria's Diamond Jubilee. Here Italian inventor Guglielmo Marconi gleefully received the first wireless transatlantic message from Cornwall, England in 1901. There are guides and displays in the tower; an amateur radio society operates a station here in summer.

In midsummer, several dozen soldiers dressed as the 19th-century Royal Newfoundland Company perform a **tattoo** (www.rnchs.ca/tattoo; admission $5; ☺11am & 3pm Wed, Thu, Sat & Sun Jul–mid-Aug) on O'Flaherty Field next to the interpretive center. It wraps up with the firing of historic cannons.

An awesome way to return to downtown is along the **North Head Trail** (1.7km) that connects Cabot Tower with the harborfront Battery neighborhood. The walk departs from the tower's parking lot and traces the cliffs, imparting tremendous sea views and sometimes whale spouts. Because much of the trail runs along the bluff's sheer edge, this walk isn't something to attempt in icy, foggy or dark conditions.

The site sits 1.5km from downtown, up Signal Hill Rd.

The Rooms

MUSEUM

(📞709-757-8000; www.therooms.ca; 9 Bonaventure Ave; adult/child $7.50/4; ☺10am-5pm Mon-Sat, to 9pm Wed, noon-5pm Sun, closed Mon mid-Oct–May) Not many museums offer the chance to see a giant squid, hear avant-garde sound sculptures and peruse ancient weaponry all under one roof. But that's the Rooms, the province's all-in-one historical museum, art gallery and archives. Frankly, the building is much more impressive to look at than look in, since its frequently changing exhibits are sparse. But whoa! The views from this massive stone-and-glass complex, which lords over the city from a breath-sapping hilltop, are eye-poppers; try the 4th-floor cafe for the best vistas. There's free admission Wednesday evenings.

Johnson Geo Centre

MUSEUM

(📞709-737-7880; www.geocentre.ca; 175 Signal Hill Rd; adult/child $11.50/5.50; ☺9:30am-5pm Mon-Sat, noon-5pm Sun) Nowhere in the world can geo-history, going back to the birth of the earth, be accessed so easily as in Newfoundland, and the Geo Centre does a grand job of making snore-worthy geological information perk up with appeal, through its underground, interactive displays.

The center also has an exhibit on the *Titanic,* and how human error and omission caused the tragedy, not just an iceberg. For instance, the ship's owners didn't supply with enough lifeboats so as not to 'clutter the deck,' and the crew ignored myriad

---

TEA TOMB

All around the Anglican Cathedral you'll see signs for 'tea in the crypt.' Sound spooky? It is a bit when you first arrive at the church's basement, what with all the women in flowery dresses and sensible shoes flurrying to and fro. But give it a chance, and **high tea** ($8; ☺2:30-4:30pm Mon-Fri mid-Jul–early Sep) here becomes more than home-baked cookies and mini-scones. It's a chance to chat with the older generation about jam recipes, tips for summer holidays and the way things used to be (actually, you'll be listening and eating, and they'll do all the talking). The crypt, by the way, has never been used for burials.

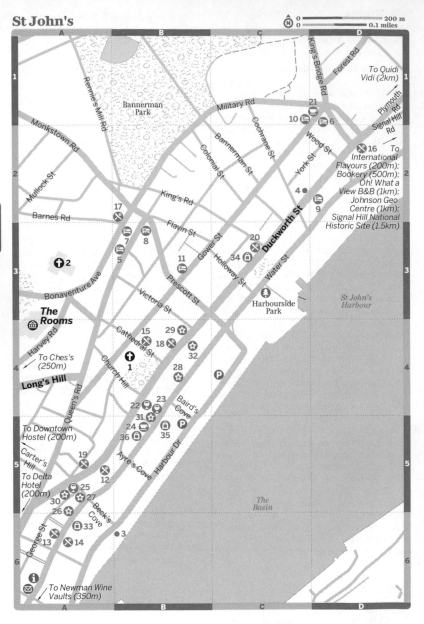

ice warnings. What any of this has to do with geology remains unclear, but who cares? It's fascinating.

Trails with interpretive panels wind around outside. The Geo Centre is up Signal Hill Rd, about 1km beyond downtown.

Basilica of St John the Baptist CHURCH
(☎709-754-2170; www.thebasilica.ca; 200 Military Rd; admission free; ⊙8am-3pm Mon-Fri, to 6pm Sat, to 12:30pm Sun) Built in 1855, the soaring twin spires of the basilica pierce the sky and are visible all the way from

NEWFOUNDLAND & LABRADOR SIGHTS

Signal Hill. Its design marks the revival of classical architecture in North America. Inside, 65 unique stained-glass windows illuminate the remarkable polychromatic Italianate ceiling and its gold-leaf highlights. The honor of being named a 'basilica' was bestowed on the church by Pope Pius XII on its centennial anniversary. Free half-hour tours are offered 10am to 5pm Monday to Saturday in July and August, according to demand.

Anglican Cathedral of St John the Baptist   CHURCH
(☑709-726-5677; www.stjohnsanglicancathedral.org; 16 Church Hill; admission free; ◎10am-noon & 2-4pm Mon-Fri, 10am-noon Sat Jul & Aug) Serving Canada's oldest parish (1699), the Anglican cathedral is one of the finest examples of ecclesiastical Gothic architecture in North America. Although originally built in the 1830s, all but its exterior walls were reduced to ashes by the Great Fire of 1892. It was rebuilt in 1905. The Gothic ribbed

ceiling, graceful stone arches and long, thin, stained-glass windows are timeless marvels. A gargoyle dating from the 12th century – a gift from the Diocese of Bristol – stands guard over the south transept. Students offer tours, organists play **concerts** (◎1:15pm Wed) and elderly church ladies serve tea and crumpets (see the boxed text, p167).

Quidi Vidi   BREWERY & HISTORICAL SITE
Over Signal Hill, away from town, is the tiny picturesque village of Quidi Vidi. Make your first stop **Quidi Vidi Brewery** (☑709-738-4040; www.quidividibrewery.ca; 35 Barrows Rd; tours $10; ◎10am-4:30pm Mon-Sat, noon-4pm Sun), which cooks up Newfoundland's most popular microbrews. Located in an old fish-processing plant on the small wharf, it's a scenic place to slake one's thirst. The fee includes ample tastings and a bottle to sip while touring. Be sure to try the Iceberg brand, made with water from the big hunks.

Nearby you'll find the oldest cottage in North America, the 1750s-era **Mallard Cottage** (☎709-576-2266; 2 Barrows Rd; ☺9:30am-4:30pm May-Sep), now a charmingly cluttered antique/junk shop. Profits go to maintenance.

The 1762 **Quidi Vidi Battery** (☎709-729-2977; www.seethesites.ca; Cuckhold's Cove Rd; admission $3; ☺10am-5:30pm late May–mid-Oct) atop the hill was built by the French after they took St John's. The British quickly claimed it, and it remained in military service into the 1800s. Period-garbed interpreters dole out historical information.

Inland from the village, **Quidi Vidi Lake** is the site of the city-stopping St John's Regatta. The **Royal St John's Regatta Museum** (☎709-576-8921; cnr Lakeview Ave & Clancy Dr, off Forest Rd; admission free; ☺Jul & Aug) is on the 2nd floor of the boathouse. Opening hours vary. A popular walking trail leads around the lake.

Quidi Vidi is about 2km from the northeast edge of downtown. Take Plymouth Rd, go left on Quidi Vidi Rd, then right on Forest Rd (which becomes Quidi Vidi Village Rd). For the brewery, bear right onto Barrows Rd. For the battery, veer off on Cuckold's Cove Rd. For the regatta museum, take a left off Forest Rd onto Lakeview Ave. You can also walk from Signal Hill via the Cuckold's Cove Trail, which takes about 30 minutes.

Newman Wine Vaults　　HISTORICAL SITE
(☎709-739-7870; www.historictrust.com; 436 Water St; admission by donation; ☺10am-5:30pm mid-Jun–Aug) Dating from the 1780s, these dark cool wine vaults are where the Newman company aged its port until 1996 (when EU regulations forced the process back to Portugal). Tour guides relay stories such as how English noblemen, who wanted to be buried in their homeland, got shipped back after death in barrels of port, since the alcohol preserved their bodies. There are no tastings, but you can purchase bottles. The vaults often host literary events.

CA Pippy Park　　PARK
(www.pippypark.com) The feature-filled, 13-sq-km CA Pippy Park coats downtown's northwestern edge. Recreational facilities include walking trails, picnic areas, playgrounds, a golf course and a campground. **Memorial University**, the province's only university, is here too.

The university's **botanical garden** (☎709-737-8590; www.mun.ca/botgarden; adult/child $6/2.50; ☺10am-5pm May-Sep, reduced hr rest of yr) is at Oxen Pond, at the park's western edge off Mt Scio Rd. There's a cultivated garden and a nature reserve. Together, these and the park's **Long Pond** marsh give visitors an excellent introduction to Newfoundland's flora, habitats (including boreal forest and bogs) and animals (look for birds at Long Pond and the occasional moose). Take the 3km **Long Pond Walk** for the full effect.

The **Fluvarium** (☎709-754-3474; www.fluvarium.ca; Nagle's Pl; adult/child/family $7/4/20; ☺9am-5pm Mon-Fri, from 10am Sat & Sun late Jun-early Sep, reduced hr rest of yr), a glass-sided cross-section of a 'living' river, is located across the street from the campground. Viewers can peer through large windows to observe the undisturbed goings-on beneath the surface of Nagle's Hill Brook. Numerous brown trout and the occasional eel can be seen. If there has been substantial rain or high winds, all visible life is lost in the murkiness.

To get here from downtown, take Bonaventure Ave north to Allandale Rd and follow the signs; it's about 2km.

🏃 Activities

For whale watching and sea kayaking, see opposite. Golf and cross-country skiing enthusiasts can partake in CA Pippy Park.

Excellent walking trails zigzag across the area. The **Grand Concourse** (www.grandconcourse.ca) is an ambitious 95km-long trail network throughout St John's and environs. Many hikes are in the CA Pippy Park and Quidi Vidi Lake areas. Definitely make time for the sea-hugging North Head Trail on Signal Hill. The concourse website has route details for all walks.

The epic **East Coast Trail** (www.eastcoasttrail.com) stretches 220km from Fort Amherst south to Cappahayden; a further 320km is to be developed. It's part easy coastal walking, part tough wilderness trail. The website has details on free weekly guided hikes; on some you can also volunteer to do trail cleanup. An excellent stretch runs along the coast from Cape Spear (p177).

👉 Tours
Boat

For most tours, you need to head south of town to Witless Bay (see p178).

Iceberg Quest (☎709-722-1888; www.icebergquest.com; Pier 7; 2hr tours adult/child $55/25) Departs from St John's harbor and makes a run down to Cape Spear in

St John's will keep the wee ones entertained, rain or shine. **CA Pippy Park** (opposite) is a kids' haven, with a huge playground, lots of trails and, of course, the Fluvarium. The ever-hungry ducks at the pond in **Bowring Park** (Waterford Bridge Rd) love company, as do the sea creatures at the **Ocean Sciences Centre** (p177). Just knowing a cannon will blast at the end of the tattoo should keep kids riveted at **Signal Hill** (p167). The various **boat tours** (opposite) are also a great bet, but inquire if there are icebergs and whales in the area first. While geology may not initially spark their interest, the fact that the **Johnson Geo Centre** (p167) is underground may do the trick. Older kids will enjoy the ghostly tales of the **St John's Haunted Hike** (see below).

search of icebergs in June, whales in July and August.

O'Brien's (☑709-753-4850, 877-639-4253; www.obriensboattours.com; 126 Duckworth St; 2hr tours adult/3-10yr/11-17yr $55/25/30) See whales, puffins and icebergs at Witless Bay. Boats launch from Bay Bulls 31km south, but O'Brien's has a shuttle service (round-trip $25) that picks up from hotels throughout St John's. Buy tickets at O'Brien's shop.

Outfitters (☑709-579-4453, 800-966-9658; www.theoutfitters.nf.ca; 220 Water St; half-/full-day tours $69/169) Popular kayak tours at Bay Bulls, with shuttle service (round-trip $25) from Outfitters' store downtown.

Bus

Ann's Tours (☑709-682-0754; www.ann stours.ca) Ann offers a variety of tours covering the Irish Loop ($160 including whale-watch boat, seven hours) and Cape St Mary's ($110, seven hours), plus shorter city jaunts and customized tours.

HI St John's Tours (☑709-754-4789; www.hihostels.ca; 8 Gower St) The hostel arranges Cape Spear/Ferryland/Witless Bay tours ($99, five hours) daily, if enough people sign up.

Legend Tours (☑709-753-1497; www.legend tours.ca; 3hr tours $59) This award-winning operator covers St John's, Cape Spear and the northeast Avalon Peninsula. The commentary is richly woven with humor and historical tidbits. Call to reserve; they'll pick you up at your hotel or B&B.

Cultural

Cape Race Cultural Adventures (www.caperace.com; 10-day package per person $2600) Immerse yourself in life as a local. You get the keys to three houses (in St

John's, Heart's Delight and Bonavista), a car and a guidebook to do it yourself.

Walking

The visitors center has brochures for self-guided walking tours in town.

East Coast Trail (www.eastcoasttrail.com) Check the website for free guided hikes.

TOP CHOICE **St John's Haunted Hike** (www.hauntedhike.com; tours $10; ⊙9.30pm Sun-Thu Jun–mid-Sep) The black-caped Reverend Thomas Wyckham Jarvis Esq leads these super-popular explorations of the city's dark corners. He'll spook you with tales of headless captains, murderers and other ghosts. Departure is from the Anglican Cathedral's west entrance.

Festivals & Events

St John's Days (www.stjohns.ca; ⊙late Jun) A long weekend of jazz and blues concerts, parades, street dances and sporting events to commemorate the city's birthday.

Sound Symposium (www.soundsymposium.com; ⊙early Jul) Held every other year, it's a big, avant-garde week of concerts, workshops, dance, theater and film experiments; next symposiums are in 2012 and 2014.

George Street Festival (www.georg estreetlive.ca; ⊙late Jul) The mighty George St becomes one big nightclub for a fabulous week of daytime and nighttime musical performances.

Newfoundland & Labrador Folk Festival (www.nlfolk.com; ⊙1st weekend Aug) This intimate, three-day event in Bannerman Park celebrates traditional Newfoundland music, dancing and storytelling.

Downtown Busker Festival (www.down townstjohns.com; ⊙1st weekend Aug) Jugglers, magicians, acrobats, comedians and more take their performances to the streets.

Royal St John's Regatta (www.stjohns regatta.org; ☼1st Wed Aug) The streets are empty, the stores are closed and everyone migrates to the shores of Quidi Vidi Lake. This rowing regatta officially began in 1825 and is now the oldest continuously held sporting event in North America.

🛏 Sleeping

Scores of B&Bs offer a place to rest your head in the heart of St John's; they're usually better value than the hotels and motels. They fill fast, so book ahead. Many have a two-night minimum stay requirement. The ones listed here all serve a hot breakfast. The city's 16% tax is not included in prices listed unless stated otherwise. Parking is available at or near all accommodations. For more lodging options, see the city's website (www.stjohns.ca/visitors/accom modation/index.jsp).

Balmoral House B&B $$
(☎709-754-5721, 877-428-1055; www.balmoral house.com; 38 Queen's Rd; d $99-179; ☼❀@) While the Balmoral is a typical B&B in many ways (cherub statues, long wooden antique tables), its owners live off-site and breakfast is self-serve, so it's more relaxed and private than many B&Bs. The beds are bestowed with super-comfy mattresses.

Abba Inn B&B $$
(☎709-754-0058, 800-563-3959; www.abbainn. com; 36 Queen's Rd; d from $85-185; ☼❀@☎) The Abba shares the same building as the Balmoral, and they even share reservations (ie if one is full, they'll hook you up with the other). Both B&Bs have similar amenities and ambience.

Cantwell House B&B $$
(☎709-754-8439, 888-725-8439; www.cantwell house.nf.net; 25 Queen's Rd; r from $85-110; ☼@) Take tea from a seat on Cantwell's deck and stare out over a colorful collage of row houses to the blue harbor. The B&B's friendly atmosphere combines with a sense of privacy amid Victorian ambience.

HI St John's HOSTEL $
(☎709-754-4789; www.hihostels.ca; 8 Gower St; dm $28-33, r $75-89; ☼@☎) It's everything a good hostel should be: well located near the action, spick 'n' span facilities, not too big (16 beds in all), and helpful. A whiteboard lists everything of interest happening in

town each day. The hostel also books reasonably priced tours.

Oh! What A View B&B B&B $$
(☎709-576-7063; www.ohwhataview.com; 184 Signal Hill Rd; r from $90; ☼@) It's a 20-minute hike (uphill) from the town center, but oh, it really is a stunning view. Several common balconies take in the harbor below. The rooms are bright and modern, if a bit small. Ask for room No 8 with its Juliet balcony or No 3 with its straight shot of the water.

Narrows B&B B&B $$
(☎709-739-4850, 866-739-4850; www.thenar rowsbb.com; 146 Gower St; d $95-175; ☼☎) Warm colors mix with elegant trims and large wooden beds in the rooms of this welcoming B&B. There are modern amenities throughout and a gorgeous sitting room and balcony where guests can mingle and swap whale stories.

Bluestone Inn B&B $$
(☎709-754-7544, 877-754-9876; www.theblue stoneinn.com; 34 Queen's Rd; d $89-189; ☼☎) Built from the same historic stone as Cabot Tower and Government House, this B&B provides towering plasterwork ceilings, fireplaces and original artwork in its rooms. It was for sale at press time, so changes may be in the offing.

Downtown Hostel HOSTEL $
(☎709-754-7658; www.hostels.com; 25 Young St; dm/r $22/55; ☼☎) It's a toss-up who has more character: the energized owner Carola or the building itself. Crooked homemade furniture resists the steeply plunging floors, and electrical cords and world maps adorn the walls. It's about 1km northwest of George St, off Carter's Hill.

At Wit's Inn B&B $$
(☎709-739-7420, 877-739-7420; www.atwitsinn. ca; 3 Gower St; d $109-139; ☼❀@☎) Polished floorboards, plasterwork ceilings, ornate fireplaces, bright-colored walls and beds you'll have trouble leaving make this B&B memorable. The living and dining rooms are as swank as they are comfy.

Leaside Manor B&B $$
(☎709-722-0387, 877-807-7245; www.leaside manor.com; 39 Topsail Rd; r $129-249; ☼❀@☎) The higher-end rooms in this old merchant's home have a canopied bed, fireplace and Jacuzzi, which explains why the *Globe and Mail* designated Leaside as one of Canada's 'most romantic destinations.' It's about a half-hour walk from downtown;

to be closer, inquire about the downtown apartments.

Delta Hotel (☑709-739-6404; www.delta hotels.com; 120 New Gower St; r $189-249; ✱@🛜🏊) The Delta is the main, amenity-laden business hotel in town; it's located next to the convention center. Parking costs $11.

Courtyard St John's (☑709-722-6636; www.marriott.com/yytcy; 131 Duckworth St; r $159-189; Ᵽ✱@🏊) It's the Marriott chain's typical property, with comfy beds. Some rooms have harbor views (about $10 extra). Wi-fi access is lobby only.

🍴 Eating

Thai, Japanese, Indian, Latin and even vegetarian restaurants pop up along Water and Duckworth Sts, providing a variety you won't find elsewhere in the province. Stroll along here and you're sure to find something to sink your teeth into.

Bistro Sofia CAFE $$
TOP CHOICE (☑709-738-2060; 320 Water St; sandwiches $7-9, mains $19-28; ⊗8am-11pm; 🛜) Bistro Sofia cooks up high-quality food and serves it casually in a bright, classy coffee-shop ambience. Order at the counter, plop down at a roomy table, and wait for your lunch (grilled sandwiches plumped to perfection) or dinner (braised lamb shank or steak and frites) while sipping coffee or wine.

Hungry Heart CAFE $
(☑709-738-6164; www.hungryheartcafe.ca; 142 Military Rd; mains $7-12; ⊗10am-2pm Mon-Sat) Eat in this warm-toned cafe and you're

helping abused women and others in need to train in food service and get back on their feet. Try the curry mango chicken or pulled pork sandwiches. Saturday brunch brings out the cheese scones with peameal bacon and cherry bread pudding. Lots of baked goodies, too.

Bacalao SEAFOOD $$$
(☑709-579-6565; www.bacalaocuisine.ca; 65 Lemarchant Rd; mains $28-35; ⊗noon-2:30pm Tue-Fri, from 11am Sat & Sun, 6-10pm Tue-Sun) Cozy Bacalao sources local, sustainable ingredients for its 'nouvelle Newfound-land cuisine.' Dishes include salt cod *du jour* and caribou in partridgeberry sauce, washed down by local beer and wines. Located 1.5km west of downtown; take Water St south to Waldegrave St, then Barters Hill Rd.

International Flavours PAKASTANI $
(☑709-738-4636; 4 Quidi Vidi Rd; mains $8-12; ⊗noon-7pm Tue-Sat; ☑) Pakistani owner Talat ladles out a whopping spicy plateful of dahl or curry with basmati rice for her daily set meal (one with meat, the other without). She's just beyond downtown, a few minutes' walk up Signal Hill Rd.

Sprout VEGETARIAN $
(☑709-579-5485; 364 Duckworth St; mains $6-12; ⊗11:30am-8pm Tue & Wed, to 9pm Thu & Fri, 9am-9pm Sat, 9am-3pm Sun; ☑) It's almost unheard of in Newfoundland: full-on vegetarian food. So savor your marinated tofu burger, spinach-pesto-melt sandwich and brown rice *poutine* (French fries topped with gravy and cheese) before leaving town.

SCRUNCHEONS, TOUTONS & FLIPPER PIE: A GASTRONOMIC GUIDE

Get ready for a whole new culinary vocabulary when you enter Newfoundland. Lesson number one: having a 'scoff' is local parlance for eating a big meal.

Two of Newfoundland's favorite dishes are fish 'n' brewis and jigg's dinner. Fish 'n' brewis is a blend of salted fish, onions, scruncheons (aka fried pork fat) and a near-boiled bread. Jigg's dinner is a right feast comprising a roast (turkey or possibly moose) along with boiled potatoes, carrots, cabbage, salted beef and pea-and-bread pudding. A touton is fried dough that you dip in gooey molasses.

Cod tongues are the tender, fleshy bits between the lower jaws served battered and fried, while cod cheeks are just that: cheeks from the fish. Fishcakes are a blend of cod, potato and onion mashed together and fried – delicious. Seal flipper pie, on the other hand, is for the brave; the strong flavor of seal meat is definitely an acquired taste.

To finish off your meal, try figgy duff, a thick fig pudding boiled in a cloth bag.

And the final lesson in gastro terminology: when you're done eating, pat your stomach and say, 'I'm full as an egg.'

Auntie Crae's
CAFE $

(☑709-754-0661; www.auntiecraes.com; 272 Water St; sandwiches $6-7; ☺8am-6pm Tue-Sat) Come to this specialty food store for a cuppa joe, baked goods, groceries or a prepared sandwich. Relax with your goodies in the adjoining Fishhook Neyle's Common Room.

Casbah
FUSION $$

(☑709-738-5293; 2 Cathedral St; mains $13-23; ☺11:30am-2:30pm Thu & Fri, from 10:30am Sat & Sun, 5:30-11pm daily) Fun, sassy waiters serve fun, sassy food in colorful Casbah. They keep everyone happy by offering small, medium and large plates, which might contain maple-roasted pumpkin soup or halibut burger with wasabi mayo.

Blue on Water
SEAFOOD $$$

(☑709-754-2583; www.blueonwater.com; 319 Water St; mains $27-35; ☺7:30am-10pm Mon-Fri, 9am-11pm Sat, 9am-9pm Sun) This hip restaurant does inventive takes on seafood dishes such as cod tongues and scruncheons and maple salmon with organic veggies. Brunch includes banana pancakes topped with rum-roasted walnuts. If nothing else, grab a drink in Blue's loungelike bar next door.

Classic Cafe East
CAFE $$

(☑709-726-4444; www.classiccafeeast.com; 73 Duckworth St; sandwiches $8-11, mains $13-21; ☺8am-10pm) Yes, many tourists eat here, but it's still a swell place to soak up harbor views and fork into Newfie standards like toutons, fish 'n' brewis, seafood chowder and fishcakes, plus omelettes and sandwiches.

India Gate
INDIAN $$

(☑709-753-6006; www.indiagate.250x.com; 286 Duckworth St; mains $12-16; ☺11:30am-2pm Mon-Fri, 5-10pm daily; ☑) This is the local Indian favorite, with loads of vegetarian options. Fill up at the weekday all-you-can-eat lunch special for $15.

Sun Sushi
JAPANESE $$

(☑709-726-8688; 186 Duckworth St; sushi rolls $4.50-7.50; ☺noon-10pm, closed Sun) This unadorned spot tops the townsfolks' list for reasonably priced sushi. The spicy tuna wins raves.

Ches's
FAST FOOD $

(☑709-726-2373; www.chessfishandchips.ca; 9 Freshwater Rd; mains $7-12; ☺11am-2am Sun-Thu, to 3am Fri & Sat) Ches's and its fish and chips are an institution in Newfoundland. No frills, just cod that will melt in your mouth.

Drinking

George St is the city's famous party lane. Water and Duckworth Sts also have plenty of drinkeries, but the scene is slightly more sedate. Bars stay open until 2am. Expect many places to charge a small cover (about $5) on weekends or when there's live music. Don't forget to try the local Screech rum.

Duke of Duckworth
PUB

TOP CHOICE (www.thedukenl.ca; McMurdo's Lane, 325 Duckworth St) 'The Duke,' as it's known, is an unpretentious English-style pub that represents all that's great about Newfoundland and Newfoundlanders. Stop in on a Friday night and you'll see a mix of blue-collar, white-collar, young and old, even band members from Great Big Sea plunked down on the well-worn, red-velour bar stools. The kitchen cooks the ultimate in chicken pot pie, fish and chips and other comfort foods, and 14 beers (including the local Quidi Vidi) flow through the taps.

Trapper John's Museum & Pub
PUB

(www.trapperjohns.com; 3 George St) It's not the most refined pub in town, but it sure is the most fun place to become an Honorary Newfoundlander, which happens after you kiss Stubby the Puffin (a variation on the

---

GETTING SCREECHED IN

Within a few days of your arrival in St John's, you'll undoubtedly be asked by everyone if you've been 'screeched in,' or in traditional Newfoundland slang, 'Is you a screecher?' It's not as painful as it sounds, and is, in fact, locals' playful way to welcome visitors to the province.

Screeching derives from the 1940s when new arrivals were given their rites of passage, and from pranks played on sealers heading to the ice for the first time. Today the ceremony takes place in local pubs, where you'll gulp a shot of rum (there's actually a local brand called Screech), recite an unpronounceable verse in the local lingo, kiss a stuffed codfish and then receive a certificate declaring you an 'Honorary Newfoundlander.' Sure it's touristy, but it's also good fun. The more the merrier, so try to get screeched in with a crowd.

usual codfish). The animal traps enshrined throughout grant the 'museum' status.

Hava Java COFFEE SHOP
(216 Water St; ⊙7:30am-11pm Mon-Fri, 9am-11pm Sat & Sun) The atmosphere at this place is refreshingly antifranchise and pro-tattoo; it focuses on making the best coffee in town.

Bookery COFFEE SHOP
(42 Powers Ct; ⊙10am-6pm Wed-Sat, noon-5pm Sun) Yes, it's a bookstore (with a fantastic selection of local authors), but it also pours rich hot chocolate and java. A clock-crazy antique shop sits upstairs. It's a 10-minute walk up Signal Hill Rd.

Grapevine WINE BAR
(206 Water St) Dark, swanky Grapevine is a wine and cocktail bar with great music and martinis.

Celtic Hearth (www.theceltichearth.com;
298 Water St; ⊙24hr) Get your Guinness and pub grub 24/7; it's underneath Bridie Molloy's.

Coffee Matters (www.coffeematters.ca; 1
Military Rd; ⊙7am-11pm Mon-Fri, from 8am Sat & Sun; 🛜) The city's swankiest coffee and tea shop.

☆ Entertainment

The Scope (www.thescope.ca) has the daily lowdown. Perhaps because this is such an intimate city, word-of-mouth and flyers slapped on light poles are also major vehicles for entertainment information. Venues are close together – have a wander and enjoy.

Live Music
Cover charges range from $5 to $10. **Mighty Pop** (www.mightypop.ca) lists cool upcoming shows.

Ship Pub (☎709-753-3870; 265 Duckworth St) Attitudes and ages are checked at the door of this little pub, tucked down Solomon's Lane. You'll hear everything from jazz to indie, and even the odd poetry reading. Wednesday is folk-music night.

Bridie Molloy's (www.bridiemolloys.com; George St) This polished Irish pub hosts an older crowd and offers Irish and Newfoundland music six nights per week.

Rose & Thistle (☎709-579-6662; 208 Water St) Pub where well-known local folk musicians strum.

Fat Cat (www.fatcatbluesbar.com; George St; ⊙closed Mon) Blues radiates from the cozy Fat Cat nightly during summer.

Rock House (☎709-579-6832; George St) When indie bands visit town, they plug in here.

Theater
Resource Centre for the Arts (☎709-753-4531; www.rca.nf.ca; 3 Victoria St) Sponsors indie theater, dance and film by Newfoundland artists, all of which plays downtown in the former longshoremen's union hall (aka LSPU Hall).

Shakespeare by the Sea Festival (www.sbts.info; tickets $15; ⊙early Jul–mid-Aug) Live outdoor productions are presented at Signal Hill, Bowring Park and other venues. Buy all tickets on-site; cash only.

Nightclubs
St John's true nightclubs, which only open on Friday and Saturday night (from between 11pm and 4am or so), cater to energetic straight and gay crowds. Cover charges do vary, but they are typically between $5 and $10.

Zone (216 Water St) This is the premier gay dance bar in Newfoundland. Straights are equally welcome to soak up the fun energy; located above Hava Java.

Liquid Ice (186B Water St) If you like your house, drum and bass or hip-hop, wade into this gay-friendly nightspot.

🛍 Shopping

You'll find traditional music, berry jams and local art in the nooks and crannies of Water and Duckworth Sts.

Fred's MUSIC STORE
(☎709-753-9191; www.freds.nf.ca; 198 Duckworth St) This is the premier music shop in St John's. It features local music such as Hey Rosetta, Buddy Wasisname, Ron Hynes, The Navigators and Great Big Sea.

Living Planet CLOTHING
(☎709-739-6810; www.livingplanet.ca; 197 Water St) For quirky tourist T-shirts and buttons even locals are proud to wear.

Downhome SOUVENIRS
(☎709-722-2070; 303 Water St) It may be touristy, but it does feature a fine selection of local goods such as jams, as well as the coveted *How to Play the Musical Spoons* CD.

Outfitters OUTDOOR GEAR
(☎709-579-4453; www.theoutfitters.nf.ca; 220 Water St) A camping and gear shop where

you can get the local outdoorsy lowdown (check the bulletin board).

Information

Internet Access

There is a public internet terminal for use at the visitors center (free access for 15 minutes). Several coffee shops and bars have free wi-fi, including Bistro Sofia, Hava Java and Duke of Duckworth.

Media & Internet Resources

City of St John's (www.stjohns.ca) The 'Tourism' category has descriptions of and links to attractions, accommodations, eateries and events.

Downhome (www.downhomelife.com) A folksy, *Reader's Digest*–style monthly for the region.

St John's Telegram (www.thetelegram.com) The city's daily newspaper.

The Scope (www.thescope.ca) Free alternative newspaper covering local arts and politics.

Medical Services

Health Sciences Complex (709-777-6300; 300 Prince Phillip Dr) A 24-hour emergency room.

Water St Pharmacy (709-579-5554; 335 Water St; closed Sun)

Money

Banks stack up near the Water St and Ayre's Cove intersection.

CIBC (215 Water St)

Scotia Bank (245 Water St)

Post

Central post office (709-758-1003; 354 Water St)

Tourist Information

Visitors Centre (709-576-8106; www.stjohns.ca; 348 Water St; 9am-4:30pm) Excellent resource with free provincial and city road maps, and staff to answer questions and help with bookings.

Getting There & Away

Air

Air Canada (www.aircanada.com), **WestJet** (www.westjet.com), **Provincial Airlines** (www.provincialairlines.com) and **Porter Airlines** (www.flyporter.com) are the main carriers. **Continental Airlines** (www.continental.com) offers the only direct flight from the USA. Air Canada has a daily flight to/from London.

Bus

DRL (709-263-2171; www.drl-lr.com) sends one bus daily each way between St John's and Port aux Basques ($112, cash only, 13½ hours)

via the 905km-long Hwy 1, making 25 stops en route. It leaves at 7:30am from Memorial University's Student Centre, in CA Pippy Park.

Car & Motorcycle

Avis, Budget, Enterprise, Hertz, National and Thrifty (see p265) have offices at the airport. **Practicar** (709-753-2277; www.practicar.ca; 909 Topsail Rd) is a 20-minute drive from the airport but often has lower rates.

Share Taxis

These large vans typically seat 15 and allow you to jump on or off at any point along their routes. You must call in advance to reserve. They pick up and drop off at your hotel. Cash only.

Foote's Taxi (709-832-0491, 800-866-1181) Travels daily down the Burin Peninsula as far as Fortune ($45, five hours).

Newhook's Transportation (709-682-4877, in Placentia 709-227-2552) Travels down the southwestern Avalon Peninsula to Placentia, in sync with the Argentia ferry schedule ($30, two hours).

Shirran's Taxi (709-468-7741) Plies the Bonavista Peninsula daily, making stops at Trinity ($45, 3½ hours) and Bonavista ($40, four hours), among others.

Getting Around

To/From the Airport

St John's Airport (YYT; www.stjohnsairport.com) is 6km north of the city on Portugal Cove Rd (Rte 40). A government-set flat rate of $22.50 (plus $3 for each extra passenger) is charged by taxis to go from the airport to downtown hotels and B&Bs; **Citywide Taxi** (709-722-7777) provides the official service. However, when you make the trip in reverse – ie from town to the airport – taxis run on meters and should cost around $20.

Car & Motorcycle

The city's one-way streets and unique intersections can be confounding. Thankfully, citizens are incredibly patient. A loonie ($1) will get you an hour up at the parking meters that line Water and Duckworth Sts. **Sonco Parking Garage** (cnr Baird's Cove & Harbour Dr; 6:30am-11pm) charges $1.50 for 30 minutes or $11 per day.

Public Transportation

The **Metrobus** (www.metrobus.com) system covers most of the city (fare $2.25). Maps and schedules are online and in the visitors center. Bus 3 is useful; it circles town via Military Rd and Water St before heading to the university.

Taxi

Except for the trip from the airport, all taxis operate on meters. A trip within town should cost around $7. **Jiffy Cabs** (☎709-722-2222; www. jiffycabs.com) provides dependable service.

AROUND ST JOHN'S

North of St John's

Right out of *20,000 Leagues Under the Sea*, the **Ocean Sciences Centre** (☎709-737-3708; www.mun.ca/osc; admission free; ☺10am-5pm Jun-early Sep) is operated by Memorial University and examines the salmon life cycle, seal navigation, ocean currents and life in cold oceanic regions. The outdoor visitors' area consists of local sealife in touch tanks. It's about 8km north of St John's, just before Logy Bay. From the city, take Logy Bay Rd (Rte 30), then follow Marine Dr to Marine Lab Rd and take it to the end.

Secluded and rocky, **Middle Cove** and **Outer Cove** are just a bit further north on Rte 30 – they're perfect for a beach picnic.

North at the head of **Torbay Bight** is the enjoyably short **Father Troy Path**, which hugs the shoreline. The view from **Cape St Francis** is worth the bumpy gravel road from Pouch Cove. There's an old battery and you may just luck out and see a whale or two.

West of St John's

West of town on Topsail Rd (Rte 60), just past Paradise, is **Topsail Beach** with picnic tables, a walking trail and panoramic views of Conception Bay and its islands.

Bell Island (www.bellisland.net) is the largest of Conception Bay's little landmasses, and it makes an interesting day trip. It's a 14km drive northwest from St John's to Portugal Cove to the **ferry** (☎709-895-6931) and then a 20-minute crossing (per passenger/car $2.25/6.25, hourly 6am to 10:30pm). Bell Island has the distinction of being the only place on the continent to have been nailed by German forces in WWII. Its pier and 80,000 tonnes of iron ore were torpedoed by U-boats in 1942. At low tide, you can still see the aftermath. The island sports a pleasant mélange of beaches, coastal vistas, lighthouses and trails. Miners here used to work in shafts under the sea at the world's largest submarine iron mine. The **Iron Ore Mine & Museum** (☎709-488-2880; adult/child $10/3; ☺11am-6pm Jun-Sep) details the

operation and gives visitors the chance to go underground; dress warmly.

South of St John's

CAPE SPEAR

A 15km drive southeast of town leads you to the most easterly point in North America. The coastal scenery is spectacular, and you can spot whales through much of the summer. The area is preserved as the **Cape Spear National Historic Site** (☎709-772-5367; www.pc.gc.ca/capespear; Blackhead Rd; adult/child $3.90/1.90; ☺grounds year-round) and includes an **interpretive center** (☺8:30am-9pm summer, 10am-6pm Sep–mid-Oct), the refurbished 1835 **lighthouse** (☺10am-6pm mid-May–mid-Oct) and the heavy gun batteries and magazines built in 1941 to protect the harbor during WWII. A **trail** leads along the edge of the headland cliffs, past 'the most easterly point' observation deck and up to the lighthouse. You can continue all the way to Maddox Cove and Petty Harbour along the East Coast Trail; even walking it a short way is tremendously worthwhile.

Heed all signs warning visitors off the rocks by the water, as rogue waves have been known to sweep in.

You reach the cape from Water St by crossing the Waterford River south of town and then following Blackhead Rd for 11km.

GOULDS & PETTY HARBOUR

In **Goulds**, at the junction of Rte 10 and the road to Petty Harbour, is **Bidgood's** (www. bidgoods.ca; Bidgood's Plaza; ☺9am-9pm Mon-Sat, 11am-5pm Sun). It's just a normal-looking supermarket, except for the fresh seal flipper (in pies, jars or jerky-like strips) and caribou steak purveyed at the back of the store. For the faint of heart, partridgeberry and bakeapple jams are the other Newfoundland specialties on hand.

Its back lapping up against steep rocky slopes, movie-set-beautiful **Petty Harbour** is filled with weathered boats, wharves and sheds on precarious stilts.

AVALON PENINSULA

Flung out to the east of Newfoundland and tethered to it by nothing more than a narrow isthmus, it doesn't seem like this little afterthought of a peninsula would be the province's powerhouse. But looks can be deceiving, because not only does the Avalon hold half of Newfoundland's population, it also houses four of the province's six seabird ecological reserves, one of its two wilderness reserves and 28 of its 41 national historic sites.

The landscape along the coastline's twisting roads is vintage fishing-village Newfoundland. Many visitors day-trip to the peninsula's sights from St John's, which is easily doable, but there's something to be said for burrowing under the quilt at night, with the sea sparkling outside your window, in Cupids, Branch or Dildo (you read right).

Much of the **East Coast Trail** (www.east coasttrail.com) runs through the area; keep an eye out for free guided hikes. The ferry to Nova Scotia leaves from Argentia.

Southeastern Avalon Peninsula

This area, sometimes called the South Shore, is known for its wildlife, archaeology, boat and kayak tours and unrelenting fog. Scenic Rtes 10 and 90, aka the **Irish Loop** (www.theirishloop.com), lasso the region.

WITLESS BAY ECOLOGICAL RESERVE
This is a prime area for whale-, iceberg- and bird-watching, and several boat tours will take you to see them from the towns of **Bay Bulls** (31km south of St John's) and around **Bauline East** (15km south of Bay Bulls).

Four islands off Witless Bay and southward are preserved as the **Witless Bay Ecological Reserve** (www.env.gov.nl.ca/parks) and represent one of the top seabird breeding areas in eastern North America. Every summer, more than a million pairs of birds gather here, including puffins, kittiwakes, storm petrels and the penguinlike murres. Tour boats sail to the islands, hugging the shore beneath sheer cliffs and giving you a shrieking earful as well as an eyeful.

The best months for trips are late June and July, when the humpback and minke whales arrive to join the birds' capelin (a type of fish) feeding frenzy. If you really hit the jackpot, in early summer an iceberg might be thrown in too.

Tours from Bay Bulls (ie the big operators O'Brien's and Gatherall's) visit Gull Island, which has the highest concentration of birds. Tours that depart to the south around

Bauline East head to nearby Great Island, home to the largest puffin colony. Bauline East is closer to the reserve, so less time is spent en route, but you see the same types of wildlife on all of the tours.

Kayaking is also popular in the area. You don't just see a whale while paddling, you feel its presence.

You can't miss the boat operators – just look for signs off Rte 10. Sometimes the smaller companies cancel tours if there aren't enough passengers; it's best to call ahead to reserve and avoid such surprises. The following are recommended tour companies, all operating from mid-May through mid-September. Most depart several times daily between 9:30am and 5pm.

Colbert's Seabird Tours (709-334-2098; Rte 10, Bauline East; 1hr tours adult/child $30/15) It's a 10-minute ride on a 40ft boat to see the puffins and whales.

Gatherall's (800-419-4253; www.gather alls.com; Northside Rd, Bay Bulls; 1½hr tours adult/1-8yr/9-17yr $56/8/18.50) A large, fast catamaran gives you as much time at the reserve as O'Brien's. It's also more stable and a wise choice for people prone to seasickness.

Molly Bawn Tours (709-334-2621; www.mollybawn.com; Rte 10, Mobile; 1hr tours adult/5-16yr $30/25) These tours cruise over the waves on a small, 35ft boat. Mobile is halfway between Bay Bulls and Bauline East.

O'Brien's (709-753-4850, 877-639-4253; www.obriensboattours.com; 2hr tours adult/3-10yr/11-17yr $55/25/30) O'Brien's, on the south side of Bay Bulls, is the granddaddy of tours and includes storytelling, music and more on its nice, big boat. A more expensive but exhilarating option is the two-hour tour in a high-speed Zodiac ($85). There's a shuttle service from St John's (round-trip $25).

Outfitters (709-579-4453, 800-966-9658; www.theoutfitters.nf.ca; Bay Bulls; half-/full-day tours $69/169) Popular half-day kayak tours leave at 9am and 2pm; full-day tours leave at 9:30am and go beyond the inner bay of Bay Bulls to the top of the eco reserve. There's a shuttle service (round-trip $25) from St John's that leaves from Outfitters (220 Water St).

Stan Cook Sea Kayak Adventures (709-579-6353, 888-747-6353; www.wildnfld.ca; Harbour Rd, Cape Broyle; 2½/4hr tours

$59/89) Located further south, just near Ferryland, this company offers great guided tours for beginners and advanced paddlers.

LA MANCHE PROVINCIAL PARK

Diverse birdlife, along with beaver, moose and snowshoe hare, can be seen in this lush park only 53km south of St John's. A highlight is the 1.25km trail to the remains of La Manche, a fishing village that was destroyed in 1966 by a fierce winter storm. Upon arrival, you'll see the beautiful newly built suspension bridge dangling over the narrows – it's part of the East Coast Trail. The trailhead is at the park's fire-exit road, past the main entrance.

There is excellent **camping** (🖉709-685-1823; www.nlcamping.ca; Rte 10; campsites $15-23, per vehicle $5; ⊘mid-May–mid-Sep), with many sites overlooking large La Manche Pond, which is good for swimming.

FERRYLAND

Ferryland, one of North America's earliest settlements, dates to 1621, when Sir George Calvert established the Colony of Avalon. A few Newfoundland winters later he was scurrying for warmer parts. He settled in Maryland and eventually became the first Lord Baltimore. Other English families arrived later and maintained the colony despite it being razed by the Dutch in 1673 and by the French in 1696.

The seaside surrounds of the **Colony of Avalon Archaeological Site** (🖉709-432-3200; www.colonyofavalon.ca; Rte 10; adult/child $9.50/7.50; ⊘10am-6pm mid-May–mid-Oct) only add to the rich atmosphere, where you'll see archaeologists unearthing everything from axes to bowls. The **Visitors Centre** (🖉709-432-3207) houses interpretive displays and many of the artifacts that have been recovered.

The village's former courthouse is now the small **Historic Ferryland Museum** (🖉709-432-2711; Rte 10; admission $2; ⊘10am-4pm Mon-Sat, 1-4pm Sun late Jun-early Sep). The towering hill behind the museum was where settlers climbed to watch for approaching warships, or to escape the Dutch and French incursions. After seeing the view, you'll understand why the settlers named the hill 'the Gaze.'

TOP CHOICE **Lighthouse Picnics** (🖉709-363-7456; www.lighthousepicnics.ca; Lighthouse Rd, off Rte 10; per person $25; ⊘11:30am-5pm Tue-Sun Jun-Sep) has hit upon a winning

concept: it provides a blanket and organic picnic meal (say, a curried chicken sandwich, mixed-green salad and lemonade from a Mason jar) that visitors wolf down while sitting in a field overlooking the ocean. It's at Ferryland's old lighthouse; you have to park and hike 2km to reach it, but ooh is it worth it. Reserve in advance.

AVALON WILDERNESS RESERVE

Dominating the interior of the region is the 1070-sq-km **Avalon Wilderness Reserve** (🖉709-635-4520; www.env.gov.nl.ca/parks; free permit required). Illegal hunting dropped the region's caribou population to around 100 in the 1980s. Twenty years later, there are thousands roaming the area. Permits for hiking, canoeing and bird-watching in the reserve are available at La Manche Provincial Park (left).

Even if you don't trek into the wilds, you still might see caribou along Rte 10 between Chance Cove Provincial Park and St Stevens.

MISTAKEN POINT ECOLOGICAL RESERVE

This **ecological reserve** (www.env.gov.nl.ca/parks), which Unesco has short-listed for World Heritage–site designation, protects 575-million-year-old multicelled marine fossils – the oldest in the world. The only way to reach it is via a free, ranger-guided, 45-minute hike from the **Edge of Avalon Interpretive Centre** (🖉709-438-1100; www.edgeofavalon.ca; Rte 10; ⊘mid-May–mid-Oct) in Portugal Cove South.

You can also drive the bumpy gravel road between here and Cape Race. At the end, a lighthouse rises up beside an artifact-filled, replica 1904 Marconi wireless station. It was the folks here who received the fateful last message from the *Titanic*.

The 'Mistaken Point' name, by the way, comes from the blinding fog that blankets the area and has caused many ships to lose their way over the years.

ALONG ROUTE 90

The area from St Vincent's to St Mary's provides an excellent chance of seeing whales, particularly humpbacks, which feed close to shore. The best viewing is from **St Vincent's Beach**. Halfway between the two villages is **Point La Haye Natural Scenic Attraction**, a dramatic arm of fine pebbles stretching across the mouth of St Mary's Bay – it's perfect for a walk.

FREE **Salmonier Nature Park** (☎709-229-7189; www.env.gov.nl.ca/snp; Rte 90; admission free; ☺10am-5pm Jun-early Sep, to 3pm early Sep–mid-Oct) rehabilitates injured and orphaned animals for release back into the wild. A 2.5km trail through pine woods takes you past indigenous fauna and natural enclosures with moose, caribou and cavorting river otters. There's an **Interpretive Centre** and touch displays for children. The park is on Rte 90, 12km south of the junction with Hwy 1.

Conception Bay

Fishing villages stretch endlessly along Conception Bay's scenic western shore, a mere 80km from St John's. Highlights include Brigus, in all its Englishy, rock-walled glory combined with North Pole history, and Cupids, a 1610 settlement, which is complete with an archaeological dig to explore. **Northern Avalon Tourism** (www.baccalieutourism.com) provides tourist information on accommodations and hiking trails.

BRIGUS

Resting on the water and surrounded by rock bluffs is the heavenly village of **Brigus** (www.brigus.net). Its idyllic stone-walled streams meander slowly past old buildings and colorful gardens before emptying into the serene Harbour Pond. American painter Rockwell Kent lived here during WWI, before his eccentric behavior got him deported on suspicion of spying for the Germans in 1915. The path toward his old cottage makes a great walk.

DON'T MISS

TOP PLACES FOR A SEASIDE HIKE

» North Head Trail, St John's (p167)

» Skerwink Trail, Trinity, Eastern Newfoundland (p183)

» Burnt Head Trail, Cupids, Avalon Peninsula (right)

» Boney Shore Trail, Red Bay, Labrador (p213)

» Copper Mine Trail, near Corner Brook (p205)

» Turpin's Trail, Fogo Island, Central Newfoundland (p192)

Captain Robert Bartlett, the town's most famous son, is renowned as one of the foremost arctic explorers of the 20th century. He made more than 20 arctic expeditions, including one in 1909, when he cleared a trail in the ice that enabled US commander Robert Peary to make his celebrated dash to the North Pole. Bartlett's house, **Hawthorne Cottage** (☎709-528-4004; www.pc.gc.ca/hawthornecottage; cnr Irishtown Rd & South St; adult/child $4/3.50; ☺9:30am-5:30pm mid-May–early Oct), is a national historic site and museum.

On the waterfront, below the church, is the **Brigus Tunnel**, which was cut through rock in 1860 so Robert Bartlett could easily access his ship in the deep cove on the other side.

Every perfect village needs a perfect eatery. At **North St Cafe** (☎709-528-1350; 29 North St; light meals $6-9; ☺11am-6pm May–mid-Oct), quiche, fish cakes, scones and afternoon tea are all on order. Brigus has a couple of B&Bs, but we suggest sleeping down the road in Cupids.

CUPIDS

Merchant John Guy sailed here in 1610 and staked out England's first colony in Canada. It's now the **Cupids Cove Plantation Provincial Historic Site** (☎709-528-3500; www.seethesites.ca; Seaforest Dr; adult/child $11.50/5.50; ☺10am-5pm mid-May–early Oct). Admission includes entry to the new **Cupids Legacy Centre**, stuffed with silver coins, bottle shards and some of the other 150,000 artifacts unearthed on-site. You also get to tour the active **archaeological dig**, where they're still finding treasures.

Afterward, head to the town's northern edge and hike the **Burnt Head Trail**. Climb to the rocky headlands, past blueberry thickets and stone walls that once fenced settlers' gardens, and look out over the same sea-buffeted coast that drew Guy.

The trail departs from an old Anglican church that has been converted into the divine **Cupid's Haven B&B and Tea Room** (☎709-528-1555; www.cupidshaven.ca; 169 Burnt Head Loop; r $99-149; ☺☐☎). Each of the four rooms has a private bathroom, vaulted ceilings and Gothic arched windows that let light stream in.

HARBOUR GRACE & AROUND

A mixed crowd of historic figures has paraded through Harbour Grace over the past 500 years. Notables include the pirate Peter

Easton and aviator Amelia Earhart. Learn about them at the redbrick customs house that is now the small **Conception Bay Museum** (☏709-596-5465; www.hrgrace.ca/museum.html; Water St; adult/child $3/2; ☺10am-4pm mid-Jun–early Sep). You can also visit the airstrip Amelia launched from in 1932 – **Harbour Grace Airfield** (www.hrgrace.ca/air.html; Earhart Rd) – when she became the first woman to cross the Atlantic solo.

It's hard to miss the large ship beached at the mouth of the harbor. This is the **SS Kyle** (1913), wrecked during a 1967 storm. Locals liked the look of it so much they paid to have it restored instead of removed.

Clinging to cliffs at the northern end of the peninsula are the remote and striking villages of **Bay de Verde** and **Grates Cove**. Hundreds of 500-year-old rock walls line the hills around Grates Cove and have been declared a national historic site. Further offshore, in the distance, is the inaccessible **Baccalieu Island Ecological Reserve**, which is host to three million pairs of Leach's storm petrel, making it the largest such colony in the world.

Trinity Bay

Thicker forests, fewer villages and subdued topography typify the shores of Trinity Bay and give the west coast of the peninsula a much more serene feeling than its eastern shore.

HEART'S CONTENT

The **Cable Station Provincial Historic Site** (☏709-583-2160; www.seethesites.ca; Rte 80; adult/child $3/free; ☺10am-5:30pm late May–early Oct) tells the story of the first permanent transatlantic cable that was laid here in 1866. The word 'permanent' is significant, because the first successful cable (connected in 1858 to Bull Arm, on Trinity Bay) failed shortly after Queen Victoria and US President James Buchanan christened the line with their congratulatory messages.

DILDO

Oh, go on – take the obligatory sign photo. For the record, no one knows definitively how the name came about; some say it's from the phallic shape of the bay.

Joking aside, Dildo is a lovely village and its shore is a good spot for whale watching. The **Dildo Interpretation Centre** (☏709-582-3339; Front Rd; adult/child $2/1; ☺10am-

4:30pm late May–mid-Sep) has a whale skeleton and exhibits on the ongoing Dorset Eskimo archaeological dig on Dildo Island. It's not terribly exciting, but outside are excellent photo opportunities with Captain Dildo and a giant squid. Across the street, **Kountry Kravins 'n' Krafts** (☏709-582-3888; ☺9am-8pm Mon-Sat, 10am-6pm late May–mid-Sep) sells fruit pies and knick knacks (including many 'Dildo' logoed items – always a fine souvenir for folks back home).

Two flawlessly restored oceanside houses comprise **Inn by the Bay** (☏709-582-3170; www.dildoinns.com; 78 Front Rd; d $89-199; ☺May-Dec; ☺☎), the most luxurious spot to stay on the northern Avalon Peninsula. Within the B&B, the elegant **Veranda Sunroom** (mains $15-19) is open to guests for dinner.

Cape Shore

The ferry, French history and lots of birds fly forth from the Avalon Peninsula's southwesterly leg. Newhook's Transportation (p176) connects the towns of Argentia and Placentia to St John's.

ARGENTIA

Argentia's main purpose is to play host to the **Marine Atlantic ferry** (☏800-341-7981; www.marine-atlantic.ca; adult/child $80.50/40.25, per car/motorcycle $165/83.50), which connects Argentia with North Sydney in Nova Scotia – a 14-hour trip. It operates from mid-June to late September with three crossings per week. The boat leaves North Sydney at 1am Tuesday, 9:30pm Wednesday and 1:30am Saturday. It returns from Argentia at 8pm Tuesday, 3:30pm Thursday and 7:30pm Saturday. Cabins (four-berth $153) are available. Vehicle fares do not include drivers.

A provincial **visitors center** (☏709-227-5272; Rte 100) is 3km from the ferry on Rte 100. Its opening hours vary to coincide with ferry sailings.

PLACENTIA

In the early 1800s, **Placentia** (www.placentiatourism.ca) – then Plaisance – was the French capital of Newfoundland, and the French attacks on the British at St John's were based here. Near town, lording over the shores, is **Castle Hill National Historic Site** (☏709-227-2401; www.pc.gc.ca/castlehill; adult/child $3.90/1.90; ☺10am-6pm mid-May–mid-Oct), where remains of French and British fortifications from the 17th and 18th centuries provide panoramic views over the town and the surrounding waters.

The fascinating **graveyard** next to the Anglican church holds the remains of people of every nationality who have settled here since the 1670s. The **O'Reilly House Museum** (☎709-227-5568; 48 Orcan Dr; admission $2; ⊙11:30am-7:30pm mid-Jun–Aug), within a century-old Victorian home, gives you more of an inside look at the town and its past luxuries. Wander past the other notable buildings, including the **Roman Catholic church** and the **stone convent**. A boardwalk runs along the stone-skipper's delight of a beach.

Breakfast is the highlight at the five-room **Rosedale Manor B&B** (☎877-999-3613; www.rosedalemanor.ca; 40 Orcan Dr; r $79-109; ⊛☎), cooked by the pastry-chef owner with organic eggs and grains. It's a 10-minute drive from the Argentia ferry.

CAPE ST MARY'S ECOLOGICAL RESERVE & AROUND
At the southwestern tip of the peninsula is **Cape St Mary's Ecological Reserve** (www.env.gov.nl.ca/parks; admission free), one of the most accessible bird colonies on the continent. Birders swoon over it, and it's impressive even for those who aren't bird crazy. Stop at the **Interpretive Centre** (☎709-277-1666; ⊙9am-5pm mid-May–mid-Oct) and get directions for the 1km trail to Bird Rock. It's an easy footpath through fields of sheep and blue irises, and then suddenly – whammo – you're at the cliff's edge facing a massive, near-vertical rock swarmed by squawking birds. There are 70,000 of them, including gannets, kittiwakes, murres and razorbills. The reserve is isolated, so you'll have to travel for lodging.

TOP **CHOICE** **The Cliffhouse** (☎709-338-2055; www.thecliffhouse.ca; Rte 100; r $90), in the wee town of Branch 22km away, is strongly recommended. Set high on a hill, you can see the ocean and spouting whales from everywhere: the front yard's Adirondack chairs, the porch, the front picture window and all three guest rooms. It's owned by a local family – Chris is a naturalist at the reserve, wife Priscilla is the town mayor and mum Rita cooks breakfast.

Near the reserve turnoff is **Gannet's Nest Restaurant** (☎709-337-2175; Rte 100; mains $8-15; ⊙8am-8pm), frying some of the province's crispiest fish and chips and baking a mean rhubarb pie.

EASTERN NEWFOUNDLAND

Two peninsulas seem to grasp awkwardly out to sea and comprise the sliver that is Eastern Newfoundland. The beloved, well-touristed Bonavista Peninsula projects northward. Historic fishing villages freckle its shores, and windblown walking trails swipe its coast. The **Discovery Trail Tourism Association** (www.thediscoverytrail.org/english/hikediscovery) provides the hiking lowdown; several trails are less than 5km, and they go to a maximum of 17km. **Clarenville** (www.fallfordiscovery.com) is the Bonavista Peninsula's access point and service center, though there's not much for sightseers.

To the south juts the massive but less-traveled Burin Peninsula, another region of fishing villages. These towns are struggling harder to find their way in the post-cod world. The ferry for France – yes, France, complete with wine, éclairs and Brie – departs from Fortune and heads to the nearby French islands of St-Pierre and Miquelon, a regional highlight.

Trinity
POP 250

Let's set the record straight: Trinity is the Bonavista Peninsula's most popular stop, a historic town of crooked seaside lanes, storybook heritage houses and gardens with white picket fences. **Trinity Bight** is the name given to the 12 communities in the vicinity, including Trinity, Port Rexton and New Bonaventure.

While Trinity is movie-set lovely, some visitors have complained that its perfection is a bit boring. But if you like historic buildings and theater along with your scenery – and you're keen for a whale-watch tour – this is definitely your place. It's a tiny town and easily walkable.

First visited by Portuguese explorer Miguel Corte-Real in 1500 and established as a town in 1580, Trinity is one of the oldest settlements on the continent.

⊙ Sights & Activities

Trinity Historic Sites   HISTORICAL SITE
(☎709-464-3599; adult/child $12/free; ⊙10am-5:30pm late May-early Oct)
One admission ticket lets you gorge on seven buildings scattered throughout the village.

The **Trinity Historical Society** (www. trinityhistoricalsociety.com) runs four of the sites. The **Lester Garland House** (West St) was rebuilt to celebrate cultural links between Trinity and Dorset, England – major trading partners in the 17th, 18th and 19th centuries. The **Cooperage** (West St) brings on a real live barrel-maker. The **Green Family Forge** (West St) is an iron-tool-filled blacksmith museum. The **Trinity Museum** (Church Rd) displays more than 2000 pieces, including North America's second-oldest fire wagon.

The provincial government operates the other trio of **sites** (www.seethesites.ca), which include costumed interpreters. The **Lester Garland Premises** (West St) depicts an 1820s general store; the **Interpretation Centre** (West St) provides a comprehensive history of Trinity; and **Hiscock House** (Church Rd) is a restored merchant's home from 1910.

Fort Point   HISTORICAL SITE
Further afield is Fort Point (aka Admiral's Point), where you'll find a pretty lighthouse and four cannons, the remains of the British fortification from 1745. There are 10 more British cannons in the water, all compliments of the French in 1762. An interpretive trail tells the tale. It's accessible from Dunfield, a few kilometers south on Rte 239.

Skerwink Trail   HIKING TRAIL
The Skerwink Trail (5km) is a fabulous (though muddy) loop that reveals picture-perfect coastal vistas. It's accessible from the church in Trinity East, off Rte 230.

☞ Tours
Boat tours leave from the wharf behind the Dock Restaurant.

Atlantic Adventures   BOAT
(☎709-464-2133; www.atlanticadventures.com; 2½hr tours $55; ⊙10am & 2pm late May-early Sep) Whale-watching tours on a big sailboat.

Trinity Eco-Tours   BOAT
(☎709-464-3712; www.trinityeco-tours.com; Main St; 3hr tours $80; ⊙10am, 1pm & 5pm mid-May–Oct) Whale-watching tours via Zodiac boat. The company also offers guided kayak tours (two-hour tours $59), as well as shipwreck dives for experienced divers.

Trinity Historical Walking Tours   WALKING
(☎709-464-3723; www.trinityhistoricalwalking tours.com; Clinch's Lane; adult/child $10/free; ⊙10am Mon-Sat late Jun-Aug) These entertain

ing and educational tours start behind Hiscock House.

🛏 Sleeping & Eating
There are numerous fine inns and B&Bs. Space gets tight in summer, so book ahead. Several snack shop/grocery stores have popped up and are good places to pick up a sandwich or cheese plate ($5 to $9), which you can take to the picnic tables near the Lester Garland Premises.

Artisan Inn & Campbell House B&B
                                          B&B $$
(☎709-464-3377, 877-464-7700; www.artisan nntrinity.com; High St; r incl breakfast $125-169, apt $250; ⊙May-Oct; ❀⑦) Adjacent to each other and managed by the same group, these places are gorgeous. The three-room inn hovers over the sea on stilts; the flower-surrounded, three-room B&B also provides ocean vistas. The inn's Twine Loft restaurant serves a multicourse, prix-fixe meal ($34) of local specialties; check the menu posted out front, which changes daily.

Eriksen Premises   B&B $$
(☎709-464-3698, 877-464-3698; www.trinityex perience.com; West St; r incl breakfast $95-160; ⊙May-Oct; ❀) This Victorian home offers elegance in accommodations and dining (mains $14 to $22, open lunch and dinner). It also books two nearby B&Bs: Kelly's Landing (four rooms) and Bishop White Manor (nine rooms).

Village Inn   INN $$
(☎709-464-3269; www.oceancontact.com; Taverner's Path; r incl breakfast $90-130) It's kind of like grandma's house – the 10 rooms are a bit faded but they're big and bright, with antique furnishings and weathered floorboards. The dining room (mains $9 to $16, open for dinner) makes traditional meals. The whole shebang is for sale, as the current owners are retiring, so changes may be afoot.

Dock Restaurant   SEAFOOD $$
(☎709-781-2255; Dock Lane; mains $9-19; ⊙9am-9pm May-Oct) This scenic spot sits next to the wharf and prepares great chowder and seafood, plus it serves Moo Moo's ice cream (from the popular eponymous shop in St John's).

☆ Entertainment
Rocky's Place Lounge   LIVE MUSIC
(☎709-464-3400; High St) Rocky's hosts bands from time to time, but even if the

mics are quiet it's a friendly place to hoist a brew.

Rising Tide Theatre   THEATER
(☎709-464-3232; www.risingtidetheatre.com; Water St; tickets $25; ◷Tue-Sun late Jun-early Sep) Alongside the Lester Garland Premises is the celebrated Rising Tide Theatre, which hosts the 'Seasons in the Bight' theater festival and the **Trinity Pageant** (adult/child $15/free; ◷2pm Wed & Sat), an entertaining outdoor drama on Trinity's history.

❶ Information
RBC Royal Bank (West St; ◷10:30am-2pm Mon-Thu, to 5pm Fri) No ATM.

Town of Trinity (www.townoftrinity.com) Tourism info.

❶ Getting There & Around
Trinity is 259km from St John's and is reached via Rte 230 off Hwy 1. **Shirran's Taxi** (☎709-468-7741) makes the trip daily from St John's ($45).

Bonavista
POP 3770

'O buona vista!' (Oh, happy sight!), shouted John Cabot upon spying the New World from his boat on June 24, 1497. Or so the story goes. From all descriptions, this pretty spot is where he first set foot in the Americas. Today Bonavista's shoreline, with its lighthouse, puffins and chasms, continues to rouse visitors.

◉ Sights & Activities
Cape Bonavista Lighthouse   LIGHTHOUSE
(☎709-468-7444; www.seethesites.ca; Rte 230; adult/child $3/free; ◷10am-5:30pm late May-early Oct) Cape Bonavista Lighthouse is a brilliant red-and-white-striped lighthouse dating from 1843. The interior has been restored to the 1870s and is now a provincial historic site. A **puffin colony** lives just offshore; the birds put on quite a show around sunset.

Dungeon Park   PARK
(Cape Shore Rd, off Rte 230; admission free) Nowhere is the power of water more evident than at the Dungeon, a deep chasm 90m in circumference that was created by the collapse of two sea caves, through which thunderous waves now slam the coast.

Ryan Premises   HISTORIC SITE
(☎709-468-1600; www.pc.gc.ca/ryanpremises; Ryans Hill Rd; adult/child $3.90/1.90; ◷10am-

6pm mid-May–mid-Oct) Ryan Premises National Historic Site is a restored 19th-century saltfish mercantile complex. The slew of white clapboard buildings honors five centuries of fishing in Newfoundland via multimedia displays and interpretive programs.

Ye Matthew Legacy   HISTORICAL SITE
(☎709-468-1493; www.matthewlegacy.com; Roper St; adult/child $7.50/3; ◷10am-6pm Jun-early Oct) An impressive full-scale replica of the ship on which Cabot sailed into Bonavista is at Ye Matthew Legacy. At press time, the site was at risk of closing due to lack of funding for repairs.

Natural Wonders   HIKING
(☎709-468-2523; www.puffins.ca; 42 Campbell St; 2hr tours adult/child $30/20; ◷Jun-Sep) Hike with a naturalist to see puffins and learn about local plants and ecology.

⌷ Sleeping
Check www.bonavista.net for further lodging options.

HI Bonavista   HOSTEL $
(☎709-468-7741, 877-468-7741; www.hihostels.ca; 40 Cabot Dr; dm $26-30, r $74-79; @◈) This tidy white clapboard hostel is new on the scene, offering four private rooms, two shared dorm rooms, free bike use and kitchen and laundry facilities. It's a short walk from the center. The gregarious owners also run Shirran's Taxi, which provides transport to the town from St John's ($40 each way).

White's B&B   B&B $$
(☎709-468-7018; www.bbcanada.com/3821.htm; 21 Windlass Dr; r incl breakfast $75-85; ◔@◈) Low-key White's has three rooms to choose from, all with either private bathroom or en suite. Enjoy the bike rentals, barbecue use and ocean view.

Harbourview B&B   B&B $
(☎709-468-2572; 21 Ryans Hill Rd; r incl breakfast $70; ◷May-Sep; ◔) The name doesn't lie: you get a sweet view at this simple, four-room B&B, plus an evening snack (crab legs) with owners Florence and Albert.

✖ Eating & Entertainment
TOP CHOICE **Walkham's Gate**   CAFE $
(☎709-468-7004; www.walkhamsgate pub.ca; mains $5-9; ◷24hr; ◈) One side is a coffee shop with whopping pies and hearty soups, the other side a congenial pub tend-

ELLISTON: ROOT CELLARS & PUFFINS

The Root Cellar Capital of the World, aka Elliston, lies 6km south of Bonavista on Rte 238. The teeny town was struggling until it hit upon the idea to market its 135 subterranean veggie storage vaults, and then presto – visitors came a knockin'. Actually, what's most impressive is the **puffin colony** just offshore and swarming with thousands of chubby-cheeked, orange-billed birds. A quick and easy path over the cliffside brings you quite close to them and also provides whale and iceberg views.

Stop at the **Visitor Centre** (☎709-468-7117; www.rootcellars.com; Main St) as you enter town, and the kindly folks will give you directions to the site. They also can arrange **guided walking tours** ($4) of the cellars.

Work up an appetite while you're here, because **Nanny's Root Cellar Kitchen** (☎709-468-7099; ☺8am-10pm) in historic Orange Hall cooks a mighty fine lobster, Jigg's dinner and other traditional foods, plus she's licensed.

From the adjoining hamlet of **Maberly** a gorgeous 17km **coastal hiking trail** winds over the landscape to Little Catalina.

ed by music-lover Harvey. Located in the town center, near the courthouse.

Garrick Theatre THEATER
(www.garricktheatre.ca; 18 Church St) The artfully restored Garrick shows mainstream and indie films and hosts live music performances.

ℹ Information

Bonavista Community Health Centre (☎709-468-7881; Hospital Rd)

Town of Bonavista (www.bonavista.net) Tourism info.

Scotiabank (☎709-468-1070; 1 Church St)

ℹ Getting There & Around

Bonavista is a scenic 50km drive north of Trinity along Rte 230. **Shirran's** (☎709-468-7741) drives up daily from St John's ($40).

Burin Peninsula

It's not exactly lively on the Burin Peninsula, as the besieged fishing economy has made its presence felt. Still, the coastal walks inspire, and the region is a low-key place to spend a day or two before embarking toward the baguettes of France (aka St-Pierre).

Marystown is the peninsula's largest town; it's jammed with big-box retailers but not much else. **Burin** is the area's most attractive town, with a gorgeous elevated boardwalk over the waters of its rocky shoreline. **St Lawrence** is known for fluorite mining and scenic coastal hikes. In **Grand Bank**, there's an interesting self-

guided walk through the historic buildings and along the waterfront. Just south is fossil-rich **Fortune**, the jump-off point for St-Pierre.

◉ Sights & Activities

Provincial Seamen's Museum MUSEUM
(☎709-832-1484; www.therooms.ca/museum; Marine Dr, Grand Bank) The impressive-looking Seamen's Museum depicts both the era of the banking schooner and the changes in the fishery over the years. It's set to reopen in 2011 after renovations.

Burin Heritage Museums MUSEUM
FREE (☎709-891-2217; www.burincanada.com; Seaview Dr, Burin; admission free; ☺9am-6pm Mon-Fri, 10:30am-6pm Sat & Sun) Displays in two historical homes tell of life's highs and lows in remote outports.

Fortune Head Ecological Reserve ECO RESERVE
(www.env.gov.nl.ca/parks; off Rte 220; admission free; ☺24hr) The reserve protects fossils dating from the planet's most important period of evolution, when life on earth progressed from simple organisms to complex animals some 550 million years ago. The reserve is about 3km west, by the Fortune Head Lighthouse. Kids will appreciate the **Interpretation Centre** (☎709-832-2810; adult/child $5/3; ☺9am-5pm mid-Jun–Aug) with fossils to touch; it's in town by the St-Pierre ferry dock.

Hiking Trails HIKING TRAIL
Ask at the Burin Heritage Museum about locating the **Cook's Lookout** trailhead. It's a 20-minute walk from town to the

NO FISHING ALLOWED

For hundreds of years, Newfoundland's waters – especially the Grand Banks to the south and east – were known as a place where you could dip your bucket and then hoist it back up filled with fat, slippery codfish. By 1992 that changed. Fish stocks had been declining over the years, and the government decided to take action. With the swipe of a pen, it made cod fishing illegal within a 320km radius of provincial shores. Suddenly, 20,000 fishers and plant workers were out of work overnight.

It was supposed to be a temporary measure, but the hoped-for cod rebound never happened. Almost two decades later, scientists warn that stocks remain critically low and could take years to come back. Fisherfolk say that while it may be true, they are being unfairly penalized. Just outside the 320km no-fishing zone, they reason, big trawlers from other countries continue to scoop up cod, and that's why stock numbers remain depleted.

Whether the moratorium is right or wrong, the impact on the local way of life has been staggering. Families who fished for generations have had to scramble to find new livelihoods. Many end up leaving the province to get work, fostering a trend known as 'outmigration.' Several regions have seen their populations drop by more than 20% since 1992.

Fort McMurray, Alberta, exerts the biggest pull, where people get seasonal jobs in the oil sands industry. Although the earnings are good, the lifestyle prompts a new set of problems: families are split, drugs are prevalent and money that's easily come by is also easily spent.

Newfoundland has struggled to cope with these changes. Some communities have converted their boats and fish plants to process crab and shrimp instead of cod. The province also has developed its own oil industry offshore from St John's. Finally, many communities are generating jobs by turning to tourism, an industry that was practically nonexistent prior to the codfish moratorium.

panoramic view. Off Pollux Cres in St Lawrence, the rugged, breath-draining **Cape Trail** (4km) and **Chamber Cove Trail** (4km) shadow the cliff edges and offer amazing vistas down to rocky shores and some famous WWII shipwrecks. Another good (and easier) trail is the **Marine Hike** (7km) that traces Admiral's Beach near Grand Bank. It leaves from Christian's Rd off Rte 220.

🛏 Sleeping & Eating

Options are spread thinly. For those heading to St-Pierre, Grand Bank and Fortune are the best bases. Grand Bank has better lodging but it's further, at 8km from the ferry dock. Fortune has a sweet bakery by its dock. For more choices check **The Heritage Run** (www.theheritagerun.com).

Thorndyke B&B   B&B $$
(☑709-832-0820, 877-882-0820; www.thethorn dyke.ca; 33 Water St, Grand Bank; r incl breakfast $95; ⊙mid-May–Oct; ⊜) This handsome old captain's home overlooks the harbor. Antique wood furnishings fill the four light and airy rooms (each with private bath-

room). The hosts will provide dinner with advance notice.

Fortune Inn B&B   B&B $$
(☑709-832-1774, 888-275-1098; www.granny smotorinn.ca; Bayview St, Fortune; r incl breakfast $89; ⊙mid-Jun–mid-Sep; ⊜) Antiques, shmantiques – who needs 'em? The rooms in this ex-apartment building are cheaply furnished (linoleum floors, drab colors, shared bathrooms), but they're clean and functional and, most importantly, they're only a 750m walk from the St-Pierre ferry.

Inn by the Sea B&B   B&B $$
(☑709-832-0202, 888-932-0202; www.theinnby thesea.com; 22 Blackburn Rd, Grand Bank; s/d incl breakfast $79/89; ⊙Jun–mid-Oct; ⊜@🛜) Each of the four rooms here has a plump queen-sized bed, private bathroom and desk with laptop hookup.

Sharon's Nook & the Tea Room   CAFE $
(☑709-832-0618; 12 Water St, Grand Bank; mains $7-10; ⊙7:30am-9pm Mon-Sat, 11am-7:30pm Sun) This countrified eatery serves up lasagna, chili, sandwiches and heavenly cheesecake.

Getting There & Around

The Burin Peninsula is accessed via Rte 210 off Hwy 1. The drive from St John's to Grand Bank is 359km and takes just over four hours. **Foote's Taxi** (✆709-832-0491, 800-866-1181) travels from St John's down the peninsula as far as Fortune ($45, five hours).

ST-PIERRE & MIQUELON

POP 6000

Twenty-five kilometers offshore from the Burin Peninsula floats a little piece of France. The islands of St-Pierre and Miquelon aren't just Frenchlike with their berets, baguettes and Bordeaux, they *are* France, governed and financed by the *tricolore*.

Citizens here take their national pride very seriously – some even feel it's their duty to maintain France's foothold in the New World. Locals kiss their hellos and pay in euros, while sweet smells waft from the myriad pastry shops. French cars – Peugeots, Renaults and Citroens – crowd the tiny one-way streets. It's an eye-rubbing world away from Newfoundland's nearby fishing communities.

St-Pierre is the more populated and developed island, with most residents of its 5300 living in the town of St-Pierre. Miquelon is larger geographically but has only 700 residents overall.

The fog-mantled archipelago has a 20th-century history as colorful as its canary-yellow, lime and lavender houses (see the boxed text, below). Going further back, Jacques Cartier claimed the islands for France in 1536, after they were discovered by the Portuguese in 1520. At the end of the Seven Years' War in 1763, the islands were turned over to Britain, only to be given back to France in 1816. And French they've remained ever since.

Sights & Activities

In St-Pierre, the best thing to do is just walk around and soak it up – when you're not eating, that is. Pop into stores and sample goods you'd usually have to cross an ocean for. Or conduct research as to the best chocolate-croissant maker. A couple of **walking trails** leave from the edge of town near the power station.

Île aux Marins   HISTORICAL BUILDINGS
(3hr tours adult/child €19.50/12.50; ◷9am & 1:30pm May-Sep) The magical Île aux Marins is a beautiful abandoned village on an island out in the harbor. A bilingual guide will walk you through colorful homes, a small schoolhouse museum and the grand church (1874). Book tours at the visitors center. You can also go over on the boat (€3) sans guide, but be aware most signage is in French.

L'Arche Museum   MUSEUM
(✆508-410-435; www.arche-musee-et-archives.net; Rue du 11 Novembre; adult/child €4/2.50; ◷10am-noon & 1:30-5pm Tue-Sun Jun-Sep) The well-done exhibits cover the islands' history, including prohibition times. The showstopper is the **guillotine** – the only one to slice in North America. Islanders dropped the 'timbers of justice' just once, in 1889, on a murderer. The museum also offers bilingual **architectural walking tours** (€6.50 to €8.50).

Miquelon & Langlade   ISLANDS
The island of Miquelon, 45km away, is less visited and less developed than St-Pierre.

ST-PIERRE'S BOOZY BACKSTORY

When Prohibition dried out the USA's kegs in the 1920s, Al Capone decided to slake his thirst – and that of the nation – by setting up shop in St-Pierre.

He and his mates transformed the sleepy fishing harbor into a booming port crowded with warehouses filled with imported booze. Bottles were removed from their crates, placed in smaller carrying sacks and taken secretly to the US coast by rumrunners. The piles of Cutty Sark whiskey crates were so high on the docks, clever locals used the wood both to build and heat houses. At least one house remains today and is known as the 'Cutty Sark cottage'; most tours drive by. At press time, the visitors center was setting up a new tour that would cover all the island's Prohibition sites.

St-Pierre still imports enough alcohol to pickle each and every citizen a few times over. It remains legendary to Newfoundland mainlanders as the home of cheap alcohol, including a type of grain alcohol that reputedly cleans engines or can be mixed with water to create a local moonshine. Not surprisingly, it is illegal in Canada.

The village of **Miquelon**, centered on the church, is at the northern tip of the island. From nearby **l'Étang de Mirande** a walking trail leads to a lookout and waterfall. From the bridge in town, a scenic 25km road leads across the isthmus to the wild and uninhabited island of **Langlade**. There are some wild horses, and around the rocky coast and lagoons you'll see seals and birds. **Chez Janot** (www.chezjanot.fr; adult/child €60/35; ☺Jun-Sep) offers full-day, bilingual tours by Zodiac covering both islands. Book at the visitors center.

Several landmarks merit a look:

Cemetery (Ave Commandant Roger Birot) The cemetery with its above-ground mausoleums provides an atmospheric wander.

Les Salines (Rue Boursaint & the waterfront) Old-timers hang out around this scenic cluster of multihued fishing shacks.

Fronton (Rue Maître Georges Lefèvre & Rue Gloanec) Watch locals play the Basque game of *pelote* (a type of handball) at the outdoor court here.

★☆ Festivals & Events

From mid-July to the end of August, folk dances are often held in St-Pierre's square.

Bastille Day (☺Jul 14) The largest holiday of the year.

Basque Festival (☺mid-Aug) A weeklong festival with music, marching and invigorating street fun.

🛏 Sleeping & Eating

There are about a dozen accommodations on St-Pierre; all include continental breakfast. Book ahead in summer. Not surprisingly, great eateries abound; make reservations to ensure a table. Several bars and restaurants are on Rue Albert Briand.

Auberge Quatre Temps B&B   B&B **$$**
(☎508-414-301; www.quatretemps.com; 14 Rue Dutemple; s/d €64/72; @🛜) Let's start by saying there's a bar inside and it's open all day. There's also bike rental and a fine restaurant (open to the public but reservations required). All six rooms have their own bathroom. Quatre Temps is a 15-minute schlep from the ferry dock, but don't let that deter you.

Nuits St-Pierre   B&B **$$**
(☎508-412-720; www.nuits-saint-pierre.com; 10 Rue du Général Leclerc; r €95-155; ☻🛜) St-Pierre's most upscale lodging opened in 2010, aiming for the honeymoon crowd. The five rooms, each with private bathroom and downy, above-the-norm beds, are named after famous French authors. There's free pickup from the airport or ferry.

Bernard Dodeman B&B   B&B **$**
(☎508-413-060; www.pensiondodeman.com; 15 Rue Paul Bert; s/d €45/50; ☻🛜) The Dodeman's three simple rooms share two bathrooms and a communal TV parlor. It's a 15-minute walk from the ferry, on a hill above town.

Brasserie de l'île   FRENCH **$$**
(☎508-410-350; 6 Rue Maître Georges Lefèvre; mains €15-18; ☺noon-2pm & 7:30-10:30pm) The candlelit wood bar, gauzy curtains, crooners on the stereo and cocktail list lend a sexy vibe to this restaurant. Staff chalk the daily specials on the board, say freshplucked fish or Moroccan tagines. A fine wine selection, of course, washes it down.

TOP CHOICE ⟩ **Patisserie Guillard**   BAKERY **$**
(23 Rue Marechal Foch; pastries €0.50-1; ☺7:30am-12:30pm Mon-Sat) Holy mother! These cream-plumped chocolate éclairs, macaroons and gateaux are the reason you came to France, right?

Le Feu de Braise   FRENCH **$$**
(☎508-419-160; www.cheznoo.net/feu-de -braise; upstairs, 14 Rue Albert Briand; mains €11-19; ☺noon-2pm & 6:30-11pm) French and Italian-influenced food hits the tables in this warm, diner-esque restaurant. Standouts include the thin-crust pizza and homemade pastas.

ℹ Information

Americans, EU citizens and all visitors except Canadians need a passport for entry. Those staying longer than 30 days also need a visa. Other nationalities should confirm with their French embassy if a visa is needed prior to arrival. Canadians can enter with a driver's license.

Business Hours Most shops and businesses close between noon and 1:30pm. Some stores also close on Saturday afternoons, and most are closed on Sunday.

Customs To merit the duty-free waiver on alcohol, you must stay on the islands at least 48 hours.

Language French, but many people also speak English.

Money Many merchants accept the Loonie, though they return change in euros. If you're staying more than an afternoon, it's probably easiest to get euros from the local ATMs.

Telephone Calling the islands is an international call, meaning you must dial ☑011 in front of the local number. Phone service links in to the French system, so beware of roaming charges on your mobile.

Time Half an hour ahead of Newfoundland Time.

Tourist Information (www.st-pierre-et-mique lon.com) The visitors center, near the ferry dock, provides a map showing all the banks, restaurants etc. Staff also have information on the islands' hotels and tours, and make bookings.

Voltage 220V; Canadian and American appliances need an electrical adapter.

❶ Getting There & Away

Air

Air Saint-Pierre (www.airsaintpierre.com) flies to St John's, Montréal and Halifax. There are two to three flights weekly to each city. Taxis to/from the airport cost around €5.

Boat

From Fortune on Newfoundland, **St-Pierre Tours** (☑709-832-0429, 800-563-2006; www.spm express.net; 5 Bayview St) operates the ferries (adult/child return $107/53.50, 1½ hours). From mid-June to mid-September, one departs daily at 11:30am, returning from St-Pierre at 2:15pm. From mid-July to early September, there's a day-trip service departing at 7:15am and returning at 2:15pm (except Sunday). Call for off-season times. The boats carry foot passengers only. Leave your car in the parking lot by the dock (per day $8).

❶ Getting Around

Much can be seen on foot. Roads are steep, so prepare to huff and puff. **Auberge Quatre Temps** (14 Rue Dutemple) rents bicycles (per half/full day €10/15). Local ferries head to Miquelon and Langlade; check with the visitors center for schedules and costs.

CENTRAL NEWFOUNDLAND

Central Newfoundland elicits fewer wows per square kilometer than the rest of the province, but that's because huge chunks of the region are pure bog land and trees. The islands of Notre Dame Bay – particularly Twillingate, when icebergs glide by – are exceptional exceptions.

Terra Nova National Park

Backed by lakes, bogs and hilly woods, and fronted by the salty waters of Clode and Newman Sounds, **Terra Nova National**

Park (☑709-533-2801; www.pc.gc.ca/terrano va; adult/child/family per day $5.80/2.90/14.70) is spliced by Hwy 1 running through its interior. It's not nearly as dramatic as the province's other national parks, though it does offer moose, bear, beaver and bald eagles, as well as relaxed hiking, paddling, camping and boat tours.

Make your first stop the **Visitor Centre** (☑709-533-2942; Hwy 1; ⊘9am-7pm late Jun-early Sep, 10am-5pm rest of season mid-May–early Oct), which has oodles of park information, ranger-guided programs and marine displays with touch tanks and underwater cameras. It's 1km off Hwy 1 at Salton's Day-Use Area, 80km east of Gander.

◉ Sights & Activities

Terra Nova's 14 hiking trails total almost 100km; pick up maps at the visitors center. Highly recommended is the **Malady Head Trail** (5km), which climaxes at the edge of a headland cliff offering stunning views of Southwest Arm and Broad Cove. **Sandy Pond Trail** (3km) is an easy loop around the pond – your best place to spot a beaver. The area is also a favorite for **swimming**, with a beach, change rooms and picnic tables. In winter, the park grooms trails here for cross-country skiing.

The epic **Outport Trail** (48km) provides access to backcountry campgrounds and abandoned settlements along Newman Sound. The loop in its entirety is rewarding, but be warned: parts are unmarked, not to mention mucky. A compass, a topographical map and ranger advice are prerequisites for this serious route.

Ocean Quest Adventures (p190) rents gear for **cycling** and **kayaking**. Inquire about the **Sandy Pond-Dunphy's Pond Route** (10km), a great paddle with only one small portage.

About 15km from the park's western gate, the **Burnside Archaeology Centre** (☑709-677-2474; www.burnsideheritage.ca; Main St; admission $2; ⊘9am-6pm Jul-Oct) catalogs artifacts found at local Beothuk sites; ask about **boat tours** (per person $40) to the more far-flung settlements. Also in the region is **Salvage**, a photographer's-dream fishing village with well-marked walking trails. It's near the park's north end on Rte 310, about 26km from Hwy 1.

☞ Tours

Departures are from the Visitor Centre.

NEWFOUNDLAND & LABRADOR TERRA NOVA NATIONAL PARK

Coastal Connections
BOAT

(☎709-533-2196; www.coastalconnections.ca; 2½hr tours adult/child $65/35; ⏰9:30am & 1pm mid-May–early Oct) Climb aboard for a trip through Newman Sound, where you'll pull lobster pots, examine plankton under the microscope and engage in other hands-on activities. It's common to see eagles, less so whales.

Ocean Quest Adventures
BOAT

(☎709-422-1111; www.oceanquestadventures. com; ⏰mid-May–Oct) Ocean Quest will take you cod fishing ($60, including gear). It also rents kayaks and bicycles.

🛏 Sleeping

Camping is the only option within the park itself. Those with aspirations of a bed should head to Eastport; it's near the park's north end on Rte 310, about 16km from Hwy 1. For camping reservations (recommended on summer weekends), call **Parks Canada** (☎877-737-3783; www.pccamping.ca; reservation fee $10.80) or go online.

Backcountry camping
CAMPGROUND $

(free permit required, campsites $16) There are several backcountry sites around the Outport Trail, Beachy Pond, Dunphy's Island and Dunphy's Pond, reached by paddling or hiking. Register at the Visitors Centre.

Newman Sound Campground
CAMPGROUND $

(campsites $24-30) This is the park's main (noisier) campground, with 343 sites, a grocery store and Laundromat. It's open for winter camping, too.

Malady Head Campground
CAMPGROUND $

(campsites $17-22) Located at the park's northern end, Malady Head is smaller, quieter and more primitive (though it does have showers).

Doctor's Inn B&B
B&B $$

(☎709-677-3539; www.doctors-inn.nf.ca; 5 Burden's Rd, Eastport; r $75-100; ⏰Jun-Sep; ⏰) Yes, there really is a doctor in this big old rambling house, as well as a flowery patio, gazebo and five fine rooms with private bathrooms. It's certainly the brightest spot in an otherwise dreary little town.

Gander

POP 9600

Gander sprawls across the juncture of Hwy 1 and Rte 330, which leads to Notre Dame Bay. It is a convenient stopping point and offers a couple of sights for aviation buffs.

Gander essentially germinated from its airport. The site was chosen by the British in the 1930s because of its proximity to Europe and its fogless weather. Most recently, Gander gained attention for its hospitality to the thousands whose planes were rerouted here after the September 2001 terrorist attacks in the USA.

There is a **Visitors Centre** (www.gander canada.com; ⏰8am-8pm mid-Jun–Sep, 8:30am-5pm Mon-Fri Oct–mid-Jun) on Hwy 1 at the central entry into town.

For aviation fanatics, the **North Atlantic Aviation Museum** (☎709-256-2923; www. naam.ca; Hwy 1; adult/child $5/4; ⏰9am-6pm Jun-Dec, to 4pm Mon-Fri Jan-May) has exhibits detailing Newfoundland's air contributions to WWII and the history of navigation. Just east on Hwy 1 is the sobering **Silent Witness Monument**, a tribute to 248 US soldiers whose plane crashed here in December 1985.

Sinbad's Hotel & Suites (☎709-651-2678; www.steelehotels.com; Bennett Dr; r $93-123) has clean, comfortable hotel rooms within the center of Gander. For meals, make it **Giovanni's Cafe** (☎709-651-3535; 71 Elizabeth Dr; mains $5-9; ⏰7am-5pm Mon-Thu, 8:30am-5pm Fri & Sat, 11:30am-4:30pm Sun), with coffee, wraps, sandwiches and salads.

The **Gander Airport** (YQX; www.gander airport.com) gets a fair bit of traffic. **DRL** (☎709-263-2171; www.drl-lr.com) buses stop at the airport en route to St John's (four hours) and Port aux Basques (nine hours).

Twillingate Island & New World Island

POP 5800

This area of Notre Dame Bay gets the most attention, and deservedly so. Twillingate (which actually consists of two barely separated islands, North and South Twillingate) sits just north of New World Island. The islands are reached from the mainland via an amalgamation of short causeways. It's stunningly beautiful, with every turn of the road revealing new ocean vistas, colorful fishing wharves or tidy groups of pastel houses hovering on cliffs and outcrops. An influx of whales and icebergs every summer only adds to the appealing mix.

◉ Sights & Activities

Prime Berth/Twillingate Fishing Museum
MUSEUM

(☏709-884-5925; Walter Elliott Causeway; admission $5, tour $7.50; ☉10am-5pm Jul & Aug) Make this your first stop. Run by an engaging fisherman, the private museum, with its imaginative and deceivingly simple concepts (a cod splitting show!), is brilliant, and fun for mature scholars and school kids alike. It's the first place you see as you cross to Twillingate.

Long Point Lighthouse
LIGHTHOUSE

(☏709-884-2247; admission free) Long Point provides dramatic views of the coastal cliffs. Travel up the winding steps, worn from lighthouse-keepers' footsteps since 1876, and gawk at the 360-degree view. Located at the tip of the north island, it's an ideal vantage point for spotting icebergs in May and June.

Little Harbour Trail
HIKING TRAIL

In Little Harbour, en route to the town of Twillingate, a 5km trail leads past the vestiges of a resettled community and rock arch to secluded and picturesque **Jone's Cove**.

Durrell Museum
MUSEUM

(☏709-884-2780; Museum St, off Durrell St; adult/child $2/1; ☉9am-5pm Jun-Sep) Don't neglect to take a tour of the exceptionally scenic Durrell and its museum, dwelling atop Old Maid Hill. Bring your lunch; there are a couple of picnic tables and a spectacular view.

Auk Island Winery
WINERY

(☏709-884-2707; www.aukislandwinery.com; 29 Durrell St; tastings $3, with tour $5; ☉9:30am-5:30pm, to 8:30pm Thu & Fri Jul-early Sep) Visit the grounds that produce Moose Joose (blueberry-partridgeberry), Funky Puffin (blueberry-rhubarb) and other fruity flavors by using iceberg water and local berries.

Twillingate Museum
MUSEUM

(☏709-884-2825; www.tmacs.ca; off Main St; admission by donation; ☉9am-5pm mid-May–early Oct) Housed in a former Anglican rectory, the museum tells the island's history since the first British settlers arrived in the mid-1700s. It also displays articles brought back from around the world by local sea captains. Another room delves into the seal hunt and its controversy. There's a historic **church** next door.

☞ Tours

Fun two-hour tours (per adult/child $44/22) to view icebergs and whales depart daily from mid-May to early September.

Twillingate Adventure Tours
BOAT

(☏709-884-5999; www.twillingateadventuretours.com; off Main St) Depart from Twillingate's wharf at 10am, 1pm and 4pm (and sometimes 7pm).

Twillingate Island Boat Tours
BOAT

(☏709-884-2242; www.icebergtours.ca; Main St) Depart from the Iceberg Shop (itself worth a peek, with its iceberg pictures and crafts) at 9:30am, 1pm and 4pm.

✪ Festivals & Events

Traditional music and dance, some of which goes back to the 16th century, merrily take over Twillingate during the weeklong **Fish, Fun & Folk Festival** (www.fishfunfolkfestival.com; ☉late Jul).

⏁ Sleeping

Despite having about a dozen lodging options, Twillingate gets very busy in the summer. Book early.

Captain's Legacy B&B
B&B $$

(☏709-884-5648; www.captainslegacy.com; Hart's Cove; r $89-114; ☉mid-May–Oct; ☻🛜) A real captain named Peter Troake once owned this historic 'outport mansion,' now a gracious four-room B&B overlooking the harbor.

Paradise B&B
B&B $$

(☏709-884-5683; 877-882-1999; www.capturegaia.com/paradiseb&b.html; 192 Main St; r $80-99; ☉mid-May–Sep; ☻🛜) Set on a bluff overlooking Twillingate's harbor, Paradise offers the best view in town. You can wander down to the beach below, or relax on a lawn chair and soak it all up. Oh, the three rooms are comfy too. Angle for room No 1. Cash only.

Harbour Lights Inn B&B
B&B $$

(☏709-884-2763; www.harbourlightsinn.com; 189 Main St; d $109-139; ☉May–mid-Oct; ☻🛜) South African hospitality greets you in this historical and popular nine-bedroom home. It's located right on the harbor and has amenities such as TVs and Jacuzzis.

✗ Eating & Entertainment

R&J Restaurant
SEAFOOD $$

(☏709-884-2212; 110 Main St; mains $8-14; ☉8am-11pm) Sink your teeth into fish 'n' brewis, shrimp, scallops or battered fish. Pizzas and burgers are also available.

All Around the Circle Dinner Theatre

THEATER

(☑709-884-5423; Crow Head; adult/child $29/15; ⊘6pm Mon-Sat Jun–mid-Sep) Six of Newfoundland's best will not only cook you a traditional meal, they'll also leave you in stitches with their talented performances. It's just south of the Long Point Lighthouse.

❶ Information

Town of Twillingate (www.townoftwillingate.ca)

Twillingate Tourism (www.twillingate.com)

❶ Getting There & Away

From the mainland, Rte 340's causeways almost imperceptibly connect Chapel Island, tiny Strong's Island, New World Island and Twillingate Island.

Fogo Island & Change Islands

POP 3000

Settled in the 1680s, Fogo is an intriguing and rugged island to poke around. Keep an eye on this place: it recently embarked on an ambitious, arts-oriented sustainable tourism plan that's quite progressive for the region. The rare Newfoundland pony roams the Change Islands, which float to the west.

⊙ Sights & Activities

On Fogo, the village of **Joe Batt's Arm**, backed by rocky hills, is a flashback to centuries past. A **farmers market** takes place at the ice rink on Saturday mornings.

Nearby is **Tilting**, perhaps the most engaging village on the island. The Irish roots run deep here and so do the accents. The inland harbor is surrounded by picturesque fishing stages and flakes, held above the incoming tides by weary stilts. There's also the great coastal **Turpin's Trail** (9km) that leaves from Tilting, near the beach at **Sandy Cove**.

On the opposite end of the island is the village of **Fogo** and the indomitable **Brimstone Head** (see the boxed text, below). After you take in the mystical rock's view, do another great hike in town: the **Lion's Den Trail** (5km), which visits a Marconi radio site. Keep an eye out for the small group of caribou that roams the island.

As part of the new development plan, the island is stringing **art studios** along its walking trails, and inviting painters, filmmakers and photographers from around the world for residencies. Ask about the **digital cinema**'s current location. And by all means see what the **World's End Theatre Company** (www.worldsendtheatre.org; ⊘mid-Jul–mid-Aug) has going on. The troupe stages original works, telling local stories, in pubs, churches and outdoor venues around the island.

The Change Islands are home to the **Newfoundland Pony Refuge** (☑709-621-4400; 12 Bowns Rd; admission free; ⊘by appointment), established to increase numbers of the native, endangered Newfoundland pony. Only 88 registered beasts of breeding age remain in the province, and this is the largest herd. The small creatures are renowned as hardy workers (especially in winter) with gentle temperaments.

✵ Festivals & Events

Great Fogo Island Punt Race (www.fogoislandregatta.com; ⊘late Jul) Locals row traditionally built wooden boats (called

---

ROUND OR FLAT?

Despite Columbus' stellar work in 1492 (when he sailed the ocean blue without falling off the earth's edge), and despite modern satellite photos that confirm his findings of a rounded orb, the folks at the Flat Earth Society aren't buying it. A spinning, spherical world hurtling through space would only lead to our planet's inhabitants living a confused and disorientated life, they say.

In 'reality,' the stable and calming flat earth is said to have five striking corners: Lake Mikhayl in Tunguska (Siberia); Easter Island; Lhasa (Tibet); the South Pacific island of Ponape; and Brimstone Head on Fogo Island, right here in Newfoundland. So climb up the craggy spine of Brimstone Head, stare off the abyss to earth's distant edge and judge for yourself if the earth is round or flat. If nothing else, you're guaranteed a stunning view of Iceberg Alley.

punts) 16km across open sea to the Change Islands and back.

Brimstone Head Folk Festival (www.town -fogo.ca; ⊙mid-Aug) A three-day hootenanny with Irish and Newfoundland music.

🛏 Sleeping & Eating

The high-end, 29-room, ecofriendly Fogo Island Inn is scheduled to open in 2012.

Peg's B&B   B&B **$$**
(🖉709-266-2392; www.pegsbb.com; 60 Main St, Fogo; r $75-85; ⊙May-Oct; ⊜🛜) Right in the heart of Fogo village, Peg's four-room place offers up a friendly atmosphere and harbor views.

Foley's Place B&B   B&B **$$**
(🖉709-658-7288, 866-658-7244; www. foleysplace.ca; 10A Kelley's Island Rd, Tilting; r $85; ⊜🛜) The four rooms in this tradition-al, 100-year-old home are brightly colored, furnished in modern style and have en-suite bathrooms.

🍴 Nicole's Cafe   CAFE **$$**
(🖉709-658-3663; www.nicolescafe.ca; 159 Main Rd, Joe Batt's Arm; mains $15-20; ⊙9am-9pm) Nicole uses ingredients from the island – sustainably caught seafood, root vegetables and wild berries – for her con-temporary take on dishes like Jigg's dinner, caribou pâté and the daily vegetarian plate. It's a sunny spot with big wood tables and local artwork and quilts on the walls.

ℹ Information

Change Islands (www.changeislands.ca)
Fogo Tourism (www.fogoisland.net)

ℹ Getting There & Away

Rte 335 takes you to the town of Farewell, where the ferry sails to the Change Islands (20 minutes) and then onward to Fogo (45 minutes). Five boats leave between 7:45am and 8:30pm. Schedules vary, so check with **Provincial Ferry Services** (🖉709-621-3150, 709-627-3448; www.gov.nl.ca/ferryservices). The round-trip fare to Fogo is $16.50 for car and driver, and $5.50 for additional passengers. It's $6.50 to the Change Islands.

Lewisporte
POP 3300
Stretched-out Lewisporte, known primar-ily for its ferry terminal, is the largest town on Notre Dame Bay. Other than for the boat to Labrador, there really isn't much reason

to visit, though as a distribution center it does have all the goods and services.

If you have to spend the night, the stark **Brittany Inns** (🖉709-535-2533, 800-563-8386; Main St; r $90-110; ❋🛜) is about as good as you're going to get. Several of the 34 rooms have kitchenettes.

Oriental Restaurant (🖉709-535-6993; 131 Main St; meals $6-11; ⊙11:30am-11pm) is a straightforward place, and you get a chance at a few vegetables.

DRL (🖉709-263-2171; www.drl-lr.com) stops at Brittany Inns en route to St John's and Port aux Basques.

Between mid-June and mid-September, the **MV Sir Robert Bond** (🖉709-535-0810, 866-535-2567; www.labradormarine.com) runs a weekly vehicle-and-passenger service to the Labrador towns of Cartwright (adult/child/car $73/36.50/118, 24 hours) and Happy Valley-Goose Bay (adult/child/car $118/59.25/194, 39 hours, including a four-hour stop in Cartwright). The boat leaves Lewisporte on Friday at 2pm.

Grand Falls-Windsor
POP 14,000
The sprawl of two small pulp-and-paper towns has met and now comprises the com-munity of Grand Falls-Windsor. The Grand Falls portion, south of Hwy 1 and near the Exploits River, is more interesting for visi-tors. The five-day **Salmon Festival** (www. salmonfestival.com; ⊙mid-Jul) rocks with big-name Canadian bands.

⊙ Sights

Mary March Provincial Museum   MUSEUM
(🖉709-292-4522; www.therooms.ca/museum; cnr St Catherine & Cromer Aves; adult/child $2.50/free; ⊙9am-4:45pm Mon-Sat, from noon Sun May–mid-Oct) This is worth visiting. Ex-hibits concentrate on the recent and past histories of Aboriginal peoples in the area, including the extinct Beothuk tribe. Take exit 18A south to reach it. Admission in-cludes the loggers' museum, and vice versa.

Loggers' Life Provincial Museum   MUSEUM
(🖉709-292-0492; www.therooms.ca/museum; exit 17, Hwy 1; adult/child $2.50/free; ⊙9am-4:45pm late May–mid-Sep) Experience the life of a 1920s logging camp – smells and all.

Salmonid Interpretation Centre   PARK
(🖉709-489-7350; www.exploitsriver.ca; adult/ child $6/2.50; ⊙8am-8pm mid-Jun–mid-Sep)

Watch Atlantic salmon start their mighty struggle upstream to spawn. Unfortunately, they do so under the pulp mill's shadow. To get there, cross the river south of High St and follow the signs.

Sleeping & Eating

Hill Road Manor B&B　　　　B&B $$
(☎709-489-5451, 866-489-5451; www.hillroad manor.com; 1 Hill Rd; r $109-119; ☎) Elegant furnishings, cushiony beds that will have you gladly oversleeping and a vibrant sunroom combine for a stylish stay. Kids are welcome.

Kelly's Pub & Eatery　　　　BURGERS $
(☎709-489-9893; 18 Hill Rd; mains $7-11; ⊗9am-2am) Hidden neatly behind the smoky pub is this great countrified spot. It makes the best burgers in town and the stir-fries are not too shabby either.

ℹ Information

Town of Grand Falls-Windsor (www.grand fallswindsor.com)

ℹ Getting There & Away

DRL (☎709-263-2171; www.drl-lr.com) has its bus stop at the Highliner Inn on the Hwy 1 service road. The drive to St John's is 430km, to Port aux Basques it's 477km.

Central South Coast

Rte 360 runs 130km through the center of the province to the south coast. It's a long way down to the first settlements at the end of **Bay d'Espoir**, a gentle fjord. Note there is no gas station, so fill up on Hwy 1. **St Alban's** is set on the west side of the fjord. You'll find a few motels around the end of the bay with dining rooms and lounges.

Further south is a concentration of small fishing villages. The scenery along Rte 364 to **Hermitage** is particularly impressive, as is the scenery around **Harbour Breton**. It's the largest town (population 2080) in the region and huddles around the ridge of a gentle inland bay.

　　Southern Port Hotel (☎709-885-2283; www.southernporthotel.ca; Rte 360, Harbour Breton; r $90-93; ☎) provides spacious, standard-furnished rooms; even-numbered ones have harbor views. Two doors down is **Scott's Snackbar** (☎709-885-2406; mains $7-15; ⊗10:30am-11pm Sun-Thu, to 1am Fri & Sat), serving burgers and home-cooked dishes; it's licensed.

Thornhill Taxi Service (☎709-885-2144, 866-538-3429) connects Harbour Breton with Grand Falls ($40, 2½ hours), leaving at 7:15am. Government passenger ferries serve Hermitage, making the western south-coast outports (see p209) accessible from here.

NORTHERN PENINSULA

The Northern Peninsula points upward from the body of Newfoundland like an extended index finger, and you almost get the feeling it's wagging at you saying, 'Don't you dare leave this province without coming up here.'

Heed the advice. This area could well be crowned Newfoundland's star attraction. The province's two World Heritage sites are here: Gros Morne National Park, with its fjordlike lakes and geological oddities, rests at the peninsula's base, while the sublime, 1000-year-old Viking settlement at L'Anse aux Meadows stares out from the peninsula's tip. Connecting these two famous sites is the **Viking Trail** (www.vikingtrail.org), aka Rte 430, an attraction in its own right that holds close to the sea as it heads resolutely north past the ancient burial grounds of Port au Choix and the ferry jump-off point to big, brooding Labrador. It's no wonder many people base their entire Newfoundland trip around this extraordinary region and usually end up coming back for more, year after year.

The region continues to gain in tourism, yet the crowds are nowhere near what you'd get at Yellowstone or Banff, for example. Still, it's wise to book ahead in July and August.

It's a five- to six-hour drive from Deer Lake at the peninsula's southern edge to L'Anse aux Meadows at its northern apex. Towns and amenities are few and far between so don't wait to fuel up.

Deer Lake

There's little in Deer Lake for the visitor, but it's an excellent place to fly into for trips up the Northern Peninsula and around the west coast.

B&Bers can hunker down at plain-and-simple **Lucas House** (☎709-635-3622; 22 Old Bonne Bay Rd; r $60-70; ⊗May-Sep; ⊗@); it's a five-minute ride from the airport. The biggest show in town is 56-room, dog-eared **Deer Lake Motel** (📞709-635-2108; www.deer lakemotel.com; Hwy 1; r $89-139; ❄️📶), which sits on Hwy 1 across from the **Visitors Centre** (🕙9am-7pm) and the **DRL** (📞709-263-2171; www.drl-lr.com) bus stop at the Irving gas station. A taxi from the airport to any of these spots costs about $7.

Deer Lake Airport (YDF; www.deerlakeair port.com) is a stone's throw off Hwy 1. It's a well-equipped little place with ATMs, food, free wi-fi and internet access, and a staffed tourism desk. Flights arrive regularly from St John's, Halifax, Toronto and even London. Avis, Budget and Hertz rent cars at the airport; for costs and contact information, see p265.

Gros Morne National Park

This **national park** (📞709-458-2417; www. pc.gc.ca/grosmorne; adult/child/family per day $9.80/4.90/19.60; 🕙year-round) stepped into the world spotlight in 1987, when Unesco granted it World Heritage designation. To visitors, the park's stunning flat-top mountains and deeply incised waterways are simply supernatural playgrounds. To geologists, this park is a blueprint for our planet and supplies evidence for theories such as plate tectonics. Specifically, the bronze-colored Tablelands are made of rock that comes from deep within the earth's crust. Nowhere in the world is such material as easily accessed as in Gros Morne (it's usually only found at unfathomable ocean depths). Such attributes have earned the park its 'Galapagos of Geology' nickname.

There is enough to do in and around the park to easily fill several days. The hiking, kayaking, camping, wildlife-spotting and boat tours are fantastic.

Several small fishing villages dot the shoreline and provide amenities. Bonne Bay swings in and divides the area: to the south is Rte 431 and the towns of **Glenburnie**, **Woody Point** and **Trout River**; to the north is Rte 430 and **Norris Point**, **Rocky Harbour**, **Sally's Cove** and **Cow Head**. Centrally located Rocky Harbour is the largest village and most popular place to stay. Nearby Norris Point and further-flung Woody Point also make good bases.

👁 Sights

The park is quite widespread – it's 133km from Trout River at the south end to Cow

ℹ️ VIKING TRAIL PASS

Gros Morne, L'Anse aux Meadows, Port aux Choix, Red Bay and Grenfell Historic Properties can be visited on the joint **admission pass** (adult/child/family $44/22/88), valid for seven days. It'll save you a few dollars if you're intending to see them all.

Head in the north – so it takes a while to get from sight to sight. We've listed the following places from south to north. Don't forget to stop in the park's visitors centers (see p198), which have interpretive programs and guided walks.

Tablelands   GEOGRAPHIC FEATURE
(Rte 431, near Trout River) Dominating the southwest corner of the park are the unconquerable and eerie Tablelands. This massive flat-topped massif was part of the earth's mantle before tectonics raised it from the depths and planted it squarely on the continent. Its rock is so unusual that plants can't even grow on it. You can view the barren golden phenomenon up close on Rte 431, or catch it from a distance at the stunning **photography lookout** above Norris Point. West of the Tablelands, dramatic volcanic sea stacks and caves mark the coast at **Green Gardens**.

Bonne Bay Marine Station   AQUARIUM
(📞709-458-2550; www.bonnebay.mun.ca; Rte 430, Norris Point; adult/child/family $6.25/5/15; 🕙9am-5pm late May-early Sep, by appointment rest of yr) At the wharf in Norris Point is the Bonne Bay Marine Station, a research facility that's part of Memorial University. Every half-hour there are interactive tours, and the aquariums display the marine ecological habitats in Bonne Bay. For kids, there are touch tanks and a rare blue lobster.

SS Ethie   SHIPWRECK
(Rte 430, past Sally's Cove) Follow the sign off the highway to where waves batter the rusty and tangled remains of the SS *Ethie*. The story of this 1919 wreck, and the subsequent rescue, was inspiration for a famous folk song.

Western Brook Pond   TRAIL & TOUR
(Rte 430) Park your car in the lot off the highway, then take the 3km flat, easy path inland to Western Brook Pond. 'Pond' is a

misnomer, since the body of water is huge. Many people also call it a fjord, which is technically incorrect, since it's freshwater versus saltwater. Here's the thing everyone agrees on: it's flat-out stunning. Western Brook's sheer 700m cliffs plunge to the blue abyss and dramatically snake into the mountains. The best way to experience it is on a boat tour (see Bon Tours, right).

FREE **Broom Point Fishing Camp**
HISTORICAL SITE
(Rte 430, Broom Point; admission free; ⊙10am-5:30pm mid-May–mid-Oct) This restored fishing camp sits a short distance north of Western Brook Pond. The three Mudge brothers and their families fished here from 1941 until 1975, when they sold the entire camp, including boats, lobster traps and nets, to the national park. Everything has been restored, and it's staffed by guides.

Shallow Bay   BEACH
The gentle, safe, sand-duned beach at Shallow Bay seems almost out of place, as if transported from the Caribbean by some bizarre current. The water, though, provides a chilling dose of reality, rarely getting above 15°C.

The Arches   PARK
These scenic arched rocks on Rte 430 north of Parsons Pond are formed by pounding waves and worth a look-see.

🏃 Activities

Hiking and kayaking can also be done via guided tours.

Hiking

Twenty maintained trails of varying difficulty snake through 100km of the park's most scenic landscapes. The gem is the **James Callahan Gros Morne Trail** (16km) to the peak of Gros Morne, the highest point in the area at 806m. While there are sections with steps and boardwalks, this is a strenuous seven- to eight-hour hike, and includes a steep rock gully that must be climbed to the ridgeline of the mountain. Standing on the 600m precipice and staring out over **10 Mile Pond**, a sheer-sided fjord, can only be described as sublime.

Green Gardens Trail (16km) is almost as scenic and challenging. The loop has two trailheads off Rte 431, with each one descending to Green Gardens along its magnificent coastline formed from lava and shaped by the sea. Plan on six to eight hours

of hiking or book one of the three backcountry camping areas, all of them on the ocean, and turn the hike into an overnight adventure. A less strenuous day hike (9km) to the beach and back is possible from this trail's Long Pond Trailhead.

Shorter scenic hikes are the **Tablelands Trail** (4km), which extends to Winterhouse Brook Canyon; **Lookout Trail** (5km), which starts behind the Discovery Centre and loops to the site of an old fire tower above the tree line; **Lobster Cove Head Trail** (2km), which loops through tidal pools; and **Western Brook Pond Trail** (below), the park's most popular path.

The granddaddies of the trails are the **Long Range Traverse** (35km) and **North Rim Traverse** (27km), serious multiday treks over the mountains. Permits and advice from park rangers are required.

If you plan to do several trails, invest $20 in a copy of the *Gros Morne National Park Trail Guide,* a waterproof map with trail descriptions on the back, which is usually available at the visitors centers.

Kayaking

Kayaking in the shadow of the Tablelands and through the spray of whales is truly something to be experienced. **Gros Morne Adventures** (single/double per day $50/60) provides rentals for experienced paddlers. See opposite for contact details.

Skiing

Many trails in the park's impressive 55km cross-country ski-trail system were designed by Canadian Olympic champion, Pierre Harvey. Contact the Main Visitor Centre (p198) for trail information and reservations for backcountry huts.

👉 Tours

Most tours operate between June and mid-September; book in advance. Kayaking is best in June and July.

Bon Tours   BOAT
(☑709-458-2016; www.bontours.ca; Ocean View Motel, Main St, Rocky Harbour) Bon runs the phenomenal **Western Brook Pond boat tour** (2hr trip per adult/child/family $52/25/120) at 10am, 1pm and 4pm. The dock is a 3km walk from Rte 430 via the easy Western Brook Pond Trail. If you haven't purchased a **park pass** ($9.80), you must do so before embarking. It's best to buy tickets ahead of time at Bon's office in the Ocean View Hotel, though you can also do so at the boat dock

(where it's cash only). It's about a 25-minute drive from Bon's office to the trailhead.

Bon also runs **Bonne Bay boat tours** (2hr trip per adult/child/family $39/16/90) departing from Norris Point's wharf, as well as a water taxi ($12 round-trip, foot passengers and bikes only) from Norris Point to Woody Point.

Gros Morne Adventures   MULTISPORT
(☑709-458-2722, 800-685-4624; www.grosmor neadventures.com; Norris Point wharf) It offers daily guided sea kayak tours (two/three hours $50/60) in Bonne Bay, plus full-day and multiday kayak trips and hiking, skiing and snowshoeing tours. Check the website for many additional options.

Long Range Adventures   MULTISPORT
(☑709-458-2828, 877-458-2828; www.longrange adventures.com; Sally's Cove) Another multiadventure outfitter offering daily guided sea kayaking (2½-hour tour $55), hiking and mountain-bike tours, plus winter activities. Locally owned Long Range also runs **Gros Morne Hostel/Island Traveller Tours** (www.grosmornehostel.com), a budget sister company with excursions taking in Twillingate and St John's from Deer Lake (three-day tour from $279) and others that continue on through the Northern Peninsula (seven-day tour from $749).

★ Festivals & Events

Gros Morne Theatre Festival (☑709-243-2899; www.theatrenewfoundland.com; tickets $15-30; ☺late May–mid-Sep) Eight productions of Newfoundland plays, staged both indoors and outdoors at various locations throughout the summer.

Writers at Woody Point Festival (☑709-453-2900; www.writersatwoodypoint.com; tickets $20; ☺mid-Aug) Authors from across Newfoundland, Canada and the world converge at the Woody Point Heritage Theatre to do readings.

🛏 Sleeping

Rocky Harbour has the most options. Woody Point, Norris Point and cute Cow Head are also good bets. Places fill fast in July and August.

Middle Brook Cottages   CABIN **$$**
(☑709-453-2332; www.middlebrookcottages. com; off Rte 431, Glenburnie; cabins $115-129; ☺mid-Mar–Nov; ⊜🛜🐾) These all-pinewood, spick-and-span cottages are both perfectly

romantic and perfectly kid-friendly. They have kitchens and TVs, and you can splash around the swimming hole and waterfalls behind the property.

Aunt Jane's Place B&B   B&B **$**
(☑709-453-2485; www.grosmorne.com/victo rianmanor; Water St, Woody Point; r with/without bathroom $75/65; ☺mid-May–mid-Oct; ⊜) This historic house oozes character. It sits beachside, so you may be woken early in the morning by the heavy breathing of whales.

Gros Morne Cabins   CABIN **$$**
(☑709-458-2020; www.grosmornecabins.com; Main St, Rocky Harbour; cabins $119-189; 🛜🐾) While backed by tarmac, most of these beautiful log cabins are fronted by nothing but ocean (ask when booking to ensure a view). Each has a full kitchen, TV and pull-out sofa for children. Bookings can be made next door at Endicott's variety store.

Red Mantle Lodge   HOTEL **$$**
(☑709-453-7204, 888-453-7204; www.redma ntlelodge.ca; Rte 431, near Woody Point; r $129-159; ❄🛜) Located up a steep hill looking down on Woody Point, with 17 of its 18 rooms facing the bay, the Red Mantle gives off a new ski lodge vibe. Rooms have high ceilings, wood floors and mellow, earth toned decor; ask for an upstairs one to minimize noise. The licensed bar/restaurant is handy for an evening drink.

Anchor Down B&B   B&B **$$**
(☑709-458-2901, 800-920-2208; www.the anchordown.com; Pond Rd, Rocky Harbour; r $75-90; 🐾) The home and its five rooms are pretty simple, but guests have raved about excellent hospitality and cooking from the friendly hosts.

Gros Morne Hostel   HOSTEL **$**
(☑709-458-2828, 877-458-2828; www.gros mornehostel.com; Sally's Cove; dm $25, r with/without bathroom incl breakfast $65/50; 🐾) The Long Range Adventures folks rent out extra rooms in their house. It's tight quarters, but the hosts' goodwill smooths out the roughness. Free bike use for guests.

Park Campgrounds   CAMPGROUND **$**
(☑877-737-3783; www.pccamping.ca; campsites $19-26, reservation fee $10.80) Four developed campgrounds lie within the park: **Berry Hill** (☺mid-Jun–mid-Sep), the largest, is most central; **Lomond** (☺late May–mid-Oct) is good and closest to the southern park entrance; **Trout River** (☺mid-Jun–mid-Sep) is average and closest to the Tablelands; and

Shallow Bay (⊘mid-Jun–mid-Sep) has ocean swimming (and mosquitoes). There's also a **primitive campground** (⊘year-round) at superb Green Point. Numerous **backcountry campsites** ($10) are spread along trails; reserve them at the Main Visitor Centre.

✕ Eating

Rocky Harbour and Woody Point have the most options. There's a good chip van in Sally's Cove.

TOP CHOICE **Java Jack's** CAFE $$
(🕾709-458-3004; www.javajacks.ca; Main St, Rocky Harbour; mains $9-19; ⊘7:30am-8:30pm mid-May–late Sep, closed Tue; ✔) Art-filled Jack's provides Gros Morne's best coffees, wraps and soups by day. By night, the upstairs dining room fills hungry, post-hike bellies with fine seafood, caribou and vegetarian fare. Greens come fresh from the property's organic garden.

Earle's Video & Convenience CANADIAN $
(🕾709-458-2577; Main St, Rocky Harbour; mains $8-14; ⊘9am-11pm) Earle is an institution in Rocky Harbour. Besides selling groceries and renting videos, he has great ice cream, pizza, moose burgers and traditional Newfoundland fare that you can chomp on the patio.

Lighthouse Restaurant SEAFOOD $$
(🕾709-453-2213; Water St, Woody Point; mains $9-15; ⊘11:30am-9pm Mon-Wed, from 9am Thu-Sun May-Sep) The ladies at this diner cook up a storm out back and deliver Gros Morne's best fish and chips, cod tongues and other Newfie dishes, along with cold beer.

Old Loft Restaurant SEAFOOD $$
(🕾709-453-2294; www.theoldloft.com; Water St, Woody Point; mains $15-21; ⊘11:30am-9pm Jul & Aug, to 7pm May, Jun & Sep) Set on the water in Woody Point, this tiny place is popular for its traditional Newfoundland meals and seafood.

❶ Information

Park admission includes the trails, Discovery Centre and all day-use areas.

Discovery Centre (🕾709-453-2490; Rte 431, Woody Point; ⊘9am-5pm late May–mid-Oct, to 9pm Wed & Sun Jul & Aug) Has interactive exhibits and a multimedia theater explaining the area's ecology and geology. There's also an information desk with maps, daily interpretive activities and a small cafe.

Main Visitor Centre (🕾709-458-2066; Rte 430, near Rocky Harbour; ⊘9am-9pm late Jun-early Sep, to 5pm mid-May–late Jun & early Sep–mid-Oct) As well as issuing day and backcountry permits, it has maps, books, Viking Trail materials and an impressive interpretive area.

Park Entrance Kiosk (Rte 430; ⊘10am-6pm mid-May–mid-Oct) Near Wiltondale.

Rocky Harbour (www.rockyharbour.ca)

Western Newfoundland Tourism (www.facebook.com/gowesternnewfoundland.com)

❶ Getting There & Around

Deer Lake Airport is 71km south of Rocky Harbour. For shuttle bus services to Rocky Harbour, Woody Point and Trout River, see Corner Brook (p202).

Port au Choix

Port au Choix, dangling on a stark peninsula 13km off the Viking Trail, houses a large fishing fleet, quirky museum and worthy archaeological site that delves into ancient burial grounds.

◉ Sights & Activities

Port au Choix National Historic Site
HISTORICAL SITE
(🕾709-861-3522; www.pc.gc.ca/portauchoix; Point Riche Rd; adult/child $7.80/3.90; ⊘9am-6pm Jun-early Oct) The Port au Choix National Historic Site sits on ancient burial grounds of three different Aboriginal groups, dating back 5500 years. The modern visitors center tells of these groups' creative survival in the area and of one group's unexplained disappearance 3200 years ago.

Phillip's Garden, a site with vestiges of Paleo-Eskimo houses, is a highlight. Two trails will take you there. One is the **Phillip's Garden Coastal Trail** (4km), which leaves from Phillip Dr at the end of town. From here you hopscotch your way over the jigsaw of skeletal rock to the site 1km away.

If you continue, it's another 3km to the **Point Riche Lighthouse** (1871). A plaque next to the tower recounts the many French and English conflicts in the area between the 1600s and 1900s. In 1904, France relinquished its rights here in exchange for privileges in Morocco (ah, the days when the world was a Monopoly board). The lighthouse is also accessible via the visitors center road.

The other way to reach Phillip's Garden is via the **Dorset Trail** (8km). It leaves the visitors center and winds across the barrens through stunted trees, passing a Dorset Paleo-Eskimo **burial cave** before finally reaching the site and linking to the Coastal Trail.

Ben's Studio
GALLERY
(☏709-861-3280; www.bensstudio.ca; 24 Fisher St; admission free; ☺9am-5pm Mon-Fri Jun–mid-Sep) At the edge of town is Ben Ploughman's capricious studio of folk art. Pieces like *Crucifixion of the Cod* are classic. His engaging and humorous manner complements the ever-evolving whale museum he's creating, which includes an impressive, wired-together whale skeleton.

🛏 Sleeping & Eating

Jeannie's Sunrise B&B B&B **$**
(☏709-861-2254, 877-639-2789; www.jeanniesunrisebb.com; Fisher St; r $55-89; ☺📶) Jeannie radiates hospitality through her spacious rooms, bright reading nook and demeanor as sweet as her breakfast muffins. Rooms at the lower end of the price spectrum share a bathroom.

Anchor Cafe SEAFOOD **$$**
(☏709-861-3665; Fisher St; mains $12-18; ☺11am-9pm) You can't miss this place – the front half is the bow of a boat – and don't, because it has the best meals in town. The luncheon specials offer good value and the dinner menu has a wide array of seafood.

St Barbe to L'Anse aux Meadows

As the Viking Trail nears St Barbe, the waters of the gulf quickly narrow and give visitors their first opportunity to see the desolate shores of Labrador. Ferries take advantage of this convergence and ply the route between St Barbe and the Labrador Straits (see p212). At Eddies Cove, the road leaves the coast and heads inland.

As you approach the northern tip of the peninsula, Rte 430 veers off toward St Anthony, and two new roads take over leading to several diminutive fishing villages that provide perfect bases for your visit to L'Anse aux Meadows National Historic Site. Route 436 hugs the eastern shore and passes through (from south to north) St Lunaire-Griquet, Gunners Cove, Straitsview and L'Anse aux Meadows village. Route 437 heads in a more westerly direction through Pistolet Bay, Raleigh and Cape Onion.

DON'T MISS

TOP PLACES TO GET AWAY FROM IT ALL

» Fogo Island, Central Newfoundland (p192)

» Cape Onion, Northern Peninsula (p200)

» Conche, Northern Peninsula (boxed text, p203)

» François, South Coast Outports (p209)

» Torngat Mountains, Northern Labrador (p214)

⊙ Sights & Activities

L'Anse aux Meadows National Historic Site HISTORICAL SITE
(☏709-623-2608; www.pc.gc.ca/lanseauxmeadows; Rte 436; adult/child $11.70/5.80; ☺9am-6pm Jun-early Oct) The premise may seem dull – visiting a bog in the middle of nowhere and staring at the spot where a couple of old sod houses once stood – but somehow this Viking site lying in a forlorn sweep of land turns out to be one of Newfoundland's most stirring attractions.

Its historic significance is absolute: it's the home of the first Europeans to land in North America. They were Vikings from Scandinavia and Greenland, who sailed over some 500 years before Columbus. That they settled, constructed houses, fed themselves and even smelted iron out of the bog to forge nails, attests to their ingenuity and fortitude. That it was all accomplished by a group of young-pup 20-somethings, led by Leif Eriksson, son of Eric the Red, is even more impressive.

The remains of the Vikings' waterside settlement from circa AD 1000 – eight wood-and-sod buildings, now just vague outlines left in the spongy ground – are what visitors can see, plus three replica buildings inhabited by costumed docents. The latter have names such as 'Thora' and 'Bjorn' and simulate Viking chores such as spinning fleece and forging nails.

Allow two or three hours to walk around and absorb the ambience, as well as to browse the interpretive center. While there, be sure to see the introductory film, which tells the captivating story of Norwegian explorer Helge Ingstad, who rediscovered the site in 1960, ending years of searching.

Also worthwhile is the 3km **trail** that winds through the barren terrain and along the coast surrounding the interpretive center.

Norstead   HISTORICAL VILLAGE
(☑709-623-2828; www.norstead.com; Rte 436; adult/child/family $10/6/30; ☺9:30am-5:30pm Jun-late Sep) Can't get enough of the long-bearded Viking lifestyle? Stop by Norstead, just beyond the turnoff to the national historic site. It's a recreation of a Viking village with costumed interpreters (more than at L'Anse aux Meadows) smelting, weaving, baking and telling stories around real fires throughout four buildings. Sounds cheesy, but they pull it off with class. There's also a large-scale replica of a Viking ship on hand.

🛏 Sleeping

Straitsview, Gunners Cove and St Lunaire-Griquet are all within 12km of the national historic site.

Tickle Inn   B&B $
(☑709-452-4321; www.tickleinn.net; Rte 437, Cape Onion; r with shared bathroom $65-85;

☺Jun-late Sep; ☻) This delightful seaside inn, built in 1890, is surrounded by a white picket fence, oodles of grass and your own private beach. Sit in the parlor, feel the warmth of the Franklin woodstove and enjoy great home-cooked meals. The location is wonderfully remote.

Valhalla Lodge B&B   B&B $$
(☑709-623-2018, 877-623-2018; www.valhalla-lodge.com; Rte 436, Gunners Cove; r $90-100; ☺mid-May–late Sep; ☻☎) Set on a hill overlooking the ocean, the five-room Valhalla is only 8km from the Viking site. Put your feet up on the deck and watch icebergs in comfort. This very view inspired Pulitzer Prize–winning author E Annie Proulx while she wrote *The Shipping News* here.

Viking Village B&B   B&B $
(☑709-623-2238; www.vikingvillage.ca; Hay Cove, L'Anse aux Meadows village; r from $72; ☻☎) A timbered home with ocean views, Viking Village offers comfy, quilted rooms just 1km from the Viking site. Ask for one of the rooms with balcony access and watch the sun rise.

THE SEAL HUNT DEBATE

Nothing ignites a more passionate debate than Canada's annual seal hunt, which occurs in March and April off Newfoundland's northeast coast and in the Gulf of St Lawrence around the Îles de la Madeleine and Prince Edward Island.

The debate pits animal rights activists against sealers (typically local fishers who hunt seals in the off-season), and both sides spin rhetoric like a presidential press secretary. The main issues revolve around the following questions.

Are baby seals being killed? Yes and no. Whitecoats are newborn harp seals, and these are the creatures in the horrifying images everyone remembers. But it's illegal to hunt them and has been for 20 years now. However, young harp seals lose their white coats when the seals are about 12 to 14 days old. After that, they're fair game.

Are the animals killed humanely? Sealers say yes, that the guns and/or clubs they use kill the seals humanely. Animal activists dispute this, saying seals are shot or clubbed and left on the ice to suffer until the sealers come back later and finish the job.

Is the seal population sustainable? The Canadian government says yes, and sets the yearly quota based on the total seal population in the area (estimated at 6.9 million). For 2010, the harp seal quota was 330,000. The 2009 quota was 280,000. Activists say the quotas don't take into account the actual number of seals killed in the hunt, such as those that are 'struck and lost,' or discarded because of pelt damage.

Is the seal hunt really an important part of the local economy? Activists say no, that it represents a fraction of Newfoundland's income. The province disagrees, saying for some sealers it represents up to one-third of their annual income. And in a province with unemployment near 15%, that's significant.

In 2009 the European Union banned the sale of seal products, which hurt the industry considerably. For further details on the two perspectives, see the websites of the **Canadian Sealers Association** (www.sealharvest.ca) and the **Humane Society of the United States** (www.protectseals.org).

Snorri Cabins
CABINS $$

(☑709-623-2241; www.snorricabins.com; Rte 436, Straitsview; cabins $89; ☉Jun-Sep; ☎) These modern cabins offer simple comfort and great value. They're perfect for families, with a full kitchen, sitting room and a pull-out sofa. There's a convenience store on-site.

St Brendan's Motel
MOTEL $

(☑709-623-2520; www.stbrendansmotel.com; Rte 436, St Lunaire-Griquet; s/d $75/80; ☉Jun–mid-Oct; ☎) This 11-room motel doesn't look like much, but the rooms (with TV, coffee-maker and refrigerator) are snug and the setting peaceful.

✖ Eating

[TOP CHOICE] Norseman Restaurant & Art Gallery
SEAFOOD $$$

(☑709-623-2018; www.valhalla-lodge.com; Rte 436, L'Anse aux Meadows village; mains $19-38; ☉noon-9pm mid-May–late Sep) This casual, waterfront room may well be the best restaurant in Newfoundland. Relish the butternut squash soup, peruse a few vegetarian options or sink your teeth into tender Labrador caribou tenderloin. Norseman chills all its drinks with iceberg ice. Patrons who order lobster hand-pick their dinner by donning rubber boots and heading out front to the ocean, where the freshly caught crustaceans await in crates.

Daily Catch
SEAFOOD $$

(☑709-623-2295; www.thedailycatch.ca; 112 Main St, St Lunaire-Griquet; mains $11-20; ☉11am-9pm) Set on the water overlooking a pretty bay, the Daily Catch is a stylish little restaurant serving finely prepared seafood and wine. The basil-buttered salmon gets kudos. Fish cakes, crab au gratin and cod burgers also please the palate.

Northern Delight
SEAFOOD $$

(☑709-623-2220; Rte 436, Gunners Cove; mains $9-15; ☉8am-9pm) Dine on local favorites such as turbot cheeks and pan-fried cod, fresh lobster and mussels, or just have a 'Newfie Mug-up' (bread, molasses and a strong cup of tea). There's live music on some evenings.

St Anthony

Yeehaw! You've made it to the end of the road, your windshield has helped control the insect population and you have seen two World Heritage sites. After such grandeur, St Anthony may be a little anticlimac-

tic. It's not what you'd call pretty, but it has a rough-hewn charm. And the hiking and whale- and iceberg-watching are inspiring.

Grenfell is a big name around here. Sir Wilfred Grenfell was a local legend and, by all accounts, quite a man. This English-born and -educated doctor first came to Newfoundland in 1892 and, for the next 40 years, traveling by dog-sled and boat, built hospitals and nursing stations and organized much-needed fishing cooperatives along the coast of Labrador and around St Anthony.

◉ Sights & Activities

Grenfell Historic Properties
HISTORICAL BUILDING

(www.grenfell-properties.com; West St; adult/child/family $10/3/22; ☉9am-6pm mid-Jun–mid-Sep) A number of local sites pertaining to Wilfred Grenfell are subsumed under Grenfell Historic Properties. The **Grenfell Interpretation Centre**, opposite the hospital, is a modern exhibit recounting the historic and sometimes dramatic life of Grenfell. Its **handicraft shop** has some high-quality carvings and artwork, as well as embroidered parkas made by locals – proceeds go to maintenance of the historic properties.

Grenfell Museum
MUSEUM

(☉9am-6pm mid-Jun–mid-Sep) Admission to the Properties also includes Grenfell's beautiful mansion, now the Grenfell Museum. It's behind the hospital, about a five-minute walk from the waterfront. Dyed burlap walls and antique furnishings envelop memorabilia including a polar-bear rug and, if rumors are correct, the ghost of Mrs Grenfell.

Fishing Point Park
PARK

The main road through town ends at Fishing Point Park, where a lighthouse and towering headland cliffs overlook the sea. The **Iceberg Alley Trail** and **Whale Watchers Trail** both lead to cliff-top observation platforms – the names say it all.

A **visitors center/cafe/craft shop** is also out here; in the side room there's a **polar bear display** (admission $2). Creatures like this guy have been known to roam St Anthony from time to time as pack ice melts in the spring.

☞ Tours

Northland Discovery Tours
WHALE-WATCHING

(☑709-454-3092, 877-632-3747; www.discovernorthland.com; 2½hr tours adult/child $55/20;

Each year 10,000 to 40,000 glistening icebergs break off Greenland's glaciers and enter the Baffin and Labrador currents for the three-year trip south to Newfoundland's famed 'Iceberg Alley.' This 480km-long, 98km-wide stretch of sea runs along the province's north and east coasts and is strewn with 'bergs in late spring and early summer. Fogo and Twillingate Islands in Notre Dame Bay and St Anthony on the Northern Peninsula are some of the best places for sightings. Even St John's is graced with a few hundred of the blue-and-white marvels most years (though sometimes the waters remain barren due to climate and current shifts).

To see where the behemoths lurk, check www.icebergfinder.com, the provincial tourism association's website showing where icebergs are floating; you can get weekly email updates on their locations and plan your trip accordingly. Also, the Canadian government's website www.ice-glaces.ec.gc.ca provides daily iceberg bulletins.

Locals harvest some smaller 'bergs, and if you ask in restaurants you may get a piece along with your drink. Considering the glacial ice may be more than 15,000 years old, it is indeed an ice cube to savor.

9am, 1pm & 4pm late May-late Sep) Northland offers highly recommended cruises for whale or iceberg viewing that leave from the dock behind the Grenfell Interpretation Centre on West St. If you tend to get seasick, medicate before this one.

Sleeping & Eating

Fishing Point B&B   B&B $$
(709-454-3117, 866-454-2009; www.bbcanada.com/6529.html; Fishing Point Rd; r $85;) This tiny place clings to the rocks en route to the lighthouse and offers the best harbor view in St Anthony. Get up early, enjoy a bountiful breakfast and watch the boats head out to sea. Each of the three rooms has its own bathroom.

Wildberry Country Inn   INN $$
(709-454-2662, 877-818-2662; www.wildberryadventures.com; Rte 430; r incl breakfast $75-95) Owner Lyndon Hodge hand-built this small, rustic lodge himself, and it's a winner. Hodge attempts to tread gently on the land (for instance, the on-site restaurant sources only local ingredients), and he knows the region like the back of his hand having lived here all his life. It's a bit of a trek from St Anthony, about 20km northwest on Rte 430.

Lightkeeper's Cafe   CAFE $$
(877-454-4900; Fishing Point Park; meals $8-20; 11:30am-8pm early Jun-Sep) This little gem of an eatery sits in the shadow of the lighthouse and is often graced by the sight of icebergs and whales. The chowder and scallops are legendary.

Getting There & Away

Flying to St Anthony is technically possible, but the airport is nearly an hour away. If you're leaving St Anthony by car, you have two options: backtrack entirely along Rte 430, or take the long way via Rte 432 (see the boxed text, opposite) along the east coast and Hare Bay. This will meet up with Rte 430 near Plum Point, between St Barbe and Port aux Choix.

WESTERN NEWFOUNDLAND

Western Newfoundland presents many visitors with their first view of The Rock, thanks to the ferry landing at Port aux Basques. It's big, cliffy, even a bit forbidding with all those wood houses clinging to the jagged shoreline against the roaring wind. From Port aux Basques, poky fishing villages cast lines to the east, while Newfoundland's second-largest town, Corner Brook, raises its wintry head (via its ski mountain) to the northeast.

Corner Brook

POP 20,100

Newfoundland's number-two town is pretty sleepy, though skiers, hikers and anglers will find plenty of action. The handsome Humber Valley, about 10km east, is where it's going on. Centered on the Marble Mountain ski resort, the area experienced a huge development boom – even Oprah was rumored to be buying one of the luxury condos – until the bottom fell out of the international economy. Maybe the vibe will ratchet up again one of these days. For now, the valley offers adventure-sport junkies places to play, while the city itself sprawls with big-box retailers and a smoke-belching pulp and paper mill.

◎ Sights & Activities

Marble Mountain   SKIING
(☑709-637-7616; www.skimarble.com; Hwy 1; day pass $49; ⊙10am-4:30pm Tue-Thu, 9am-9:30pm Fri, 9am-4:30pm Sat-Mon mid-Dec–early Apr) Marble Mountain is the lofty reason most visitors come to Corner Brook. With 35 trails, four lifts, a 488m vertical drop and annual snowfall of 5m, it offers Atlantic Canada's best skiing. There are snowboarding and tubing parks, as well as night skiing on Fridays, plus Oh My Jesus (you'll say it when you see the slope).

When the white stuff has departed, the **Steady Brook Falls Trail** (500m) leads from the ski area's rear parking lot, behind the Tim Hortons, to a cascade of water that tumbles over 30m.

Marble Zip Tours   ZIP-LINE
(☑709-632-5463; www.marbleziptours.com; Thistle Dr; 3hr tours adult/child $79/69) It's the highest zipline in Canada. Strap in near the mountaintop, and zigzag platform to platform down a gorge traversing Steady Brook Falls. It'll take your breath away. Tours depart three to four times daily. The company also arranges rock climbing, caving

and fishing tours. The office is past Marble Mountain's lodge, behind the Tim Hortons.

My Newfoundland Adventures   MULTISPORT
(☑709-638-0110, 800-686-8900; www.mynewfoundland.ca) If skiing doesn't get the adrenaline flowing, try snow-kiting (a windsurfing-meets-snowboarding endeavor). Or snowshoeing, ice fishing or ice climbing. Canoeing, salmon fishing and caving take place in warmer seasons. Pretty much anything is possible with these patient folks, no experience required. The office is located at Marble Mountain's base, just by the Tim Hortons.

Blow-Me-Down Cross-Country Ski Park
                                    CROSS-COUNTRY SKIING
(☑709-639-2754; www.blowmedown.ca; Lundigran Dr; day pass $13; ⊙sunrise-9pm early Dec-Apr) It has 50km of groomed trails; ski rentals (per day $12) are available. It's located about 6km southwest of downtown.

Captain James Cook Monument   PARK
(Crow Hill Rd) While this cliff-top monument is admirable – a tribute to James Cook for his work in surveying the region in the mid-1760s – it's the panoramic view over the Bay of Islands that is the real payoff. Cook's names for many of the islands, ports and waterways you'll see, such as the Humber Arm and Hawke's Bay, remain today. The site is northwest of downtown via a convoluted route. Ready? Take Caribou Rd to Poplar Rd to Country Rd, then go right on Atlantic Ave, left on Mayfair Ave and follow the signs.

WORTH A TRIP

RTE 432 & THE FRENCH SHORE

Surprises await along lonely Rte 432. First is **Tuckamore Lodge** (☑709-865-6361, 888-865-6361; www.tuckamorelodge.com; r incl breakfast $140-180; ❀@☎), a wood-hewn, lakeside retreat with ridiculously comfortable beds and home-cooked meals, located smack in the middle of nowhere. You'll pass about 20 moose on your way out to it. Owner Barb Genge arranges all manner of activities (fishing, bird-watching, hunting, photography classes) with first-rate guides.

The little towns along the coast are known as the **French Shore** (www.frenchshore.com) for the French fishermen who lived in the area from 1504 to 1904. Top of the heap is **Conche** with its intriguing gaggle of sights: a **WWII airplane** that crashed in town in 1942, the seaside **Captain Coupelongue walking trail** past old French gravemarkers, and a crazy-huge **tapestry** in the local interpretation center. A woman named Delight runs the sunny **Bits-n-Pieces Cafe** (☑709-622-5400; mains $9-14; ⊙8am-8pm, to 9pm Thu-Sat), ladling out cod cakes, Thai chicken and other fare that's, well, delightful. Two simple rooms above the cafe comprise the **Stage Cove B&B** (www.stagecovebandb.ca; r $90; ☎) if you want to spend the night. It's about 68km from Tuckamore Lodge; take Rte 433 to unpaved Rte 434.

Corner Brook

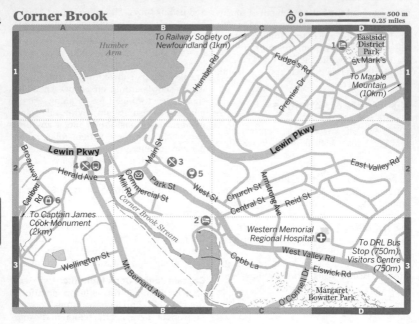

To Railway Society of Newfoundland (1km)

Corner Brook

🛏 Sleeping

🍴 Eating

🍷 Drinking

🛍 Shopping

Railway Society of Newfoundland MUSEUM
(☎709-634-2720; Station Rd, off Humber Rd;
admission $2; ⏱9am-9pm Jun-Aug) With-
in historic Humbermouth Station, the
Railway Society of Newfoundland has a
good-looking steam locomotive and some
narrow-gauge rolling stock that chugged
across the province from 1921 to 1939.

🛏 Sleeping

Bell's Inn B&B **$$**
(☎709-634-1150, 888-634-1150; www.bellsinn.
ca; 2 Ford's Rd; r $80-110; ⊜🐾) Gordon Bell's

rambling green house tops a hill that's a
15-minute walk from downtown. The eight
smallish, comfy rooms all have private bath-
rooms; Nos 1 and 4 have harbor views. Sip
your morning coffee on the breezy veranda.

Glynmill Inn HOTEL **$$**
(☎709-634-5181, 800-563-4400; www.glynmil
linn.ca; 1 Cobb Lane; r $102-130; ✳@🐾) Lawns,
gardens and graciousness surround the
Tudor-style Glynmill. It was built originally
for the engineers supervising the pulp mill's
construction in the 1920s, at that time the
largest project in the history of paper making. The inn retains an elegant if somewhat
faded ambience.

Two riverside B&Bs provide peace in the
valley, a stone's throw from the ski area
(about 10km east of Corner Brook).

Edgewater B&B (☎709-634-3474; www.
visittheedge.com; 14 Forest Dr, Steady Brook; r
$65-85; ⊜@🐾) Four rooms.

Wilton's B&B (☎709-634-5796; www.
wiltonsbandb.com; 57 Marble Dr, Steady Brook; r
$69-89; ⊜🐾) Three rooms.

🍴 Eating & Drinking

Thistle's Place CAFE **$**
(☎709-634-4389; www.thistledownflorist.com;
Millbrook Mall, Herald Ave; sandwiches $6-11;

⊙9am-5pm Mon-Sat; @🍴🛜) Walk through the front flower shop to reach the smoked meat, curried chicken and whole-wheat veggie wraps at the wee cafe in the back.

Gitano's   MEDITERRANEAN **$$**
(📞709-634-5000; www.thistledownflorist.com; Millbrook Mall, Herald Ave; tapas $7-13, mains $18-25; ⊙11:30am-2pm Mon-Fri, 5-10pm Sun-Fri, to midnight Sat; 🛜) Behind Thistle's and owned by the same family, Gitano's dishes up Spanish-themed mains such as *estofado* (stewed sweet potatoes, chickpeas and figs over couscous), tapas (try the saltfish cakes) and pastas. Live jazz wafts through the supper-club-esque room on weekends.

Bay of Islands Bistro   NEW CANADIAN **$$$**
(📞709-634-1300; www.bayofislandsbistro.com; 13 West St; sandwiches $11-17, mains $30-37; ⊙11:30am-11pm Sun & Tue-Fri, to midnight Sat, closed Mon; 🛜) Inventive meals grace the plates at this hip bistro, say bacon and fava-bean-cushioned halibut for dinner, or a lobster and cornbread sandwich for lunch. Vegetarians even get a couple of choices.

Brewed Awakening   CAFE **$$**
(www.brewedawakening.ca; 35 West St; ⊙7am-10pm Sun-Wed, 7:30am-11pm Thu-Sat; 🛜) This small, funky, art-on-the-wall coffee shop pours fair-trade, organic java done right. It's attached to a bike shop that runs local cycling and caving tours.

🛍 Shopping

Newfoundland Emporium   SOUVENIRS
(📞709-634-9376; 7 Broadway) Step over Flossie, the owner's massive Newfoundland dog, to get at the local crafts, music, antiques and books found here.

ℹ Information

CIBC Bank (9 Main St)

Post office (14 Main St)

Visitors Centre (www.cornerbrook.com; cnr Confederation Dr & West Valley Rd; ⊙9am-5pm) Just off Hwy 1 at exit 5. Has a craft shop.

ℹ Getting There & Away

Corner Brook is a major hub for bus services in Newfoundland. **DRL** (📞709-263-2171; www.drl-lr.com) stops on the outskirts of town at the **Irving gas station** (Confederation Dr), just off Hwy 1 at exit 5 across from the visitors center.

All other operators use the **bus station** (📞709-634-2659; Herald Ave) in the Millbrook Mall building. The following are shuttle vans. Prices are one-way. You must make reservations.

Burgeo Bus (📞709-886-6162, 709-634-4710) Runs to Burgeo ($38 cash only, two hours) departing at 3pm Monday through Friday. Leaves Burgeo between 8am and 9am.

Eddy's (📞709-643-2134) Travels to/from Stephenville ($20, 1¼ hours) twice daily on weekdays, once daily on weekends.

Gateway (📞709-695-2222, 709-695-7777) Runs to Port aux Basques ($33, three hours) on weekdays at 3:45pm. Departs Port aux Basques at 7:45am.

Martin's (📞709-453-7269) Operates weekdays, departing for Woody Point ($16, 1½ hours) and Trout River ($18, two hours) at 4:30pm. Returns from Trout River at 9am.

Star Taxi (📞709-634-4343) Picks up from various hotels en route to Deer Lake Airport ($22, 45 minutes) three to five times daily.

Viking 430 Shuttle (📞709-458-8186) Runs to Rocky Harbour ($20, two hours) via Deer Lake on weekdays at 4:15pm. Departs Rocky Harbour at 9am.

Around Corner Brook

BLOMIDON MOUNTAINS

The Blomidon Mountains (aka Blow Me Down Mountains), heaved skyward from a collision with Europe around 500 million years ago, run along the south side of the Humber Arm. They're tantalizing for hikers, providing many sea vistas and glimpses of the resident caribou population. Some of the trails, especially ones up on the barrens, are not well marked, so topographical maps and a compass are essential for all hikers.

Many trails are signposted off Rte 450, which runs west from Corner Brook along the water for 60km. One of the easiest and most popular is **Blow Me Down Brook Trail** (5km), which begins west of Frenchman's Cove at a parking lot. The trail can be followed for an hour or so; for more avid hikers it continues well into the mountains, where it becomes part of the International Appalachian Trail (IAT). The moderately difficult **Copper Mine Trail** (7km), by York Harbour, provides awesome views of the Bay of Islands and also links to the IAT.

Further on, **Blow Me Down Provincial Park** (📞709-681-2430; www.nlcamping.ca; Rte 450; campsites $15, per vehicle $5; ⊙late May-early Sep) has beaches and scenery.

STEPHENVILLE

As the drive into town past deserted hangars, piles of rusted pipes and tract housing portends, Stephenville is in the running

ℹ NEWFOUNDLAND APPALACHIAN

Think the **International Appalachian Trail** ends in Québec just because it runs out of land at Cap Gaspé? Think again. It picks up in Newfoundland, where another 1200km of trail swipes the west coast from Port aux Basques to L'Anse aux Meadows. The province has linked existing trails, logging roads and old rail lines through the Long Range Mountains, part of the Appalachian chain. It's a work in progress, but some of the most complete sections are around Corner Brook and the Blomidon Mountains. See www. iatnl.ca for trail details.

for Newfoundland's least appealing town. There's not much reason to stop, except for the **Stephenville Theatre Festival** (www. stf.nf.ca). It sweeps into town during July and August toting along the Bard, Broadway and – to stir the pot – some cutting-edge Newfoundland plays.

PORT AU PORT PENINSULA

The large peninsula west of Stephenville is the only French-speaking area of the province, a legacy of the Basque, French and Acadians who settled the coast starting in the 1700s. Today, the culture is strongest along the western shore between **Cape St George** and **Lourdes**. Here children go to French school, preserving their dialect, which is now distinct from the language spoken in either France or Québec.

In **Port au Port West**, near Stephenville, the gorgeous **Gravels Trail** (3km) leads along the shore, passing secluded beach after secluded beach. Nearby in Felix Cove, stop at **Alpacas of Newfoundland** (www. alpacasofnfld.ca; admission free; Rte 460; ⊙9am-6pm) and meet the fluffy namesake critters on a farm tour.

BARACHOIS POND PROVINCIAL PARK

This popular **park** (☎709-649-0048; www. nlcamping.ca; Hwy 1; campsites $15, per vehicle $5; ⊙mid-May–mid-Sep), sitting just south of Rte 480 on Hwy 1, is one of the few in the province to offer a backcountry experience. From the campground, the **Erin Mountain Trail** (4.5km) winds through the forest and up to the 340m peak, where there are back-country campsites and excellent views. Allow two hours for the climb.

Not far away are a couple of leisurely nature trails and a nice swimming area.

Port aux Basques

POP 4300

It's all about the ferry in Port aux Basques. Most visitors come here to jump onto the Rock from Nova Scotia, or jump off for the return trip. That doesn't mean the town isn't a perfectly decent place to spend a day or night. Traditional wood houses painted brightly in aqua, scarlet and sea-green clasp the stony hills. Laundry blows on the clotheslines, boats moor in backyard inlets and locals never fail to wave hello to newcomers.

Port aux Basques (occasionally called Channel-Port aux Basques) was named in the early 16th century by Basque fishers and whalers who came to work the waters of the Strait of Belle Isle.

The town is a convenient place to stock up on food, fuel and/or money before journeying onward.

⊙ Sights & Activities

Several scenic fishing villages lie to the east (see p208).

Grand Bay West Beach   BEACH
(Kyle Lane) Located a short distance west of town, the long shore is backed by grassy dunes, which are breeding grounds for the endangered piping plover. The **Cormack Trail** (11km) leaves from here and flirts with the coast all the way to John T Cheeseman Provincial Park.

Scott's Cove Park   PARK
(Caribou Rd) This park, with its restored boardwalk, candy-colored snack shacks and boat-shaped amphitheater, is the place to mingle with townsfolk and listen to live music.

Railway Heritage Centre   MUSEUM
(☎709-695-7560; off Hwy 1; museum $2, railcars $5; ⊙10am-8pm Jul & Aug) The center has two things going on. One is a museum stuffed with shipwreck artifacts. Its showpiece is the astrolabe, a striking brass navigational instrument made in Portugal in 1628. The device is in remarkable condition and is one of only about three dozen that exist in the world. Restored railway cars are the center's other facet.

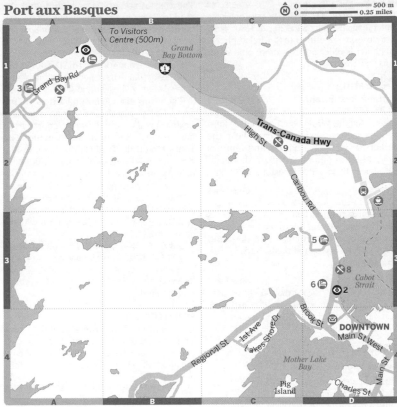

🛏 Sleeping

With all the ferry traffic, reservations are a good idea.

Radio Station B&B   B&B $
(📞709-695-2906; www.radiostationbedandbreak
fast.intuitwebsites.com; 100 Caribou Rd; r $69-79;
🕐May-Oct) Up on the bluff overlooking the
harbor, the five-room Radio Station is the
closest lodging to the ferry (a 10-minute
walk). Three rooms have their own bathroom, the other two share, and there's a
kitchen for guest use.

Caribou B&B   B&B $
(📞709-695-3408; www.bbcanada.com/2225.
html; 42 Grand Bay Rd; r $70-80; 🕐May-Sep;
🍽🛜) There's nothing fancy going on here,
but the five rooms are clean, bright and car-
peted; two share a bathroom.

St Christopher's Hotel   HOTEL $$
(📞709-695-3500, 800-563-4779; www.stchrisho
tel.com; Caribou Rd; r $93-140; ❄🛜) This is the

Port aux Basques

⊚ Sights

1 Railway Heritage Centre	A1
2 Scott's Cove Park	D3

🛏 Sleeping

3 Caribou B&B	A1
4 Hotel Port aux Basques	A1
5 Radio Station B&B	D3
6 St Christopher's Hotel	D3

🍽 Eating

7 Alma's	A1
8 Harbour Restaurant	D3
9 Tai Hong	C2

most professional digs in town, with a small
fitness room and a fine seafood restaurant
called the Captain's Room (meals $10 to $16,
open breakfast, lunch and dinner). Odd-
numbered rooms have harbor views.

Hotel Port aux Basques HOTEL $$
(☎709-695-2171, 877-695-2171; www.hotelpab.com; 1 Grand Bay Rd; r $85-120, ste $130; ❄🛜) The closest competition to St Christopher's, this hotel is older but has more character. Kids stay free.

✖ Eating

Harbour Restaurant CANADIAN $
(☎709-695-3238; 121 Caribou Rd; mains $8-15; ⊗8am-midnight) While you'll get better food and service elsewhere, you can't beat the harborside view here. Pizzas and *donairs* (spiced beef in pita bread) share the menu with fried chicken. It's licensed, too.

Alma's CANADIAN $
(☎709-695-3813; Mall, Grand Bay Rd; mains $7-13; ⊗8am-8pm, closed Sun) Follow the locals into this no-frills family diner for heaping portions of cod, scallops, fishcakes and berry pies. It serves breakfasts, burgers and sandwiches, too.

Tai Hong CHINESE $
(☎709-695-3116; 77 High St; mains $7-12; ⊗11am-10:30pm) Tai Hong stir-fries standard Chinese fare. Vegetarians will find a couple of fried rice options.

❶ Information

Bank of Montréal (83 Main St)

Hospital (☎709-695-2175; Grand Bay Rd)

Post office (3 Main St)

Visitors Centre (☎709-695-2262; www.portauxbasques.ca; Hwy 1; ⊗6am-8pm mid-May–mid-Oct) Information on all parts of the province; sometimes open later for ferry traffic.

❶ Getting There & Away

The **Marine Atlantic ferry** (☎800-341-7981; www.marine-atlantic.ca) connects Port aux Basques with North Sydney in Nova Scotia (adult/child/car $29/14.50/81.50). It operates year-round, typically with two sailings daily during winter and three or four between mid-June and mid-September. Crossings take about six hours. The terminal has no ATMs, food or car rentals.

DRL (☎709-263-2171; www.drl-lr.com) has its stop at the ferry terminal. Buses leave at 8am for Corner Brook ($38, 3½ hours) and St John's ($112, 13½ hours); cash only.

Around Port aux Basques

CAPE RAY

Adjacent to John T Cheeseman Provincial Park 14km north of town is Cape Ray.

The coastal scenery is engaging, and the road leads up to the windblown **Cape Ray Lighthouse** (admission free; ⊗8am-8pm late Jun-early Sep, closed Mon). This area is the southernmost known Dorset Paleo-Eskimo site, dating from 400 BC to AD 400. Thousands of artifacts have been found here and some dwelling sites can be seen.

There are also some fine **hikes** in the area. The Cormack Trail (from Port aux Basques) will eventually stretch north from here to Flat Bay near Stephenville. The **Table Mountain Trail** (12km) is more like a rugged road (but don't even think about driving up it) and begins on Hwy 1 opposite the exit to Cape Ray. The hike leads to a 518m plateau, where there are ruins from a secret US radar site and airstrip from WWII. It's not a hard hike, but allow three or four hours.

John T Cheeseman Provincial Park (☎709-695-7222; www.nlcamping.ca; Rte 408; campsites $15-23, per vehicle $5; ⊗late May–mid-Sep) rests next to the beach and has top-notch facilities.

SOUTH COAST

Visitors often ignore Rte 470, and that's a shame because it's a beauty. Heading east out of Port aux Basques for 45km and edging along the shore, the road rises and falls over the eroded, windswept terrain, looking as though it's following a glacier that plowed through yesterday.

Isle aux Morts (Island of the Dead) got its label compliments of the many shipwrecks that occurred just offshore over some 400 years. Named after a family famous for daring shipwreck rescues, the **Harvey Trail** (7km) twists along the rugged shore and makes a stirring walk. Look for the signs in town.

Another highlight is the last settlement along the road, **Rose Blanche**, an absolutely splendid, traditional-looking village nestled in a cove with a fine natural harbor – a perfect example of the classic Newfoundland fishing community. From here follow the signs to the restored **Rose Blanche Lighthouse** (www.roseblanchelighthouse.ca; adult/child $3/2; ⊗9am-9pm May-Oct). Built in 1873, it's the last remaining granite lighthouse on the Atlantic seaboard. Close by, the **Friendly Fisherman Cafe** (☎709-956-2022; mains $8-14; ⊗11am-9pm) serves huge portions of fish and chips, and also boasts a great view out over the coastal scenery.

For those without a vehicle, **Gateway** (☎709-695-3333) offers flexible van tours from Port aux Basques that visit Rose Blanche. Prices start at $90 and go up depending on how many villages you want to visit en route.

SOUTH COAST OUTPORTS

If you have the time and patience, a trip across the south coast with its wee fishing villages – called outports – is the best way to witness Newfoundland's unique culture. These little communities are some of the most remote settlements in North America, reachable only by boat as they cling to the convoluted shore. An anomaly is Burgeo (population 1600), connected by an easy road trip; it has an unspoiled, isolated feel, yet good amenities for travelers. Ramea (population 620) is another uncomplicated option. It's an island just offshore from Burgeo with lodging and activities.

Other outports along the coast include Grey River, François and McCallum. But hurry: the villages are dwindling fast as government pressure and lack of employment force residents to relocate to more accessible areas. The community of Grand Bruit was the latest to call it quits. Down to just 18 residents, they packed up and left for good in 2010.

◎ Sights & Activities

When the sun is out and the sea shimmers between endless inlets and islands, Burgeo is a dream. Climb the stairs to **Maiden Tea Hill** and look out in admiration. The 7km of white-sand beaches at **Sandbanks Provincial Park** may be the best in the entire province (at least the piping plover who dawdle there think so).

Boat tours (2hr per person $25) and **sea-kayak rentals and tours** (per half-day single/double kayak $40/50, guide per hr $20) are available from Burgeo Haven B&B.

Author Farley Mowat lived in Burgeo for several years, until he penned *A Whale for the Killing* and pissed off the locals. The book tells the story of how Burgeo's townsfolk treated an 80-tonne fin whale trapped in a nearby lagoon. Let's just say the whale's outcome was not a happy one. Locals can point out the lagoon and Mowat's old house, though expect to get an earful about it.

The other outports are great areas for remote **camping**, **hiking** and **fishing**; ask locals or at the Visitors Centre in Port aux Basques about arranging a guide. Tiny **François**, surrounded by towering walls of rock, is particularly gorgeous.

⌂ Sleeping & Eating

Burgeo Haven B&B   B&B $$
(☎709-886-2544; www.burgeohaven.com; 111 Reach Rd, Burgeo; r $80-100; @☜) Right across from Maiden Tea Hill, this large house backs onto an inlet and offers a serene setting in which to stay. Some of the five rooms have views.

Ramea Retreat   HOSTEL/B&B $
(☎709-625-2522; www.ramea.easternoutdoors. com; 2 Main St, Ramea; dm/r incl breakfast $30/59; ☺May-Nov; ☜) The owners have 10 hostel beds at their lodge, where they arrange kayaking, bird-watching, hiking and fishing tours. In addition, they rent rooms in various vintage clapboard houses scattered around Ramea.

Gillett's Motel   MOTEL $$
(☎709-886-1284; www.gillettsmotel.ca; 1 Inspiration Rd, Burgeo; r $92; ☜) The sole motel in town is, well, motel-like, with all the usual room amenities. It's just fine, as is the on-site Galley Restaurant (meals $7 to $15), where you'll eat cod likely caught that morning.

Sandbanks Provincial Park   CAMPGROUND $
(☎709-886-2331; www.nlcamping.ca; off Rte 480, Burgeo; campsites $15, per vehicle $5; ☺late May–mid-Sep) Two-thirds of the 25 campsites here are nestled in the forest, while the remainder are in a grassy area. The flies can be brutal.

Joy's Place   CANADIAN $
(☎709-886-2569; Reach Rd, Burgeo; mains $6-11; ☺11am-11pm) Near Burgeo Haven B&B, Joy whips up fried chicken, Chinese dishes, burgers and pies in addition to her ever-present fish dishes.

❶ Information

Burgeo (www.burgeonl.com)

❶ Getting There & Away

Lonely, 148km-long Rte 480 shoots off Hwy 1 south of Corner Brook and then runs straight into Burgeo. Note there is no gas station and barely any civilization, just glacier-cut boulders and ponds and a whole lotta moose.

The Burgeo Bus (p205) shuttle van runs between Corner Brook and Burgeo once daily.

Access to the other towns is by boat only. While the ferries run all year, the routes described here are for mid-May through September. Schedules change, so check with **Provincial Ferry Services** (☎709-292-4302; www.tw.gov.nl.ca/ferryservices). Note that the ferries do not take vehicles (except Burgeo to Ramea).

With careful planning a trip through the islands is doable.

Burgeo to Ramea ($3.75, 1½ hours) Goes twice a day; times vary but there's usually one around 11am and another in the evening.

Burgeo to Grey River to François ($7.50, five hours) Goes daily (except Tuesday and Thursday) at 1:45pm.

François to McCallum to Hermitage ($6.75, four hours) Goes on Thursday only at 7am.

At Hermitage, you'll have to suss out transportation back to Rte 360. You can then hook up with **Thornhill Taxi Service** (☎709-885-2144, 866-538-3429), which runs between Harbour Breton and Grand Falls, and connects with DRL in the latter.

LABRADOR

POP 27,000

It's called the Big Land, and with 293,000 sq km sprawling north toward the Arctic Circle, it's easy to see why. Undulating, rocky, puddled expanses form the sparse, primeval landscape. If you ever wanted to see what the world looked like before humans stepped on it, this is the place to head. Adding to the Great Northern effect, four huge caribou herds, including the world's largest (some 750,000 head), migrate across Labrador to their calving grounds each year.

Inuit and Innu have occupied Labrador for thousands of years, and until the 1960s the population was still limited to them and a few longtime European descendants known as 'liveyers.' They eked out an existence by fishing and hunting from their tiny villages that freckled the coast. The interior was virgin wilderness.

Over the past few decades, the economic potential of Labrador's vast natural resources has earned it a new degree of attention. Companies have tapped into the massive iron-ore mines in Wabush and Labrador City and the hydroelectric dam at Churchill Falls.

The simplest way to take a bite of the Big Land is via the Labrador Straits region, which connects to Newfoundland via a daily ferry. From there, a solitary road –

the stark, rough Trans-Labrador Hwy – connects the interior's main towns. The aboriginal-influenced northern coast is accessible only by plane or supply ferry.

Labrador is a cold, wet and windy place, and its bugs are murderous. Facilities are few and far between throughout the behemoth region, so planning ahead is essential. Note that the Labrador Straits (not including the Québec portion) are on Newfoundland Time, while the rest of Labrador (starting at Cartwright) is on Atlantic Time, ie 30 minutes behind Newfoundland. Québec is on Eastern Time, which is an hour behind Atlantic Time. These variations can make ferry and airplane schedules a headache.

Labrador Straits

And you thought the Northern Peninsula was commanding? Sail the 28km across the Strait of Belle Isle and behold a landscape even more windswept and black-rocked. Clouds rip across aqua-and-gray skies, and the water that slaps the shore is so cold it's purplish. Unlike the rest of remote Labrador, the Straits region is easy to reach and exalted with sights such as Red Bay and Battle Harbour and a slew of great walking trails that meander past shipwreck fragments and old whale bones.

'Labrador Straits' is the colloquial name given to the communities that comprise the southern coastal region of Labrador. Note that your first stop in the area will not actually be in Labrador at all, as the ferry terminal and airport are both in Blanc Sablon, Québec. Once in Labrador, Rte 510 is the road that connects the Straits' communities. South of Red Bay, it is sealed and open all year. From Red Bay north, it's hard-packed gravel and often closed in winter, depending on conditions. Check with the **Department of Transportation & Works** (☎709-729-2300; www.roads.gov.nl.ca).

BLANC SABLON TO L'ANSE AU CLAIR

After arriving by ferry or plane in Blanc Sablon and driving 6km northeast on Rte 510 you come to Labrador and the gateway town of L'Anse au Clair. Here you will find the Straits' excellent **Visitors Centre** (☎709-931-2013, 877-931-2013; www.labradorcoastaldrive.com; Rte 510, L'Anse au Clair; ⊙9am-5pm mid-Jun–mid-Oct) in an old church that doubles as a small museum. Be sure to pick up hiking trail information for the region.

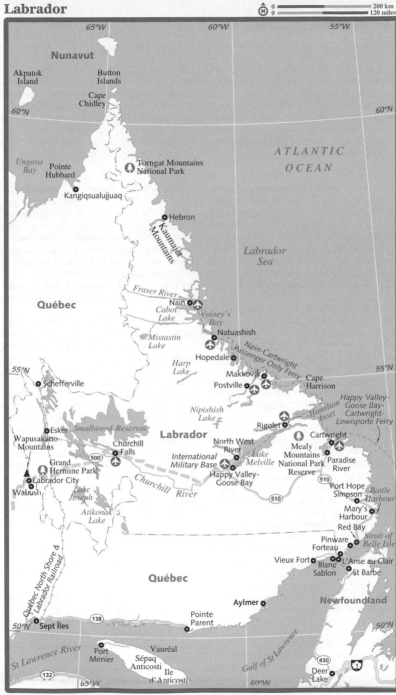

0 200 km
0 120 miles

Nunavut

Akpatok Island
Button Islands
Cape Chidley

Ungava Bay
Pointe Hubbard

Kangiqsualujjuaq

Torngat Mountains National Park

Hebron

Kaumajet Mountains

Labrador Sea

ATLANTIC OCEAN

Québec

Fraser River
Nain
Cabot Lake
Voisey's Bay

Natuashish

Mistastin Lake
Hopedale
Nain-Cartwright Passenger Only Ferry

Harp Lake

Makkovik
Postville
Cape Harrison

Scheffervile

Nipishish Lake

Rigolet

Hamilton Inset

Happy Valley-Goose Bay-Cartwright-Lewisporte Ferry

Esker
Wapusakatto Mountains
Smallwood Reservoir
Churchill Falls
Labrador
North West River
Lake Melville
Mealy Mountains National Park Reserve
Cartwright
Paradise River

Grand Hermine Park
500
International Military Base
Happy Valley-Goose Bay
510
Port Hope Simpson
Battle Harbour

Labrador City
Wabush
Lake Joseph
Churchill River
510
Mary's Harbour
Red Bay

Atikonak Lake
Pinware
Forteau
Strait of Belle Isle

Vieux Fort
Blanc Sablon
L'Anse au Clair
St Barbe

Québec

Aylmer

Newfoundland

138
Pointe Parent

Sept Îles

St Lawrence River

Port Menier
Vauréal
Sépaq Anticosti
Ile d'Anticosti

132

Gulf of St Lawrence

430
1
Deer Lake

NEWFOUNDLAND & LABRADOR **LABRADOR**

SCENIC DRIVE: QUÉBEC'S ROUTE 138

Yes, we know: this book concentrates on the Atlantic provinces, but this drive is most easily accessed from Québec.

Route 138 (the Québec incarnation of Labrador's Rte 510) runs down the Lower North Shore, the name given to the wild, remote chunk of La Belle Province that extends south of Blanc Sablon. From the ferry landing until the road ends abruptly 65km later at Vieux Fort, Rte 138 makes a beautiful swing past several roadside **waterfalls** and lookouts from which to see the crashing surf and offshore **puffin colonies**.

For those wanting to do more than just drive through the region, **Tourism Lower North Shore** (www.tourismlowernorthshore.com) provides information on attractions and accommodations.

The town makes a good pre- or post-ferry base. Norm at **Beachside Hospitality Home** (☎709-931-2338; normanletto@yahoo.ca; 9 Lodge Rd; r with shared bathroom $48-58) plays the accordion for guests in the evening. Quilts await on the beds, while homemade jams await in the kitchen at this three-bedroom, two-bathroom B&B.

The modern, well-kept **Northern Light Inn** (☎709-931-2332, 800-563-3188; www.northernlightinn.com; 56 Main St; s/d $89/109; ❋❀) is a tour-bus favorite. The even-numbered rooms have harbor views. The **dining room** (mains $12-18; ☉7am-9pm Sun-Thu, to 10pm Fri & Sat) at the inn is your best bet for food in town.

The **MV Apollo** (☎709-535-0810, 866-535-2567; www.labradormarine.com; adult/child/car $7.50/6/15.25) sails the two hours between St Barbe in Newfoundland and Blanc Sablon between May and early January. The boat runs one to three times daily between 8am and 6pm. Schedules vary from day to day. In July and August, it's not a bad idea to reserve in advance (though there's a $10 fee). Note that the ferry terminal in Blanc Sablon operates on Newfoundland Time and not Eastern Time.

Provincial Airlines (www.provincialairlines.com) has flights to Blanc Sablon from St John's and St Anthony. Just to confuse you, departure times from the airport are on Eastern Time versus Labrador Straits (ie Newfoundland) Time.

Rental cars are available at the airport from **Eagle River Rent-a-Car** (☎709-931-3300, 709-931-2352).

FORTEAU TO PINWARE

Continuing northeast on Rte 510 you'll pass Forteau, L'Anse Amour, L'Anse au Loup, West St Modeste and Pinware.

Forteau-based **Labrador Adventures** (☎709-931-2055; chancock@tourlabrador.ca; tours $15-85) provides truly knowledgeable guides for Straits-oriented hikes or day tours by SUV. It also arranges all-inclusive overnight packages (from $240). This is a terrific way to see the area, especially if you're short on time or car-less.

In Forteau, the **Overfall Brook Trail** (4km) shadows the coast and ends at a 30m waterfall.

Six houses in total comprise the village of L'Anse Amour, but it holds more than its fair share of sights. **L'Anse Amour Burial Mound** (L'Anse Amour Rd), a pile of stones placed here by the Maritime Archaic Aboriginals, is the oldest burial monument in North America. A small roadside plaque marks the 7500-year-old site. On the same road is **Point Amour Lighthouse Provincial Historic Site** (☎709-927-5825; www.seethesites.ca; L'Anse Amour Rd; admission $3; ☉10am-5:30pm mid-May–late Sep). Taking four years to build and with 127 steps to climb, this is the tallest lighthouse in Atlantic Canada. When you reach the top, you will be rewarded with a spectacular 360-degree view of the coastline. The lighthouse-keeper's house has exhibits on maritime history. The HMS *Raleigh* went aground here in 1922 and was destroyed in 1926. The **Raleigh Trail** (2km) takes you by the site and warship fragments on the beach.

Past L'Anse au Loup is the **Battery Trail** (4km), which meanders through a stunted tuckamore forest to the summit of the Battery, unfurling panoramic sea views.

The road veers inland at Pinware, and skirts along the western side of the Pinware River, until it crosses a one-lane iron bridge, and then runs along the eastern side, high above the rushing whitewater. This stretch of the Pinware is renowned for its **salmon fishing**. About 10km before reaching Red Bay, the land becomes rocky and barren, except for the superfluity of blueberries and bakeapples (and pickers) in August.

Forteau's **Grenfell Louie A Hall B&B** (709-931-2916; www.grenfellbandb.ca; Willow Ave; r $60-70; May-Oct) is in the old nursing station where generations of Labrador Straits folk were born. The five simple rooms (a couple with sea views) share two bathrooms. The **Seaview Restaurant** (Rte 510; mains $8-17; 9am-8pm) is nearby in Forteau. Chow down on the famous fried chicken and tender caribou. A grocery store and jam factory are also on-site.

Up and over the hills in L'Anse au Loup, **Dot's Bakery** (709-927-5311; Rte 510; breakfasts $4-6.50, pizzas $23; 7am-11pm Mon-Sat) caters to all your needs with her donuts, pies, breakfast dishes and pizzas.

RED BAY

Spread between two venues, **Red Bay National Historic Site** (709-920-2051; www.pc.gc.ca/redbay; Rte 510; adult/child/family $7.80/3.90/19.60; 9am-6pm early Jun–mid-Oct) uses different media to chronicle the discovery of three 16th-century Basque whaling galleons on the seabed here. Well preserved in the ice-cold waters, the vestiges of the ships tell a remarkable story of what life was like here some four centuries ago. Red Bay was the largest whaling port in the world, with more than 2000 people residing here. Have a look at the reconstructed *chalupa* (a small Basque dingy used for whale hunting) and some of the other relics in the museum. Then hop in a small boat ($2) to nearby **Saddle Island**, where there is a self-guided interpretive

trail around the excavated land sites. Allow at least two or three hours for the museum and island.

Across the bay, the amazing **Boney Shore Trail** (2km) skirts the coast and passes ancient whale bones (they pretty much look like rocks) scattered along it. The **Tracey Hill Trail** climbs a boardwalk and 670 steps to the top of American Rockyman Hill for a bird's-eye view of the harbor; it takes about 20 minutes each way.

Between the trails and the historic site, a 15m, 400-year-old **North Atlantic right whale skeleton** sprawls through the **Selma Barkham Town Centre** (admission $2; 9am-5pm Jul–mid-Sep).

Basinview B&B (709-920-2022; blancheearle@hotmail.com; 145 Main St; r $50-80) is a simple four-room, shared-bathroom home right on the water.

Remember, Red Bay is the end of the paved road. It's hard-packed gravel from here all the way to Labrador City.

BATTLE HARBOUR

Sitting on an island in the Labrador Sea is the elaborately restored village and saltfish premises of **Battle Harbour** (709-921-6216; www.battleharbour.com; adult/child $9/4.50, mid-Jun–mid-Sep). Now a national historic district, it used to be the unofficial 'capital' of Labrador during the early 19th century, when fishing schooners lined its docks. Another claim to fame: this is the place where Robert E Peary gave his first news conference after reaching the North Pole in 1909.

It's accessed by boat ($60 round-trip) from Mary's Harbour (departures 11am and 6pm, one hour) and you can come for the day or spend a few nights. Accommodations are spread among various heritage homes

---

BONKERS FOR BAKEAPPLES

You keep hearing about it: bakeapple jam, bakeapple pie, bakeapple syrup. But what's a bakeapple?

We'll tell you this much: it's not a red fruit that's been placed in the oven. Rather, a bakeapple (sometimes called a cloudberry) is an orangey-yellow fruit similar in shape and size to a large raspberry. It grows wild on small plants in moist northern tundra and bog lands – ie Labrador. The taste is often compared to apricot and honey.

Bakeapples ripen in mid-August, and that's when aficionados from Newfoundland pile over to the Labrador Straits and start picking. Get your fill – breakfast, lunch and dinner – at Forteau's **Bakeapple Folk Festival** (adult/child $5/3; mid-Aug), a three-day event featuring music, dance, crafts and buckets of the eponymous fruit. Or buy bakeapple products at the Seaview Restaurant, where they're made on-site (see above).

and cottages, operated by the **Battle Harbour Inn** (☎709-921-6325; www.battleharbour. com; r incl breakfast $125-155; ☺mid-Jun–mid-Sep). A store and **restaurant** (mains $9-18; ☺served at 8am, noon & 6pm) are on-site.

MARY'S HARBOUR TO CARTWRIGHT

After departing Mary's Harbour you'll pass through Port Hope Simpson 53km up the gravel road, and then there's nothing for 186km until Cartwright.

Cartwright-based **Experience Labrador** (☎877-938-7444; www.experiencelabrador.com; ☺Jul & Aug) runs kayaking trips that range from day paddles (six-hour tour $120) to multiday trips (three-day tour $840) along the northern coast, where you glide by the endless sands of the Wonderstrands that mesmerized the Vikings so long ago. The company also offers hiking, fishing and berry-picking tours.

The federal government recently created the **Mealy Mountains National Park Reserve** from 11,000 sq km of caribou-crossed boreal forest between Cartwright and Happy Valley-Goose Bay. Once the park gets up and running, paddlers, snowshoers, cross-country skiers and hikers will have access to an unblemished wilderness.

The simple **Cartwright Hotel** (☎709-938-7414; www.cartwrighthotel.ca; 3 Airport Rd, Cartwright; r $88-130; ☎) has 10 rooms, a **dining room** (mains $7-17; ☺6am-10pm) and a lounge.

Other than that, Cartwright is about the ferry. Passenger boats depart for the remote villages that sprinkle the Northern Coast (opposite). Vehicle ferries stop here on their route between Goose Bay and Lewisporte (see p193). **Labrador Marine** (☎709-535-0810, 866-535-2567; www.labradormarine.com) has the schedules.

Rte 510 continues west to Happy Valley-Goose Bay. Contact the **Department of Transportation & Works** (☎709-729-2300; www.roads.gov.nl.ca) for the latest conditions.

Northern Coast

North of Cartwright up to Ungava Bay there are a half-dozen small, semitraditional Inuit communities accessible only by sea or air along the rugged, largely unspoiled mountainous coast. Torngat Mountains National Park is the (literal) high point.

In 1993 on the shores of Voisey's Bay, near Nain, geologists discovered stunningly rich concentrations of copper, cobalt and especially nickel. A giant mine has been built to extract the goods, and it is expected to pump $11 billion into the provincial economy over 30 years. This likely will open up the north – for better or worse.

◎ Sights & Activities

The first port of call on the north coast is **Makkovik**, an early fur-trading post and a traditional fishing and hunting community. Both new and old-style crafts can be bought.

Further north in **Hopedale** visitors can look at the old wooden Moravian mission church (1782). This **national historic site** (admission $5; ☺8:30am-8pm Jun-Sep) also includes a store, residence, some huts and a museum collection; it's all operated by the **Agvituk Historical Society** (☎709-933-3777).

Natuashish is a new town that was formed when the troubled village of Utshimassit (Davis Inlet) was relocated to the mainland in 2002. The move was made after a 2000 study showed that 154 of 169 youths surveyed had abused solvents (ie sniffed gasoline) and that 60 of them did it on a daily basis.

The last stop on the ferry is **Nain**, and it's the last town of any size as you go northward. Fishing has historically been the town's main industry, but this is changing due to the Voisey's Bay nickel deposit.

From Nain, you can try to arrange boat transportation to otherworldly **Torngat Mountains National Park** (☎709-922-1290; www.pc.gc.ca/torngat) at Labrador's wintry tip. The park headquarters is in town, and staff can direct you to local Inuit guides. The mountains are popular with climbers because of their altitude (some of the highest peaks east of the Rockies) and isolation. The **Kaumajet Mountains**, south of the park, also make for an out-of-this-world hiking experience.

🛏 Sleeping & Eating

Most travelers use the ferry as a floating hotel. For those wishing to get off and wait until the next boat, it usually means winging it for a room, as only Postville, Hopedale and Nain have official lodging.

Atsanik Lodge　　　　　　　　HOTEL **$$**
(☎709-922-2910; atsaniklabrador@msn.com; Sand Banks Rd, Nain; r $138-165; ☎) This large, 25-room lodge and its restaurant (meals $14 to $19) are your best bet in Nain.

Amaguk Inn
HOTEL $$

(☎709-933-3750; Hopedale; r $130-180; 🛜)
This 18-room inn also has a dining room
(meals $11 to $16), and a lounge where
you can get a cold beer.

❶ Getting There & Away

Provincial Airlines (www.provincialairlines.
com) serves most of the northern coast's vil-
lages from Goose Bay.

The passenger-only MV *Northern Ranger*
plies this section of coast from mid-June to
mid-November. It leaves once per week, mak-
ing the three-day (one-way) journey between
Happy Valley-Goose Bay and Nain, stopping
in Makkovik, Hopedale and Natuashish along
the way. Check with **Labrador Marine** (☎709-
535-0810, 866-535-2567; www.labradorma
rine.com) for the ever-evolving schedule and
fares.

Central Labrador

Making up the territorial bulk of Labrador,
the central portion is an immense, sparsely
populated and ancient wilderness. Para-
doxically, it also has the largest town in
Labrador, **Happy Valley-Goose Bay** (www.
happyvalley-goosebay.com), home to a mili-
tary base. The town (population 7570) has
all the usual services, but unless you're an
angler or hunter, there isn't much to see or
do and it is very isolated.

Goose Bay was established during
WWII as a staging point for planes on
their way to Europe, and has remained an
aviation center. The airport is also an of-
ficial NASA alternate landing site for the
space shuttle.

◉ Sights & Activities

FREE **Northern Lights Building** MUSEUM
(☎709-896-5939; 170 Hamilton River Rd;
admission free; ⊙10am-5:30pm Tue-Sat) The
Northern Lights Building hosts a military
museum, interesting lifelike nature scenes
and simulated northern lights.

FREE **Labrador Interpretation Centre**
MUSEUM
(☎709-497-8566; www.therooms.ca/museum;
2 Portage Rd, North West River; admission free;
⊙noon-4:30pm Jun–mid-Sep, 1-4pm Wed-Sun
rest of yr) Officially opened by Queen Eliza-
beth II in 1997, the Labrador Interpretation
Centre is the provincial museum, which
holds some of Labrador's finest works of
art. In North West River, via Rte 520.

🛏 Sleeping & Eating

Everything listed here is in Happy Valley-
Goose Bay.

Royal Inn & Suites
HOTEL $$

(☎709-896-2456; www.royalinnandsuites.ca;
5 Royal Ave; r incl breakfast $94-149; 🏵🛜) The
good-looking Royal has a variety of rooms
to choose from. Many of them have kitchens. The 'inn' side has wi-fi; the suites side
has hard-wired high-speed access.

Davis' B&B
B&B $

(☎709-896-5077; www.bbcanada.com/davisbb;
14 Cabot Crescent Rd; r $50-70; 🛜) Family at-
mosphere and caribou sausages await you
at Davis' four-room home. It's near restaurants and amenities.

El Greco
PIZZA $$

(☎709-896-3473; 133 Hamilton River Rd; pizzas
$16-22; ⊙4pm-1am Sun-Wed, to 3am Thu-Sat)
This is a decent joint serving pizzas near
the Royal Inn.

❶ Getting There & Away
Air

Air Canada (www.aircanada.com) flies to St
John's and Gander. **Provincial Airlines** (www.
provincialairlines.com) flies to St John's, Deer
Lake and most towns around Labrador.

Boat

You can reach Goose Bay by two different fer-
ries: the vehicle carrier MV *Robert Bond* (p193)
and the passenger-only MV *Northern Ranger*
(left).

Car & Motorcycle

From Happy Valley-Goose Bay you can take
gravel Rte 500 west to Churchill Falls and then
on to Labrador City. The drive to Labrador City
takes about 10 hours. There are no services until
Churchill Falls, so stock up. The road can also be
very, very rough. Rte 510 is the newly built gravel
road heading southeast toward Cartwright
(383km) and L'Anse au Clair (623km). Before
leaving, contact the **Department of Transpor-
tation & Works** (☎709-729-2300; www.roads.
gov.nl.ca) for the latest conditions.

Trucks can be rented at the airport from **Na-
tional** (☎709-896-5575), but due to road condi-
tions, you cannot buy insurance.

Labrador West
POP 9000

Just 5km apart and 15km from Québec,
the twin mining towns of Labrador City
(population 7250) and Wabush (population

1750) are referred to collectively as Labrador West, and this is where the western region's population is concentrated. The largest open-pit iron-ore mine in the world is in Labrador City, and another operates in Wabush. The landscape is massive and the celestial polychromatic artwork can take up the entire night sky.

◉ Sights & Activities

Gateway Labrador   MUSEUM
(☎709-944-5399; www.gatewaylabrador.ca; adult/child $3/2; ◉9am-9pm mid-Jun–Aug, reduced hr rest of yr) In the same building as the visitors center is Gateway Labrador and its Montague Exhibit Hall, where 3500 years of human history and culture, including the fur trade, are represented with intriguing artifacts and displays.

Wapusakatto Mountains   SKIING
The Wapusakatto Mountains are 5km from town, popping up off the vast landscape interspersed with flat northern tundra. A good, cold dry snow falls from late October to late April, so the ski season here is much longer than anywhere else in Canada. For trail information and fees for world-class cross-country skiing (the Canadian national team trains in the region), check with the **Menihek Nordic Ski Club** (☎709-944-5842; www.meniheknordicski.ca); for alpine skiing, check with the **Smokey Mountain Ski Club** (☎709-944-2129).

Grande Hermine Park   PARK
(☎709-282-5369; admission $3; ◉Jun–mid-Sep) From Wabush, 39km east on Rte 500 is Grande Hermine Park, with a beach and fine scenery. The **Menihek hiking trail** (15km) goes through wooded areas with waterfalls and open tundra. Outfitters can take anglers to excellent fishing waters.

Mines   MINE TOURS
(tours $10; ◉1pm Wed & Sun Jul-Sep) If big holes and trucks the size of apartment buildings make your heart flutter, you can tour the mines by contacting the visitors center.

🛏 Sleeping & Eating

PJ's Inn by the Lake   B&B $
(☎709-944-3438; www.pjsinnbythelake.com; 606 Tamarack Dr, Labrador City; r $70-95; ☜) Pete and Jo's home is your home: they'll let you use their treadmill, rowing machine and/or guitar. Each of the B&B's six rooms has its own bathroom; the Green Room has a Jacuzzi.

Wabush Hotel   HOTEL $$
(☎709-282-3221; www.wabushhotel.com; 9 Grenville Dr, Wabush; r $119-124; ✳☜) Centrally located in Wabush, this chalet-style 68-room hotel has spacious and comfortable rooms. The dining room (meals $9 to $21, open 6:30am to midnight) has a popular dinner buffet.

Carol Inn   MOTEL $$
(☎709-944-7736, 888-799-7736; 215 Drake Ave, Labrador City; d $110; ✳✳) All 20 rooms here have kitchenettes. There's also a fine dining room (meals $20 to $30, open 5:30pm Tuesday to Saturday), pub (meals $8 to $12, open 8am to midnight) and small pizza franchise.

❶ Information

Destination Labrador (www.destinationlabrador.com)

Visitors Centre (☎709-944-5399; www.labradorwest.com; 1365 Rte 500) Just west of Labrador City, in the Gateway Labrador building.

❶ Getting There & Away

Air
Air Canada (www.aircanada.com), **Provincial Airlines** (www.provincialairlines.com) and **Air Inuit** (www.airinuit.com) fly into the twin cities' airport (in Wabush).

Car & Motorcycle
Fifteen kilometers west from Labrador City along Rte 500 is Fermont, Québec. From there Rte 389 is mainly paved (with some fine gravel sections) and continues south 581km to Baie Comeau. Happy Valley-Goose Bay is a rough 10-hour drive east on Rte 500.

Budget (☎709-282-1234) has an office at the airport; rental cars may not be driven on Rte 500.

Understand Nova Scotia, New Brunswick & Prince Edward Island

population per sq km

👤 ≈ 4 people

Nova Scotia, New Brunswick & Prince Edward Island Today

There's No Place Like Home

Until recently, you could sit down at any dinner table in Atlantic Canada, and hear the same thing:

'My ____ [fill in the blank: sister, cousin, neighbor] just left for Alberta to work in the oil fields.'

Outward migration, or 'outmigration,' has been the single biggest issue facing the Atlantic provinces over the last 15 to 20 years, but the region is finally experiencing a small rebound. As the provinces' traditional industries – fishing, logging and mining – continue to fall deeper into decline, a small glimmer of hope is coming from newer industries – particularly gypsum mining and offshore oil and natural gas. Although Alberta's oil fields offer high-paying industrial jobs, and plenty of people still leave to make their living where it makes economic sense, the quality of life, low cost of living and hope of finding work closer to home is keeping an increasing number of folks on the Atlantic coasts.

Nova Scotia has been the mover and shaker of the crowd by becoming a hub for Canada's defense and aerospace sector (which also tips into Prince Edward Island). In fact, a surprising 40% of the country's military assets are found in this low-key province. Meanwhile, the artsy folk of its capital, Halifax, have hurdled the city into the fourth-largest film industry in the nation, and small businesses, manufacturing and technology are all growing sectors that are keeping more and more young graduates from the city's universities employed. In other provinces, small-scale businesses add to the ever-plodding-along agricultural economy.

» Population: 2.34 million

» Unemployment rate: 10.5%

» Median family income: $60,236

» Average life expectancy: 82 years

Top Nonfiction

» *A Whale for the Killing*, Farley Mowat

» *The Hermit of Africville: The Life of Eddie Carvery*, Jon Tattrie

» *My Cross-Country Checkup*, Walter Stewart

Good-Read Novels

» *The Shipping News*, E Annie Proulx

» *Mercy among the Children*, David Adams Richards

» *Fall on Your Knees*, Anne-Marie MacDonald

» *Anne of Green Gables*, Lucy Maud Montgomery

Modern Artists

» Alex Colville, realist

» Mary Pratt, still life

» Alan Syliboy, aboriginal

» Maud Lewis, folk

» Graeme Patterson, industrial

» Mario Doucette, Acadian

belief systems
(% of population)

65   13

Roman Catholic   United Church

9.5   8   3.5

Anglican   Other   No religion

if Atlantic Canada were 100 people

32 would be Scottish	14 would be French
28 would be English	2 would be Aboriginal
23 would be Irish	1 would be African

Getting Creative

Despite recent progress, these provinces still have the highest unemployment rates in Canada, with Newfoundland leading the pack at around 14%. At present it's a conservative government that's figuring out how to deal with the situation; each of the provinces is led by a center-right party, in line with Canada's current federal administration and the area's general conservative leaning. This conservatism was on show when Nova Scotians went to the polls in 2004 to vote on whether stores should be allowed to open on Sundays. The result? The province decided to keep them shuttered on the 'Lord's Day' to encourage family time. In 2006 the law was overturned after too many big-name businesses managed to open on Sundays by finding loopholes in the system and now all stores can legally open every day of the week.

It's true that many people bemoan the waning economy and population decline, and that some expect the government to bail them out. But this is also a region that embraces an independent and entrepreneurial spirit. Plenty of creative folks see it all as an opportunity: they refurbish fishing boats into whale-watch boats, or turn mines into attractions that teach about ecology. The region's abundant natural resources are still there to be used, but this is taking on new forms; codfishing may be on its way out, for example, but offshore oil drilling has arrived to take its place. What remains to be seen is how these resources are developed from now on; whether the region has learned from past mistakes and whether it will move forward responsibly and sustainably. It's this struggle that will loom largest over Atlantic Canada in the coming years.

» Nova Scotia's percentage of Canada's overall seafood production: 25

» New Brunswickers for whom French is their mother tongue: 33%

» Number of annual moose-vehicle collisions in Newfoundland: 700

» Potato production per capita on PEI: 8000kg

Films Shot Here
» *The Shipping News* (2001)
» *Titanic* (1997)
» *The Memory Keeper's Daughter* (2008)
» *Scotland, PA* (2001)
» *The River King* (2004)
» *The Weight of Water* (2000)

Hockey Teams
» Halifax Mooseheads
» Cape Breton Screaming Eagles
» PEI Rockets
» Moncton Wildcats
» Saint John Sea Dogs
» Acadie-Bathurst Titans

Dos & Don'ts
» Don't drive over the speed limit
» Do stop for pedestrians
» Do smile and talk to people; it's the local way
» Don't forget to put your bib on for your lobster supper – it'll save your shirt

History

Atlantic Canada has always been home to hardy folk whose lives have revolved around the sea. Early Aboriginal people lived on seals and fish, and the first European arrivals could hardly believe their luck when they discovered the plentiful cod stocks. Through the millennia Canadian Aboriginal tribes, the British and the French have all vied for control of the region with the British eventually getting the upper hand, and Canadian Aboriginal people and French-speaking Acadians sticking to the fringes. American Loyalists, including many freed slaves, were taken in after the American Civil War and over time thousands of other immigrants from Europe and around the world have joined the cultural mix.

Today, with the closure of mines and the moratorium on the now depleted cod stocks, the region has faced outward migration and economic hard times – yet the natural beauty and quality of life still encourages many to stay put and others to move here from 'away.'

The First Fishermen

Atlantic Canada's first inhabitants, the Paleoindians, walked into Labrador 9000 years ago. The harsh, frozen land didn't make life easy or lengthy for these folks. Next came the Maritime Archaic Indians, hunters and gatherers who survived on the sea's bountiful fish-and-seal dinners. They ranged throughout Atlantic Canada, Maine and into parts of Labrador between 7500 and 3500 years ago and are known for their ceremonial burials and other religious and magical practices, evidenced at sites such as Newfoundland's Port au Choix. They mysteriously disappeared around 1000 BC.

The next to tend the land were the Mi'kmaw and Maliseet peoples in the Maritimes and the Beothuk people in Newfoundland – all members of the Algonquin-speaking eastern woodlands tribes. The Mi'kmaq and Maliseet practised agriculture and lived in fairly per-

Discover First Nation Culture

» Lennox Island, PEI

» Port au Choix National Historic Site, Newfoundland

» Heritage & Cultural Centre, Bear River, Nova Scotia

» First Nation room at Louisbourg, Nova Scotia

TIMELINE

1000 BC	AD 1000	1492
After hanging around for a few thousand years eating fish and seals and developing complex ceremonial practices, the Maritime Archaic Indians inexplicably disappear.	Viking Leif Eriksson and crew wash up at L'Anse aux Meadows, create the New World's first European settlements, repair their ships and smelt iron.	Christopher Columbus, under the crown of Spain, stumbles upon the Bahamas and gets credit for 'discovering' America; John Cabot sails five years later and lands on Cape Breton and Newfoundland.

manent settlements. The Beothuk were seminomadic and paddled the area in their birch-bark canoes. It was the Beothuk and their ceremonially ochre-coated faces who were dubbed 'red men' by the arriving Europeans, a name soon applied to all of North America's indigenous groups.

None of these people fared well once Europeans arrived and introduced diseases, land conflict and war to the mix. While the Mi'kmaq and Maliseet still occupy parts of Atlantic Canada, the Beothuk died out in 1829.

Age of European Discovery

Viking celebrity Leif Eriksson was the first European to reach Atlantic Canada's shores. Actually, he and his tribe of adventurous seafarers from Iceland and Greenland were the first Europeans in all of North America. Around AD 1000 they poked around the eastern shores of Canada, establishing winter settlements and way stations for repairing ships and restocking supplies, such as at L'Anse aux Meadows (p199) in Newfoundland. The local Canadian Aboriginal tribes did not exactly roll out the welcome mat for these intruders, who eventually tired of the hostilities and withdrew. There would be no more visits from the outside for another 300 to 400 years.

The action heated up again in the late 15th century. In 1492, backed by the Spanish crown, Christopher Columbus went searching for a western sea route to Asia and instead stumbled upon some small islands in the Bahamas. Other European monarchs, excited by his 'discovery,' quickly sponsored expeditions of their own. In 1497 Giovanni Caboto, better known as John Cabot, sailed under a British flag as far west as Newfoundland and Cape Breton. Although there's no evidence of where he first made landfall, the village of Bonavista (p184) in eastern Newfoundland usually gets the nod.

Cabot didn't find a passage to China but he did find cod, then a much-coveted commodity in Europe. In short order, hundreds of boats were shuttling between Europe and the fertile new fishing grounds. Basque whalers from northern Spain soon followed. Several were based at Red Bay (p213) in Labrador, which became the world's biggest whaling port during the 16th century.

About this time, French explorer Jacques Cartier also was sniffing around Labrador. He was looking for gold and precious metals, but found only 'stones and horrible rugged rocks,' as he wrote in his journal in 1534. So he moved on to Québec – but not before bestowing Canada with its name. Scholars say it comes from *kanata,* a Huron-Iroquois word for 'village' or 'settlement,' which was written in Cartier's journal and later transformed by mapmakers to 'Canada.'

HISTORY

Newfoundland's Viking Sites

» L'Anse aux Meadows National Historic Site

» Norstead

1528

Fishing village of St John's bobs up as North America's first European settlement but belongs to no nation; instead it serves fishing fleets from around the world.

1755

English round up and deport thousands of French Acadians from Bay of Fundy region for not pledging allegiance to the crown. Many move to Louisiana to become known as Cajuns.

» St John's Harbour (p166), Newfoundland

Settlers Move In

So we've got fish, furs and nice juicy chunks of land – is it any wonder Europe starts salivating?

St John's lays claim to being the oldest town in North America, first settled in 1528. It belonged to no nation; rather it served fishing fleets from all over Europe. By 1583 the British claimed it, and St John's had the distinction of being the first colony of the Empire. The Brits also threw down stakes in Trinity (in the mid-1500s, though this was an unofficial group of merchants living together versus a chartered colony), Cupids (1610) and the Colony of Avalon (1621), all in Newfoundland.

The French weren't just sitting on their butts during this time. In 1604 explorer Samuel de Champlain and his party spent the winter on St Croix Island, a tiny islet in the river on the present international border with Maine. The next year Champlain and his fur-trader patron Sieur de Monts moved their small settlement to Port Royal in the Annapolis Valley, which would soon become an English-French flash point.

The French revved up their colonization in 1632 by bringing in a load of immigrants to LaHave on Nova Scotia's south shore. More settlers arrived in 1635, and soon the French had spread throughout the Annapolis Valley and the shores of the Bay of Fundy – a rich farming region they called Acadia.

French & English At War

The French were galling the English, and the English were infuriating the French. Both had claims to the land – hadn't Cabot sailed here first for England? Or was it Cartier for France? – but each wanted regional dominance. They skirmished back and forth in hostilities that mirrored those in Europe, where wars raged throughout the first half of the 18th century.

Things came to head in 1713 with the Treaty of Utrecht, which ended Queen Anne's War (1701–13) overseas. Under its provisions the majority of Nova Scotia and Newfoundland went to the British, and Cape Breton Island, Prince Edward Island and what is today New Brunswick went to the French. That Acadia was now British was a particularly bitter spoonful for the French; the Brits had even overtaken Port Royal and renamed it Annapolis Royal (p60), after Queen Anne.

The French reorganized and decided to give regional dominance another shot. In 1719 they began construction of a fortress at Louisbourg (p86) on Cape Breton Island to protect their interests. Bit by bit the fortified town grew.

1763	1769	1784	1812
Treaty of Paris boots France out of Canada after France loses the Seven Years' War. France retains St-Pierre and Miquelon, however, which remain an overseas French territory to this day.	The colony of Prince Edward Island is created from the larger Nova Scotia and will one day be Canada's smallest province; English is the official language.	New Brunswick is created as a separate province from Nova Scotia in order to appease the tension between the huge influx of Loyalists from the USA with the original settlers.	Halifax's local government takes advantage of the War of 1812 by sponsoring 'Privateers' to plunder ships then store it all at along the city's waterfront.

The British took note and in 1745 sent out a colonial army from Massachusetts to capture Louisbourg. It fell after a 46-day siege. A treaty a few years later returned it to France.

And so it went, with control of the region ping-ponging, until 1754 when the French and Indian Wars (sometimes called the Seven Years' War) began and ramped up the fighting to a new level.

Memo to Acadians: Get Out

Charles Lawrence, the security-conscious British governor of Nova Scotia, had had enough. A war was going on, and when the French Acadian citizens in his territory refused to swear allegiance to Britain, his suspicions mounted to a fever pitch. In 1755, he ordered the Acadians to be rounded up and deported.

AVAST! PIRATES ON THE HORIZON

Pirates began to ply and plunder Atlantic Canada's waters soon after Europeans arrived to colonize the area.

Peter Easton was one of the region's most famous pirates. He started out as an English naval officer in 1602. But when King James downsized the Royal Navy the next year, stranding Easton and his men in Newfoundland without any money, they – perhaps understandably – got pissed off and decided to use the resources at hand (ie boats and a bad attitude) to become pirates. By 1610 Easton was living large in Harbour Grace (p180), commanding a fleet of 40 ships and a crew of 5000 men. The money piled in for several more years, until he eventually retired to France, married a noblewoman and became the Marquis of Savoy.

Black Bart, aka Bartholomew Roberts, was another boatsman who made quite a splash in the local plundering business. He became a pirate after being captured by another, and he took to the lifestyle. Sort of. He liked the booty and the clothing it enabled (crimson waistcoat, scarlet plumed hat, gold necklaces), but he disliked booze and gambling. He also encouraged prayer among his employees. No one mutinied though, because his pirating prowess was legendary. For example, in 1720 he sailed into Newfoundland's Trepassey Bay aboard a 10-gun sloop with a crew of 60 men, and they were able to capture 21 merchant ships manned by 1200 sailors. He died in battle off the coast of Africa a few years later.

Halifax, always a well-sailored port, put a unique spin on its pirate history when the local government began sponsoring the plunder. The pirates were called 'privateers,' and during the War of 1812 the government sanctioned them to go out and get the goods and then provided them with waterfront warehouses to store it all. You can see where the action took place at the Privateer's Warehouse (p33). The South Shore town of Liverpool commemorates the era by hosting a rollicking Privateer Days festival (p51).

1840	**1864**
Cunard Line shipping company founded in Halifax providing the fastest link to England and boosting the region's economy; immigrants from around Europe and the UK arrive in droves.	Fathers of the Confederation meet in Charlottetown and create the framework for a new country called Canada. The deal is sealed by the British North America Act in London, 1867.

JIM WARK

» Charlottetown (p137), Prince Edward Island

In a tragic chapter of history known as the Great Expulsion, the British burned villages and forced some 14,000 men, women and children onto ships. (The exact number varies, but scholars agree somewhere between 10,000 and 18,000 people were displaced.) Grand Pré (p65) was the heart of the area from which the Acadians were removed. Many headed for Louisiana and New Orleans; others went to various Maritime points, Martinique in the Caribbean, Santo Domingo in the Dominican Republic, or back to Europe.

The government gave their lands in the Annapolis Valley to 12,000 New England colonists called 'planters.' After peace was restored, some Acadians chose to return from exile but they were forced to settle on the less favorable 'French Shore' between Yarmouth and Digby.

Ultimately the English won the French and Indian Wars, and the French colonial era in the region ended. At the Treaty of Paris in 1763, France handed Canada over to Britain – except for two small islands off the coast of Newfoundland named St-Pierre and Miquelon (p187), which remain staunchly French to this day.

A Perfect Union in PEI

All through the first half of the 19th century, shipbuilding made New Brunswick and Nova Scotia wealthy, and Nova Scotia soon boasted the

See Where Canada Was Born

» Province House National Historic Site, Charlottetown, PEI

LOYALIST COLONIES IN THE MARITIMES

Some Acadians returned to Canada but *merde alors,* they hadn't seen the end of English-speaking colonization. Many American colonists who remained loyal to the King of England during the American Revolutionary War fled or were driven out of the USA once the British were defeated; these families resettled throughout the British Empire, including the Maritime Provinces while others went to the British West Indies.

Loyalists were offered free land by the British and their arrival meant a sudden influx of English-speakers west and east of Québec. This new division of language and culture divided the country into predominantly British 'Upper Canada' and French 'Lower Canada.' It also led to the division of Nova Scotia into two provinces, modern-day Nova Scotia and New Brunswick.

Meanwhile, many Loyalists from the American South brought their slaves as they were assured, by law, that their slaves would remain their property. However, there were also freed black Loyalists who had been granted their freedom by fighting for the British during the Revolution. The government helped these ex-slaves resettle in Canada but they were not met as kindly as their white compatriots (see p53).

Ultimately, the influx of Loyalists to Canada helped strengthen ties with Britain and increased antipathy to the United States, which contributed to keeping Canada an independent country in North America.

1912

Titanic sinks off the southern coast of Newfoundland and rescue ships are sent from Halifax – most of the recovered bodies are buried in Halifax.

1917

A munitions ship collides with another ship in the Halifax Harbour creating the 'Halifax Explosion,' the largest man-made explosion before the A-bomb, killing some 1900 people.

ANDREW BAIN

» Graves of *Titanic* victims (p35), Halifax, Nova Scotia

world's fourth-largest merchant marine. The Cunard Line was founded at Halifax in 1840, and immigration from Scotland and Ireland flourished (as a look at the lengthy Mac and Mc sections of today's phone book confirms).

In 1864, Charlottetown, Prince Edward Island (PEI), served as the birthing room for modern Canada. At the town's Province House (p137), a group of representatives from Nova Scotia, New Brunswick, PEI, Ontario and Québec got together and hammered out the framework for a new nation. It took two more meetings – one in Québec City, the other in London – before Parliament passed the British North America Act in 1867. And so began the modern, self-governing state of Canada, originally known as the Dominion of Canada. The day the act became official, July 1, is celebrated as Canada's national holiday; it was called Dominion Day until it was renamed Canada Day in 1982.

Newfoundland, ever true to its independent spirit, did not join the confederation until 1949.

World Wars

During both world wars Atlantic Canada played a key role as a staging area for the convoys that supplied Britain. The wars also boosted local economies and helped transition the region from an agricultural to an industrial base.

Halifax was the only city in North America to suffer damage during WWI. In December 1917, the *Mont Blanc,* a French munitions ship carrying TNT and highly flammable benzol, collided with the *Imo* in Halifax Harbour. The 'Halifax Explosion' ripped through the city, leveling most of Halifax' north end, injuring 9000 and killing 1900 people. It was the world's biggest man-made explosion prior to A-bombs being dropped on Japan in 1945.

Newfoundland had the dubious honor of being the only place in North America directly attacked by German forces during WWII. Just offshore from Bell Island (p177) near St John's, German U-boats fired on four allied ore carriers in 1942. All of them sank, with a loss of 69 lives. The Germans fired a torpedo at yet another carrier, but the projectile missed and instead struck inland at Bell Island's loading pier – thus making it the sole spot on the continent to take a straight-on German hit. That same year the Germans also torpedoed a Newfoundland ferry sailing in the Cabot Strait near Port aux Basques; 137 people died.

Modern Times

It wasn't until 1960 that Canada's Aboriginal people – including the Mi'kmaq, Maliseet and Innu – were finally granted Canadian citizenship. Even into the late 1960s Aboriginal children were being removed from

Early-20th-Century Sites

» Fort Amherst, Newfoundland

» Cape Spear National Historic Site, Newfoundland

» *Titanic* Graveyards, Nova Scotia

» Pier 21 Centre, Nova Scotia

» Maritime Museum of The Atlantic, Halifax, Nova Scotia

1925	1942	1962	1969
Fed up and hungry Cape Breton coal miners stage a 155-day strike and end up with a 7% pay cut. The industry continues to decline from here on.	Bell Island, Newfoundland, torpedoed by German forces and 69 people are killed; this is the only location to get a German hit on the American continent during WWII.	Trans-Canada Hwy officially opens, spanning 7821km from St John's to Victoria, BC and linking Canada's 13 provinces – it will be completed in 1971.	New Brunswick extends its Equal Opportunity Plan when it passes the Official Languages Act making it the only constitutionally bilingual province in Canada.

their families and sent away to residential schools to 'civilize' them; many were abused. Land-rights claims and settlements regarding the schools are still winding their way through Canadian courts, while the damage such policies inflicted continues to haunt the Aboriginal communities.

Meanwhile, in Newfoundland in the 1950s the provincial government also was enforcing a resettlement program upon its citizens. People living in small, isolated fishing communities (aka outports) were being strongly 'encouraged' to pack it up and move inland where the government could deliver schools, health care and other services more economically. One method for 'encouraging' villagers was to cut ferry services to their communities, thus making them inaccessible since there were no roads. Many people were squeezed out of their ancestral homes in this way.

The later 20th century was particularly harsh to two of the region's biggest industries: coal mining and fishing. Cape Breton's coal mines started to tank in the 1960s as their high-sulphur, high-pollution product fell out of favor in the marketplace; the mines shuttered for good in the 1990s. In 1992, the codfishing moratorium (see the boxed text, p186) was put in place, and many fisherfolk and fish-plant workers – a huge percentage of the population, especially in Newfoundland – lost their livelihoods. The offshore oil and tourism industries have been trying to pick up the slack, but many people are leaving the region to find work elsewhere in Canada.

The Nova Scotia government maintains a website (http://titanic.gov.ns.ca) of all things *Titanic,* including a list of passengers buried in local graveyards and artifacts housed in the local museums.

TITANIC

1992

Cod moratorium imposed and thousands of fisherfolk lose their livelihood. While hoped to be only a temporary measure, the cod stocks do not make a comeback.

RICHARD CUMMINS

» Port of Sydney (p84)

2001

Cape Breton's last coal mine shuts down, paving the way for outward migration and clean-up of Sydney Tar Ponds, North America's largest toxic waste site.

2003

Hurricane Juan hits Halifax passing through central Nova Scotia and PEI leaving extensive destruction, eight fatalities and $30 million worth of damage.

Rockin' the Atlantic Coast

If Atlantic Canada were bowl of chowder, music would be the stock in which everything floats. During the winter, fiddle, accordion, piano, vocal harmonies and vivid storytelling keep folks warm and happy; come spring the doors burst open and well-oiled skills are let out in the sunshine. As a visitor you'll run into live performances everywhere be they called 'ceilidhs' (*kay*-lees), 'shindigs' or 'kitchen parties'; even if you never gave fiddle music a thought, the festive ambiance will make you want to join in, sing along or tap your feet surreptitiously in time.

This region has been mixing cultures since humans have had the technology to cross oceans. It seems that everyone who has come to these shores has brought some sort of instrument, be it a drum, fiddle or bagpipe, along with a bit of rhythm and even more soul. Throughout the centuries music has been a force that has brought these folks from all corners of the globe, and today, everyone from Aboriginal to Scottish and Acadian musicians produce compositions that define the region.

Men of the Deeps, a choral group of retired coal miners in Nova Scotia, can be found playing around the province and invariably pull a crowd.

Aboriginal

Aboriginal cultures who populated the Atlantic coast for thousands of years are known to have sung, played music and danced, but details are few. Today, native music has been strongly influenced by the power of the fiddle. The most recent famous Mi'kmaq musician was Lee Cremo (1939–1999), whose fiddle-playing talents mixing Mi'kmaq, Scottish and Irish music took him as far as Nashville and Hollywood; it's said that no one played quite like Lee, and he was ranked by many as one of the top 10 fiddle players of his time in North America.

PARTYING AT THE PUB

Pubs are by far the best way to experience local music and, fortunately, finding a good one is about as easy as finding a public restroom. With Halifax and St John's vying for the title of most pubs per capita, you'll actually have a harder time finding a nightspot that's not hosting a live gig. The following is a list of our favorites:

» Rare Bird Pub (p87), Guysborough, Nova Scotia; folk & fiddle
» Red Shoe Pub (p77), Mabou, Cape Breton, Nova Scotia; folk & fiddle
» Seahorse Tavern (p41), Halifax, Nova Scotia; indie, punk & metal
» Benevolent Irish Society (p142), Charlottetown, PEI; Irish
» O'Leary's (p117), Saint John, New Brunswick; open-mic nights
» The Old Cosmo (p124), Moncton, New Brunswick; punk & rock
» Ship Pub (p175), St John's, Newfoundland; anything & everything
» Rock House (p175), St John's, Newfoundland; indie

Your best chance of hearing traditional music is at one of several powwows held around the region; for modern aboriginal sounds, head to music festivals that highlight the region's culture, such as Celtic Colours (see boxed text, opposite) in Nova Scotia. One of the best acts is the Newfoundland band Tipatshimun whose lyrics are in the Innu language.

Scottish & Irish

Bagpipes wail mysteriously from a blustery hilltop and a lone fiddler serenades you at lunch. Yes, Scottish music is the dominant influence in the region, particularly in Nova Scotia and Prince Edward Island (PEI). Highland Scots who settled here didn't leave their fiddles at home, and the lively, fun piano and fiddle combos were quick to catch on. To this day these folksy sounds define the Atlantic Canadian music scene. Most modern music produced from the music-heavy regions of Cape Breton Island and Halifax still sound quite a bit like the folk music of old, blending the fiddle with some electric guitar but still little percussion. Popular Cape Breton musicians include fiddlers Ashley MacIsaac, Buddy MacMaster and Natalie MacMaster, and multi-instrumentalist JP Cormier.

Bagpipes might not often be found in popular music but you will hear them in the area– a lot. Between the College of Piping and Celtic Arts in PEI (p157) and the Gaelic College of Celtic Arts and Crafts on Cape Breton (p82), bagpipers are pumped out by the dozen to play at historical sites, busk along the streets of cities and create a mysterious air in some of the most out of the way places, taking you away to the Scottish Highlands.

Up Newfoundland and Labrador way expect to hear more Irish-tinged tunes that move at a faster pace and generally tell a story, with the dialogue dominating the accompaniment – if you've ever listened to the Pogues, you know what we're talking about. This music generally emanates from Irish pubs where accents start to lilt as more beer is consumed. Singer-songwriter Ron Hynes embodies the local style and can be found strumming his guitar in St John's pubs; the Navigators play driving Celtic tunes; while the Novaks evoke Tom Petty with the whoop-ass amped up. But the band that most successfully translates this music to a larger stage is Great Big Sea. They tour throughout the

CEILIDHS AND KITCHEN PARTIES

"So what exactly is a ceilidh?" you might ask. Well, in the broadest sense, a ceilidh is a gathering where traditional Gaelic music is played and people can dance – kind of like a rural, family-style disco with an accordion instead of heavy bass. Sometimes it's just a solo fiddle player playing during lunch hours at a restaurant; other times it can be families dressed fully in their clan tartan performing for folks in town halls, or larger, more professional groups playing in front of big audiences. Whatever the size, ceilidhs are always laid-back affairs where the musicians mingle with the audience and hold no airs of being anything more than another local who just happens to play an instrument rather well. There are usually many more locals in the audience than visitors, and everyone goes crazy when, say, Cyril and Betty's seven-year-old son Timmy gets up and step dances – and you'll be into it too because chances are little Timmy is really, really good.

The term 'ceilidh' and 'kitchen party' are often used interchangeably but the latter is a term more likely to be used by Acadians (along with the Acadian French term: 'party de cuisine'), non-Celtic folks or by anyone on Cape Breton Island in Nova Scotia. A kitchen party is also more likely to actually be at someone's house and to have food and drink, although this is not always the case.

Beyond pubs and concerts, Canada's Atlantic provinces swell with music festivals, especially during the summer. The following are the most renowned:

» **Evolve** (www.evolvefestival.com; Antigonish, Nova Scotia) Voted best festival in Canada by the listeners of CBC Radio 3 in 2010, this three-day music and awareness festival showcases everything from grassroots music to modern, big-name performers in styles from folk to hip-hop.

» **Stan Rogers Folk Festival** (www.stanfest.com; Canso, Nova Scotia) Camp out in remote Canso for three days of live music from fine bluegrass and folk songwriters and performers.

» **Celtic Colours International Festival** (www.celtic-colours.com; Cape Breton, Nova Scotia) Watch the trees turn color in several Cape Breton locations while enjoying nine days of Celtic music from around the world.

» **Cavendish Beach Music Festival** (www.cavendishbeachmusic.com; Cavendish, Prince Edward Island) Big names like Taylor Swift make it to this five-day camp out, which features a big stage and an audience that pours in from all around Canada and the USA.

» **Deep Roots** (www.deeproots.ca; Wolfville, Nova Scotia) Folk and roots music is highlighted at this weekend festival, which also includes music workshops.

» **Indian River Festival** (www.indianriverfestival.com; Indian River, New Brunswick) Classical, folk, jazz and world music resonate through the acoustically blessed St Mary's Church.

» **Sound Symposium** (www.soundsymposium.com; St John's, Newfoundland) Amazing diversity from jazz, world music and classical musicians; nine days and nights of artistic jamming.

United States and Canada, filling mighty venues with their Celtified rave-ups and kitchen-party enthusiasm. They are a definite must-see.

Acadian

The Acadians are scattered in small groups throughout Atlantic Canada, and were often very remote and isolated before the modern advent of roads; Acadian music has therefore evolved in many different directions. Scottish influences are very apparent in areas like Cape Breton, and, as you move up the Cabot Trail from Mabou's Scottish fiddling to Chéticamp's Acadian kitchen parties, you'll be struck by how similar the sounds are. Generally, Acadian music is a little more soulful than Scottish music, with more percussion from tricky hand-clapping, foot-tapping and the spoons. The lyrics, of course, are in French.

In southwestern Nova Scotia the local music is far more influenced by rock, bluegrass and country, as well as Cajun styles introduced by descendants of those caught up in the Great Expulsion. The most popular Acadian band today, Blou, is from this region, and they call their sound 'Acadico' – a mix of Acadian, Cajun and Zydeco (an American Creole folk music). The group's accordion-based rock tunes regularly win the East Coast Music Award title for Best Francophone recording of the year. Meanwhile, from the same region, Jacobus et Maleco, which eventually became Radio Radio, was the first Acadian rap group, and internationally renowned Grand Dérangement sings movingly of Acadian reality through its traditional tunes.

Many Acadian groups head to Montréal where there's a much stronger Francophone music scene and it's easier to get recognized. New Brunswick Acadian groups are often very influenced by the traditional Québecois poetic style. Acts from Atlantic Canada that have made

Find Out What's On
» Nova Scotia: www.thecoast.ca
» Newfoundland: www.thescope.ca
» New Brunswick: www.girafecycle.com
» Prince Edward Island: www.buzzon.com

This playlist will get you right in the mood for highland hills, long stretches of Atlantic coastline and perhaps a stop for some step-dancing on the way. These old and new favorites are a little bit folk and a little bit country:

» 'Guysborough Train,' Stan Rogers
» 'The Silver Spear,' Natalie MacMaster
» 'These Roads,' David Gunning
» 'Rant and Roar,' Great Big Sea
» 'Home I'll Be,' Rita MacNeil
» 'Walk With Me,' Pogey
» 'My Nova Scotia Home,' Hank Snow
» 'Wrong Side of the Country,' Old Man Luedecke
» 'Maritime Express,' Eddie LeGere
» 'Maple Sugar,' Don Messer
» 'Snow Bird,' Anne Murray

names for themselves include Marie-Jo Thério (soothing and lyrical from New Brunswick), Suroît (Cajun and fiddle from the Magdalen Islands), Borlico and Barachois (lively kitchen-party-style duo from PEI), and Felix and Formanger (an accordion and guitar group from Newfoundland).

African Influences

Just when you were getting tired of the fiddle, in come more cultures. Many Black Canadians arrived as freed slaves and Loyalists to the British Crown during the American War of Independence (see p224). Social inequalities and marginalization (Nova Scotia's racism earned it the moniker 'Mississippi of the North') stopped the black community from making a huge mark in the Maritime music scene in the past, but nowadays it's adding a lot of spice to the region's music scene. The influence had been largely gospel music, but today hip-hop, jazz, blues, R&B, pop and classical music are all holding some cultural sway.

Portia White from Truro, Nova Scotia, was one of the first African-Canadians to make it big in the region when she won a silver cup at the Nova Scotia Music Festival in 1928 at the age of 17. She went on to become a powerful and well-known contralto classical vocalist and stage presence through the early '40s. In more recent years, Nova Scotian R&B musician Gary Beals placed second in the first season of *Canadian Idol,* and Faith Nolan, a mixed-heritage African, Mik'maq and Irish jazz singer, songwriter and guitarist, has made music with powerful political statements.

What's For Supper?

Until recently, this corner of Canada was noted solely for its seafood rather than the rest of the plentiful bounty on offer. This is changing, particularly in Prince Edward Island (PEI), where Charlottetown's Holland College is churning out more renowned chefs by the year, many interested in making the most of the region's bounty. Even so, for the most part Atlantic Canada's food and drink remains plain and simple; inventive Canadian and international chefs tend to congregate in cities, only occasionally cropping up in remote outposts. A quintessential Atlantic Canadian meal is fish or shellfish, fried or boiled, with a veggie thrown in for good measure, and perhaps a bowl of chowder. Odd local specialties liven up many menus; don't be shy to give them a try.

Bounty from the Sea

The sea defines Atlantic Canada, so it's no surprise that seafood defines the local cuisine.

Cod gets battered and fried and brought to your table as fish and chips; it's the one dish you can trust to be on every menu. Atlantic salmon, cousin of the better-known Pacific salmon, usually arrives broiled

Signature Sea Critters

» Mussels, Prince Edward Island

» Digby scallops, Nova Scotia

» Malpeque Oysters, Prince Edward Island

» Lobster, everywhere

DO-IT-YOURSELF SEAFOOD CHOWDER

You've sipped and slurped chowder throughout the region and now you want to do it yourself. The ingredients below await your cooking pot.

Ingredients

500mL lobster meat
500g fish fillets
125mL chopped onions
50mL butter or margarine
25mL all-purpose (plain) flour
1L peeled and diced potatoes
500g mussels or clams, steamed and shucked.

250mL water
500g scallops
1L cream
750g milk
5mL salt
pinch of white cayenne pepper

Method

If frozen, thaw lobster and reserve the water. Remove any bits of shell or cartilage and cut into bite-size pieces. De-bone fish fillets and cut into 2.5cm pieces. Set aside.

In a heavy saucepan, sauté onions in butter until tender. Stir in flour and cook for one minute. Add potatoes and enough water to cover, bring to a boil and cook until tender. Add fish and scallops, and simmer for five minutes, stirring once or twice. Add cream, milk, lobster, lobster juice, mussels and seasonings. Heat gently and serve.

Makes 12 servings.

Recipe from *Taste of Nova Scotia* © 2006 www.tasteofnovascotia.ns.ca

Some of the best restaurants in these provinces are located in out-of-the-way villages or bucolic areas that make you combine your meal with a road trip. Locals as well as visitors don't seem to find this a hardship, though, as many of these eateries have been open for years and manage to stay full throughout summer (most shut in winter).
   Our favorites include:
» Ship to Shore (p156), Darnly, Prince Edward Island
» Chanterelle Country Inn (p82), St Ann's Loop, Nova Scotia
» Inn at Bay Fortune (p146), Bay Fortune, Prince Edward Island
» Shipwright's Cafe (p156), Margate, Prince Edward Island
» Chez Christophe Guesthouse & Restaurant (p56), Grosses-Coques, Nova Scotia
» Doctor's Inn (p159), Tyne Valley, Prince Edward Island

and sauced, perhaps with dill or hollandaise. 'Nova' is lightly smoked salmon (akin to lox), for which Nova Scotia is deservedly famous.

Nova Scotia, New Brunswick and PEI boil more lobster than you can shake a stick of butter at. One of the best places to get down and dirty with the crustacean is at a community-hall lobster supper (see p234). Don't eat too much; you'll need to leave room for the bulging fruit pie that'll come your way afterward.

Nova Scotia visitors should also save their appetites for Digby scallops. Those touring PEI will find succulent oysters that grow around the island's shore and have a different flavor depending on when and where they're harvested (see p155).

The sea doesn't limit itself to meat either – the Maritime provinces harvest seaweeds that are eaten or used for their medicinal properties. Stop by Roland's Sea Vegetables (p111) on Grand Manan Island, New Brunswick, for a bag of dulse to eat as-is or to sprinkle on fish; Seaweed Cafe (p160), on the west coast of PEI, for a slice of seaweed pie that's thickened with local carrageen; or to Point Prim (p144), PEI, for a 'Seaweed Experience', where you collect, learn about and eat the region's vegetables from the sea.

Earthly Delights

Eastern Canada gets much less fame for its land-based food than for its seafood, but that doesn't mean it can't cook up some tasty non-fish-based dishes. French Acadians in particular have invented several specialties over the centuries. In Acadian towns you might see menu items such as rappie pie (also known as *la rapure*), a potato and salted-pork dish. *Tourtière* is a meat pie. *Poutine râpée* is a mixture of grated raw and mashed potatoes wrapped around fresh pork.

Newfoundland and Labrador may be boggy, rocky and cruddy for growing most things, but berries flourish here. Thus blueberries, partridgeberries (similar to cranberries) and bakeapples (p213) get shoveled into muffins, pies and jams. For more on the province's cuisine, see p173. PEI rivals Idaho for being the potato capital of North America and it's said the island's tubers have a unique flavor due to the rich, red soil.

Bottoms Up!

Moosehead is the region's best-known beer, brewed in Saint John, New Brunswick. In Newfoundland, Quidi Vidi microbrews (p169) flow through the provincial taps; try Eric the Red. Beer lovers will also enjoy Alexander Keith's crisp beer from the eponymous, good-time brewery (p33) in Halifax.

Farmers Markets Forages

» Halifax Farmers' Brewery Market (p42), Halifax, Nova Scotia

» Dieppe Market (p122), Moncton, New Brunswick

» Boyce Farmers' Market (p96), Fredericton, New Brunswick

» Old City Market (p116), Saint John, New Brunswick

» Charlottetown Farmers' Market (p142), Charlottetown, Prince Edward Island

» Bidgood's (p177), Goulds, Newfoundland

Boutique wineries are also uncorking their bottles in Nova Scotia, mostly in the Annapolis Valley, Bear River area and on the Malagash Peninsula. Domaine de Grand Pré (p65), Blomidon Estate Winery (p62) and Jost Vineyards (p72) are the biggest, and these are the wines that you'll find in many fine restaurants in Nova Scotia and occasionally beyond. Rossignol Winery (p144) on PEI specializes in delicious and well-respected fruit wines but has begun to focus more on regular wines as well.

The Glenora Distillery (p76) on Cape Breton Island produces a very sip-worthy single-malt whiskey. Newfoundland is famous for its Screech (p174), a brand of rum that's actually made in Jamaica; and PEI now has two distilleries, one piping out fine potato vodka and the other a tonsil-searing barely legal moonshine (see p147).

You can get quality coffee, including espresso and cappuccino, in cities. Barring that, the ubiquitous Tim Hortons doughnut shops brew a respectable cup.

Celebrations

Food and drink are a big part of celebrating in Atlantic Canada. Summer's seafood festivals, autumn's Thanksgiving, winter's Christmas get-togethers and spring's Easter holidays traditionally feature generous family feasts with plenty of meat dishes, salad bowls, giant desserts, and beer and wine. A hearty, family-focused Sunday dinner is also a common event.

Several towns showcase their special cuisines with annual festivals:
Lobster Carnival (p73) Pictou, Nova Scotia; early July.
Tyne Valley Oyster Festival (p159) Tyne Valley, PEI; early August.
Digby Scallop Days (p58) Digby, Nova Scotia; mid-August.
PEI International Shellfish Festival (p140) Charlottetown, PEI; late September.

Where to Eat & Drink

Even the smallest town usually has a midpriced restaurant. In places where this is not the case, your lodging host will likely serve food; for instance, many B&Bs serve meals beyond breakfast for a price and if you prearrange it. Atlantic Canada doesn't feature many fine-dining establishments outside of cities and college towns, but a few do turn up in unexpected, out-of-the-way places; see the boxed text, opposite, for further information. A pub is often the cheapest place to get a good meal.

While there are many variations, most restaurants open for lunch (usually between 11.30am and 2:30pm) and dinner from 5:30pm (some fancy establishments only open for dinner). Midrange and family restaurants often stay open all day. In small towns and rural areas many restaurants close at 8pm but times vary and often depend on how busy the restaurant is that day.

Budget eateries include takeouts, cafes, markets and basic restaurants where you can fill up for less than $15. At midrange establishments you get full menus, beer and wine lists and a bill that shouldn't

Regional Specialties

» Bakeapple, Newfoundland

» Fiddleheads, New Brunswick

» Oat Cakes, Cape Breton, Nova Scotia

» Solomon Gundy, Southshore, Nova Scotia

» Dulce, Grand Manan Island, New Brunswick

» Éclairs, St-Pierre & Miquelon, Newfoundland

» Cod Tongues, Newfoundland

TRAVEL YOUR TASTEBUDS

Head-scratching foods you may encounter in Nova Scotia and Prince Edward Island include Solomon Gundy (a pickled-herring and chopped-meat combo) and Lunenburg pudding (pork and spices cooked in the intestines of a pig). Dulce is an edible seaweed; New Brunswick's Grand Manan Island (p110) is famous for it. Fiddleheads are a fern's first shoots that are served like vegetables in the region. Figgy duff and jig's dinner are just a few of Newfoundland's colorfully named dishes.

exceed $25 per person for an appetizer, main course and one drink, not including tax and tip. Top-end places are typically gourmet affairs with fussy service, and freshly prepared and creative food. At these establishments, main courses alone can cost $25 or more.

Quick Eats

In addition to farmers markets in cities, roadside stands offer enticing seasonal produce in rural areas. Do yourself a favor and pick up a container of strawberries (best in June) or blueberries (August).

You might come across the occasional roadside van selling fish and chips, and lots of seafood markets serve inexpensive lobster rolls, sandwiches and chowder. *Poutine* (French fries topped with gravy and cheese) isn't as prevalent here as in some other areas of Canada but it is on a few menus and there's a popular food cart that whips it up right next to the library in downtown Halifax. Barring that, well, there's always Tim Hortons.

Vegetarians & Vegans

Vegetarians will be well catered for in the region's principal cities such as Halifax, Fredericton and St John's, but as you move away from urban areas your options become extremely limited. Vegans can expect an even rougher ride. Strict adherents should stick to any vegetarian-only eateries they come across, since 'vegetarian' items in mainstream restaurants may well have been prepared with meat stock or lard. We have marked restaurants that cater particularly well to vegetarians with a vegetarian icon (🖉) throughout this book.

Specialty health food shops are found almost exclusively in the larger cities so you'll want to stock up on supplies before going to more remote regions. Chinese eateries occasionally pop up in remote areas and may be another option. Many fine restaurants (some that pop up in very unexpected rural locations – see p232) will nearly always cater to dietary restrictions, as will many B&Bs.

Eating with Kids

Everywhere you turn in Atlantic Canada you'll find fast food, fried fare and Tim Hortons, Canada's favorite stop for doughnuts, sandwiches and coffee. If you're health conscious, one of your biggest hurdles with kids will be finding more wholesome options; in small towns your only choice might be to self-cater. Fortunately there are plenty of cabin and family-suite-style options that allow you to cook for yourself, and some

Top Five Foodie Restaurants

» Fleur de Sel (p50), Lunenburg, Nova Scotia

» Fid (p39), Halifax, Nova Scotia

» Lot 30 (p141), Charlottetown, Prince Edward Island

» Norseman Restaurant (p201), L'Anse aux Meadows, Newfoundland

» Rossmount Inn (p107), St Andrews By-the-Sea, New Brunswick

LOBSTER SUPPERS

You don't need to change out of your jeans or get the kids a babysitter to gorge yourself on the Maritime province's most delicious shellfish. The classic Nova Scotia, New Brunswick and PEI dining experience is a no-frills lobster supper, held in dining halls, churches and community centers. The lobster is generally unadorned of sauces and fanfare; the suppers are a place to enjoy these critters in the buff (or perhaps with a little melted butter), for their own divine flavors and texture. Kids are not only welcome, they are well-catered for, with half-sized suppers and other menu options like beef or scallops. Just to make sure no one goes hungry, there is a slew of accompaniments from chowder and mussels to potato salad and oven-fresh rolls. Held daily for dinner from roughly mid-June to mid-October, the most suppers per capita are found on PEI. The cost of dinner depends on the market price of lobster but generally hovers around $28 for an all-inclusive meal with a 1lb crustacean.

Tip around 15% (pretax) in restaurants and bars with good table service but don't tip the full 15% unless the service has been worth it. Also check that a gratuity hasn't been automatically added to your bill – a growing practice.

B&Bs will also let you prepare your own food. In cities, pretty much every restaurant option is available, from vegan to steakhouses.

Most Canadian restaurants are adept at dealing with families, offering booster seats and child-friendly servers as soon as you steer your progeny through the door. As an alternative to chicken fingers and burgers on the kids menu, you can usually ask for a half-order of something from the adult menu. Families with even the most well-behaved children may not feel comfortable at fine-dining establishments.

See p251 for further details on prices and resources for children.

Habits & Customs

Atlantic Canadians follow the tradition of eating morning breakfast, midday lunch and early-evening dinner. Expect the generally high standards of North American restaurant and bar service to apply throughout the region. Table service is common at most pubs, although you can still order at the bar as well. Don't forget to give a tip to your table server, and consider dropping some change in the bar-server's pot if you stick around for a few beers.

All of the Atlantic provinces have adopted widespread smoking bans. Nova Scotia's law is the toughest in the nation, prohibiting smoking at outdoor eating and drinking establishments in addition to all indoor public areas.

Get Out!

Atlantic Canada has only recently begun to harness its cliffy, marine-mammaled terrain for outdoor adventures. Visitors can now get out in the sun (or rain or fog, as the case may be) to hike, kayak, whale-watch, or even surf. The season is short for most activities (May to October in a good year), but you'll find plenty of tour operators eager to set you up for action. It's also easy to arrange independent adventures with your own or rented equipment.

Hiking

Trails – from gentle jaunts around an interpretive path to breath-sapping slogs up a mountain – crisscross the area's national and provincial parks. And hiking – aside from being low-cost – is the most enjoyable way to absorb the region.

The hiking season runs from May to October, with optimal conditions from July onward, when the trails have dried out. Maps are available at park information centers, although for extended hikes you may need topographic maps (see p255).

And don't forget that Canada is also home to one of the most ambitious paths ever conceived, the **Trans Canada Trail** (www.tctrail.ca), an 18,078km-long ribbon from Cape Spear (p177) in Newfoundland that runs all the way across the country to Victoria, British Columbia. It's still a work in progress, but trails in the provinces sometimes coincide with it.

Kayaking & Canoeing

Atlantic Canada is chock-full of possibilities to get out on the water, be it a lazy canoe trip or a battle with roiling white water. Sea kayaking has exploded here, with myriad places to paddle; see the boxed text, p239, for details. A unique activity in the region is tidal-bore rafting, where you harness the blasting force of the famous Fundy tides; see p66 for how to get outfitted.

National and provincial parks are excellent places to start if you've never dipped an oar. Maps and equipment rentals are usually available from the park information centers, where the staff can also give route recommendations.

Canoeing doesn't have the cachet of sea kayaking in the region, but there are still some lovely opportunities. The sport is best suited to inland lakes and rivers, so it's no shocker that Kejimkujik National Park (p51) ranks high on the list. It's a good place to paddle into the backcountry and camp. In New Brunswick, canoeing in untouched, moose- and bear-trodden Mt Carleton Provincial Park (p100) is sweet, while those who wish to remain closer to city life can push off from Fredericton (p95) and paddle through the Saint John River. Canoeing in Newfoundland centers on the region's Terra Nova National Park (p189).

MARINE CONDITIONS

Kayakers, fisherfolk and anyone else sailing out to sea can check www.buoyweather.com for marine conditions all around Atlantic Canada.

Whale Watching

The region's most precious gift to visitors is whale watching. The thrill of spotting a whale's spout followed by its giant tail flukes arching and descending is unbeatable.

More than 22 species of whale and porpoise lurk offshore throughout Atlantic Canada, drawn to the rich fishy feeding waters. The standout species include the humpback whale, the highly endangered North Atlantic right whale and the largest leviathan of all, the blue whale.

Whale-watch boat operators are ubiquitous and will bring you close to the creatures. The most common sightings around Cape Breton, Nova Scotia are humpback, minke and pilot whales. In New Brunswick, there is excellent whale watching along the eastern Fundy Shore and around the Fundy Isles; right whales and blue whales are viewable. Newfoundland pretty much has whales swimming all around its shores, with humpback and minke commonly seen.

Most tours last about two hours and cost around $45 to $60 per adult. The sighting success rate is often posted, and you should ask if there's any sort of money-back guarantee if you do not see whales. Remember,

GET OUT!

BEST PLACES TO STRAP ON YOUR HIKING BOOTS

Nova Scotia
Nova Scotia holds so much variety of terrain and well-tended backcountry that you'll be spoilt with options.

» **Cape Breton Highlands National Park** (p79) offers exquisite hiking over dramatic coastline; the Skyline Trail is the most popular path, but it's hard to go wrong with any of them.

» **Cape Split** (p62) is one of the best hikes to view the Fundy tides plus pastoral to wilderness scenery.

» **Taylor Head Provincial Park** (p89), which occupies a slender sprig of land on the eastern shore and has trails traversing forest and beach.

New Brunswick
Rugged, forested New Brunswick holds an unlistable number of hiking options ranging from mountains and river valleys to the dramatic Fundy coastline.

» **Fundy National Park** (p120) and **Fundy Trail Parkway** (p119) have a variety of paths along the wooded coastline.

» **Mt Carleton** (p101) offers adventurous hikes over mountain peaks to river valleys and lakes. Expect to see wildlife but few humans.

» **Grand Manan Island** (p111) shines as the provincial jewel for seaside-themed mellow hikes. Cliffs, marshes and lighthouses are all on the paths.

Newfoundland
Remnants of old walking paths that used to connect local communities and provided escape routes inland from pirates now make for fantastic hiking since most clutch the shoreline and often provide whale views.

» **East Coast Trail** (p170) on the Avalon Peninsula

» **Discovery Trail** (p182) on the Bonavista Peninsula

» **Gros Morne National Park** (p196) is renowned for its vistas

Prince Edward Island (PEI)
PEI is very flat so there are far less hiking opportunities than the other provinces in this book. That said, there are plenty of beaches to stroll.

» **Prince Edward Island National Park** (p149) is the best choice if you feel the need to use your feet.

you're heading out on open sea for many of these tours, so be prepared for a wavy ride. If you're at all prone to seasickness, medicate beforehand. It's also cold out there, so take a jacket or sweater. The season varies by location but usually is in July and August.

And while whale-watch tours are great, never underestimate what you can see from shore, especially from places such as Cape Breton's Cabot Trail and throughout Newfoundland's Avalon Peninsula.

A good resource is the *Pocketguide to Whale Watching on Canada's East Coast* (2003; Formac Publishing), by Jeffrey C Domm.

Cycling & Mountain Biking

Cycling is where PEI shines. Several years ago, the province converted a defunct 357km railway bed into a cycling route called the Confederation Trail (p143), and it landed PEI on the map as an international cycling destination. The trail runs along the length of the island, with feeder paths down to most towns. Good services and facilities line it, many provided in reconditioned train stations. This easy service availability, combined with compact distances and flat terrain, make cycling here doable even for those with limited experience. The seaside stretch from St Peters to Mt Stewart (p147) is particularly inspiring.

New Brunswick is working hard to do something similar, and you'll find finished but as yet unconnected sections of the New Brunswick Trail (www.nbtrail.com) around the province. Rewarding rides include the Fundy Trail Parkway (p119) along coastal wilderness, and paths through the backcountry in Kouchibouguac National Park (p127).

In Nova Scotia the area around Lunenburg (p48) is a cyclist's dream with few hills, sweet ocean views and little vehicle traffic. Cape Breton Highlands National Park (p79) certainly has the scenery going for it, but it's tough riding due to the hilliness and traffic – not a good place for beginners.

Rugged terrain, high winds, poor road conditions and long stretches of road between towns make Newfoundland a difficult cycling destination. If you want to give it a try, Gros Morne National Park (p196) and CA Pippy Park (p170) in St John's are options.

For cycling regulations and costs, see p263.

Fishing

Fly-fishing in this region is downright mythical. Avid anglers get all slack-jawed and weak-kneed when names such as 'Miramichi' and 'Margaree' are invoked. No, these aren't beautiful women, but rather places to cast a line for Atlantic salmon and trout (speckled and brown, among the many).

On the tranquil Miramichi River (p129) in New Brunswick, everyone from Prince Charles to Dick Cheney to Marilyn Monroe has reeled one in. The Humber River (p203) in Newfoundland and Pinware River

---

KNOTS

Unleash your inner sailor (or fisherperson or rock climber) by learning to tie a half hitch, bowline and others with *Knots and Splices* (2006) by Cyrus Day and Colin Jarman. Also helpful for budding escape artists.

FISHING RULES & LICENSES

Staff at any tourist office will have the most current information about fishing regulations and outfitters. Each province also produces its own 'angler's guide' booklet that includes licensing rules. License prices vary by province and by species fished; a seven-day license costs anywhere from $30 to $90. Check with each province's environmental or natural resources department for further information:

Newfoundland & Labrador (☎709-637-2409; www.env.gov.nl.ca)
New Brunswick (☎506-453-2440; www.gnb.ca)
Nova Scotia (☎902-426-5433; www.gov.ns.ca/nsaf)
Prince Edward Island (☎902-368-6080; www.gov.pe.ca)

If there's any one activity that is Atlantic Canada's specialty, it's sea kayaking. It's everywhere; it's absolutely the best way to see the remarkable coastlines, and you'll often be kayaking alongside whales.

Most companies cater to beginners, so no need to feel unworthy if you've never kayaked before. Conversely, advanced paddlers can rent crafts and head out on their own. It can be very rough out there due to volatile weather, high winds and strong currents, so know your limits. The Canadian government publishes an excellent resource titled *Sea Kayaking Safety Guide*, available via download from **Transport Canada** (www.tc.gc.ca/BoatingSafety/pubs/kayak/menu.htm). It details each province's weather and kayaking terrain, and also provides trip-planning tips.

(p212) in Labrador Straits are known for salmon fishing. If the latter isn't remote enough, Labrador offers several fly-in lodges that host the likes of George Bush Sr.

These places all have experienced ups and downs with overfishing, poaching and unknown causes (perhaps climate change) affecting stocks, but they seem to be at sustainable levels presently.

And finally, lobster fishing provides a unique experience, one that kids will love. Haul up crustacean-filled pots in Lunenburg (p48) in Nova Scotia. Then grab a bucket and a shovel to go clamming in PEI (p148).

Bird-watching

No need to be a binocular-toting ornithologist to get into the scene here. Birds swarm the region, and whether you're a birder or not, you'll find it tough to resist the charm of a funny-looking puffin or common murre.

Seabirds are the top draw. Many whale-watch tours also take visitors to seabird colonies; since whales and birds share a taste for the same fish, they often lurk in the same areas. So you'll be able to feast your eyes upon razorbills, kittiwakes, arctic terns, and yes, puffins and murres. The colonies can be up to one million strong, their shrieks deafening and their smell, well, not so fresh. Still, it's an amazing sight to behold.

Also impressive to watch are the Arctic-nesting shorebirds that migrate south through the Bay of Fundy. Each year millions of tiny sandpipers refuel in the rich mudflats exposed by the world's highest tides. The prime time is mid-August, and the prime places are around Windsor and Grand Pré in Nova Scotia's Annapolis Valley.

The *Sibley Field Guide to Birds of Eastern North America* (2003) by David Sibley makes an excellent, illustrated and portable companion for bird-watchers.

Surfing

Surfing seems an unusual sport for Atlantic Canada – too damn cold, right? Think again. People do surf here and not only is it cold, it's bloody freezing, since the best waves break in winter.

The place to partake of the madness is Lawrencetown Beach (p44) on Nova Scotia's eastern shore. L-town, as it's called, faces due south and picks up stormy weather from hundreds of kilometers away; this results in exceptional wrapping waves, especially plentiful in the colder months. So bundle up in your 7mm wetsuit, try not to freeze your ass off in the 0°C water, and join the line-up. People do surf at warmer times of the year, too. Board rentals cost about $25 per day, lessons about $75.

Kejimkujik Seaside Adjunct (p52) provides additional waves and the prices are similar.

Paddlers' Delight

» Eastern and south shores, Nova Scotia

» Cape Breton, Nova Scotia

» Fundy Isles, New Brunswick

» Eastern Fundy shore, New Brunswick

» Cartwright, Labrador

» Witless Bay, Newfoundland

» North Rustico, PEI

This will impress the friends at the next beer-up: tell them you went snow-kiting in Newfoundland. Of course, it will entail actually going to Newfoundland – in winter – but you'll be going to Corner Brook, near the renowned ski resort of Marble Mountain, so you won't feel too out of place.

Snow-kiting is sort of a windsurfing-meets-snowboarding endeavor, and the patient folks at **My Newfoundland Adventures** (☑866-469-6353; www.mynewfoundland.ca) teach you how to do it, no experience required. Just bring some very, very warm clothes for the 3½-hour lesson ($99) and off you'll zip across the tundra. (OK, it's not really tundra, but it's cold enough to be!)

Perhaps even more radical than surfing is kite-surfing, in which you cruise in, over and out of waves using some funky equipment. Shippagan (p131) in northeastern New Brunswick is a good place to try it.

Check www.wavewatch.com for wave forecasts for the region.

Skiing & Snowboarding

Atlantic Canada's best skiing and snowboarding take place at Newfoundland's **Marble Mountain** (☑709-637-7616; www.skimarble.com; Hwy 1; day pass $45; ☉10am-4:30pm Tue-Thu, 9am-9:30pm Fri, to 4:30pm Sat-Mon mid-Dec–early Apr) outside Corner Brook (p202). It may not have the height of Whistler or other top resorts, but it's lower cost with far fewer queues, so you get more time on the slopes.

Marble has 35 trails, four lifts, a 488m vertical drop and annual snowfall of 4.8m. There are snowboarding and tubing parks, as well as night skiing on Friday. The region caters to cross-country skiers at **Blow-Me-Down Cross Country Ski Park** (☑709-639-2754; www.blowmedown.ca; ☉sunrise-9pm early Dec-Apr), about 10 minutes from the mountain.

Serious cross-country skiers will want to head far north to where the Canadian national team trains in Labrador West. The Wapusakatto Mountains (p216) let loose with good, cold, dry snow from late October to late April, a much longer season than elsewhere in the region – or anywhere in Canada.

For further information contact the **Canadian Ski Council** (☑905-212-9040; www.canadianskicouncil.org).

Top 5 Places to Whale-watch

» Twillingate Island, Newfoundland

» Digby Neck, Nova Scotia

» Grand Manan Island, New Brunswick

» Pleasant Bay, Nova Scotia

» Witless Bay Ecological Reserve, Newfoundland

Lay of the Land

From unexplored wilderness to dramatic coastlines and phenomenal wildlife, the provinces of Atlantic Canada are a nature-lover's dream. It's a place where you are as likely to see thousands of seabirds resting on a passing iceberg as a moose crossing the road, and, if you're lucky, you may spot feeding blue whales or a wandering polar bear. This rich and varied landscape is easily explored courtesy of the region's many parks, ranging from the alluring sandy beaches of Prince Edward Island National Park to the soaring fjords of Gros Morne National Park in Newfoundland.

A Geologist's Dream

The spectacular landscapes of Atlantic Canada are both their charm and their challenge. Due to the rugged land and crumpled coastlines, the traditions of isolated villages and homesteads have been preserved to a greater extent than perhaps anywhere else in North America, but the difficulty of coaxing crops from the rocky soil or transporting goods to market keeps much of the region economically depressed to this day.

For geologists this region hides great wealth, not just in rich ore deposits but in the record of earth history preserved by the rocks. This is where two significant geologic provinces converge: Labrador forms the eastern rim of the vast Canadian Shield, the greatest exposure of ancient rocks on the earth's surface; while the other Atlantic provinces perch themselves at the northern tip of the Appalachian Mountains, which is the single most important topographic feature of eastern North America.

Sitting at this great convergence, Atlantic Canada offers a visually dramatic snapshot of more than one billion years of earth history, ranging from the red sandstone cliffs of Northumberland Strait to the famed granite headlands at Peggy's Cove, Nova Scotia. And perhaps even more fascinating for the visitor are the many signs of the massive Pleistocene ice sheet that smothered the region with ice a mile deep as recently as 20,000 years ago: the thrilling fjords of the north, the rounded mounds of Nova Scotia (known locally as drumlins), the tens of thousands of small shallow lakes.

DINOSAURS

At the Fundy Geological Museum (http://museum. gov.ns.ca/fgm/ index.html; p68), 'time travel' with interactive exhibits and visit a lab where dinosaur bones are being cleaned and assembled.

FABULOUS FOSSILS

Kids will probably be especially intrigued by the region's fossils, many of which are on display in various parks and museums. They include fossil footprints, dinosaur bones, and fossilized creatures that look like they're from outer space. In New Brunswick province, you can see remains of the first life to walk on land in North America (a giant centipede, just in case you're wondering) as well as evidence of the most primitive terrestrial plants.

ATLANTIC CANADA'S TOP NATURAL AREAS

PARK	FEATURES
Nova Scotia	
Cape Chignecto Provincial Park	largest and newest park in province, rugged wilderness; old growth forest, deer, moose, eagles
Kejimkujik National Park	pristine wilderness, network of glacial lakes; otter, loon, bald eagles
Cape Breton Highlands National Park	dramatic oceanside cliffs, world-famous scenic drive; whales, bald eagles, seabirds, bear, moose, wild orchids
New Brunswick	
Fundy National Park	sandstone cliffs, extensive beach; dramatic tides, bear, moose, beaver, peregrine falcons
Kouchibouguac National Park	lagoons, white-sand beaches; moose, deer, bear
Prince Edward Island	
Prince Edward Island National Park	red sandstone bluffs, dunes, beaches; red foxes, piping plover, sandpipers
Newfoundland	
Cape St Mary's Ecological Reserve	rugged ocean cliffs; one of the most accessible seabird colonies in North America, nesting gannets, whales
Terra Nova National Park	craggy cliffs and many sheltered inlets; lakes, bogs; moose, beaver, bald eagles, whales
Witless Bay Ecological Reserve	offshore islands; over a million breeding seabirds, feeding whales, icebergs

In its simplest form, the geologic story is that Atlantic Canada formed from the fragments and pieces left over after North America and Africa collided and crushed an ocean between them 400 million years ago. In the process of swinging into each other with tremendous force, the two continents compressed and folded seafloor sediments into a giant mountain chain that has eroded over millions of years into the rolling hills we now call the Appalachian Mountains. Mixed into this mélange are the many different pieces of smaller land masses trapped between the colliding continents.

When North America and Africa went their separate ways 180 million years ago, they each left part of their coastline behind. This may be best observed in Newfoundland, for its western third is a remnant of the ancestral North American coastline, its middle third is a slice of ancient seafloor, and its eastern third once belonged to northern Africa.

But geology never stops at the simple story, and for the traveler who's enthusiastic about the subject, this region never runs out of surprises. Even if you don't study rocks or get excited by fossils, you cannot ignore the stunning outcroppings and rock types visible at nearly every stage of your journey. There are, for example, sea stacks, drowned coastlines, glacial grooves, and erratics everywhere – what more could you ask for?

ACTIVITIES	BEST TIME TO VISIT	PAGE
hiking and back-country camping	Jun–Oct	(p70)
canoeing, camping, hiking	late Sep–early Oct	(p51)
hiking, camping, sightseeing, whale watching	May–Oct	(p77)
mountain biking, bird-watching, hiking	year-round	(p119)
strolling, clam digging, bicycling, skiing, kayaking, bird-watching	year-round	(p127)
bird-watching, beach walking, swimming, picnicking	May–Sep	(p149)
bird-watching	Mar–Aug	(p182)
kayaking, fishing, camping	mid-May–mid-Oct	(p189)
bird-watching, whale watching	Jun–Aug	(p178)

Critters of the Great North

Whether you come for a glimpse of caribou, whales or moose, Atlantic Canada will not disappoint the wildlife enthusiast. Many people travel to the region to see the incredible numbers of seabirds and whales that can be spotted from coastal bluffs or on whale-watch trips, but some of the most unusual wildlife is seen in the far north where few travelers journey.

The plants and animals of Atlantic Canada are even more amazing when you realize that the entire region was completely buried in ice only 20,000 years ago and was not accessible for life until about 10,000 years ago. Where all these critters came from and how they got here so quickly is anybody's guess!

Animals

If you needed one single reason to visit Atlantic Canada, it might be the world-class encounters with whales that gather in these food-rich waters. Around 22 species of whale and porpoise can be seen on whale-watch tours, which are offered from countless coastal harbors. Leaping and diving humpback whales are most common throughout the region, but you might also catch a glimpse of the highly endangered North Atlantic right whale or even the largest leviathan of all, the blue whale.

POLAR BEARS

Closer to shore or hauled out on the ice, it is common to see seals, including in winter the snowy white young of the harp seal. Harbor and gray seals are easily observed, though in winter they seek out the edges of the pack ice.

Land animals are also a powerful draw. Fox, bear, and otter are widespread throughout the region. On Newfoundland there are more than 100,000 moose and there are many more on Cape Breton Island, so you'd have to work hard *not* to see one. As you travel north the animals become even more exotic. From Newfoundland north you will find polar bear, arctic fox, wolf, lynx, and musk oxen. Labrador has the largest herd of caribou in the world, as well as wolves that follow the long lines of migrating caribou.

Birds

Seabirds are the primary wildlife attraction in Atlantic Canada, and rightly so. There are few places in North America where it's easier to see outstanding numbers of seabirds such as razorbill, Atlantic puffin, common murre, and northern gannet. Huge nesting colonies on rocky islands and promontories may contain more than a million birds, but these merely hint at the numbers that once nested here before market hunters slaughtered uncounted millions of birds.

Mudflats and shorelines, especially along the Bay of Fundy, are famous for the tremendous quantities of shorebirds they attract during the May and August migration. Upwards of two million birds stop here annually. On nearby beaches, the endangered piping plover tries to hold its own against the trespass of invading sunbathers and beach walkers – please respect signs that warn you of this bird's home.

The white hairs on a polar bear are hollow and trap sunlight to help keep the animal warm in frigid temperatures.

Fish

More than any other animal, fish have placed Atlantic Canada on the map, in particular the northern cod (see the boxed text, below). With the collapse of the great cod fishery, other species such as halibut, mackerel, haddock, and herring have grown in economic importance. In the region's many lakes and rivers, fishermen seek out trout, bass, salmon, and river herring (with the quaint name alewives).

Insects

Although it is easy to focus on the region's showiest animals, we cannot ignore the one that is smallest but not least in Atlantic Canada. It has been said that the diminutive black fly has single-handedly maintained the wild splendor of Labrador. This may sound like an exaggeration until

---

THE GRAND BANKS

Banks are a funny name for a shallow area, but in the case of the Grand Banks off Newfoundland's southeast coast it's no laughing matter. Until recently this was considered the greatest site in the world for ocean fish and the animals that came to feed on them. Even today, with the fish nearly hunted out, millions of seabirds and uncounted whales come to feed in the rich waters. This area is incredibly productive because the continental shelf off the coast of Newfoundland sticks out like a thumb to intercept the south-flowing waters of the frigid Labrador Current right at the point where they mingle with the warm north-flowing waters of the Gulf Stream. The mix of warmth and nutrient-rich Arctic waters creates an explosion of plankton that feeds everything from the smallest fish to the biggest whale. And because the shallow waters allow sunlight to penetrate to the ocean floor, the food chain is active at all depths.

Atlantic Canada has taken its park systems seriously and many important sites are protected within both national and provincial parks. Nova Scotia alone has more than 120 parks, but even Newfoundland and Labrador, which are so sparsely settled as to be parks in their own right, have a total of 34 parks.

Not all parks are set up for camping, but they are all worthy of a visit. In a few parks it is possible to plan extended hiking and camping trips, but all of them offer splendid opportunities for activities ranging from picnicking to beachcombing to kayaking and cycling. Those that are open in the winter are favored by cross-country skiers and snowshoers.

you step foot onto the shore in midsummer and are blanketed in insects against which you are defenseless. Second only to the black fly are prolific mosquitoes. If it's any consolation, every animal from ant to moose is tormented equally by these creatures, so they're not picking on you.

Plants

Although Atlantic Canada presents some tree diversity in its southern reaches with a mix of birch, maple, and ash, vast areas of forest are completely dominated by spruce as you head north. And at some point even those homogenous forests give way to soggy tundra that stretches to the Arctic. Surprisingly the area can be rich with abundant wildflowers during the short growing season.

The yellow dandelion-like flowers of the coltsfoot may be the first ones to come out each spring, but far more attention is given to the region's delightful midsummer orchid displays, including showy lady's slipper, which may carpet entire boggy areas. Blue lupines seem to bloom everywhere, and many other varieties and colors can be found.

The most common shrubs, especially in Newfoundland and Labrador, are those in the heath family, including blueberries, cranberries, and other delicious berries that grow in profusion in August.

Perhaps the most curious plant is the odd lichen called caribou moss. Growing in such a dense spongy carpet that other plants cannot get a toehold, this pale greenish moss may be the most dominant plant in the northern forests. It is an important food source for caribou, hence its name, and is often mixed with seal meat to vary the diets of sled dogs.

Environmental Issues

Early Europeans explorers were dumbfounded by the apparently inexhaustible numbers of animals they encountered in Atlantic Canada. It was a scene of such incredible abundance that they thought it would never end, so they bent their will toward exploiting and profiting from the natural wealth in every way possible. The result is only too predictable and sad: animals lost forever include the mythical great auk, the Labrador duck and the sea mink. Today Atlantic Canada is facing the horrifying prospect that the greatest fishery in the world, the uncounted millions of cod that sustained their provincial livelihood for 400 years, may have come to an end when cod were listed as endangered in 2003. In the end, not only has the environment suffered great damage, but so have the villages and traditions that needed the fish for their survival.

Unfortunately resource exploitation continues unabated on several other fronts. Some $3 billion a year is generated from logging, with half of the production coming from New Brunswick. Vast ore deposits are

LAY OF THE LAND

World Heritage Sites

» Gros Morne National Park, Newfoundland

» L'Anse aux Meadows National Historic Site, Newfoundland

» Old Town Lunenburg, Nova Scotia

» Joggins Fossil Cliffs, Nova Scotia

being explored and developed all the time, with huge areas stripped of their forest and soil cover to access coal, iron, nickel and other mineral resources. Recently there has been a spate of oil and natural gas development, especially on the ocean floor, with untold consequences for marine life. What is particularly troubling is how much exploitation occurs in seldom-visited parts of Labrador, where there is little public scrutiny or attention.

Survival
Guide

Directory A-Z

Accommodations

In this part of Canada, you'll be choosing from a wide range of B&Bs, chain motels, hotels and hostels. Provincial tourist offices (see Tourist Information, p258) publish comprehensive directories of accommodations, and take bookings online or from visitor information centers.

Seasons

» Peak season is summer, from mid-June to early September, when prices are highest.

» It's best to book ahead during summer and during holidays (see Public Holidays, p256) and major events (see Month by Month, p16), as rooms can be scarce.

Prices

» Prices listed in this book are for peak-season travel and, unless stated otherwise, do not include taxes (which can be up to 17%). If breakfast is included and/or a bathroom is shared, that information is included in our listing.

» The budget category comprises campgrounds, hostels and simple hotels and B&Bs where you'll likely share a bathroom. Rates rarely exceed $100 for a double room.

» Midrange accommodations, such as most B&Bs, inns, motels and some hotels, generally offer the best value for money. Expect to pay between $100 and $180 for a comfortable, decent-sized double room with a private bathroom and TV.

» Top-end accommodations (more than $180 per double) offer an international standard of amenities, including fitness and business centers and other upmarket facilities.

Amenities

» Most properties offer in-room wi-fi. It's typically free in budget and midrange lodgings, while top-end hotels often charge a fee.

» Many smaller properties, especially B&Bs, ban smoking. Marriott and Westin brand hotels are 100% smoke free. All other properties have rooms set aside for nonsmokers. In this book, we have used the nonsmoking icon (☺) to mean that *all* rooms within a property are nonsmoking.

» Air-conditioning is not a standard amenity at most budget and midrange places. If you want it, be sure to ask about it when you book.

Discounts

» In winter, prices can plummet by as much as 50%.

» Membership in the American Automobile Association (AAA) or an associated automobile association, American Association of Retired Persons (AARP) or other organizations also yields modest savings (usually 10%).

» Check the hotel websites listed throughout this book for special online rates. The usual suspects also offer discounted room prices throughout Canada:

Priceline (www.priceline.com)

Hotwire (www.hotwire.com)

Expedia (www.expedia.com)

Travelocity (www.travelocity.com)

Tripadvisor (www.tripadvisor.com)

B&Bs

» **Bed & Breakfast Online** (www.bbcanada.com) is the main booking agency for properties nationwide.

» In Canada, B&Bs (known as *gîtes* in French) are essentially converted private homes whose owners live on site. People who like privacy may find B&Bs too intimate, as walls are rarely soundproof and it's usual to

---

BOOK YOUR STAY ONLINE

For more reviews by Lonely Planet authors, check out hotels.lonelyplanet.com. You'll find independent reviews, as well as recommendations on the best places to stay. Best of all, you can book online.

mingle with your hosts and other guests.

» Standards vary widely, sometimes even within a single B&B. The cheapest rooms tend to be small with few amenities and a shared bathroom. Nicer ones have added features such as a balcony, a fireplace and an en suite bathroom. Breakfast is always included in the rates (though it might be continental instead of a full cooked affair).

» Not all B&Bs accept children while others cater to them.

» Minimum stays (usually two nights) are common, and many B&Bs are only open seasonally.

Camping

Canada's Maritime and Atlantic provinces are filled with campgrounds – some federal or provincial, others privately owned. Private campgrounds sometimes cater only to trailers (caravans) and RVs, and may feature convenience stores, playgrounds and swimming pools. It is a good idea to phone ahead to make sure the size of sites and the services provided at a particular campground are suitable for your vehicle.

» **Season** varies by location but most camp sites are open from May to September. Some campgrounds remain open for maintenance year-round and may let you camp at a reduced rate in the off-season. This can be great in late autumn or early spring when there's hardly a soul tramping about. Winter camping, though, is only for the hardy.

» **Facilities** vary widely. Backcountry sites offer little more than pit toilets and fire rings, and have no potable water. Unserviced (tent) campgrounds come with access to drinking water and a washroom with toilets and sometimes showers. The best-equipped sites feature

Newspapers & Magazines

The most widely available newspaper is the Toronto-based *Globe and Mail* and *Maclean's* (www.macleans.ca) is Canada's weekly news magazine. Regional principal dailies:

» *The Chronicle Herald* in Halifax
» *The New Brunswick Telegraph Journal* in Saint John
» *The Guardian* in Charlottetown
» *The Telegram* in St John's

Television

The Canadian Broadcasting Corporation (CBC) is the dominant nationwide network for both radio and TV. The Canadian TV Network (CTN) is the major competition.

Measurements

Canada officially uses the metric system, but imperial measurements are used for many day-to-day purposes. To convert between the two systems, see the chart on the inside front cover.

Smoking

Smoking is banned in all restaurants, bars and other public venues nationwide.

flush toilets and hot showers, and water, electrical and sewer hookups for recreational vehicles (RVs).

» **Fees** in national and provincial parks range from about $20 to $30 for tents up to $39 for full hookup sites per night; fire permits often cost a few dollars extra. Backcountry camping costs about $14 per night. Private campgrounds tend to be a bit pricier. BC's parks, in particular, have seen a hefty rate increase in recent years.

» **Availability** is on a first-come-first-served basis at most government-run sites and fills up quickly, especially in July and August. Several national parks participate in Parks Canada's **camping reservation program** (☑877-737-3783; www.pccamping.ca; reservation fees $10.80), which is a convenient way to make sure you get a spot. Provincial park

reservation information is provided in destination chapters throughout this book.

Homestays

How do you feel about staying on the couch of a perfect stranger? If it's not a problem, consider joining an organization that arranges homestays. The following groups charge no fees to become a member, and the stay itself is also free.

Couch Surfing (www.couchsurfing.com)

Hospitality Club (www.hospitalityclub.org)

Hostels

Canada has independent hostels as well as those affiliated with Hostelling International (HI). All have dorms ($25 to $35 per person on average), which can sleep from two to 10 people, and many have private rooms (from $60) for couples and families. Rooms in HI hostels

THE CHAIN GANG

Budget
Days Inn (☎800-329-7466; www.daysinn.com)
Econo Lodge (☎877-424-6423; www.econolodge.com)
Super 8 (☎800-800-8000; www.super8.com)

Midrange
Best Western (☎800-780-7234; www.bestwestern.com)
Clarion Hotel (☎877-424-6423; www.clarionhotel.com)
Comfort Inn (☎877-424-6423; www.comfortinn.com)
Fairfield Inn (☎800-228-2800; www.fairfieldinn.com)
Hampton Inn (☎800-426-7866; www.hamptoninn.com)
Holiday Inn (☎888-465-4329; www.holidayinn.com)
Howard Johnson (☎800-446-4656; www.hojo.com)
Quality Inn & Suites (☎877-424-6423; www.qualityinn.com)
Travelodge/Thriftlodge (☎800-578-7878; www.travelodge.com)

Top End
Delta (☎877-814-7706; www.deltahotels.com)
Fairmont (☎800-257-7544; www.fairmont.com)
Hilton (☎800-445-8667; www.hilton.com)
Hyatt (☎888-591-1234; www.hyatt.com)
Marriott (☎888-236-2427; www.marriott.com)
Radisson (☎888-201-1718; www.radisson.com)
Ramada (☎800-272-6232; www.ramada.com)
Sheraton (☎800-325-3535; www.sheraton.com)
Westin (☎800-937-8461; www.westin.com)

are gender segregated and alcohol and smoking are prohibited; nonmembers pay a surcharge of about $4 per night.

Bathrooms are usually shared, and facilities include a kitchen, lockers, internet access, laundry room and common TV room. Most hostels, especially those in big cities, are open 24 hours. If not, ask if you can make special arrangements if you're arriving late.

For additional information and online reservations:
Backpackers Hostels Canada (www.backpackers.ca) Independent hostels
Hostelling International Canada (www.hihostels.ca)
Hostels.com (www.hostels.com) Includes independent and HI hostels

Hotels & Motels
Most hotels are part of international chains, and the newer ones are designed for either the luxury market or business people. Rooms have cable TV and wi-fi; many also have swimming pools and fitness and business centers. Rooms with two double or queen-sized beds sleep up to four people, although there is usually a small surcharge for the third and fourth person. Many places advertise that 'kids stay free' but sometimes you have to pay extra for a crib or a rollaway (portable bed).

In Canada, like the US (both lands of the automobile), motels are ubiquitous. They dot the highways and cluster in groups on the outskirts of towns and cities. Although most motel rooms won't win any style awards, they're usually clean and comfortable and offer good value for travelers. Many regional motels remain your typical 'mom and pop' operations, but plenty of North American chains have also opened up around the region (see the boxed text, left, for contact information).

University Accommodations
In the lecture-free summer months, some universities and colleges rent beds in their student dormitories to travelers of all ages. Most rooms are quite basic, but with rates ranging from $25 to $40 a night, often including breakfast, you know you're not getting the Ritz. Students usually qualify for small discounts.

Activities
Snowboarding, sea kayaking, mountain biking – there's so much to do we've devoted a whole chapter to Nova Scotia, New Brunswick, PEI and Newfoundland's Outdoor Activities (see p236). Other resources:
Parks Canada (www.pc.gc.ca) National park action
Canada Trails (www.canadatrails.ca) Hiking, biking, cross-country skiing
Canadian Ski Council (www.skicanada.org) Skiing and snowboarding
Paddling Canada (www.paddlingcanada.com) Kayaking and canoeing
Alpine Club of Canada (www.alpineclubofcanada.ca) Climbing and mountaineering

Business Hours
The following list provides 'normal' opening hours for businesses. Reviews throughout this book show

specific hours only if they vary from these standards. Note, too, that hours can vary by season. The listings in this book are for peak season operating times.

Banks: 10am to 5pm Monday to Friday; some open 9am to noon Saturday

General office hours: 9am to 5pm Monday to Friday

Museums: 10am to 5pm daily, sometimes closed on Monday

Restaurants: breakfast 8am to 11am, lunch 11:30am to 2:30pm Monday to Friday, dinner 5pm to 9:30pm daily; some open for brunch 8am to 1pm Saturday to Sunday

Bars: 5pm to 2am daily

Clubs: 9pm to 2am Wednesday to Saturday

Shops: 10am to 6pm Monday to Saturday, noon to 5pm Sunday, some open to 8pm or 9pm Thursday and/or Friday

Supermarkets: 9am to 8pm, some open 24 hours

Children

These Canadian provinces were made for kids. As if seeing moose, eagles and whales or running around in the snow, on the beach or in the woods all day wasn't fun enough, everywhere you turn those crafty Canadians have cooked up some hands-on learning experience, living history lesson or child-oriented theater.

Lonely Planet's *Travel with Children* offers a wealth of tips and tricks. The website **Travel With Your Kids** (www.travelwithyourkids.com) is another good, general resource.

Practicalities

Children who are traveling to Canada without both parents need authorization from the nonaccompanying parent (see p264).

Once in Canada, kids receive a wide range of discounts on attraction admissions and transportation fares. Usually kids aged six to 17 are half price; younger children are free. Ask about 'family' admissions if your posse consists of two adults and two or more kids.

Kids often stay for free in hotels and motels. B&Bs are not so gracious, and may even refuse to accept pint-sized patrons. Ask when booking. Most restaurants other than fine-dining establishments will usually offer you booster seats and anything else you might need as soon as you steer your family through the door. Children's menus are widely available as well.

Baby food, infant formula, milk, disposable diapers (nappies) and the like are widely available in drugstores and supermarkets. Breastfeeding in public is legal. In all vehicles, children under 18kg must be restrained in safety seats (p266).

For specific suggestions, see the For Children sections throughout the regional chapters of this book. In addition, most tourist offices can lead you to resources for children's programs, childcare facilities and pediatricians.

Customs Regulations

The **Canada Border Services Agency** (CBSA; www.cbsa.gc.ca) has the customs lowdown. A few regulations to note:

Alcohol You can bring in 1.5L of wine, 1.14L of liquor or 24 355mL beers duty free.

Gifts You can bring in gifts totaling up to $60.

Money You can bring in/take out up to $10,000; larger amounts must be reported to customs.

Personal effects Camping gear, sports equipment, cameras and laptop computers can be brought in without much trouble. Declaring these to customs as you cross the border might save you some hassle when you leave, especially if you'll be crossing the US-Canadian border multiple times.

Pets You must carry a signed and dated certificate from a veterinarian to prove your dog or cat has had a rabies shot in the past 36 months.

Prescription drugs You can bring in/take out a 90-day supply for personal use (though if you're bringing it to the USA, know it's technically illegal, but overlooked for individuals).

Tobacco You can bring in 200 cigarettes, 50 cigars, 200g of tobacco and 200 tobacco sticks duty free.

Discount Cards

Discounts are commonly offered for seniors, children, families and people with disabilities, though no special cards are issued (you get the savings on site when you pay). AAA and other automobile association members also receive various travel-related discounts. Many cities have discount cards for local attractions; see the destination information for details.

International Student Identity Card (ISIC; www.isiccard.com) Provides students with discounts on travel insurance and admission to museums and other sights. There are also cards for those who are under 26 but not students, and for full-time teachers.

Parks Canada Discovery Pass (www.pc.gc.ca/voyage-travel/carte-pass/index_e.asp; adult/child 6-16yr/family $68/33/136) Provides access to 27 national parks throughout Canada (seven in the regions covered in this book) and 77 historic sites (a whopping 22 of them in the Atlantic and Maritime provinces) for a year. It can pay for itself in as few as seven visits over daily entry fees; also provides quicker entry into sites.

Embassies & Consulates

All countries have their embassies in Ottawa although a few maintain consulates in Nova Scotia, New Brunswick and/or Newfoundland.

Ottawa

Australia (☎613-236-0841; www.ahc-ottawa.org; ste 710, 50 O'Connor St, Ottawa, ON K1P 6L2)

New Zealand (☎613-238-5991; www.nzembassy.com; ste 727, 99 Bank St, Ottawa, ON K1P 6G3)

UK (☎613-237-2008; www.ukincanada.fco.gov.uk; 80 Elgin St, Ottawa, ON K1P 5K7)

Nova Scotia

France (☎902-494-0999; ngilfoy@progresscorp.com; 1660 Hollis St, Halifax, NS B3J 1V7)

Germany (☎902-420-1599; achapman@coxandpalmer.com; 1100 Purdy's Wharf Tower 1 1959 Upper Water St, Halifax, NS B3J 3E5)

Italy (☎902-494-3934; itconsul@netcom.ca; 1100 Purdy's Wharf Tower 1 1959 Upper Water St, Halifax, NS B3J 3E5)

Japan (☎902-421-1330; www.ca.emb-japan.go.jp; Robertson-Surette Ltd Cornwallis House 5475 Spring Garden Rd 6th fl Halifax, NS B3J 3T2)

Mexico (☎902-466-3678; gcarrera@ns.sympatico.ca; 130 Lakeshore Park Trc, Dartmouth, NS B3A 4Z4)

Netherlands (☎902-422-1485; dutchconsulatehalifax.ns.sympatico.ca; 2000 Barrington St ste 801, Halifax, NS B3J 3K1)

USA (☎902-429-2480; http://ottawa.usembassy.gov; Purdy's Tower II, ste 904, 1969 Upper Water St, Halifax NZ B3J 3R7)

New Brunswick

France (☎506-857-4191; cmoncton@nbet.ca.nb; 777 Main St ste 100, Moncton, NB E1C 1E9)

Netherlands (☎506-453-7771; Cox & Palmer, 371 Queen Street Fredericton, NB E3B 4Y9)

Newfoundland

France (☎709-758-8190; ngilfoy@progresscorp.com; 115 Cavendish Sq, St John's, NF A1C 5W8)

Germany (☎709-739-9727; 2 Winter Pl, St John's, NF A1C 5W8)

Ireland (☎709-738-6280; 34 Harvey Rd 5th fl, St John's, NF A1C 5W8)

Italy (☎709-368-8800; delcontracting@nl.rogers.com; 8 Circular Rd, St John's, NF A1C 5W8)

Japan (☎709-722-4166; viciyoung@hotmail.com; 9 Primrose Pl, St John's, NF A1C 5W8)

Electricity

120v/60hz

120v/60hz

Gay & Lesbian Travelers

Canada is tolerant when it comes to gays and lesbians, though this outlook is more common in the big cities than in rural areas. Same-sex marriage is legal throughout the country (Canada is one of only 10 nations worldwide that permits this).

Halifax is by far this region's gayest city, with a humming nightlife scene, publications and lots of associations and support groups. It has a sizeable Pride celebration, too, which attracts big crowds. For more details, see the boxed texts on p41. While very low-key, PEI also has a decent-sized gay population and has a small pride event in July.

The following are good resources for gay travel; they include Canadian information, though not all are exclusive to the region.

Damron (www.damron.com) Publishes travel guides-*Men's Travel Guide, Women's Traveller* and *Damron Accommodations;* gay-friendly tour operators are listed on the website, too.

Gay Canada (www.gaycanada.com) Search by province or city for queer-friendly businesses and resources.

Gay Travel News (www.gaytravelnews.com) Website listing gay-friendly destinations and hotels.

Out Traveler (www.outtraveler.com) Gay travel magazine.

Purple Roofs (www.purpleroofs.com) Website listing queer accommodations, travel agencies and tours worldwide.

Queer Canada (www.queercanada.ca) A general resource.

Xtra (www.xtra.ca) Source for gay and lesbian news nationwide.

Health
BEFORE YOU GO
INSURANCE
Canada offers some of the finest health care in the world. The problem is that, unless you are a Canadian citizen, it can be prohibitively expensive. It's essential to purchase travel health insurance if your regular policy doesn't cover you when you're abroad. Check www.lonelyplanet.com/travel_services for supplemental insurance information.

Bring medications you may need clearly labeled in their original containers. A signed, dated letter from your physician that describes your medical conditions and medications, including generic names, is also a good idea.

RECOMMENDED VACCINATIONS
No special vaccines are required or recommended for travel to Canada. All travelers should be up to date on routine immunizations, listed in the boxed text, below.

MEDICAL CHECKLIST
» acetaminophen (eg Tylenol) or aspirin
» anti-inflammatory drugs (eg ibuprofen)
» antihistamines (for hay fever and allergic reactions)
» antibacterial ointment (eg Neosporin) for cuts and abrasions
» steroid cream or cortisone (for poison ivy and other allergic rashes)
» bandages, gauze, gauze rolls
» adhesive or paper tape
» safety pins, tweezers
» thermometer
» DEET-containing insect repellent for the skin
» permethrin-containing

insect spray for clothing, tents and bed nets
» sunblock
» motion-sickness medication

WEBSITES
Canadian resources:
Public Health Agency of Canada (www.publichealth.gc.ca)
General resources:
MD Travel Health (www.mdtravelhealth.com)
World Health Organization (www.who.int) Government travel health websites:
Australia (www.smarttraveller.gov.au)
United Kingdom (www.nhs.gov/healthcareabroad)
United States (www.cdc.gov/travel/)

IN CANADA
AVAILABILITY & COST OF HEALTH CARE
Medical services are widely available. For emergencies, the best bet is to find the nearest hospital and go to its emergency room. If the problem isn't urgent, call a nearby hospital and ask for a referral to a local physician, which is usually cheaper than a trip to the emergency room (where costs can be $500 or so before any treatment).

IMMUNIZE YOURSELF

VACCINE	RECOMMENDED FOR	DOSAGE	SIDE EFFECTS
chickenpox	travelers who've never had chickenpox	two doses one month apart	fever, mild case of chickenpox
influenza	all travelers during flu season (November through March)	one dose	soreness at the injection site, fever
measles	travelers born after 1956 who've had only one measles vaccination	one dose	fever, rash, joint pains, allergic reactions
tetanus-diphtheria	all travelers who haven't had booster within 10 years	one dose lasts 10 years	soreness at injection site

Pharmacies are abundant, but prescriptions can be expensive without insurance. However, Americans may find Canadian prescription drugs to be cheaper than drugs at home. You're allowed to take out a 90-day supply for personal use (though know it's technically illegal to bring them into the USA, but overlooked for individuals).

INFECTIOUS DISEASES
Most are acquired by mosquito or tick bites, or environmental exposure. The **Public Health Agency of Canada** (www.publichealth.gc.ca) has details on all listed below.

Giardiasis Intestinal infection. Avoid drinking directly from lakes, ponds, streams and rivers.

Lyme Disease Occurs mostly in southern Canada. Transmitted by deer ticks in late spring and summer. Perform a tick check after you've been outdoors.

Severe Acute Respiratory Syndrome (SARS) At the time of writing, SARS has been brought under control in Canada.

West Nile Virus Mosquito-transmitted in late summer and early fall. Prevent by keeping covered (wear long sleeves, long pants, hats, and shoes rather than sandals) and apply a good insect repellent, preferably one containing DEET, to exposed skin and clothing.

ENVIRONMENTAL HAZARDS
Cold exposure This can be a significant problem, especially in the northern regions. Keep all body surfaces covered, including the head and neck. Watch out for the 'Umbles' – stumbles, mumbles, fumbles and grumbles – which are signs of impending hypothermia.

Heat exhaustion Dehydration is the main contributor. Symptoms include feeling weak, headache, nausea and sweaty skin. Lay the victim flat with their legs raised, apply cool, wet cloths to the skin, and rehydrate.

Insurance
See p253 for health insurance and p265 for car insurance.

Travel Insurance
Make sure you have adequate travel insurance, whatever the length of your trip. At a minimum, you need coverage for medical emergencies and treatment, including hospital stays and an emergency flight home. Medical treatment for non-Canadians is very expensive.

Also consider insurance for luggage theft or loss. If you already have a homeowners or renters policy, check what it will cover and only get supplemental insurance to protect against the rest. If you have prepaid a large portion of your vacation, trip cancellation insurance is worthwhile.

Worldwide travel insurance is available at www.lonelyplanet.com/travel_services. You can buy, extend and claim online at anytime – even if you're already on the road. Also check the following providers.

Insure.com (www.insure.com)

Travelex (www.travelex.com)

Travel Guard (www.travelguard.com)

Internet Access
It's easy to find internet access. Libraries, schools and community agencies in practically every town provide free high-speed internet terminals for public use, travelers included. The only downsides are that usage time is limited (usually 30 minutes), facilities have erratic hours and you may not be able to upload photos (it depends on the facility). The government's **Community Access Program** (http://www.ic.gc.ca/eic/site/cap-pac.nsf/eng/home) provides the services.

Internet cafes are limited to the main tourist areas, and access generally costs $3 to $4 per hour.

Wi-fi is widely available. Most lodgings have it (in-room, with good speed), as do many urban coffee shops and bars. We've identified sleeping, eating and drinking listings that have wi-fi with a 🛜. We've denoted lodgings that offer internet terminals for guest use with a @.

Check the regional Information sections throughout the book for suggested facilities where you can go online.

Legal Matters
Police
If you're arrested or charged with an offense, you have the right to keep your mouth shut and to hire any lawyer you wish (contact your embassy for a referral, if necessary). If you cannot afford one, be sure to ask to be represented by public counsel. There is a presumption of innocence.

Drugs & Alcohol
The blood-alcohol limit is 0.08% and driving cars, motorcycles, boats and snowmobiles while drunk is a criminal offense. If you are caught, you may face stiff fines, license suspension and other nasty consequences.

Consuming alcohol anywhere other than at a residence or licensed premises is also a no-no, which puts parks, beaches and the rest of the great outdoors off limits, at least officially.

Avoid illegal drugs, as penalties may entail heavy fines and possible jail time, as well as a criminal record. The only exception is the use of marijuana for medical purposes, which became legal in 2001. Meanwhile, the decriminalization of pot possession for personal use remains a subject of ongoing debate among the general public and in the parliament.

Other

» Abortion is legal.

» Travelers should note that they can be prosecuted under the law of their home country regarding age of consent, even when abroad.

Maps

Most tourist offices distribute free provincial road maps.

For extended hikes or multiday backcountry treks, it's a good idea to carry a topographic map. The best are the series of 1:50,000 scale maps published by the government's **Centre for Topographic Information** (http://maps.nrcan.gc.ca). These are sold by around 900 map dealers around the country; check the website for vendors.

You can also download and print maps from **Geo-Base** (www.geobase.ca).

Money

All prices quoted throughout this book are in Canadian dollars ($), unless stated otherwise.

Canadian coins come in 1¢ (penny), 5¢ (nickel), 10¢ (dime), 25¢ (quarter), $1 (loonie) and $2 (toonie or twoonie) denominations. The gold-colored loonie features the loon, a common Canadian water bird, while the two-toned toonie is decorated with a polar bear.

Paper currency comes in $5 (blue), $10 (purple), $20 (green) and $50 (red) denominations. The $100 (brown) and larger bills are less common, and are tough to change.

The Canadian dollar has seen fluctuations over the last decade, though since 2007 it has tracked quite closely to the US dollar.

For changing money in the larger cities, currency exchange offices may offer better conditions than banks.

See Need to Know (p11) for exchange rates and costs.

ATMs

Many grocery and convenience stores, airports, and bus, train and ferry stations have ATMs. Most are linked to international networks, the most common being Cirrus, Plus, Star and Maestro.

Most ATMs also spit out cash if you use a major credit card. This method tends to be more expensive because, in addition to a service fee, you'll be charged interest immediately (in other words, there's no interest-free period as there is with purchases). For exact fees, check with your own bank or credit card company.

Visitors heading to Canada's more remote regions (such as in Newfoundland) won't find an abundance of ATMs, so it is wise to cash up beforehand.

Scotiabank, common throughout Canada, is part of the Global ATM Alliance. If your home bank is a member, fees may be less if you withdraw from Scotiabank ATMs.

Cash

Most Canadians don't carry large amounts of cash for everyday use, relying instead on credit and debit cards. Still, carrying some cash, say $100 or less, comes in handy when making small purchases. In some cases, cash is necessary to pay for rural B&Bs and shuttle vans; inquire in advance to avoid surprises. Note that shops and businesses rarely accept personal checks.

Credit Cards

Major credit cards such as MasterCard, Visa and American Express are widely accepted in Canada, except in remote, rural communities where cash is king. You'll find it hard or impossible to rent a car, book a room or order tickets over the phone without having a piece of plastic. Note that some credit card companies charge a 'transaction fee' (which is around 3% of whatever you purchased); ensure you check with your provider to avoid surprises.

For lost or stolen cards, these numbers operate 24 hours:

American Express (866-296-5198; www.americanexpress.com)

MasterCard (800-307-7309; www.mastercard.com)

Visa (800-847-2911; www.visa.com)

Taxes & Refunds

Canada's federal goods and services tax (GST), variously known as the 'gouge and screw' or 'grab and steal' tax, adds 5% to just about every transaction. Most provinces also charge a provincial sales tax (PST) on top of it. Several provinces have combined the GST and PST into a harmonized sales tax (HST). Whatever the methodology, expect to pay 10% to 15% in all. Unless otherwise stated, taxes are not included in prices given.

You might be eligible for a rebate on some of the taxes. If you've booked your accommodations in conjunction with a rental car, plane ticket or other service (ie if it all appears on the same bill from a 'tour operator'), you should be eligible to get 50% of the tax refunded from your accommodations. Fill out the GST/HST Refund Application for Tour Packages form available from the **Canada Revenue Agency** (☎902-432-5608, 800-668-4748; www.cra-arc.gc.ca/E/pbg/gf/gst115).

TAX RATES (GST + PST)

New Brunswick*	13%
Newfoundland*	13%
Nova Scotia*	15%
Prince Edward Island	15%

*has a combined HST

Tipping
Tipping is standard practice.

TIPPING RATES

Restaurant waitstaff	15% to 20%
Bar staff	$1 per drink
Hotel bellhop	$1 to $2 per bag
Hotel room cleaners	$2 per day
Taxis	10% to 15%

Traveler's Checks
Traveler's checks are becoming obsolete in the age of ATMs. Traveler's checks issued in Canadian dollars are generally treated like cash by businesses. Traveler's checks in most other currencies must be exchanged for Canadian dollars at a bank or foreign currency office. The most common issuers:

American Express (www.americanexpress.com)
MasterCard (www.mastercard.com)
Visa (www.visa.com)

POSTAL ABBREVIATIONS

PROVINCES & TERRITORIES	ABBREVIATIONS
New Brunswick	NB
Newfoundland & Labrador	NL
Nova Scotia	NS
Prince Edward Island	PE

Post
Canada's national postal service, **Canada Post/Postes Canada** (www.canadapost.ca), is neither quick nor cheap, but it is reliable. Stamps are available at post offices, drugstores, convenience stores and hotels.

Postcards or standard letters cost 57¢ within Canada, $1 to the USA and $1.70 to all other countries. Travelers often find they have to pay high duties on items sent to them while in Canada, so beware.

Public Holidays
Canada observes 10 national public holidays a year and more at the provincial level. Banks, schools and government offices close on these days.

National Holidays
New Year's Day January 1
Good Friday March or April
Easter Monday March or April
Victoria Day Monday before May 25
Canada Day July 1; called Memorial Day in Newfoundland
Labour Day First Monday of September
Thanksgiving Second Monday of October
Remembrance Day November 11
Christmas Day December 25
Boxing Day December 26

Provincial Holidays
Some provinces also observe local holidays, with Newfoundland leading the pack.
St Patrick's Day Monday nearest March 17
St George's Day Monday nearest April 23
National Day Monday nearest June 24 in Newfoundland
Orangemen's Day Monday nearest July 12 in Newfoundland
Civic Holiday First Monday of August everywhere *except* Newfoundland and PEI

School Holidays
Children break for summer holidays in late June and don't return to school until early September. University students get even more time off, usually from May to early or mid-September. Most people take their big annual vacation during these months.

Telephone
Canada's phone system is almost identical to the USA's system.

Domestic & International Dialing
Canadian phone numbers consist of a three-digit area code followed by a seven-digit local number. In many parts of Canada, you must dial all 10 digits preceded by ☎1, even if you're calling across the street. In other parts of the country, when you're calling within the same area code, you can dial

the seven-digit number only, but this is slowly changing. The pay phone or phone book where you are should make it clear which system is used.

For direct international calls, dial ☑011 + country code + area code + local phone number. The country code for Canada is ☑1 (which is the same as for the USA, although international rates still apply for all calls made between the two countries).

Toll-free numbers begin with ☑800, ☑877 or ☑866 and must be preceded by ☑1. Some of these numbers are good throughout Canada and the USA, others only work within Canada, and some work in just one province.

Emergency Numbers

Dial ☑911. Note it is *not* the emergency number in the Yukon, Northwest Territories or Nunavut.

Cell Phones

Local SIM cards can be used in European and Australian phones. Other phones must be set to roaming.

If you have a European, Australian or other type of unlocked GSM phone, buy a SIM card from local providers such as **Telus** (www.telus.com), **Rogers** (www.rogers.com) or **Bell** (www.bell.ca).

US residents can often upgrade their domestic cell phone plan to extend to Canada. **Verizon** (www.verizonwireless.com) provides good results.

Reception is poor in rural areas no matter who your service provider is.

Public Phones

Coin-operated public pay phones are fairly plentiful. Local calls cost 25¢ (sometimes 35¢); many phones also accept prepaid phonecards and credit cards. Dialing the operator (☑0) or directory assistance (☑411 for local calls, ☑1 + area code + ☑555-1212 for long-distance calls) is free of charge from public phones; it may incur a charge from private phones.

Phonecards

Prepaid phonecards usually offer the best per-minute rates for long-distance and international calling. They come in denominations of $5, $10 and $20 and are widely sold in drugstores, supermarkets and convenience stores. Beware of cards with hidden charges such as 'activation fees' or a per-call connection fee. A surcharge ranging from 30¢ to 85¢ for calls made from public pay phones is common.

Time

Canada spans six of the world's 24 time zones. The Eastern zone in Newfoundland is unusual in that it's only 30 minutes different from the adjacent zone. The time difference from coast to coast is 4½ hours.

Canada observes daylight saving time, which comes into effect on the second Sunday in March, when clocks are put forward one hour, and ends on the first Sunday in November.

UNIQUELY CANADIAN CELEBRATIONS

» **National Flag Day** (February 15) Commemorates the first time the maple-leaf flag was raised above Parliament Hill in Ottawa, at the stroke of noon on February 15, 1965.

» **Victoria Day** (late May) This day was established in 1845 to observe the birthday of Queen Victoria and now celebrates the birthday of the British sovereign who's still Canada's titular head of state. Victoria Day marks the official beginning of the summer season (which ends with Labour Day on the first Monday of September). Some communities hold fireworks.

» **National Aboriginal Day** (June 21) Created in 1996, it celebrates the contributions of Aboriginal peoples to Canada. Coinciding with the summer solstice, festivities are organized locally and may include traditional dancing, singing and drumming; storytelling; arts and crafts shows; canoe races; and lots more.

» **Canada Day** (July 1) Known as Dominion Day until 1982, Canada Day was created in 1869 to commemorate the creation of Canada two years earlier. All over the country, people celebrate with barbecues, parades, concerts and fireworks.

» **Thanksgiving Day** (mid-October) First celebrated in 1578 in what is now Newfoundland by explorer Martin Frobisher to give thanks for surviving his Atlantic crossing. Thanksgiving became an official Canadian holiday in 1872 to celebrate the recovery of the Prince of Wales from a long illness. These days, it's essentially a harvest festival involving a special family dinner of roast turkey and pumpkin, very much as it is practiced in the US.

Occasionally and especially in francophone areas, times for shop hours, train schedules, film screenings etc are usually indicated by the 24-hour clock.

TIME DIFFERENCE BETWEEN CITIES

Vancouver	3pm
New York City	6pm
Halifax, Fredericton & Charlottetown	7pm
Newfoundland	7:30pm
London	11pm

Tourist Information

The **Canadian Tourism Commission** (www.canada. travel) is loaded with general information, packages and links.

All provincial tourist offices maintain comprehensive websites packed with information helpful in planning your trip. Staff also field telephone enquiries and, upon request, will mail out free maps and directories about accommodations, attractions and events. Some offices can also help with making hotel, tour or other reservations.

For detailed information about a specific area, contact the local tourist office, aka visitors center. Just about every city and town has at least a seasonal branch with helpful staff, racks of free pamphlets and books and maps for sale. Visitor center addresses are listed in the Information sections for individual destinations throughout this book.

Provincial tourist offices include:

Tourism New Brunswick (☏800-561-0123; www.tourism newbrunswick.ca)

Newfoundland & Labrador Tourism (☏800-563-6353; www.newfoundlandlabrador. com)

Tourism Nova Scotia (☏800-565-0000; www. novascotia.com)

Prince Edward Island Tourism (☏800-463-4734; www.peiplay.com)

Travelers with Disabilities

Canada is making progress when it comes to easing the everyday challenges facing people with disabilities, especially the mobility impaired.

Many public buildings, including museums, tourist offices, train stations, shopping malls and cinemas, have access ramps and/or lifts. Most public restrooms feature extra-wide stalls equipped with hand rails. Many pedestrian crossings have sloping curbs.

Newer and recently remodeled hotels, especially chain hotels, have rooms with extra-wide doors and spacious bathrooms.

Interpretive centers at national and provincial parks are usually accessible, and many parks have trails that can be navigated in wheelchairs.

Car rental agencies offer hand-controlled vehicles and vans with wheelchair lifts at no additional charge, but you must reserve them well in advance. See p265 for a list of rental agencies.

For accessible air, bus, rail and ferry transportation check **Access to Travel** (www.accesstotravel.gc.ca), the federal government's website. In general, most transportation agencies can accommodate people with disabilities if you make your needs known when booking.

Other organizations specializing in the needs of travelers with disabilities:

Access-Able Travel Source (www.access-able. com) Lists accessible lodging, transport, attractions and equipment rental by province.

Canadian National Institute for the Blind (www. cnib.ca)

Canadian Paraplegic Association (www.can paraplegic.org) Information about facilities for mobility-impaired travelers in Canada.

Mobility International (www.miusa.org) Advises travelers with disabilities on mobility issues and runs an educational exchange program.

Society for Accessible Travel & Hospitality (www. sath.org) Travelers with disabilities share tips and blogs.

Visas

For information about passport requirements, see p261.

Citizens of dozens of countries – including the USA, most Western European nations, Australia, New Zealand, Japan and South Korea – do not need visas to enter Canada for stays of up to 180 days. US permanent residents are also exempt. **Citizenship & Immigration Canada** (CIC; www.cic.gc.ca) has the details.

Nationals of other countries – including China, India and South Africa – must apply to the Canadian visa office in their home country for a temporary resident visa (TRV). A separate visa is required if you plan to study or work in Canada.

Single-entry TRVs ($75) are usually valid for a maximum stay of six months from the date of your arrival in Canada. Multiple-entry TRVs ($150) allow you to enter Canada from all other countries multiple times while the visa is valid (usually two or three years), provided no single stay exceeds six months.

Visa extensions ($75) need to be filed with the **CIC Visitor Case Processing Centre** (☏888-242-2100; ⊗8am-4pm Mon-Fri) in Alberta at least one month before your current visa expires.

Visiting the USA

Admission requirements are subject to rapid change. The **US State Department** (www.travel.state.gov) has the latest information, or check with a US consulate in your home country.

Under the US visa-waiver program, visas are not required for citizens of 36 countries – including most EU members, Australia and New Zealand – for visits of up to 90 days (no extensions allowed), as long as you can present a machine-readable passport and are approved under the **Electronic System for Travel Authorization** (ESTA; www.cbp.gov/esta).

Canadians do not need visas, though they do need a passport or document approved by the **Western Hemisphere Travel Initiative** (www.getyouhome.gov). Citizens of all other countries need to apply for a US visa in their home country before arriving in Canada.

All visitors, regardless of their country of origin, are subject to a US$6 entry fee at land border crossings. Note that you don't need a Canadian multiple-entry TRV for repeated entries into Canada from the USA, unless you have visited a third country.

Volunteering

Volunteering provides the opportunity to interact with local folks and the land in ways you never would just passing through. Many organizations charge a fee, which varies depending on the program's length and the type of food and lodging it provides. The fees usually do not cover travel to Canada. Groups that use volunteers:
Churchill Northern Studies Centre (www.churchillscience.ca) Volunteer for

six hours per day (anything from stringing wires to cleaning) and get free room and board at this center for polar bear and other wildlife research.
Earthwatch (www.earthwatch.org) Help scientists track whales off the coast of British Columbia, track moose and deer in Nova Scotia, and monitor climate change in Churchill, Manitoba or the Mackenzie Mountains of the Northwest Territories. Trips last between seven and 14 days and cost from $2250 to $5050.
Volunteers for Peace (www.vfp.org) Offers tutoring stints in Aboriginal communities in Canada's far north, as well as projects in Québec.
World-Wide Opportunities on Organic Farms (www.wwoof.ca; application fee $45) Work on an organic farm, usually in exchange for free room and board; check the website for locations throughout Canada.

Women Travelers

Canada is generally a safe place for women to travel, even alone and even in the cities. Simply use the same common sense as you would at home.

In bars and nightclubs, solo women are likely to attract a lot of attention, but if you don't want company, most men will respect a firm 'no thank you.' If you feel threatened, protesting loudly will often make the offender slink away – or will at least spur other people to come to your defense. Note that carrying mace or pepper spray is illegal in Canada.

Physical attack is unlikely, but if you are assaulted, call the police immediately (☎911 except in the Yukon, Northwest Territories and Nunavut) or contact a rape crisis center. A complete list is available from the

Canadian Association of Sexual Assault Centres (☎604-876-2622; www.casac.ca). Has hotlines in some of the cities:
Halifax (☎902-425-0122)
St John's (☎800-726-2743)
Fredericton (☎506-454-0437)
Charlottetown (☎800-289-5656)

Resources for women travelers:
Journeywoman (www.journeywoman.com)
Her Own Way (www.voyage.gc.ca/publications/woman-guide_voyager-feminin-eng.asp) Published by the Canadian government for Canadian travelers, but it contains a great deal of general advice.

Work
Permits

In almost all cases, you need a valid work permit to work in Canada. Obtaining one may be difficult, as employment opportunities go to Canadians first. Before you can even apply, you need a specific job offer from an employer who in turn must have been granted permission from the government to give the position to a foreign national. Applications must be filed at a visa office of a Canadian embassy or consulate in your home country. Some jobs are exempt from the permit requirement. For full details, check with **Citizenship & Immigration Canada** (www.cic.gc.ca/english/work/index.asp).

Employers hiring temporary service workers (such as hotels, bars, restaurants or resorts) and construction, farm or forestry workers sometimes don't ask for a permit. If you get caught, however, you can kiss Canada goodbye.

Finding Work

Students aged 18 to 30 from over a dozen countries,

including the USA, UK, Australia, New Zealand, Ireland and South Africa, are eligible to apply for a spot in the **Student Work Abroad Program** (SWAP; www.swap.ca). If successful, you get a six-month to one-year, nonextendable visa that allows you to work anywhere in Canada in any job you can get. Most 'SWAPpers' find work in the service industry as waiters or bartenders.

Even if you're not a student, you may be able to spend up to a year in Canada on a 'working holiday program' with **International Experience Canada** (www. international.gc.ca/iyp-pij/ intro_incoming-intro_entrant. aspx). The Canadian government has an arrangement with several countries for people aged 18 to 35 to come over and get a job; check the website for participants. The Canadian embassy in each country runs the program, but basically there are quotas and spaces are filled on a first-come first-served basis.

Transportation

GETTING THERE & AWAY

Flights, tours and rail tickets can be booked online at www.lonelyplanet.com/bookings.

Entering the Country

Entering Canada is pretty straightforward. First, you will have to show your passport (and your visa if you need one; see p258). The border officer will ask you a few questions about the purpose and length of your visit. After that, you'll go through customs. See **Going to Canada** (www.goingtocanada.gc.ca) for details.

Note that questioning may be more intense at land border crossings and your car may be searched.

For updates (particularly regarding land-border crossing rules), check the websites for the **US State Department** (www.travel.state.gov) and **Citizenship & Immigration Canada** (www.cic.gc.ca).

Having a criminal record of any kind, including a DUI (driving under the influence) charge, may keep you out of Canada. If this affects you, you should apply for a 'waiver of exclusion' at a Canadian consulate in your country. The process costs $200 and takes several weeks.

Passport

Most international visitors require a passport to enter Canada. US citizens at land and sea borders have other options besides using a passport, such as an enhanced driver's license or passport card. See the **Western Hemisphere Travel Initiative** (www.getyouhome.gov) for approved identification documents.

Visitors from selected countries also require a visa to enter Canada (see p258).

Air

Airports & Airlines

Halifax has the region's largest airport and it's the only one so far to have US preclearance privileges (ie nonstop passengers to the US are processed through customs prior to departure, thus ensuring a no-fuss arrival on the US side). Moncton is also busy, and may offer lower fares than Halifax. For visitors heading to Newfoundland, Deer Lake is a great option if you are centering your travels on the west coast.

Atlantic Canada's main airports:

Charlottetown, Prince Edward Island (YYG; ☎902-566-7997; www.flypei.com)

Deer Lake, Newfoundland (YDF; ☎709-635-3601; www.deerlakeairport.com)

Fredericton, New Brunswick (YFC; ☎506-460-0920; www.frederictonairport.ca)

Halifax, Nova Scotia (YHZ; ☎902-873-4422; www.hiaa.ca)

Moncton, New Brunswick (YQM; ☎506-856-5444; www.gma.ca)

St John's, Newfoundland (YYT; ☎709-758-8581; www.stjohnsairport.com)

Sydney, Nova Scotia (YQY; ☎902-564-7720)

AIRLINES FLYING TO & FROM NOVA SCOTIA, NEW BRUNSWICK & PRINCE EDWARD ISLAND

The region is not particularly well serviced, and flight and airline choices are limited. Most visitors will need to fly into Montréal or Toronto, and then connect with another flight to reach their destination in Atlantic Canada. Most flights are via the national flagship carrier Air Canada; it's one of the world's safest airlines, though locals often gripe about its stiff prices. Subsidiary Air Canada Jazz operates the majority of flights to and within the Atlantic region.

Other companies that are based in Canada and are serving international destinations are the charter airline Air Transat and discount airline WestJet. There are numerous US airlines that also serve Atlantic Canada, which are worth researching.

Airlines operating to/from the region:

Air Canada & Air Canada Jazz (AC; ☎888-247-2262; www.aircanada.com)

Every form of transport that relies on carbon-based fuel generates CO_2, the main cause of human-induced climate change. Modern travel is dependent on aeroplanes, which might use less fuel per per person than most cars but travel much greater distances. The altitude at which aircraft emit gases (including CO_2) and particles also contributes to their climate change impact. Many websites offer 'carbon calculators' that allow people to estimate the carbon emissions generated by their journey and, for those who wish to do so, to offset the impact of the greenhouse gases emitted with contributions to portfolios of climate-friendly initiatives throughout the world. Lonely Planet offsets the carbon footprint of all staff and author travel.

Air St-Pierre (PJ; ☎902-873-3566, 877-277-7765; www.airsaintpierre.com)

Air Transat (TS; ☎866-847-1919; www.airtransat.com)

American Airlines (AA; ☎800-433-7300; www.aa.com)

Austrian Airlines (OS; ☎800-843-0002; www.austrian.com)

British Airways (BA; ☎800-247-9297; www.ba.com)

British Midlands (BD; ☎800-788-0555; www.flybmi.com)

Continental Airlines (CO; ☎800-231-0856; www.continental.com)

Delta Airlines (DL; ☎800-241-4141; www.delta.com)

Finn Air (AY; ☎800-950-5000; www.finnair.com)

Iberia (IB; ☎800-772-4642; www.iberia.com)

Lufthansa (LH; ☎800-563-5954; www.lufthansa.com)

Porter Airlines (PD; ☎888-619-8622; www.flyporter.com)

Qantas (QF; ☎800-227-4500; www.qantas.com)

United Airlines (UA; ☎800-241-6522; www.united.ca)

US Airways (US; ☎800-428-4322; www.usairways.com)

WestJet (WS; ☎888-937-8538; www.westjet.com)

Land

Border Crossings

The three major border crossings into Atlantic Canada are between Maine, USA, and New Brunswick at Calais/St Stephen, Mada-waska/Edmundston and Houlton/Woodstock. The website for the **Canadian Border Services Agency** (www.cbsa-asfc.gc.ca/general/times/menu-e.html) has details on estimated wait times. In general, waits rarely exceed 30 minutes, except during the peak summer season and holidays.

When returning to the USA, check the website for the **US Department for Homeland Security** (http://apps.cbp.gov/bwt) for border wait times.

For information on documents needed to enter Canada, see p261.

Bus

Greyhound (☎800-231-2222; www.greyhound.com) and its Canadian equivalent, **Greyhound Canada** (☎800-661-8747; www.greyhound.ca), operate the largest bus network in North America, with services to 3600 destinations. Alas, the Atlantic provinces are not among them, so you'll have to take Greyhound to a gateway city such as Montréal or Bangor (Maine) and then switch to an **Acadian Lines** (☎902-454-9321, 800-567-5151; www.acadianbus.com) bus. The changeover is pretty seamless, and Acadian even honors Greyhound's discounted Discovery Pass (p264). From Halifax, Acadian runs once daily to Bangor ($105, 11 hours), where there are sporadic connections for New York and Boston.

Car & Motorcycle

The USA's extensive highway network connects directly with the Canadian system at numerous key points along the border. These Canadian highways then go on to meet up with the east–west Trans-Canada Hwy, an excellent way to traverse the country.

If you're driving into Canada, you'll need the vehicle's registration papers, proof of liability insurance and your home driver's license. Cars rented in the USA usually can be driven into Canada and back, but make sure your rental agreement says so. If you're driving a car registered in someone else's name, bring a letter from the owner authorizing use of the vehicle in Canada. For general information about border crossings, see p262. For details about driving within Canada, see p265.

Train

Via Rail (☎888-842-7733; www.viarail.ca), Canada's national rail line, offers one service to the Atlantic region: a Montréal to Halifax train (advance purchase adult/child two to 11 years $182/80, 21 hours) that runs daily except Tuesday, and includes several stops in New Brunswick and Nova Scotia. It leaves Montréal at 6:30pm, and arrives in Halifax at 4:20pm the next day.

Visitors coming from the USA can hop aboard America's national rail line, **Amtrak** (☎800-872-7245; www.amtrak.com), and its daily service connecting New York City with Montréal.

Sea

Ferry

Various ferry routes connect Atlantic Canada to the USA and even France:

Nova Scotia The Yarmouth/Maine Ferry was not running at the time of writing but plans were in the works for starting it up again with a new boat in 2011. The ferry previously ran from the towns of Bar Harbor and Portland, Maine and it looks likely that those ports will be used for the service again.

New Brunswick East Coast Ferries links Deer Island to Eastport, Maine (p109).

Newfoundland From the Burin Peninsula, you can reach the French territory of St-Pierre & Miquelon (p189).

GETTING AROUND

Air

Airlines in Nova Scotia, New Brunswick & Prince Edward Island

Most regional flights within the Maritimes are operated by Air Canada's subsidiary, Air Canada Jazz. Small provincial airlines fly out to the more remote portions

of the region. Fares in such noncompetitive markets can be high.

See the Getting There & Away sections of the destination chapters for specific route and fare information. The following are the main carriers flying within Atlantic Canada:

Air Canada & Air Canada Jazz (AC; ☑888-247-2262; www.aircanada.com) Flights throughout the region.

Air Labrador (WJ; ☑709-738-5441, 800-563-3042; www.airlabrador.com) Flights within Newfoundland and Labrador.

Air St-Pierre (PJ; ☑902-873-3566, 877-277-7765; www.airsaintpierre.com) Flights from the French island of St-Pierre to St John's, Halifax, Sydney and Moncton.

Provincial Airlines (PB; ☑800-563-2800; www.provincialairlines.ca) Services throughout Newfoundland and Labrador, as well as to Halifax.

WestJet (WS; ☑888-937-8538; www.westjet.com) Nationwide discount carrier with a route between St John's and Halifax.

Air Passes

Star Alliance (www.staralliance.com) members Air Canada, Continental Airlines, United Airlines and US Airways have teamed up to offer the North American Airpass, which is available to anyone not residing in the USA, Canada, Mexico, Ber-

muda or the Caribbean. It's sold only in conjunction with an international flight operated by any Star Alliance–member airline. You can buy as few as three coupons (US$399) or as many as 10 (US$1099).

Bicycle

The Maritime provinces, particularly Prince Edward Island, are ideal for bicycle touring. See p238 for more on routes and resources.

Transportation

» By air: most airlines will carry bikes as checked luggage without charge on international flights, as long as they're in a box. On domestic flights they usually charge between $30 and $65. Always check details before you buy the ticket.

» By bus: you must ship your bike as freight on Greyhound Canada. In addition to a bike box ($10), you'll be charged according to the weight of the bike, plus an oversize charge ($30) and GST. Bikes only travel on the same bus as the passenger if there's enough space. To ensure that yours arrives at the same time as (or before) you do, ship it a day early.

» By train: VIA Rail will transport your bicycle for $20, but only on trains offering checked-baggage service (which includes all long-distance and many regional trains).

263

TRANSPORTATION SEA

CYCLING RULES & RESOURCES

» Cyclists must follow the same rules of the road as vehicles, but don't expect drivers to always respect your right of way.

» Helmets are mandatory for all cyclists in British Columbia, New Brunswick, Prince Edward Island and Nova Scotia, as well as for anyone under 18 in Alberta and Ontario.

» The **Better World Club** (☑866-238-1137; www.betterworldclub.com) provides emergency roadside assistance. Membership costs $40 per year, plus a $12 enrollment fee, and entitles you to two free pick-ups, and transport to the nearest repair shop, or home, within a 50km radius of where you're picked up.

» For information on Canada's sweetest mountain biking and cycling trails, see p238.

Rental

Outfitters renting bicycles exist in most tourist towns; many are listed throughout this book. Rentals cost around $15 per day for touring bikes and $25 per day for mountain bikes. The price usually includes a helmet and lock. Most companies require a security deposit of $20 to $200.

Purchase

Buying a bike is easy, as is reselling it before you leave. Specialist bike shops have the best selection and advice, but general sporting-goods stores may have lower prices. Some bicycle stores and rental outfitters also sell used bicycles. To sniff out the best bargains, scour flea markets, garage sales and thrift shops, or check the notice boards in hostels and universities. These are also the best places to sell your bike.

Boat

The watery region hosts an extensive ferry system. For details, see the Getting There & Away and Getting Around sections of the destination chapters. Walk-ons and cyclists should be OK anytime, but call ahead for vehicle reservations or if you require a cabin berth. This is especially important during peak season (July and August). Main operators:

Bay Ferries (☎888-249-7245; www.bayferries.com) Year-round service between Saint John, New Brunswick, and Digby, Nova Scotia.

Coastal Transport (☎506-662-3724; www.coastaltransport.ca) Ferry from Blacks Harbour to Grand Manan in the Fundy Isles, New Brunswick.

CTMA Ferries (☎418-986-3278, 888-986-3278; www.ctma.ca) Daily ferries to Québec's Îles de la Madeleine from Souris, Prince Edward Island.

East Coast Ferries (☎506-747-2159, 877-747-2159; www.eastcoastferries.nb.ca) Connects Deer Island to Campobello Island, both in the Fundy Isles, New Brunswick.

Labrador Marine (☎709-535-0810, 866-535-2567; www.labradormarine.com) Connects Newfoundland to Labrador.

Marine Atlantic (☎800-341-7981; www.marine-atlantic.ca) Connects Port aux Basques and Argentia in Newfoundland with North Sydney, Nova Scotia.

Northumberland Ferries (☎902-566-3838, 888-249-7245; www.peiferry.com) Connects Wood Islands, Prince Edward Island and Caribou, Nova Scotia.

Provincial Ferry Services (www.gov.nl.ca/ferryservices) Operates coastal ferries throughout Newfoundland.

Bus

Greyhound Canada does not operate within the Atlantic provinces. The main bus lines in the region:

Acadian Lines (☎902-454-9321, 800-567-5151; www.acadianbus.com) Operates a network throughout Nova Scotia, New Brunswick and Prince Edward Island.

DRL Coachlines (☎709-263-2171; www.drl-lr.com) Service throughout Newfoundland.

Bus frequency ranges from one to two buses per day along most routes. Buses generally are clean, comfortable and reliable. They usually have onboard toilets, air-conditioning (bring a sweater), reclining seats and onboard movies.

A series of small, regional shuttle vans comprises the rest of bus service in the area. These services are detailed in the Getting There & Away sections of the destination chapters. For major shuttle routes see Halifax (p43), Charlottetown (p143), St John's (p176) and Corner Brook (p205).

Bus Passes

Neither Acadian nor DRL offers any special discount passes, though Acadian does honor Greyhound's Discovery Pass (www.discoverypass.com), valid for travel in both the USA and Canada. Note that for short-haul trips, the pass is not necessarily more economical than buying individual tickets. However, it can be worthwhile for onward, long-haul travel.

Costs

Bus travel is cheaper than other means of transport. Advance purchases (four, seven or 14 days) save quite a bit, too. For specific route and fare information, see the Getting There & Away sections of the regional chapters.

Sample fares on Acadian:
Halifax to North Sydney ($79, seven hours)
Halifax to Charlottetown ($70, 5½ hours)
Charlottetown to Moncton ($38, 3½ hours)

Sample fares on DRL Coachlines:

St John's to Corner Brook ($91, 10½ hours)

St John's to Port aux Basques ($131, 13½ hours).

Reservations

Tickets must be bought at bus terminals for Acadian and on the bus (cash only) for DRL; there are no phone or online sales. Show up at least 30 to 45 minutes prior to departure.

Car & Motorcycle

Automobile Associations

Auto-club membership is a handy thing to have in Canada. Try the following:

Better World Club (☏866-238-1137; www.betterworld club.com) donates 1% of its annual revenue to environmental cleanup efforts. It offers service throughout the USA and Canada, and also has a roadside-assistance program for bicycles.

Canadian Automobile Association (CAA; ☏800-268-3750; www.caa.ca) offers services, including 24-hour emergency roadside assistance, to members of international affiliates such as AAA in the USA, AA in the UK and ADAC in Germany. The club also offers trip-planning advice, free maps, travel-agency services and a range of discounts on hotels, car rentals etc.

Bring Your Own Vehicle

There's minimal hassle driving into Canada from the USA as long as you have your vehicle's registration papers, proof of liability insurance and your home driver's license.

Driver's License

In most provinces visitors can legally drive for up to three months with their home driver's license. In some, such as British Columbia, this is extended to six months.

If you're spending considerable time in Canada, think about getting an International Driving Permit (IDP), which is valid for one year. Your automobile association at home can issue one for a small fee. Always carry your home license together with the IDP.

Fuel & Spare Parts

Essentials:

Gas is sold in liters.

At the time of writing, the average for midgrade fuel was $1.08 per liter (about C$4.10 per US gallon).

Prices are higher in remote areas.

Fuel prices in Canada are usually higher than in the USA, so fill up south of the border.

Most gas stations are self-service.

Finding a gas station is generally easy except in sparsely populated areas such as Labrador and Newfoundland's south coast.

Finding spare parts can be difficult far from big cities.

When traveling in remote regions, always bring some tools and at least a spare tire.

Insurance

Canadian law requires liability insurance for all vehicles, to cover you for damage caused to property and people.

The minimum requirement is $200,000 in all provinces except Québec, where it is $50,000.

Americans traveling to Canada in their own car should ask their insurance company for a Nonresident Interprovince Motor Vehicle Liability Insurance Card (commonly known as a 'yellow card'), which is accepted as evidence of financial responsibility anywhere in Canada. Although not mandatory, it may come in handy in an accident.

Car-rental agencies offer liability insurance. Collision Damage Waivers (CDW) reduce or eliminate the amount you'll have to reimburse the rental company if there's damage to the car itself. Some credit cards cover CDW for a certain rental period, if you use the card to pay for the rental, and decline the policy offered by the rental company. Always check with your card issuer to see what coverage they offer in Canada.

Personal accident insurance (PAI) covers you and any passengers for medical costs incurred as a result of an accident. If your travel insurance or your health-insurance policy at home does this as well (and most do, but check), then this is one expense you can do without.

Rental

CAR

To rent a car in Canada you generally need to:

» be at least 25 years old

» hold a valid driver's license (an international one may be required if you're not from an English- or French-speaking country; see Driver's License, left)

» have a major credit card Some companies will rent to drivers between the ages of 21 and 24 for an additional charge.

You should be able to get an economy-sized vehicle for about $35 to $65 per day. Child safety seats are compulsory (reserve them when you book) and cost about $8 per day.

Car-rental prices can double in July and August, and it's essential to book ahead in prime tourist spots such as Charlottetown or St John's, as there often just aren't enough cars to go around.

International car-rental companies usually have branches at airports and in city centers; note that ferry terminals often do not have branches.

Avis (☑800-437-0358; www.avis.com)

Budget (☑800-268-8900; www.budget.com)

Dollar (☑800-800-4000; www.dollar.com)

Enterprise (☑800-736-8222; www.enterprise.com)

Hertz (☑800-263-0600; www.hertz.com)

National (☑800-227-7368; www.nationalcar.com)

Thrifty (☑800-847-4389; www.thrifty.com)

Practicar (☑800-327-0116; www.practicar.ca), formerly known as Rent a Wreck, often has lower rates. It's also affiliated with Backpackers Hotels Canada and Hostelling International.

In Canada, on-the-spot rentals often are more expensive than pre-booked packages (ie rental cars booked online or with your flight).

MOTORCYCLE

Nova Scotia's tourism office produces a free **motorcycle guide** (☑800-565-0000; www.novascotia.com/ride); take a look at **Motorcycle Tour Guide Nova Scotia** (www.motorcycletourguide.com) for online information. Unfortunately there are no Harley rentals available in this region, the nearest are in Montréal, Québec and Bangor, Maine.

Northeastern Motorcycle Tours (www.motorcycletours.com) runs tours along the Cabot Trail from Maine, USA.

RECREATIONAL VEHICLES

Rentals cost roughly $160 to $265 per day in high season for midsize vehicles although insurance, fees and taxes add a hefty chunk. Diesel-fueled RVs have considerably lower running costs.

Canadream Campers (☑403-291-1000, 800-461-7368; www.canadream.com) Rentals from Halifax.

Islander RV (☑709-364-7368, 888-848-2267; www.islanderrv.com) Rentals from St John's.

Road Conditions & Hazards

Road conditions are generally good, but keep in mind:

» Fierce winters can leave potholes the size of landmine craters. Be prepared to swerve. Winter travel in general can be hazardous due to heavy snow and ice, which may cause roads and bridges to close periodically. **Transport Canada** (☑800-387-4999; www.tc.gc.ca/road) provides links to road conditions and construction zones for each province.

» If you're driving in winter or in remote areas, make sure your vehicle is equipped with four-seasonal radial or snow tires, and emergency supplies in case you're stranded.

» Distances between services can be long in sparsely populated areas so keep your gas topped up whenever possible.

» Moose, deer and elk are common on rural roadways, especially at night. There's no contest between a 534kg bull moose and a Subaru, so keep your eyes peeled.

Road Rules

» Canadians drive on the right-hand side of the road.

» Seat-belt use is compulsory. Children under 18kg must be strapped in child-booster seats, except infants, who must be in a rear-facing safety seat.

» Motorcyclists must wear helmets and drive with their headlights on.

» Distances and speed limits are posted in kilometers. The speed limit is generally 40km/h to 50km/h in cities and 90km/h to 110km/h outside town.

» Slow down to 60km/h when passing emergency vehicles (such as police cars and ambulances) stopped on the roadside with their lights flashing.

» Turning right at red lights after coming to a full stop is permitted in all provinces.

» Driving while using a hand-held cell phone is illegal in Newfoundland, Nova Scotia and Prince Edward Island.

» Radar detectors are not allowed. If you're caught driving with a radar detector, even one that isn't being operated, you could receive a fine of $1000 and your device will be confiscated.

» The blood-alcohol limit for drivers is 0.08%. Driving while drunk is a criminal offense.

Hitch-hiking & Ride Sharing

Hitch-hiking

Hitch-hiking is never entirely safe in any country and we don't recommend it. That said, in remote and rural areas in Canada it is not uncommon to see people thumbing for a ride.

» If you do decide to hitch, understand that you are taking a small but potentially serious risk. Remember that it's safer to travel in pairs and let someone know where you are planning to go.

» Hitch-hiking is illegal on some highways and in the provinces of Nova Scotia and New Brunswick although you'll see people hitching there anyway.

Ride Sharing

Many hostels have ride-share boards that can be a boon if you're traveling without a car.

Digihitch (www.canada.digihitch.com) is a decent, if dated, resource.

Autotaxi (www.autotaxi.com) lists rides within Canada and to the USA. You can advertise a ride yourself or make arrangements with drivers going to your destinations.

Local Transportation

Bicycle

Cycling is more of a recreational activity than a means of local transportation in Atlantic Canada. City bike paths are not common. Still, most public transportation allows bicycles to be brought on at certain times of day. See p238 and p263 for more on cycling in the region.

Bus

The only cities in the region with municipal bus services are Fredericton, Saint John, Moncton, Halifax, Sydney and St John's. The Annapolis Valley has an excellent regional bus service between Wolfville and Bridgetown. Elsewhere the private car is king.

Taxi

All the main cities have taxis, which are detailed in the Getting Around sections throughout this book. Taxis usually are metered, with a flag-fall fee of $2.70 and a per-kilometer charge around $1.75. Drivers expect a tip of between 10% and 15%. Taxis can be flagged down or ordered by phone.

Tours

Group travel can be an enjoyable way to go, especially if you're traveling solo. Try to pick a tour that will suit you in terms of age, interest and activity level. For additional packages, check the Tours section for individual destinations throughout this book.

Arctic Odysseys (☎20 6-325-1977, 800 574-3021; www.arcticodysseys.com) Arctic-oriented company with yacht trips up the Newfoundland and Labrador coast.

Backroads (☎510-527-1555, 800-462-2848; www.backroads.com) Guided and self-guided bicycle tours worldwide, including Nova Scotia and Prince Edward Island.

Elderhostel (☎800-454-5768; www.elderhostel.org) Nonprofit organization offering study tours for active people over 55, including bus and walking tours in Atlantic Canada.

Freewheeling Adventures (☎902-857-3600, 800-672-0775; www.freewheeling.ca) Nova Scotia–based company with bicycle tours throughout Atlantic Canada, including bike-and-yoga getaways.

Routes to Learning (☎613-530-2222, 866-745-1690; www.routestolearning.ca) Explore Newfoundland's Vikings, New Brunswick's Acadians or Nova Scotia's lighthouses with this Canadian nonprofit's educational tours.

Salty Bear Adventure Tours (☎902 202-3636, 888-425-2327; www.saltybear.ca) Backpacker-oriented van tours through the Maritimes with jump-on-jump-off flexibility. There's a two-day circuit around Nova Scotia, or a more stimulating four-day route into Cape Breton and beyond.

Train

Train travel is limited within the region. Prince Edward Island and Newfoundland have no train services. Nova Scotia and New Brunswick are served along the **VIA Rail** (☎888-842-7245; www.viarail.ca) Montréal-to-Halifax route. For a train schedule, check the website. Most stations have left-luggage offices.

Western Labrador is also accessible by train: a privately owned service operated by the **Iron Ore Company of Canada** (☎709-944-8400, ask for operator & then 'train service') goes once weekly from Sept Îles, Québec, to Labrador City ($64).

Train buffs should also check out **Canada by Rail** (www.canadabyrail.ca), an excellent portal packed with information on regional excursion trains, railroad museums and historical train stations.

Classes

There are four main classes:

» Economy Class buys you a fairly basic, if indeed quite comfortable, reclining seat with a headrest. Blankets and pillows are provided for overnight travel.

» Sleeper Class is available on shorter overnight routes. You can choose from compartments with upper or lower pullout berths, and private single, double or triple roomettes, all with a bathroom.

» Touring Class is available on long-distance routes and includes Sleeper Class accommodations plus meals, access to the sightseeing car and sometimes a tour guide.

Costs

Taking the train is more expensive than the bus, but most people find it a more comfortable way to travel. June to mid-October is peak season, when prices are about 40% higher. Buying tickets in advance (even just five days before) can yield significant savings.

Reservations

Tickets and train passes are available for purchase online, by phone, at VIA Rail stations and from many travel agents. Seat reservations are highly recommended, especially in summer and for sleeper cars.

Train Passes

The Canrailpass buys 12 days of comfort-class travel within a 30-day period beginning with the first day of travel. It costs $926 during peak season (June to mid-October), and $579 at other times.

The North America Rail Pass allows unlimited travel in the USA and Canada for 30 consecutive days and costs $1149 from June to mid-October and $815 at all other times. All passes can be purchased through VIA Rail.

VIA Rail offers the Canrail-pass-System, good for seven trips on any train during a 21-day period. All seats are in Economy Class; upgrades are not permitted. You must book each leg at least three days in advance (doable online). It costs $941/588 in high/low season.

behind the scenes

SEND US YOUR FEEDBACK

We love to hear from travelers – your comments keep us on our toes and help make our books better. Our well-traveled team reads every word on what you loved or loathed about this book. Although we cannot reply individually to postal submissions, we always guarantee that your feedback goes straight to the appropriate authors, in time for the next edition. Each person who sends us information is thanked in the next edition – and the most useful submissions are rewarded with a free book.

Visit **lonelyplanet.com/contact** to submit your updates and suggestions or to ask for help. Our award-winning website also features inspirational travel stories, news and discussions.

Note: We may edit, reproduce and incorporate your comments in Lonely Planet products such as guidebooks, websites and digital products, so let us know if you don't want your comments reproduced or your name acknowledged. For a copy of our privacy policy visit lonelyplanet.com/privacy.

OUR READERS

Many thanks to the travelers who used the last edition and wrote to us with helpful hints, useful advice and interesting anecdotes:

Emily Alma, Alan Baker, Joan Blore, Julian Brown, Jill Dixon, Louise DuRepos, Philip Eicher, Holley Grant, Martin Greenberg, John Groom, Sandy Hagan, Gerald Shea, Nicole van Wassenaer, Kathi Walsh, Edward Wendt, Mike Young

AUTHOR THANKS

Celeste Brash

Thanks to tourism's best: Emily Kimber at Destination Halifax and Pamela Beck with PEI Tourism. Special thanks to crazy hitchhikers Caitlin and Courtney, the good folks of Digby Backpackers and Kiwi Kaboodle, John Tattrie (an awsome writer), Darcy in Cape d'Or, Doug in Guysburough, Cailin O'Neill in Halifax, John Bil in PEI, the Tysons in Parsborro and Sandra in Creignish. I wish I could work with Karla Zimmerman, Emily Matchar and Jennye Garibaldi on every book. Mean-

while husband Josh moved our life to the US in the whirlwind and my dad Trace picked up trailing details.

Emily Matchar

A huge thanks to Jennye Garibaldi and Celeste Brash, who made this whole thing happen, and to the rest of the LP team in California and Oz. Thanks to all the New Brunswickers who pointed me towards the best hikes, hidden beaches, pubs and poutine râpée. Thanks as always to Jamin Asay, the best travel (and life) companion anyone could ask for. And thanks to my grandmother, Evelyn Matchar, who passed away during the writing of this book, for imparting her sense of wonder and her deep-seated appreciation for the unconventional.

Karla Zimmerman

Thanks to St John's gurus Bryan Curtis and Sarah Mathieson; Harvey in Bonavista; Gillian Marx and Laura Walbourne at Newfoundland Tourism; and the countless locals who stopped to tell me their tales. Thanks to

THIS BOOK

This 2nd edition of Lonely Planet's *Nova Scotia, New Brunswick & Prince Edward Island* was researched and written by Celeste Brash, Emily Matchar and Karla Zimmerman. Karla and Celeste also wrote the 1st edition. This guidebook was commissioned in Lonely Planet's Oakland office, and produced by the following:

Commissioning Editor Jennye Garibaldi

Coordinating Editor Katie O'Connell

Coordinating Cartographer Corey Hutchison

Coordinating Layout Designer Carlos Solarte

Managing Editors Sasha Baskett, Liz Heynes

Managing Cartographers David Connolly, Alison Lyall

Managing Layout Designers Indra Kilfoyle, Celia Wood

Assisting Editors Judith Bamber, Helen Koehne, Alison Ridgway

Cover & Internal Image Research Sabrina Dalbesio

Thanks to Mark Adams, Imogen Bannister, Stefanie Di Trocchio, Heather Dickson, Frank Diem, Janine Eberle, Joshua Geoghegan, Mark Germanchis, Michelle Glynn, Lauren Hunt, Laura Jane, David Kemp, Lisa Knights, Nic Lehman, John Mazzocchi, Wayne Murphy, Adrian Persoglia, Piers Pickard, Raphael Richards, Lachlan Ross, Michael Ruff, Julie Sheridan, Laura Stansfeld, John Taufa, Sam Trafford, Juan Winata, Emily Wolman, Nick Wood

righteous babe Lisa Beran for woman'ing the wheel once again. Über gratitude to fellow scribes Celeste and Emily, and LPers Jennye, Bruce and the editorial crew. Thanks most to Eric Markowitz, the world's best partner-for-life, without whom these travels wouldn't be possible.

ACKNOWLEDGMENTS

Climate map data adapted from Peel MC, Finlayson BL & McMahon TA (2007) 'Updated World Map of the Köppen-Geiger Climate Classification', *Hydrology and Earth System Sciences*, 11, 163344.

Cover photograph: Peggy's Cove/ Christopher Drost, Getty Images. Many of the images in this guide are available for licensing from Lonely Planet Images: www.lonelyplanetimages.com.

index

000 Map pages
000 Photo pages

how to use this book

These symbols will help you find the listings you want:

⊙ Sights
🏃 Activities
🎓 Courses
👉 Tours

🎉 Festivals & Events
🛏 Sleeping
🍴 Eating
🍷 Drinking

☆ Entertainment
🛍 Shopping
ℹ Information/Transport

These symbols give you the vital information for each listing:

- ☎ Telephone Numbers
- ☺ Opening Hours
- Ⓟ Parking
- ⊖ Nonsmoking
- ❄ Air-Conditioning
- @ Internet Access

- 🔊 Wi-Fi Access
- ⊜ Swimming Pool
- 🌱 Vegetarian Selection
- 📖 English-Language Menu
- 👪 Family-Friendly
- 🐾 Pet-Friendly

- 🚌 Bus
- ⛴ Ferry
- Ⓜ Metro
- Ⓢ Subway
- ⊖ London Tube
- 🚊 Tram
- 🚆 Train

Reviews are organised by author preference.

Map Legend

Sights
- ❷ Beach
- ❹ Buddhist
- ❸ Castle
- ❶ Christian
- ⓦ Hindu
- ⓒ Islamic
- ❸ Jewish
- ❶ Monument
- ⊜ Museum/Gallery
- ❽ Ruin
- ⓦ Winery/Vineyard
- ❽ Zoo
- ⊙ Other Sight

Activities, Courses & Tours
- ⊖ Diving/Snorkelling
- ⊙ Canoeing/Kayaking
- ⊕ Skiing
- ⊕ Surfing
- ⊜ Swimming/Pool
- ⊘ Walking
- ⊗ Windsurfing
- • Other Activity/Course/Tour

Sleeping
- ⊜ Sleeping
- ⊙ Camping

Eating
- 🍴 Eating

Drinking
- ⊙ Drinking
- ⊙ Cafe

Entertainment
- ⊙ Entertainment

Shopping
- ⊙ Shopping

Information
- ⊜ Post Office
- ❶ Tourist Information

Transport
- ⊙ Airport
- ⊗ Border Crossing
- ⊜ Bus
- ⊕ Cable Car/Funicular
- ⊙ Cycling
- ⊙ Ferry
- Ⓜ Metro
- ⊙ Monorail
- Ⓟ Parking
- Ⓢ S-Bahn
- ⊙ Taxi
- ⊕ Train/Railway
- ⊜ Tram
- ⊜ Tube Station
- Ⓤ U-Bahn
- • Other Transport

Routes
- Tollway
- Freeway
- Primary
- Secondary
- Tertiary
- Lane
- Unsealed Road
- Plaza/Mall
- Steps
- Tunnel
- Pedestrian Overpass
- Walking Tour
- Walking Tour Detour
- Path

Boundaries
- International
- State/Province
- Disputed
- Regional/Suburb
- Marine Park
- Cliff
- Wall

Population
- ❂ Capital (National)
- ◉ Capital (State/Province)
- ● City/Large Town
- ○ Town/Village

Geographic
- ⊙ Hut/Shelter
- ⊙ Lighthouse
- ⊜ Lookout
- ▲ Mountain/Volcano
- ⊙ Oasis
- ❶ Park
-)(Pass
- ⊜ Picnic Area
- ⊙ Waterfall

Hydrography
- River/Creek
- Intermittent River
- Swamp/Mangrove
- Reef
- Canal
- Water
- Dry/Salt/Intermittent Lake
- Glacier

Areas
- Beach/Desert
- +++ Cemetery (Christian)
- ××× Cemetery (Other)
- Park/Forest
- Sportsground
- Sight (Building)
- Top Sight (Building)

OUR STORY

A beat-up old car, a few dollars in the pocket and a sense of adventure. In 1972 that's all Tony and Maureen Wheeler needed for the trip of a lifetime – across Europe and Asia overland to Australia. It took several months, and at the end – broke but inspired – they sat at their kitchen table writing and stapling together their first travel guide, *Across Asia on the Cheap*. Within a week they'd sold 1500 copies. Lonely Planet was born.

Today, Lonely Planet has offices in Melbourne, London and Oakland, with more than 600 staff and writers. We share Tony's belief that 'a great guidebook should do three things: inform, educate and amuse'.

OUR WRITERS

Celeste Brash

Coordinating author, Nova Scotia, Prince Edward Island 'So this is where people from Tahiti go on vacation?' is a question often asked of Celeste – who's proud to say that she's been an *Anne of Green Gables* fan since she was nine years old – during her voyages through the Maritime provinces. Lighthouses, blueberries and lupine are a far cry from the palm trees, coconuts and hibiscus of her Polynesian island home of 15 years, but even with a tropical bias Celeste thinks that Atlantic lobster is the best food on Earth. Right after this trip to Canada, Celeste moved from the tropics to a more Maritime latitude in Oregon to start temperate adventures involving snow, salmon and blackberries. You can find out about her travels for this book and for several other Lonely Planet titles, including *Southeast Asia on a Shoestring* and *South Pacific*, at www.celestebrash.com.

Read more about Celeste at:
lonelyplanet.com/members/celestebrash

Emily Matchar

New Brunswick Though American by birth, Emily has long suffered acute Canada-envy (and not just for the healthcare, either!). She's had some of her best adventures in the True North, from paddling with seals off the coast of British Columbia to eating poutine at 3am in Montréal to hanging out with canoe-makers in rural New Brunswick. These days, she makes her home quite a bit further south, in Chapel Hill, North Carolina, where she writes for a variety of magazines, newspapers and websites. She's contributed to half a dozen Lonely Planet guides, including *USA, Mexico* and *Trips: The Carolinas, Georgia and the South*.

Read more about Emily at:
lonelyplanet.com/members/emilymatchar

Karla Zimmerman

Newfoundland & Labrador Karla is an Honorary Newfoundlander, with a rum-soaked certificate to prove it. During her years covering the province, she has paddled by icebergs, come nose-to-beak with puffins, hiked in polar bear territory and driven by most of Newfoundland's 120,000 moose. She's visited Dildo, Come by Chance and Heart's Delight, and intends to get to Jerry's Nose one day soon. When she's not north of the border, Karla lives in Chicago, where she writes travel features for newspapers, books, magazines and websites. She has authored or co-authored several Lonely Planet guidebooks to the USA, Canada, Caribbean and Europe.

Read more about Karla at:
lonelyplanet.com/members/karlazimmerman

Published by Lonely Planet Publications Pty Ltd
ABN 36 005 607 983
2nd edition – Apr 2011
ISBN 978 1 74179 171 6
© Lonely Planet 2011   Photographs © as indicated 2011
10 9 8 7 6 5 4 3 2 1
Printed in Singapore